W9-BIO-030

NETWORK POWER

DAVID SINGH GREWAL

Network Power

THE SOCIAL DYNAMICS OF GLOBALIZATION

YALE UNIVERSITY PRESS   NEW HAVEN & LONDON

A Caravan book. For more information, visit www.caravanbooks.org.

Published with assistance from the Louis Stern Memorial Fund.

Copyright © 2008 by David Singh Grewal.
All rights reserved.
This book may not be reproduced, in whole or in part, including illustrations, in any form
(beyond that copying permitted by Sections 107 and 108 of the U.S. Copyright Law and
except by reviewers for the public press), without written permission from the publishers.

Set in Scala and Scala Sans by Duke & Company, Devon, Pennsylvania.
Printed in the United States of America by Sheridan Books, Ann Arbor, Michigan.

Library of Congress Cataloging-in-Publication Data

Grewal, David Singh, 1976–
Network power : the social dynamics of globalization / David Singh Grewal.
p. cm.
Includes bibliographical references and index.

ISBN 978-0-300-11240-5 (cloth : alk. paper)
1. Globalization—Social aspects. 2. Globalization—Economic aspects. 3. Social networks.
4. Business networks. 5. Communication, International. 6. Cosmopolitanism. I. Title.
JZ1318.G792 2008
303.48′2—dc22   2007040499

A catalogue record for this book is available from the British Library.

The paper in this book meets the guidelines for permanence and durability of the Committee on Production Guidelines for Book Longevity of the Council on Library Resources.

10 9 8 7 6 5 4 3 2 1

For my parents

CONTENTS

ACKNOWLEDGMENTS

THIS BOOK has benefited a great deal from the criticism of friends, colleagues, and teachers. Of course, none of them are responsible for any of its shortcomings. Sanjay Reddy first sparked my interest in the themes I take up here, and I have enjoyed with him a decade-long conversation about globalization, modernity, and cultural diversity. Jedediah Purdy has also been an invaluable and long-standing interlocutor on these and related issues, and his frequent contributions have been critical to the development of the ideas presented here.

I began writing systematically on these themes while studying legal philosophy and multiculturalism with Paul Kahn, who was an excellent reader and critic. I am also very grateful to Tony Kronman, who first encouraged me to think of this subject as worthy of a book-length treatment and supported me in what may have sometimes seemed a quixotic project at some distance from the principal avenues of legal scholarship.

I have twice had the opportunity to be a teaching fellow in courses on globalization. Both were structured as ongoing discussions: first between Roberto Mangabeira Unger and Richard Freeman, and then among Michael Sandel, Larry Summers, and Thomas Friedman. I learned a great deal listening to these debates. Roberto Unger and Michael Sandel have my particular gratitude, as do the many dedicated Harvard undergraduates whom I have been fortunate enough to teach. I also want to thank Richard

Tuck, whose instruction in the history of political and social thought has had a profound impact on my thinking in ways he will surely recognize.

Daniela Cammack arrived late, but decisively, in the course of writing this book, and her incisive criticism improved it a great deal. I especially want to thank her for taking time out of her own projects to edit every chapter at a late stage, painstakingly clarifying the text and arguing out important ideas with me, many of which she seemed to grasp better than I did. Others from whom I have received valuable suggestions, criticism, and encouragement include Christian Barry, Paul Cammack, Kirsten Edwards, Bill Eskridge, Dario Gil, Robin Goldstein, Tinker Green, Andrew Grewal, Susan Hamilton, Royal Hansen, Adam Haslett, Bob Hockett, Stanley Hoffmann, Malgorzata Kurjanska, Sidney Kwiram, Roland Lamb, Carlos Lopez, Stephen Marglin, Daniel Mason, Pratap Mehta, David Menschel, Kirsty Milne, Karthik Muralidharan, Ian Simmons, Marco Simons, Peter Spiegler, Rahul Sagar, Talli Somekh, Lydia Tomitova, and Jason Woodard. Each of them contributed in important ways to this work, and they have my warm thanks. I would also like to acknowledge Joe Hing Kwok Chu, Barbara Dinesen, and William Ackerly, who provided personal support while I was involved in writing this book.

Finally, I wish to note with gratitude the help I have received from many people at Yale University Press, and especially the contributions of my editor, John Kulka, who was a consistently supportive and intelligent reader and critic, and helped to sharpen my argument through many successive drafts. I also want to acknowledge the assistance and encouragement of Keith Condon, Jessie Hunnicutt, Katherine Scheuer, Lindsay Toland, and three anonymous reviewers, who saw this book in draft form perhaps more times than they would care to remember.

Introduction

IMAGINE FOR A MOMENT that you are lost in New York City without a cell phone or any other way to contact a friend whom you were planning to meet that very same day. Expecting to coordinate at the last minute, you failed to specify a meeting place in advance. You might think it absurd to suppose that the two of you—lacking any way to communicate and lost in the middle of several million people—will ever find a way to meet up. But if you had to pick a time and location in the hope that your friend might be waiting for you at that same place and hour, where would you go, and when?

A common practice would be to wait beneath the clock tower at the information booth in the center of the Main Concourse in Grand Central Station. Is there something particularly suitable about that clock—or even that station—that makes the choice obvious? Certainly, Grand Central Station is well known and, at least since its restoration, very beautiful. It is centrally located, and tourists and commuters routinely pass through it. Perhaps other reasons, too, could be adduced for its attractiveness.

Yet while all of these reasons may matter, none of them matters decisively. None of them makes that particular location a uniquely compelling spot for an unplanned rendezvous, particularly in a city filled with possible places to meet. What does is the established expectation that the clock in the middle of the Main Concourse simply *is* the default place to meet a friend. And at what time of day would you head to Grand Central? If you are like most people, you would wait under that clock tower at 12 noon—and you would likely find your friend waiting there for you at the same time.

This story about an unplanned meeting in Grand Central Station is adapted from an earlier account that economist Thomas Schelling used to illustrate his idea of "focal points," which are points of reference that coordinate expectations in the absence of prior agreement. Schelling asked an "unscientific sample of respondents" to name a time and location at which they would attempt to meet a friend in New York City without having specified the details in advance and without any way to communicate. An absolute majority of Schelling's interviewees responded that they would go to the clock tower at the information booth in Grand Central Station, and nearly all of them said they would do so at 12 noon. Schelling used this (and similar examples) to illustrate the "tacit coordination" through which, in the absence of express agreement, we nevertheless find ourselves able to coordinate our activities.[1]

Throughout the world, billions of people are similarly looking for places to "meet"—either literally or figuratively—often without having specified the details in advance. Across the globe we ask ourselves a question whose answer in New York City is that clock in the center of Grand Central Station: how should I best position myself in order to "meet up" with other people without a prior agreement? If that omnibus term "globalization" captures anything—and I argue in this book that it does capture something important about our contemporary circumstances—then what it highlights are the diverse but increasingly shared answers to that question.

Globalization involves a game of social coordination similar to that of meeting a lost friend in New York City, except that we are not usually deciding on a location but rather on the languages, laws, technologies, and frames of reference—or, as I refer to them in this book, the *standards*—by which we can best facilitate our newly global activities. We are not so much asking *where* to meet, as *how*. Of course, the "meeting" that these standards facilitate is more complex than locating a friend, but the logic of tacit social coordination is common to both.

For the most part, we are not yet at a stage where the global standards we will use have become clearly known. But in every area of global activity, as some standards gain prominence, alternative ones become less attractive choices for social coordination. This process can prove self-reinforcing, with the result that a single standard can become the established choice, the convention on which we settle to coordinate global access. Globalization is, among other things, the uneven process by which such conventions are determined, the way in which we construct (or, in many cases, simply receive) the settled terms of access to each other that make international cooperation possible.

The word "globalization" has become impossible to escape and yet remains difficult to define. Indeed, the term now functions in a great deal of scholarship and commentary as a residual category: since almost any contemporary phenomenon of importance crosses some kind of border, the word has become a catchall. Even many serious studies of globalization rapidly degenerate into simple analyses of immediately identifiable global institutions and actors, with little inquiry into their deeper inter-relationships or the logic that underlies them. Thus, perhaps *the* defining characteristic of our era receives only piecemeal theorization across various academic disciplines, and little beyond platitudes from public commentators.

GLOBALIZATION AND NETWORK POWER

In this book, I present an argument about how we should understand globalization, claiming that many contemporary phenomena now loosely grouped under this rubric can helpfully be viewed through a single lens. Prominent elements of globalization can be understood as the rise to dominance of shared forms of social coordination, and these global conventions can prove difficult to alter once in place. In areas as diverse as trade, media, legal procedures, industrial control, and perhaps even forms of thought, we are witnessing the emergence of international standards that enable us to coordinate our actions on a global scale. What we are experiencing now, in "globalization," is the creation of an international in-group that welcomes the entire globe on settled terms: a new world order in which we clamor for connection to one another using standards that are offered up for universal use. Yet, while we may all come to share these new global standards—to the extent, at least, that we desire access to the activities that they mediate—we may not all have much influence over their establishment in the first place.

The standards that enable such global coordination display what I call *network power*.[2] The notion of network power consists in the joining of two ideas: first, that coordinating standards are more valuable when greater numbers of people use them, and second, that this dynamic—which I describe as a form of power—can lead to the progressive elimination of the alternatives over which otherwise free choice can effectively be exercised. It is support for, and criticism of, both of these elements, in various guises, combinations, and degrees of self-consciousness, that fuels contemporary debates over globalization.

Network power emerges with the possibility of social coordination via new global standards, made possible by the compression of space and imagination that technological advances have brought. At both the global and the local level, coordination is based largely on expectations. Consider again the problem of meeting your lost friend in New York City. The decision to head to Grand Central Station (and at 12 noon) is determined by a series of reciprocal expectations: where you think your friend will go, which depends upon where he thinks you will go, which depends upon where you think that he thinks you think he will go, and so on.[3] Globally, we face a similar problem: how we are all to "meet" in the global landscape which is now opening up before us requires making best guesses about reciprocal expectations. As any one of the possible solutions to a coordination game becomes a point of reference reflected in these expectations, it generates a form of power, with the capacity to pull in people who might otherwise rely on other conventions.

Although I introduce the idea of network power in the context of a discussion of contemporary globalization, I do not mean to suggest that it is a new phenomenon, but simply that it is one that has become more visible in the contemporary world. Networks, even global ones, are not new—and neither is the power present in the social interactions that generate them. Human history plentifully records intercultural trade, communication, and migration, spanning continents and millennia. But what *is* new about our age is the accelerated emergence of, and linkages among, these global networks. From trade to communication to domestic regulations, what was once mainly, even exclusively, "local" is becoming increasingly global. More precisely, certain versions of local practices, routines, and symbols are being catapulted onto a global stage and offered as a means by which we can gain access to one another. They have become the standards by which we render each other's actions comprehensible and comparable, and through which we are enabled to engage in forms of beneficial cooperation, such as the exchange of goods or ideas.

Emerging global standards solve our problems—or at least compete to do so—and those standards that gain the most prominence become *focal points* in which we find the solution to the problem of global coordination. This "solution" is, of course, double-edged: it offers coordination among diverse participants but it does so by elevating one solution above others and threatening the elimination of alternative solutions to the same problem. Inherent in the use of any standard is a tension between the cooperation that it allows users to enjoy and the check on innovation that it also imposes, since innovation would constitute a break in an ongoing cooperative regime.

This double-edged aspect allows us to make sense of a seeming paradox at the heart of debates over globalization. On the one hand, globalization is often celebrated as an advance of human freedom in which individuals become ever more able to lead lives of their own choosing. Transnational flows of money, goods, and ideas accompany an increasingly liberal international order in which (it is claimed) individuals are ever freer to participate in a global economy and culture. At the same time, the complaint that globalization is based on power has become widespread, and is developed especially pointedly in recent accusations of "empire." At the center of these seemingly contradictory claims lies a difficulty in untangling voluntary choice-making from coercion, with allegations of both frequently being attached to the same action. For example, the choices of people to learn English or of nations to join the World Trade Organization (WTO) may seem, on the face of it, well reasoned, freely made choices. Yet it is also argued that these choices stem from a kind of domination that they may in turn reinforce, reflecting the systemic power of already privileged actors or institutions. The idea of network power allows us to maintain our common-sense view of people as reasonable, choosing agents while simultaneously allowing that those doing the choosing may be subject to a form of external compulsion. It does so by treating the context of a choice as part of any adequate description of it. On this account, convergence on a set of common global standards is driven by an accretion of individual choices that can be considered both free and unfree. Of course, the claim that our choices can manifest freedom, in that they express formal consent, and yet still reflect oppression in their recapitulation of systemic unfreedom, is relatively commonplace in modern social theory. It is, however, a claim largely missing from today's discussion of globalization.

Contemporary commentators too often treat the emergence of globalization as either a rational act of global self-construction or an agentless process in which standards spread like free-floating viruses across the planet. In the former case, human agents are conceived as global institution-builders; in the latter, as the hapless victims of a brave new world beyond their control. The idea of network power rejects both of these descriptions as inadequate, but incorporates certain aspects of each, allowing us to see that convergence on a set of global standards can occur purely as the result of the accretion of decentralized choices—choices that can feel both free and forced at the same time.

GLOBALIZATION AS EMPIRE?

Many people greet the arrival of global standards with ambivalence, not only because local practices often get edged out, but because the standards gaining global prominence are not the products of common deliberation and collective effort, but seem to emanate from and privilege certain countries, particularly the United States. One of the complaints about globalization that Americans understand least is that it represents a new empire, or works to the hegemonic advantage of the United States. Some of this incomprehension comes from parochialism and inattention. But it may also seem puzzling that, by all appearances, many of the fiercest critics of globalization either participate in, or aspire to, a global and even "Americanized" way of life. How, one might ask, can such people complain that their free choices are also a form of oppression? These malcontents, it is often said, act in confusion or bad faith, perhaps both.

Network power starts from a different premise, taking seriously the charge that billions live as subjects to a power they feel but whose nature they may not be able to articulate clearly. On this account, the globalization to which we are now witness cannot be described as a straightforwardly voluntary process. Neither can resentment against it be said to represent merely envious discontent. It is rather a challenging response to the global expansion of a form of power that may not have been characterized adequately but which is increasingly dominant in our social relations.

Indeed, the assertion that globalization is imperial has lately become the subject of mainstream and conservative discussion in the United States and elsewhere; it is no longer a charge made by anti-globalization activists alone.[4] The characterization rests on two claims: first, the fact that many important choices (even those taken at the level of whole nations or peoples) can seem to have been already decided on account of the effects of globalization; and second, that many already privileged countries benefit disproportionately from processes of globalization. Both parts of this allegation of imperialism become easier to understand if we consider them in the light of the network power of dominant global standards. Coordination is both liberating and entrapping: liberating because it offers greater access to others, and entrapping because it does so—often necessarily—in a way that privileges one mode of access rather than another.

Of course, the characterization of a form of entrapping coordination as "imperial" may seem exaggerated, given that the term is usually invoked to describe a situation in which one society openly dominates another. The most obvious examples of this control are the political conquest and occupation of foreign societies—as in many cases of the "new imperialism" of the nineteenth century—but the control of one society by another does not require such direct means.[5] The very word "empire" comes from the Latin word *imperium,* which was used to describe the mixture of territorial conquest, informal commercial domination, and cultural hegemony characterizing Rome's rule of the Mediterranean in the early phase of its expansion.

The distinction between formal and informal empire is now a familiar one, serving to contrast a situation in which direct political control is necessary to secure benefits from a subordinated society with one in which it is not.[6] In the latter case, the subordinate society cooperates willingly in serving the interests of the controlling society, whether through relations of economic dependency, military alliance, or some other form of "indirect" control. In any case, the control of one society by another is the same, but the way in which such control is maintained varies. Certainly, as many studies of imperial history conclude, formal and informal imperial strategies should not be thought of as opposed, but may be pursued simultaneously in different geographic contexts or at different moments in time.

The claim that contemporary globalization represents a new kind of empire rests on the concept of informal empire (or hegemony), since direct imperial control is absent in most of the world. But this idea of informal empire—while intuitively appropriate and often persuasive—leaves unarticulated the precise mechanism of control. Part of the problem is conceptual. To each idea of empire is necessarily tied a model of the power that underlies the control of the subordinate society. Formal domination suggests a model of power operating as the command of a political superior, and which is backed up by outright force. In certain regions of the world, this kind of analysis will seem more plausible than in others. As an account of globalization overall, however, a focus on the political control of territory will fail to offer insight into the economic, cultural and institutional aspects of globalization that are perhaps most interesting —albeit difficult—to capture.

The insight that the relations that seem to liberate us may also bind us emerges clearly in the work of certain theorists of modernity such as Max Weber. But unlike the forms of unfreedom associated with an internally generated modernity, global standards often come (or appear to come) from the outside. They also impose their costs unevenly, and frequently privilege the already powerful. Therefore globalization may appear to many who feel its effects most acutely not as the iron cage of modernity manifest on a newly global scale, but as foreign imposition in the familiar mold of empire. Given these dynamics, we should not expect the accusation of empire to disappear any time soon. But neither should we pretend that it consists of nothing more than confusion and bad faith in a moment of unambiguous global advance. Globalization is Janus-faced, generating new forms of freedom and new problems of entanglement.

TWO FORMS OF POWER

Any account of globalization as empire—or indeed any that sees it as constituted, at least in part, by relations of domination—must confront the problems inherent in theorizing any power relations that do not resemble the command of a political superior over a subordinate. Perhaps the most important of these problems is one that recurred repeatedly in debates in social thought during the nineteenth and twentieth centuries: the difficulty of describing how power can operate through social structures rather than as the express will of a well-defined agent. The concept of network power may have something to contribute to this debate. It can help us to see how individual actions can create structures that, in turn, limit individual agency in a way that resembles the more familiar exercise of power by one person over another.

Here we can usefully draw a distinction between two dynamics of power that correspond to two different ways in which social activity occurs. One way in which we organize our social life is through the construction of a political will, which allows us to make decisions collectively. Final decisions might still be taken by only one person, by several, or by the entire collectivity, but the process itself can still be described as collective decision-making since it follows a procedure which the entire group accepts as producing decisions that are valid for everyone. The dynamic of power that operates when we take decisions collectively in this way—that is, through a political procedure—can be described as reflecting relations of *sovereignty*. A sovereign decision can reshape social outcomes directly through the exercise of a form of power that resembles the command of a political superior. In the case of democratic government, for example, this occurs when a majority determines an outcome for everyone.

The second dynamic of power operates through what we might call relations of *sociability*. In this case, aggregate outcomes emerge not from an act of collective decision-making, but through the accumulation of decentralized, individual decisions that, taken together, nonetheless conduce to a circumstance that affects the entire group. Market activity and linguistic evolution are paradigmatic instances of the construction of a collective outcome via relations of sociability. This cumulative social construction may—because it rests on voluntary individual cooperation—appear to represent a form of uncoerced participatory activity. While this may sometimes be the case, I argue that such relations of sociability do not generally represent a form of social activity free from the exercise of power. However, the power at work in sociability is not well understood. The idea of network power offers a way to conceptualize the power at work in these relations of sociability, which has today become most visible in the emergence of new global networks. The distinction between sociability and sovereignty has been developed in a variety of important social and political theories, but the distinction between the ways that power operates in each remains underdeveloped. Without a clearer grasp of both of these dynamics, and particularly the differences between them, we cannot properly understand the processes driving contemporary globalization.

OUTLINE OF THE BOOK

In this book, I develop the idea of network power by first offering a general formulation of the concept in broad terms and then analyzing examples drawn from contemporary globalization. However, the book does not proceed by first developing a theory and then offering "applications." Rather, a single argument advances, initially through the abstract presentation of network dynamics, and later in the examination of concrete instances of global networks. It should also be noted that I do not attempt to offer a survey of globalization (or of the ever expanding literature on the subject) but merely select those problems and themes that seem most relevant to my purposes.

In the first chapter, I introduce the concept of network power, the power that a successful standard possesses when it enables cooperation among members of a network. In the way I use the terms, a *network* is united by a *standard,* which is a shared norm or practice that facilitates cooperation among members of a network. Since the reason we use standards is to gain access to others for the sake of cooperation, the more people who adopt a given standard, the more valuable it will be for others to adopt the same one. For example, a language is more valuable for us to learn if many other people already speak it. In general, therefore, the larger the network, the more powerful the standard underlying it will be—and the more pressure non-users will feel to adopt that standard. In extreme cases, this pressure can represent a kind of compulsion to join a dominant network. It is this form of power that generates much of the resentment against globalization, since it may entail a loss of local autonomy and the suppression of alternative modes of coordination.

A standard that possesses network power can develop into a universal standard. A universal standard is a convention on which all members of a network have settled. It reflects a particular kind of cooperative behavior emerging from an interdependence of choice, in which people seek a way to coordinate their actions with one another. The idea of network power attempts to capture the dynamic behind this universalization—the way in which interdependent choices can tend to favor the emergence of a single standard.

As a standard develops toward conventionality, it follows a particular trajectory. This trajectory involves three factors: *reason, force,* and *chance.* The path of any real-world network is, of course, highly contingent upon historical trends and may well involve all three factors in combination. Studying the trajectory along which standards move reveals that the power of any particular standard may be unrelated to the inherent benefits it has to offer. For example, the English language is today poised to become the global language in many domains not because of anything intrinsically special about it, but because of Britain's imperial history and the success of American mass media. After an initial push that may come from a variety of causes, the network power of a standard alone may be sufficient to drive it toward conventionality.

In Chapter 2, I locate the idea of network power in relation to the distinction between *sociability* and *sovereignty,* and then set that distinction in the context of the history of social thought more generally. The idea of network power may be understood as an attempt to analyze the dynamics of the power operative in sociability: that is, as a way of understanding how power is structured through social relations outside the formal politics of sovereignty. An analysis of this sort is particularly important in order to characterize globalization adequately. Indeed, we can understand the process of globalization as one in which the relations of sociability tend to outstrip the relations of sovereignty, the latter being contained within the boundaries of nation-states in a way that the former are not. Such an understanding also allows us to think clearly about individual agency and social structure together in the context of contemporary globalization, neither exalting individual agency while neglecting the possibility of entrapment in social structures, nor elucidating social structures without considering how individual agents can transform them.

In Chapter 3, I make these arguments more concrete by examining the dominance of the English language today and the dominance of the gold standard in the nineteenth and early twentieth centuries. Both of these cases provide interesting examples of social coordination via shared standards. Language allows communication, and money facilitates economic exchange. The symbolic tokens that enable linguistic and monetary coordination possess network power, and English and gold are particularly interesting examples of standards that have attained (or did once attain) global dominance. Studying the contemporary rise of English shows us a standard as it progresses toward universality. Examining the rise and fall of the gold standard reveals the tensions generated when a universal standard is unable to accommodate the need for local autonomy and innovation.

As a given standard becomes dominant and moves to universality, it eclipses rival standards that formerly facilitated the same activity. It may also prevent the emergence of alternative forms of coordination in the future. The choice to adopt the dominant standard then becomes an increasingly coerced one, for the only options are to join it or face social isolation. It is the prevalence of this kind of choice—a circumstance in which I argue a kind of power is at work—that makes the emergence of global networks something other than a large-scale act of international voluntarism, or the free enactment of a global social contract. Accordingly, a standard may be selected not for its intrinsic properties but for the access it provides to the network it coordinates—or even, in extreme cases, on account of the concomitant risk of losing access to any social network whatsoever. A dominant standard may even prove intrinsically disadvantageous in terms of the activity which it coordinates, and yet possess enough network power to compel non-users to adopt it.

In Chapter 4, I explore the idea of network power *as power* more systematically, examining different conceptions of power and situating the idea of network power within these ongoing debates. An understanding of the distinction between sociability and sovereignty is present (if only implicitly) in many of the most important social theories of the nineteenth and twentieth centuries, and especially in attempts to develop heterodox theories of power. For instance, the idea of *hegemony* presents a model of power in which consent and domination are not opposed, but in which people who are subjected to domination consent in some way to the power exercised over them. Yet ideas of power based on hegemony or related concepts have had a mixed reception, in part because they can be evocative but vague, depriving us of a clear way of thinking about human agency and social structure together. I suggest that the idea of network power can provide a theory of power in which consent and domination are also joined, but in which the relationship between human agency and social structure is better elucidated.

Of course, arguing that something constitutes "power" says little about whether that power is normatively justified. We cannot be *against* power independent of an evaluation of the uses to which it is put, or the legitimacy of the circumstances that give rise to it. In Chapter 5, I outline the elements of a normative assessment of network power, focusing on two general classes of concerns: first, a concern about the extent to which different people are able to realize their interests, and second, a concern about the maintenance of cultural identity. With regard to the former, I discuss theories of distributive justice, and to the latter, theories of recognition, in order to consider how an inequality of network power might be evaluated in these frameworks.

Where we judge an instance of network power abusive, how best are we to counter it? In Chapter 6, I turn to possible strategies for defusing network power where we judge it harmful. It is difficult to determine which strategies to deploy against network power because, unlike in cases of straightforward coercion, this kind of power is driven by consent. Against many forms of power we rely on the elaboration of rights—both *negative rights* that guarantee a zone of individual autonomy and *positive rights* that guarantee a minimum level of resources. I argue that the provision of negative rights will fail to remedy abuses of network power, precisely because network power is consent-driven. The strategy of elaborating positive rights also leaves much to be desired since it is difficult to specify how the state (or some other party) might intervene in support of a threatened standard. Instead, we need to reconceive both kinds of rights relationally, asking who we think ought to be free, from what constraints or because of what enabling conditions, to undertake which actions.

Adopting a relational approach along these lines, I propose that the best way to counter network power is through institutional changes to the configuration of networks. Since we are clamoring for access to one another, the only way to manage network power is to provide alternative and multiple channels for such access, refusing to privilege any single one. The question of whether this is possible takes us far from the idea of rights, whether positive or negative, and suggests instead a more contextual, institutional analysis that understands the extent of our effective liberty to depend, not on any abstract conception of right, but on the details of the institutions in which we make our lives. Accordingly, defusing network power in any concrete instance requires that we first understand how it inheres in different network configurations. I examine three "network properties"—availability, compatibility, and malleability—and suggest how different combinations of these properties affect the power of a given network. Understanding at a deeper level of specificity what kinds of standards gain network power may enable us to change the institutional context in which that power arises.

In Chapter 7, I examine the spread of global technologies, including technical standards and practices. The most striking technological development of the last few decades has been the emergence of telecommunications technology and personal computing on a global scale. These technologies are dependent on underlying standards for technical coordination and therefore present striking examples of the dynamics of network power in action. I discuss the anti-trust case *United States v. Microsoft*, and its implications for the regulation of network power in high technology. I then turn to the "open-source" movement prominent in new forms of collaborative digital production. I argue that these egalitarian relations of production can be preserved only by embracing, rather than rejecting, politics. I therefore criticize the anarchistic tendencies of many adherents of the open-source movement, arguing that only if the democratic politics of sovereignty are mobilized on its behalf will a free digital world be able to survive.

In Chapter 8, I analyze the network power of the World Trade Organization. To some, the WTO is a major achievement of the international community: a victory of progressive forces over parochialism and unenlightened self-interest. To others, it is a telling example of a world driven to undemocratic centralization by economic forces beyond the control of ordinary people. Understanding the WTO as a standard that exerts network power will make these divergent views intelligible and allow us deeper insight into the organization and its possible future. The debate over the WTO is obviously related to the debate over trade liberalization more generally, so I also take this opportunity to look more deeply into arguments in favor of such liberalization and the ends it serves, in order to explicate further the network power dynamics at work in this domain.

The WTO is the most visible institutional embodiment of neoliberalism or, as it is sometimes referred to, the "Washington Consensus." Neoliberalism serves as a portmanteau term for a set of economic policy proposals that privilege markets and criticize collective interventions in the economy. In Chapter 9, I discuss these policies and argue that neoliberalism is not one standard but a host of related standards, the network properties of which are not generally configured to provide them with network power. Neoliberal economic policies sometimes govern access to others—to the benefits of foreign aid, foreign markets, and foreign recognition—and when they do they may coordinate access via a standard that possesses network power. At other times, however, countries adopt neoliberal policies for reasons unrelated to network power—for example, because a particular policy seems persuasive to a country's decision-makers, or because of direct pressure from a foreign country or international agency. Because neoliberal policies possess varying degrees of network power, the Washington Consensus is not a "take it or leave it" standard. Rather, it can be broken down, adopted piecemeal, and revised, as many successful economies have managed to do. The way in which neoliberal policies can become coordinating standards that do possess network power is through a process that I term *juridification*—the creation of formal legal principles governing a mode of access, as in the example of the WTO. I explore the process of juridification in the negotiations over a global agreement governing international investment, which produced the dramatic and controversial failure of the Multilateral Agreement on Investment (MAI).

One of the widespread complaints against globalization is that it produces, or hastens, cultural loss and homogenization, moving us toward a dystopic "McWorld." Accordingly, in Chapter 10 I turn to the subject of cultural globalization. Unlike specific economic policies or technological platforms in which the governing standard and the power it exerts may be relatively clear, this form of globalization is governed by complex standards in which the dynamics of network power are much less obvious. Of course, the constituent elements of "culture" are very diverse; I adopt the framework introduced by the sociologist Peter Berger in order to examine the "four faces of global culture" in the light of network power. I then explore what are sometimes called "epistemic communities," networks of people with shared expertise, such as the international community of scientists. If we can understand the shared conceptual frames linking these communities as standards, then network power may generate cultural convergence, not just at the level of consumer preferences but even in forms of thought.

The rise of universal standards such as the ones I discuss in this book link us together in global networks that are often in tension with many of our important "local" commitments. This is most significantly and, in my view, worryingly the case in the mismatch between the global scope of these relations of sociability and the domestic locus of democratic sovereignty. It is clear that the globalization of social relations cannot be straightforwardly balanced by a concomitant globalization of the structures of political authority. But whether a globalized sociability will mollify or exacerbate antagonisms among different sovereign states is a long-standing question to which history offers unsettling answers.

For it is not the first time that the world has been in this situation. John Maynard Keynes's famous description of the world before the "Great War" may seem eerily familiar to contemporary eyes:

> The inhabitant of London could order by telephone, sipping
> his morning tea in bed, the various products of the whole
> earth, in such quantity as he might see fit, and reasonably
> expect their early delivery upon his doorstep; he could at the
> same moment and by the same means adventure his wealth
> in the natural resources and new enterprises of any quarter of
> the world, and share, without exertion or even trouble, in their
> prospective fruits and advantages . . . [he] could then proceed
> abroad to foreign quarters without knowledge of their religion,
> language or customs, bearing coined wealth upon his person,
> and would consider himself greatly aggrieved and much sur-
> prised at the least interference. But, most important of all, he
> regarded this state of affairs as normal, certain and permanent,
> except in the direction of further improvement, and any devia-
> tion from it as aberrant, scandalous and avoidable.[7]

If we are to avoid the bloodshed that ended this earlier episode of globalization, we must press forward to a global modernity that we can live with. This is a task for politics above all, but our political strategies may be limited by our conceptual analysis. Our first step, then, is coming to terms with globalization as it is now unfolding.

CHAPTER ONE

Defining Network Power

WITH THE END OF THE COLD WAR, a world divided into hostile halves suddenly became "one world" in the middle of a historic transformation: the integration and consolidation of activities not just at the national or even continental level, but on the global scale too. Commerce, technology, media, and cultural imagery spilled across national borders in what appeared to some commentators to be a new worldwide free-for-all. Thus was the revolution of "globalization" suddenly upon us—as it has been, in fact, for the past few centuries.

In most contemporary discussions, globalization is presented as constituting a break from the past, a contemporary circumstance without precedent. But as the historian Emma Rothschild reminds us, not only does the idea of globalization have a history—even the idea of globalization as a phenomenon *without a history* has a history.[1] The failure to grasp the long history of globalization epitomizes an ongoing failure to understand its real significance today. Part of the problem is that we lack a plausible framework in which to understand the diverse but arguably interrelated phenomena that constitute "globalization," past or present. In this chapter, I suggest a framework for making sense of these diverse phenomena, as they have unfolded historically and as they appear in the world today.

THEORIES OF GLOBALIZATION

The social processes that we group together under the rubric "globalization" stretch back to the early modern period, and often before. Writers in Western Europe—which has sometimes been a fairly isolated corner of the world—have been commenting since at least the sixteenth century on the increasing internationalization of their commercial, intellectual, and cultural affairs, and on the changes in the subjective identities of people and peoples that such internationalization brought about.[2] These early commentators on what we now call globalization were aware that technological and social changes had led to a compression of space (as it might be put today) and that this compression had myriad consequences for their commerce, their political and social life, and their self-understanding. The French writer and diplomat François-René de Chateaubriand made an argument that sounds strikingly contemporary when he wrote, in 1841, that technological advances could be expected to bring about an international society: "When steam power will be perfected, when, together with telegraphy and railways, it will have made distances disappear, it will not only be commodities which travel, but also ideas which will have wings. When fiscal and commercial barriers will have been abolished between different states, as they have already been between the provinces of the same state; when different countries, in daily relations, tend toward the unity of peoples, how will you be able to revive the old mode of separation?"[3]

It is a rather parochial conceit of contemporary commentators, therefore, that globalization is something unique to our time. But while the processes of globalization are not new, its theorization under this name is of more recent provenance—and this fact helps to account for the claim that globalization is itself novel. The word "globalization" in its current usage goes back only as far as the 1960s, while even the related word "international" only originated (with Jeremy Bentham) in the late eighteenth century.[4] Sustained analyses of globalization are of even more recent vintage, most fewer than two or three decades old.

Any idea of globalization—whether in Chateaubriand's time or in the present—must begin with the compression of space, a change in geographic distance as it is lived and conceived. At a subjective level, at least, this change is undeniable. The widespread feeling that "the world is getting smaller" attests to the fact that technological and social advances have made the distance between points—and people—on the globe feel far less significant than they did only a short time ago. Objectively, the distances *are* shorter, at least if we think of the time required to traverse them. With modern transport, no two cities in the world are, any longer, any more than about a day's travel apart. The world no longer seems to hold points unfathomably far away, geographically or culturally.

The sociologist Anthony Giddens, an able contemporary commentator on this feature of globalization, offers a much-cited definition in these terms: "Globalisation can . . . be defined as the intensification of world-wide social relations which link distant localities in such a way that local happenings are shaped by events occurring many miles away and vice versa. This is a dialectical process. . . . Local transformation is as much a part of globalisation as the lateral extension of social connections across time and space."[5]

Giddens understands globalization as a process through which distant localities become linked in a way that constitutes a "lateral extension of social connections across time and space." This process also transforms the nature of these localities in relation to the global. In a similar way, one of the first scholars to discuss "globalization" under that name, Roland Robertson, emphasizes this compression of distance: "Globalization as a concept refers both to the compression of the world and the intensifica-tion of consciousness of the world as a whole . . . both concrete global interdependence and consciousness of the global whole."[6] Drawing on both these descriptions, the social theorist Malcolm Waters has defined globalization as a "social process in which the constraints of geography on social and cultural arrangements recede and in which people become increasingly aware that they are receding."[7] These scholars recognize that our experience of global geography has changed, that we are collectively aware of this change, and that it alters many "local" aspects of our lives that have now come to possess a new "global" dimension.

The idea of network power originates with this observation of geo-graphic compression, but treats it only as a prelude. In its most essential aspects, globalization occurs *after* this change in the experience of global geography. The release from geographic constraint does not in itself bring about many transformations in the way that people live and relate to each other without a second set of social changes that enable them to cooperate in international and transnational activities. Chateaubriand writes that when "distances disappear," then "ideas have wings." But, of course, ideas do not really have wings: it is people who promote particular ideas, and who come into contact with other people who may at some point come to share them. It is not technological advances themselves that "tend toward the unity of peoples," but the fact that social relations can now be conducted on a global level, among greater masses of people, thanks in part to those advances.

What the compression of geography enables but does not provide is social coordination. That coordination, I argue, is achieved in the adoption of shared *standards* that allow global social networks to emerge following the technological changes that bring people into contact with one another, but do not (in themselves) generate everything else that people require to become mutually intelligible and beneficial partners in cooperation. This social coordination is achieved via standards that provide the frameworks for global cooperation—the languages, points of reference, customs, rules, laws and regulations—that must follow the compression of space for the creation of a global society.[8]

On this account, globalization is the disruptive and uneven process by which we come to share common standards after the eclipse of distance. Because there are usually multiple possible standards that might enable global cooperation in any specific domain, the choice of any one of them is socially and politically consequential. Unsurprisingly, then, the struggle over these standards—over the forms that our emerging globalization could take—is one of the defining features of our age.

STANDARDS AND NETWORKS

In this book, I advance an argument about how we might understand the social coordination that standards provide, focusing on the power that standards have in bringing into being new global networks. The idea of a "network" has come into greater usage in recent discussions of globalization. However, since the concept is used differently in different scholarly disciplines, let me be explicit about how I will use the term. A *network* is an interconnected group of people linked to one another in a way that makes them capable of beneficial cooperation, which can take various forms, including the exchange of goods and ideas. While every network is ultimately composed of people, the way in which these people gain access to one another may include mediation, for example through computers or corporations. Networks can also exist in many different forms with important implications for network dynamics, a point to which I will return in Chapter 6.[9]

A *standard* defines the particular way in which a group of people is interconnected in a network. It is the shared norm or practice that enables network members to gain access to one another, facilitating their cooperation.[10] A standard must be shared among members of the network to a sufficient degree that they can achieve forms of reciprocity, exchange, or collective effort. Consider, for example, networks of English speakers, Internet chat room participants, consumers in the Euro zone, or people who use the metric system. In every case, a standard is central to the existence of the network, serving as a convention common to all its members. Without it, we would see a collection of isolated individuals rather than a connected group capable of achieving something together.

A network can be, but is not necessarily the same thing as, a "community," at least if we mean by that term a geographically proximate and socially integrated group. Global networks may well not function or feel like communities to those participating in them. When we imagine a community, we tend to envision a close-knit group of people who share a great deal—values, language, and, usually, some specific geographic location. By contrast, a network may be rather "thin," united in one particular fashion and perhaps in that fashion only, linking participants who may be scattered physically across the globe. At its most diffuse, networks of computer users around the world "meet" over a network of wires and satellite signals constituting a virtual network of people who have never actually met one another personally—nor are ever likely to do so. But global networks need not be technologically based; they may result from the common use of a particular currency, language, regulatory regime, or other convention.[11]

It is important to differentiate between two kinds of standards: what I call "mediating" standards and "membership" standards. These two types of standards are not mutually exclusive, and distinguishing between them can be considerably complex in any given instance.[12] Both of these kinds of standards can exert network power: mediating standards do so inherently while membership standards need to be configured in a particular manner in order to do so, as I will explain further in Chapter 6.

What I mean by a *mediating standard* is a standard that governs access to others by its very nature; some particular social activity is inherently regulated by it. Language is perhaps the most obvious example of a mediating standard: to join the network of English speakers, you must learn English. Mediating standards are ones that cannot be avoided if users wish to engage in certain activities: they form a part of that very activity itself. Thus they serve as solutions to the problem of social coordination, thereby enabling beneficial cooperation in a network.

We also use the term "standard" in a second sense, to refer to a specific ideal, exemplar, or required level of attainment, as in discussions of a "standard" in fashion, hygiene, education, environmental protection, or industrial manufacture. This second kind of standard is not necessarily basic or inherent to a given activity (as the English language is to communication with people who only speak English) but rather establishes an ideal or target. Thus, these standards do not generally govern the access that we can have to others, except where membership in a network is predicated upon the common acceptance of such a standard as a precondition for access. When it is, we can identify it as a membership *standard*. Membership standards do not enable beneficial cooperation by serving as coordinating standards, but they do govern access to an in-group by specifying criteria for admission to a network.

Mediating standards, because they inhere in a given social activity, are self-enforcing standards. No one needs to insist on the use of English in London or U.S. dollars in Florida; the logic of decentralized social coordination is inherently regulative in these cases. By contrast, membership standards usually require enforcement by some actor or set of actors to exclude all but those who adopt particular norms. For example, membership in the European Union (EU) is predicated on the acceptance of the *acquis communautaire*, which is the minimum set of regulations required of all EU states. (The *acquis* consists of the entire body of laws of the EU, including all treaties, regulations, directives passed by the EU institutions, and the judgments of the European Court of Justice.) The *acquis* serves as the membership standard regulating the entry of new countries to the EU, each of which is required to "adopt, implement, and enforce" it upon its accession.[13]

STANDARDS AND ECONOMIES OF SCALE

This description of standards may give the impression that they are relatively unremarkable, little more than social facts the general existence of which we all take for granted. Standards exist everywhere, and we have a sense of how they work: by making things comparable, commensurable, comprehensible, and thus accessible and available. But the most interesting feature of standards—and the one that gives rise to what I call "network power"—is that they can "spread," propelled by people's desire for access to members of a network. A commonly used standard uniting a desirable network will be attractive to any outsiders wanting to gain access to that network and such outsiders may well decide to adopt it for that purpose alone.

To illustrate this point, suppose for a moment that you are the head of a manufacturing company, *Bolt Inc.*, which produces small mechanical parts, such as bolts. In the United States, bolts are identified by two measurements: their diameter in fractions of an inch, and the number of threads per inch. Now imagine that a large conglomeration of the major producers and corporate consumers of mechanical parts calling itself the "Alliance for Rational Standards" commits itself to switching over from the imperial standard of measurement to the metric standard. Metric bolts are described by their diameter and "pitch"—the distance between two threads—given in millimeters. Members of the Alliance claim that the adoption of the metric standard will bring them into conformity with mainstream global practice, and bridge the gap between the production of precision scientific instruments, which are always designed in metric, and that of retail products sold to Americans, which are designed according to the imperial standard. A credible announcement of this kind will force other producers and consumers of small mechanical parts to make a decision about the standards they will use. For Bolt Inc., the question now is whether or not to follow the Alliance and switch from the imperial to the metric standard, manufacturing bolts in thicknesses measured not in fractions of an inch, but in millimeters. Making this switch may require reconfiguring or replacing existing bolt manufacturing machines, which we will assume can only produce bolts according to one specification and so would not be able to produce in both metric and imperial measures. But your overriding concern will not, in all likelihood, be with the potential mechanical difficulties of switching over. Your principal consideration will be your expectations about Bolt Inc.'s customers, who own machines designed to take a particular kind of bolt, built to imperial specifications. If these customers go metric and Bolt Inc. does not, Bolt Inc. will lose their business. Will Bolt Inc. go metric?

Assuming that the market share that the Alliance represents is significant—and further, that you expect that other non-Alliance companies in the market will also want to switch to metric—you will almost surely adopt the metric standard too. Otherwise, you risk losing a large part of your business: that is, all the clients for whom your bolts will no longer prove compatible once they have switched, as well as any future clients who switch over at a later point. Of course, this might mean losing some clients who prefer the imperial measurements that you currently use, but your considered choice might necessarily involve such a loss. It might also mean accepting the cost of changing some equipment. But if the Alliance's total market share passed a critical threshold, you would probably be forced to make the switch to metric anyway, in order to continue to compete. Fortunately, your clients would presumably do so as well: in fact, they may decide that they are at risk of losing Bolt Inc. as their supplier of bolts if they do not join the Alliance, even in advance of any decision you make.

The power of standards generates these reciprocally determining decisions in the market for bolts. Borrowing a concept from economics, we might say that there are *economies of scale* in the adoption of metric, as proposed by the Alliance. (The notion of economies of scale is formally distinct from, but intuitively similar to, the more familiar notion of "increasing returns to scale."[14]) A production process exhibits such economies of scale if there is a decreasing cost for each additional unit of output over some range of production. In this case, it is more efficient to produce on a larger scale since each additional unit of production costs less than the previous unit did.

The value of a telephone offers an example of economies of scale. How much is a telephone worth? One answer might be that a phone is worth what it costs to produce, the sum total of its parts plus the labor needed to assemble them. However, we do not buy the telephone for the machine itself, but for the *connection* that it offers to others who also have telephones. So how much it is worth depends on how much we want it, which depends in turn on the number of people who already have a telephone (or whom we expect to get one). If the world contained only one single telephone, it would be worth nothing to us—even though it costs something to produce—for there would be nobody in the world we could call. Given the existence of other telephone users in the world, however, our phone begins to look more valuable. And when billions of other people own telephones, that same telephone, far from being worthless, becomes extremely valuable—so much so that many people might even be prone to claim that they "could not live" without one.

The economies of scale that we see in the telephone network are also exhibited in the example of Bolt Inc. The greater the number of people who use a particular standard, the more valuable it becomes for others to adopt the same one. Expectations play a critical role in this process. Even if the Alliance does not currently control a large market share, its announcement may well make large numbers of people believe that the metric standard will become widely used—leading many of them to adopt it preemptively. Expecting that its customers (and its competitors) will go metric, Bolt Inc. will probably decide do so. In turn, this will confirm the expectations of other market participants, who, anticipating Bolt Inc.'s switchover, will likely have done so too. Generalizing this dynamic, we can easily imagine a scenario in which, before long, there may be no companies left which are still using the imperial standard: most likely every company will have either made the switch or gone out of business. In this example, we see how decentralized, individual decisions to participate in the adoption of a particular standard can conduce to a circumstance in which the standard becomes effectively compulsory for everyone in a given market—and all without any collective decision to produce such an outcome ever having been taken.

THE NETWORK POWER OF STANDARDS

The economies of scale driving the adoption of a standard result from a "positive feedback" dynamic in which each new user increases the desirability of that standard in the eyes of other potential users. A system is said to exhibit positive feedback when a change in one variable leads to a further change in that same variable, and in the same direction. For example, an increase in the number of people who own a telephone increases the value of the telephone network as a whole, which then attracts new telephone users. Or, the greater number of people who speak a given language, say, the more attractive that language is likely to appear to those who wish to learn a foreign tongue. It is the positive feedback generated by the adoption of a standard that constitutes its power, the "pull" that a standard has because it underlies a network of users to whom others are likely to want to gain access. The concept of *network power* joins two ideas: first, that standards are more valuable when greater numbers of people use them because they offer a form of coordination that exhibits economies of scale; and second, that one effect of this coordination is, over time, to eliminate alternative standards that might have been freely chosen. When these ideas are considered together, the central premise of network power is that the benefits that come from using one standard rather than another increase with the number of users, such that domi- nant standards can edge out rival ones. This process exhibits a positive feedback dynamic and can prove self-reinforcing: the value of a standard increases with the addition of each new user to its network, which means that it has the power to draw in additional users from other networks, each of which further increases its network power. Importantly, when a user switches from one network to another, she will not only increase the value of the network she joins, but will also decrease the value of her previous network by leaving it with one fewer member (in turn, making it less attractive for the remaining members of that standard to continue using it, and more attractive for them to copy her defection).

Although there is a sort of social "momentum" behind network power, the growth of a network is driven by the active *choices* of individuals, rather than by their passive acceptance of something external to them. An anal- ogy to physical momentum (describing network power as a "snowball effect") can tend to obscure the agency of the people involved, and direct attention away from the decisions of network members and toward prop- erties considered at the aggregate level. But the concept of network power should not tempt us to locate active agency in aggregate social phenomena such as "the network" rather than in the people who compose it. Networks do not grow of their own volition, or "spread" in an impersonal way, even though it is easy to drift into employing that kind of language when we want to describe how network power leads to growth in network size, and how that, in turn, increases network power. It is *our* choices that lie behind network power, and nothing beyond or outside them—a point I will return to in the discussion of modern social thought in the next chapter.[15]

It is easy to see network power at work in the technological examples I introduced above. But in many forms of social exchange, too, a relatively specific standard underlies a network and regulates access to the benefits of cooperation with members of that network.[16] The network power of these standards is a measure of the attractiveness of that network to outsiders. Since it is via such standards that people gain access to one another in networks, whenever it is desirable to participate in a larger network rather than a smaller one, *standards have a power that grows in proportion to the size of the network they unite.*

In computing, the idea that the value of a network is related to its size has been given technical elaboration in "Metcalfe's Law," which asserts that the value of a computer network increases exponentially with the number of its users. However, the broader point can be made more generally: standards attract new users in proportion to the size of the network they underlie, and sometimes in greater proportion.[17] Of course, the fact that a standard has network power does not mean that non-users will necessarily adopt it. A standard is attractive as a gatekeeper to a network of users, even if that network is not large or otherwise significant enough to induce non-users to switch onto that standard. Importantly, network power is always a *comparative* notion, based on the different sizes of rival networks—that is, networks based on different standards, each of which facilitates the same activity. Even the standard underlying a small network generates network power, for any standard that mediates access to others is valuable. Whether it is valuable enough to adopt is another question.[18]

The size of the network that a standard unites is not the only factor that can lead one standard to dominate over others. A network may be attractive to outsiders not only because of its size but because of the desirability of the particular standard that unites it—a point to which I will return below. Also, the idea of "size" requires further elaboration, for it is always a comparative measure. It refers to the proportion of people engaged in a particular activity who use one standard rather than another, not the absolute number of people using a standard. For example, if there were only ten people in the world participating in a certain activity, seven by one standard and three by another, the seven-person network would be considered a "large" one. Networks may also vary in significance not on account of their relative size, but on account of the significance of their members in the activity that the standard mediates: a small handful of elite financiers may have much more effect on the use of a particular currency than numerically larger networks of currency users in poor countries who command fewer resources. The network power of standards that mediate especially important or desirable activities will also be greater than that of those that mediate less central or important activities. The benefits of being part of the club, so to speak, are greater in some fields of endeavor than others.

SWITCHING NETWORKS

Network power can induce people to "switch" networks—to do things like learn foreign languages, use different currencies, or join organizations that require adherence to new rules of conduct, all of which occur frequently in contemporary globalization. To illustrate more precisely how network power can lead to such changes, consider in the abstract two standards, Standard A and Standard B, which unite their respective networks, Network A and Network B. These standards enable the same activity, and function in roughly equivalent ways: that is, the difficulty of the activity does not change depending on which standard is used. People in Network A would gain access to everyone in Network B if they used Standard B. Likewise, members of Network B would need to use Standard A to deal with people in Network A. Individual members of either network will, whenever it is desirable to gain access to a greater rather than a smaller number of people, encounter strong incentives to use both standards or, where they must use only one or the other, to use the one that provides access to the larger network.

For example, suppose that Network A has many more members than Network B. Any member of either network would want to be able to use both Standards A and B if they are compatible, thereby gaining access to all the members of both networks. But if these standards are incompatible, such that they govern the same mode of social interaction without allowing complementary or parallel structures—an assumption I will re-examine in Chapter 6—then network power will push members of Network B to adopt Standard A and join Network A. The incentive to do so will come from the possibility of gaining access to the larger number of members of Network A, even at the cost of losing access to the remaining members of Network B.

Examining the incentives faced by an individual member of Network B makes the point clearer. The member of Network B will need to consider the benefits of cooperating with the larger body of members in Network A that she would gain if she adopted Standard A. These benefits would be offset by whatever costs she would incur in the process of switching over from Standard B to Standard A, which might include losing access to the remaining members of Network B and the difficulty of adjusting to the new standard. (We might call the first set of costs "opportunity costs," and the second "switching costs," but remember that staying put in Network B also generates its own set of "opportunity costs"—the loss of potential cooperation with members of Network A.) So any member of Network B contemplating the move into Network A will have to compare the value of accessing Network A against the costs of adopting Standard A and losing the value of current membership in Network B. Since the value of a network is related to its size, we can conclude that when Network A is larger than Network B, any member of B will face pressure to join A.

A greater disparity in the size of the two networks will translate into a greater discrepancy in network power. This does not mean that Standard B has *no* network power. Because cooperation with members of Network B is desirable, Standard B will exert some pull on members of Network A. But this pull must be assessed comparatively. All else being equal, users of Standard A will remain in the dominant Network A, sacrificing potential access to members of Network B in order to maintain a connection to the larger network.

So far, we have been assuming that Standards A and B are equivalent in their functioning, so that the choice between Networks A and B is based on their value as a function of their respective sizes only. In abstract models of networks (or in some actual computer networks) this assumption may hold, since the connections of which the network is made up may be considered uniform. But in the case of standards that enable social interaction, we cannot assume that standards operate similarly in different networks. Rather, the value of membership in such networks must be considered a function of both the size of that network and the quality of its standard.

We may think of this difference as one of *intrinsic* and *extrinsic* reason. We have *intrinsic* reasons to adopt a new standard if it simply functions better for our purposes, while we have *extrinsic* reasons if that standard governs access to a network that we find desirable for some other reason, most likely because of its size. Thus the decision to switch from Network B to Network A, where Standards A and B perform differently and are of differing quality, will depend on the size of the two networks *and* the different levels of performance of the standards in comparison, an analysis that includes both intrinsic and extrinsic reasons. I will discuss extrinsic and intrinsic reasons at greater length below.

So far, assuming a picture of the two networks at one moment in time—a snapshot that shows Network A to be larger than Network B—the costs and benefits facing a member of Network B considering the switch to Standard A will look as I have described. But taking a dynamic approach that examines how networks grow and decline over time—and incorporates the expectations of such growth or decline—reveals the positive feedback effect which generates network power. Given the economies of scale in the adoption of a standard, members of Network B who do not switch to Network A will face *increasing*, rather than constant, costs for staying put.

Suppose that members of Network B, the smaller network, face costs of different magnitudes in switching over to Standard A. Very plausibly, the adoption of a new standard will prove difficult in varying degrees for different people, depending on a whole host of factors, including their capacity for learning, their attachment to and position in the original network, and so on. We might imagine the members of Network B distributed along a line illustrating the costs to each member of switching over: from near zero, where we put those to whom the cost of switching to Standard A will be least, to some large number at the other end, where we put those to whom the cost of switching over will be greatest. Those with the least cost of switching will presumably do so first, since they face only the opportunity cost of losing access to Network B, and very few switching costs of any magnitude. But this first wave of departures will make the value of Network A increase, precisely because of the increase in its size. Thus the opportunity cost of remaining in Network B will not remain constant. It will increase every time a member of Network B defects to Network A, since with each lost member, Network B will become smaller in comparison to Network A, and hence less attractive to potential members, while Network A will grow in attractiveness. Each new defection from Network B to Network A will likely trigger another wave of defections, drawn from those members of Network B for whom the cost of switching over is now least. As this process continues, the costs incurred by those members of Network B for whom switching over was always more difficult will themselves increase—perhaps even at an increasing rate—as the opportunity cost of staying in the declining network continue to mount up. This means not only that Network A will progressively increase in size (and hence attractiveness) but that Network B will become progressively less viable as a real alternative to A.

Of course, members of a small network will not always wait until mounting costs make switching to the dominant network necessary. Frequently, they will anticipate this dynamic and act in advance of it, expecting waves of defections to occur, and not wanting to be the last to switch over. Members of Network B will rationally expect that, given some minimum necessary level of imbalance between Network A and Network B, Network B will progressively lose members to Network A, and that holdouts in Network B will face steadily mounting costs so long as they do not adopt Standard A. These expectations then become self-confirming and reinforce the power of a dominant standard; especially if the switch comes to be viewed as inevitable, members of Network B can be expected to start scrambling to join Network A in the hope of avoiding being the last to switch over, since any delay in switching will be ever more costly in terms of lost access to the growing Network A. The expectations of members of both networks will determine the expected consequences for any individual member's decision, which will be reciprocally factored into the expectations of all other members in turn.

Understanding the role of expectations in network power helps to explain how the promulgation of standards can be a form of strategic interaction. For example, in the case of the "Alliance for Rational Standards" discussed above, even the expectation that the Alliance's standards will become dominant may push them to becoming so in actual fact. With a credible commitment to these new standards by key companies, the network power of the Alliance's standards will induce non-users to adopt them, even if the dominance of these standards is not already accomplished but merely expected.

INTRINSIC AND EXTRINSIC REASONS

So far, my presentation of the concept of network power has focused on cases of competition between two existing networks, each of which possesses some network power. But in order to clarify the process through which particular standards come to be adopted, we need to take a step back. Whenever a new standard emerges, the reasons for which it is used will have little to do with network power, since a standard will develop that power only once the network it unites is itself substantial enough to seem attractive to potential users. Leaving network power aside for the moment, then, we can say that there are three main causes for which a particular standard might be adopted: *reason, force,* and *chance.* The origination and development of any actual network will be highly contingent, and may well involve all three causes in different combinations at different times throughout its history. Put differently, we can say that whenever we enter into cooperative arrangements, we will either be pursuing our interests or values (using reason), acting under duress (being subject to force), or doing so by accident (being subject to chance). Reason, force, and chance will continue to act as contributing factors in a network's development, and one way of understanding network power is to describe it as a combination of one kind of reason—extrinsic reason—and one kind of force—indirect force.[19]

By *reason,* I mean simply that one standard is preferred to the alternatives, because it *better meets the goals that an agent has when entering into cooperative relations.* The reason for the preference of one standard over another may be *intrinsic* or *extrinsic.* By intrinsic reasons, I mean that a given standard is attractive for its inherent properties and not because it happens to unite an already large network. For example, certain standards may simply function better, facilitating easier and richer forms of social interaction, or allowing their users to gain access to each other with less difficulty. The claim that one standard is, strictly speaking, superior to another will often be very contentious, requiring a careful delineation of the evaluative framework in question as well as the empirical content of the standards being compared. But it will usually be the case that a standard that enables the desired coordination easily will be intrinsically preferable to more difficult alternatives. For example, in eighteenth-century Sweden, the monetization of copper meant that people had to cart around wheelbarrow loads of coinage (rather than simply carry a small purse of gold) in order to conduct large transactions. For such transactions, a gold standard rather than a copper one would better facilitate economic exchange.

A standard is adopted for *extrinsic reasons* when it is selected not for its internal characteristics, but because of the size of the network it unites. If a greater number of potential partners for cooperation use one standard rather than another, that standard will be more attractive extrinsically. It is not unreasonable to adopt a standard for the value of the network it unites, but this consideration is rather different from choosing based on its intrinsic properties. Indeed, in many cases, the only reason to adopt one standard rather than another may be extrinsic, particularly if there are no important intrinsic differences between the standards. In the example above, the decision to switch from Network B to the larger Network A was owing to extrinsic reason, determined by the size of the network rather than anything about the underlying standard, since I specified at the outset that the two standards were of roughly equivalent functioning—that is, of roughly equal intrinsic value.

This distinction between intrinsic and extrinsic reasons generalizes a set of insights from linguistics about the nature of words as arbitrary conventions. The Swiss linguist Ferdinand de Saussure based his analysis on the arbitrary nature of the sign. He insisted that the choice of particular sounds or letters to serve as a linguistic sign was wholly arbitrary in that there is no necessary or intrinsic relation between a word and that to which it refers. By arbitrary, Saussure did not mean that signification was open to individual revision, but that there was no intrinsic relationship between what he called a signifier and what it signified; he rejected the possibility "that a signal depends on the free choice of the speaker."[20]

The use of words is both conventional and arbitrary: there is no reason that we should indicate the animal *canis lupus familiaris* by the word "dog" in English and "*chien*" in French—or *canis lupus familiaris,* in biological nomenclature, for that matter—other than that we do so conventionally in order to be understood by other English or French speakers. A given word "has no natural connexion in reality" to that to which it refers; nothing in the sound pattern (or textual elaboration) of a word ties it intrinsically to what it is used to indicate. Thus, in the terms I have introduced here—which follow Saussure's own reference to the possible "intrinsic" qualities of a sign[21]—words have only extrinsic and not intrinsic reasons for their adoption, leaving aside the odd case of onomatopoeia like *bang* or *quack.* Saussure recognized that some signs do bear a connection to their referent, and he called these signs *symbols.* A symbol always retains what Saussure described as "a vestige of natural connexion between the signal and its signification," possessing what he elsewhere identified as a "rational connexion with what it symbolizes."[22] Although he did not discuss symbols at length in his *Course in General Linguistics,* it is possible to make (as later work in semiology has done) the argument that symbols are conventional, but not entirely arbitrary. Symbols may be taken up for a combination of extrinsic and intrinsic reasons: extrinsic because they are conventional and thus take their ultimate value from common use, and intrinsic because they can nevertheless do a better or worse job representing something.

Saussure clearly recognized the conventional and non-arbitrary value of symbols: "any means of expression accepted in a society rests in principle upon a collective habit or a convention, which comes to the same thing. Signs of politeness, for instance, although often endowed with a certain natural expressiveness . . . are none the less fixed by rule. It is this rule which renders them obligatory, not their intrinsic value."[23] For the sake of expositional clarity, however, Saussure focused his attention on linguistic signs because "signs which are entirely arbitrary convey better than others the ideal semiological process," even while acknowledging that other conventions may be distinguished according to their intrinsic qualities.[24]

Later work in semiotics has distinguished the purely arbitrary conventions of signification (such as words in natural languages) from the iconic mode (in which the sign is supposed to resemble that to which it refers, as in onomatopoeia or in models) and the indexical mode (in which the sign is directly connected to its referent, as in a photograph or a recording). Consider the difference between gold coins and paper money: both are used to represent value, but the former retains a direct connection to something intrinsically valued (bullion) while the latter is a purely arbitrary convention. The insight here is that not everything that is conventional—that is, governed by social conventions—is for that reason arbitrary, lacking any intrinsic connection between the signifier and signified.

My distinction between extrinsic and intrinsic reasons is meant to capture these basic semiotic insights and generalize them beyond language alone. Other than in systems of purely arbitrary signification, such as language as described by Saussure or paper currencies, standards will be selected for a combination of intrinsic and extrinsic reasons. But as the network power of a standard grows, the intrinsic reasons why it should be adopted become less important relative to the extrinsic benefits of coordination that the standard can provide: the conventional value of a standard will come to outweigh any intrinsic merits or demerits.

The British adoption of the metric system offers a good example of the role of extrinsic reason in the choice among (non-linguistic) conventions, since the switch from imperial to metric measurements was made in order to allow smoother exchange with Britain's European neighbors. Certainly, we can imagine intrinsic reasons for the adoption of metric, such as the ease of calculating with a decimal system. But the extrinsic coordination—the fact that the metric standard was used in the rest of Europe—proved decisive. Indeed, even if the metric system had provided an intrinsically *less* reasonable standard, Britain would still probably have adopted it for the sake of easier coordination with its trading partners. By the same token, had the opposite had been the case and if the metric system had been used only in Britain, with imperial measurements used throughout the rest of Europe, Britain would most likely have abandoned the metric system, regardless of its intrinsic advantages.

Over the course of the rise of a standard, the importance of extrinsic reasons in deciding whether or not to adopt that standard increases relative to the importance of the relevant intrinsic reasons. The initial growth of a network may be based on intrinsic reasons, but as that network grows over time, the attraction of its size will provide a sufficient extrinsic reason for its adoption. This does not mean that an extrinsic reason displaces any intrinsic reason for choosing a standard, but simply that the matter becomes overdetermined. The intrinsic merits of a standard will usually remain relevant even with the increased effects of network power, but they will be supplemented—and perhaps, eventually, wholly outweighed—by extrinsic reasons. For example, it may have been *intrinsically* reasonable for Britain to adopt the metric system at any point in the history of the decimal-base measurement standard, whether in the year 1800, following the French Revolution that introduced it, in the year 1900, at the height of the British Empire, or in the year 2000, with European economic integration the order of the day. The intrinsic merits of metric have not changed over the last two hundred years, but the weight of extrinsic reason bearing down on the British did—and that is what proved decisive.

FORCE AND CHANCE

Of course, the early growth of a network does not usually depend on the intrinsic reasons for adopting one standard rather than another; history seldom presents such a straightforward choice. Another major factor in the early adoption of one standard rather than another is *force*. By force, I mean the *use of coercion* to compel the adoption of a standard. Force may be either direct or indirect: direct force should be understood as the imposition of costs unrelated to network membership that compel a switch, while indirect force is the imposition of (opportunity) costs resulting from membership in one network rather than another.

Direct force involves imposing "costs" such as violence or punishment for failing to adopt a given standard, or denying benefits unrelated to the immediate standard-governed activity. For example, in the category of direct force, we can include not only threats or acts of physical violence but also coercive socialization, such as education in which pupils are not allowed to speak to one another in their native language, or are punished for retaining traditional dress or customs. If direct force is the motivation for switching networks, then we can say that a person adopting a new standard has been compelled to do so outright and not because of anything about the configuration of networks. In such cases, the person making the switch is forced to do so by the threat of punishment or deprivation unrelated to her membership in the network, although this factor will, of course, have an impact on any decisions she has to make about her network membership.

Indirect force, by contrast, is the pressure to adopt a standard that comes from the threat of losing access to others, the social isolation from people who use a different standard. Indirect force comes not from the imposition of costs unrelated to network membership, but from the imposition of costs driven by the structure of network membership itself. The opportunity costs that I described above as mounting on those who hold out against a dominant standard should be understood as a form of indirect force. A member of one network faces overwhelming indirect force when these opportunity costs mount to such an extent that she is deprived of real opportunities for cooperation in any network except the dominant one. But a lesser degree of indirect force may also be felt in any case of the rise of one standard over another. Importantly, the penalties extant in indirect force consist not just of lost access to users of a dominant standard by users of a smaller one but, in the case of great inequality or disproportion in network power, lost access to former users of one's own standard who have defected to the larger network as well.

Early in the rise of a network, only direct rather than indirect force may be used to increase network size; if force is to be used, new adherents must be added by direct coercion, since indirect force emerges only once a network of sufficient size exists that non-users feel compelled to join it or face social isolation. The crux of the formulation of network power *as power*—a theme I discuss in Chapter 4 at length—is that beyond a certain point, members of a small network are "forced" to adopt the standard of a dominant network or else face isolation. For example, an individual's decision to adopt a majority language (when it is not driven by direct compulsion) comes from the desire to communicate with other speakers of that language, but also because a minority language becomes progressively less viable as the population of its speakers dwindles. To be a part of a viable network *at all* may require defecting to a larger one.

On this account, indirect force can be seen as equivalent to extrinsic reason, for the same benefits of coordination that draw in new users based on extrinsic considerations also generate the structure of opportunity costs that I describe here as indirect force. The attraction of a standard underlying a dominant network constitutes both a form of indirect force and an extrinsic reason, either or both of which can be used to describe choices made because of network power. Thus, early on in the rise of a network, we may see either intrinsic reasons or direct force augmenting its membership, but after the network passes a certain size, both extrinsic reasons and indirect force will come into play, since the standard that unites it will have become valuable for the social coordination it provides.

Indeed, indirect force and extrinsic reason may be said to merge at the highest levels of network power, for the demand of reason is to adopt a dominant standard rather than lose access to others, and yet this reason dictates a selection that, while rational, is chosen under the compulsion of having no viable alternatives. When reason and force merge under conditions of great disparities in network power, it becomes a matter of semantics whether we should best describe the situation as determined by "reason" or determined by "force." Recognizing the equivalence of indirect force and extrinsic reason enables us see both at work in the same process: intrinsic reason becomes irrelevant and direct force unnecessary once a standard has surpassed a critical threshold and its continued rise is driven by network power.

Finally, a standard may attract early adherents merely by *chance*, by which I mean the *accidental convergence on a routine*. We may accidentally converge upon a standard that provides the solution to a problem of coordination, whose resolution in any one of many possible ways is desirable. And once we have stumbled upon such a solution, even if we suppose it is not the best solution possible, it may well continue to have some staying power. Consider in this regard the arbitrary nature of spoken words: if there is no intrinsic connection between the phonetic qualities of a word and its referent, then we may suppose its emergence to have been an accident. (Therefore, Saussure proposed studying signs synchronically rather than diachronically, rejecting the historical approach of nineteenth-century comparative grammar and arguing instead that words have meaning as they are used in relation to a system of signification at a given moment in time.[25]) Other standards, too, may emerge as the result of happenstance or fortunate convergence, as in the case of "pure conventions," which will be discussed in the next chapter. The literature on industrial organization is filled with stories of products that gained market dominance because of seemingly insignificant differences in initial market share that later became magnified because of economies of scale. In such circumstances, an early lead gained by accident can generate unexpectedly large differences in final outcomes. However, although we may fall into the use of one standard rather than another by chance, we cannot always adopt a new standard just as easily. While chance may be responsible for the initial emergence of a standard, it will be transformed into network power—into indirect force and extrinsic reason—as the standard gains new users. For, once on the trajectory of network power, it is not accident that will increase the size of a network, but its own amassed power. Put differently, even arbitrary signs possess network power, precisely because of their conventionality.

THRESHOLDS IN NETWORK POWER

After a standard gains its initial push from reason, force, or chance, it exerts network power and moves along to conventionality, buoyed by an influx of new users. We have examined how this process begins, but two further thresholds on this trajectory remain to be delineated in order to complete the trajectory of a standard. Like "tipping point" phenomena, a standard can surpass critical thresholds in the path of network power, exhibiting new properties after gaining critical mass.[26] Importantly, these thresholds are subjective and not necessarily determinate or objective;

I introduce them in order to capture the social and phenomenological evaluation of successful standards.

The first threshold is what I call the *threshold of visibility*, signifying the point past which a network is sufficiently large to become attractive to non-users. Below this threshold, a standard has no network power because it is effectively invisible to those outside its network. Network power arises beyond this threshold, once the standard has attracted a large enough number of users that its network becomes visible and attractive to others. Reason, force, or chance (or some combination thereof) may push a standard past this threshold. Beyond it, the network begins generating network power, exerting a pull on members of other networks for extrinsic reasons. Below it—though the network exists—it is not large enough even to register with outsiders.

Language offers a convenient way of exemplifying what I mean by a threshold of visibility. Many English speakers would like to learn French or Spanish, two languages with large populations of speakers both in France and Spain and in their former colonies abroad. Both French and Spanish have passed the threshold of visibility and prove attractive to English speakers. (Whether they prove attractive enough for English speakers to make the effort to learn them is another question.) But the language of the Eyak, now known only to the elderly Marie Smith of Cordova, Alaska, remains below the threshold of visibility—so far below that it seems certain that with Marie's death it will be extinguished altogether as a living language.[27]

As this example illustrates, standards do not only rise above the threshold of visibility; they can fall below it, too. Indeed, when smaller networks decline, whether through the death of their members or their members' absorption into larger networks, these smaller networks can fall below the threshold of visibility and become "invisible," powerless in the broader sphere of social relations.[28] These standards may still have users but they have no network power: total effacement of a standard is not necessary for it to lose all effective relevance to non-users. Not only Eyak, but a very large number of dying languages have fallen below this threshold, as I discuss in Chapter 3. A small community may still speak them, but they are effectively invisible to outsiders, even in a very local geographic setting.

Below the threshold of visibility, standards do not exhibit economies of scale in their adoption; they do not possess network power. Hence, the maintenance of such a standard may suffer many of the problems of non-conventional cooperative behavior: for example, familiar problems of collective action. Individual defection from the standard may be individually preferable to cooperation, even if cooperation is in everyone's collective interest. (However, it should be noted that this suggestion depends, in part, on a view of "free riding" that may be philosophically untenable.[29]) It is perhaps unsurprising, then, that when standards are deliberately created—work that may involve large initial investments—the effort will often have been made by powerful players with strategic ambitions and a long-term planning horizon, such as large companies, government agencies, or industry consortia. The move beyond the threshold of visibility requires such a subsidy. Network power will take over beyond it, but cannot be counted on before the network attains some minimum size.

The second threshold is what I call the *threshold of inevitability*, signifying the point past which a network has become so dominant that we can expect virtually all non-users to adopt its standard. Convergence on the dominant network has become inevitable; this threshold comes before convergence on a universal standard, but after its imminent arrival has come to be expected by everyone. This threshold is a kind of tipping point, as we see in studies of non-linear dynamic systems, beyond which the diversity of possible alternatives is quickly distilled into a single unified network. We may understand this threshold as occurring at the point at which the expected value of joining the dominant network to all remaining non-users (as a function of both its size and the quality of its standard) is equal to that of any lesser network plus switching costs. Remember that by this point, the value of a smaller network to its members may be very small indeed, as its total size will have decreased due to prior defections, and its current value will reflect a general expectation of further attrition.

A critical question to consider is whether one network's movement beyond the threshold of inevitability will tend to push competing networks below the threshold of visibility. As a general matter, the movement of one standard past the threshold of inevitability will tend to displace competing standards to the extent that they prove incompatible with it.[30] In the extreme case, if two standards are *strictly* incompatible—such that a user can use only one at a time—then as the dominant standard moves toward universality, any rival standards will necessarily fall below the threshold of visibility and may even be pushed to extinction, for a universal standard that is strictly incompatible with its rivals will be (by definition) the only game in town. But the movement of one standard to universal status does not require the elimination of compatible alternatives, only incompatible ones. For example, the rise of English as a global language should prove compatible with the continued existence of other languages, if it is used as a global *second* language rather than the sole global language. However, in other cases—for example, some technical or monetary conventions—the rise of a universal standard may lead to the effective elimination of alternatives that prove incompatible.

Again, these thresholds may be identified through phenomenological or social assessment: they are not necessarily distinct points, and they are certainly not invariant across different standards. Rather, they represent loose concepts whose actual content will vary given the empirical circumstances of any particular network. There is probably no abstract formula by which we can determine the network size at which either tipping point occurs, unlike in some models of non-linear systems. For example, whether the threshold of inevitability is passed after a network gains a precise minimum size or is a more gradual process occurring once a network is recognized as clearly dominant cannot be addressed out of context. Similarly, whether the threshold of visibility is as small as two people using a standard with each other in a purely private communication, or as great as a large minority of a given population is also an empirical, not an abstract matter, and depends on the relevant network configuration in question. But these thresholds capture two defining aspects of network power: first, that a network requires a minimum size to exert power over members of other networks, and second, that beyond a certain size, a network pulls all other networks with it toward convergence on a universal convention.

THE UNIVERSAL STANDARD

It should be obvious from the discussion so far that network power will push different networks toward a position of convergence, in which two or more networks become one. When all members of Network B have switched over to Network A—or at least, so many that Network B no longer possesses any attraction for members of Network A—then we can say that Network B has converged with Network A. If we continue the assumption of strict incompatibility, then we can say that Network B has fallen below the threshold of visibility and Network A has surpassed the threshold of inevitability and successfully universalized.[31]

It is important to note that convergence on the same standard should not be assumed to be the only outcome possible when two networks come into contact—various other positions of equilibrium are possible, and this particular one depends on several initial assumptions, particularly of the strict incompatibility of the standards in question and their equal intrinsic value. It may not be the result, for example, if the intrinsic value of two standards differs greatly, or is perceived to differ greatly by two relatively distinct groups of people who wish to maintain separate networks. Whether someone will choose to join a large network with an inferior standard depends on a balance of intrinsic and extrinsic reasons that need not tend toward convergence.[32] In the general case, however, network power will tend to drive networks to convergence on the same standard, because standards are inherently universalizing—even though the domain in which their predominance grows may be restricted in any number of ways. The social relations embodied in cooperative arrangements like standards suggest themselves as incipient universals. Every coordinative arrangement represents an invitation to others because it proclaims a manner in which social cooperation can be accomplished.

We can call a standard whose invitation has been taken up by everyone a *universal standard*.[33] The power of a standard thus follows a peculiar trajectory on its way to universality: starting from reason, force, or chance, it grows in relation to the size of its network—even at an increasing rate—up to the point at which it replaces all competing standards. At that point, when a network is as large as it can be without becoming the only viable network, the network power of its standard is at its zenith. Beyond that point, however, we cannot properly speak of the standard retaining any power at all.[34] Rather, its power has become so total that the comparative notion of network power is no longer applicable, for all its rivals have fallen below the threshold of visibility. Such a standard admits no others against which we can compare it. It has become conventional: a commonplace, a universal.

The triumph of a universal standard is revealed in both its generality and its obscurity. It is difficult to identify a universal standard in the absence of contrasting alternatives. Put differently, we might say that *conventions are most conspicuous when partial.* A universal standard may often prove inconspicuous, appearing to its users simply as a social fact with its actual function in social coordination obscured. We notice social facts only with great difficulty for they constitute our modes of relation to others and influence our perception and interpretation of these modes themselves.[35]

The great tumult of globalization, past and present, results from the great diversity of standards brought into competition with one another and thus rendered visible in a new way. And our attention is primed to that diversity by the fact that, almost as soon as it is registered, it appears to be at risk of melting away in a series of global convergences. Understanding why this may be occurring requires examining more closely the network power at work in these newly global social relations.

CHAPTER TWO

The Power of Sociability

IN THE LAST CHAPTER, I introduced the idea of network power and suggested that this concept can help us to make sense of globalization. In my discussion, there was a notable lacuna: politics. This omission was no accident, since network power forms a crucial part of the process in which large-scale social structures emerge through the accumulation of decentralized, individual decisions without necessarily involving political intervention. The construction of the transnational networks that constitute what we commonly call "globalization" is largely based on such a cumulative pattern, rather than on constructive political effort. It is this feature of contemporary globalization that should most arrest our attention and invite critical scrutiny.

In the introduction, I suggested that there are, broadly speaking, two different ways in which we arrive at outcomes that hold good for whole groups of people: via what we might call relations of *sovereignty* or via relations of *sociability*. The idea of network power can help us to describe the power that operates in the second category, via relations of sociability; it is an attempt to sketch out the rudiments of a more developed analysis of sociability than we have had so far, and to show how power is at work in relations of sociability just as it is in relations of sovereignty, albeit in a less obvious way. Developing an analysis of sociability raises a question that has given rise to a great deal of debate in modern social theory: how it is possible to describe a kind of power that operates through social structures, rather than as the express will of a specific agent. The idea of network power may contribute to a theory of *structuration*, helping us to develop an account of social structures that understands them as both the outcome of individual choices and their constitutive foundation. Such an account will be especially helpful for analyzing the relations of sociability underlying contemporary processes of globalization.

SOCIABILITY AND SOVEREIGNTY

In Chapter 1, I showed how the dynamics of network power can lead to the universalization of a dominant standard. I did so, in part, to help us distinguish two channels or routes through which our social relations (including standards) can take a definite shape. The first is through the accumulation of decentralized, individual decisions that come to constitute, over time, large-scale social structures—perhaps even leading to the establishment of universal standards or global conventions, uniting vast numbers of users in worldwide networks. I have already argued that this dynamic should be understood as exerting a form of *power*, and I will develop this argument further in Chapter 4 with reference to philosophical theories of power. The second route through which our social relations take shape is via *political* procedures, which work not through the collection of many individual decisions aggregated together over time, but in instances of collective decision-making by specially constituted political bodies.

The difference between these two ways in which we organize our social life revolves around what we might think of as two different sets of human relations: those of *sociability* and those of *sovereignty*. These two terms have been used in overlapping, varied, and sometimes confusing ways at different historical junctures for different theoretical and conceptual purposes.[1] (This is perhaps particularly true of the term "sovereignty," whereas "sociability" has largely fallen out of contemporary use.) Before I discuss the way in which I wish to distinguish them more precisely, I want to make explicit that this distinction is one of "ideal types" of decision-making, and that any actual social structure may well be constituted by relations of both sociability and sovereignty.[2] Indeed, these relations are intertwined in a rather deep way. Excepting perhaps the most elementary or fleeting forms, the relations of sociability usually depend upon background conditions determined and enforced by the relations of sovereignty. Similarly, without the sociability that renders us mutually intelligible, we would not be able to assemble ourselves into larger decision-making bodies—that is, we would not be able to constitute our sovereignty.

The distinction between sociability and sovereignty is perhaps easy to overlook, but it is critically important to recognize that social outcomes that affect all members of a group can be arrived at in one of two ways, with very different consequences. A universal standard of the kind I described in the preceding chapter results from many decentralized, individual decisions accumulated together; to borrow Rousseau's famous terminology, the way a universal standard emerges reflects the *will of all*, the summation of all personal wills, since all the members of a network will have decided individually to participate in a common social activity.[3] Standards that have not yet achieved universality are voluntary constructions reflecting the participation of particular individuals; Rousseau called these forms of voluntarism resulting from the summation of some subset of all personal wills by the name *partial associations*. (We might think of them—to appropriate a phrase used recently in a different context—as "coalitions of the willing.")

In relations of sociability, everyone is understood as a private person, whether non- or pre-political, and whatever we pursue together results from the exercise of our individual choice to participate (or not) in a common enterprise. The accumulation of these decisions—for example, whether or not to switch to a particular standard in order to gain access to a dominant network—can result in the construction of large-scale social organizations such as multinational corporations, churches, technology networks, and perhaps even some kinds of empires. More generally, it results in the construction of the social conventions (with or without an organizational structure) that regulate our shared activities.

What sociability cannot do is to construct a political state; that task depends on an act of self-constituting sovereignty, which, to borrow the other half of Rousseau's famous contrast, marks the formation of the *general will*, which is to be distinguished from the mere summation of individual wills, and which initiates politics proper. The formation of the general will is not a mysterious process: the constitution of sovereignty results from an agreement on a set of procedural rules that create a general decision-making body, out of which further substantive rules can then issue in the form of legislation. In the relations of sovereignty, then, there is a two-tiered decision-making structure: in the first instance, a procedural commitment to the creation of a sovereign union (the "social contract" which results in a general will), through which secondary, substantive decisions may then be taken, according to the agreed-upon procedural rules.

In his *Second Treatise of Government*, John Locke presents a concise definition of (majoritarian) sovereignty along just these lines. He explains: "When any number of Men have so *consented to make one Community* or Government, they are thereby presently incorporated, and make *one Body Politick*, wherein the *Majority* have a Right to act and conclude the rest." Locke restates this basic description at several different points, and a second passage brings out clearly the nature of sovereignty: "For when any number of Men have, by the consent of every individual, made a *Community*, they have thereby made that *Community* one Body, with a Power to Act as one Body, which is only by the will and determination of the *majority*."[4]

Once relations of sovereignty are established, each person can be recognized as a citizen, and constructive projects can be undertaken by the decisions of the single, corporate body in which each individual is conceived of as being represented (for example, because they have cast a vote on what subset of the entire group should be entrusted to make decisions in the name of the whole). Thus while the relations of sociability consist in the accumulation of individual contracts that, taken together, generate a broader social setting or structure—as I have described happening through network power—those of sovereignty depend upon an initial "social contract," through which individuals fashion themselves into a unity that then provides for collective, rather than merely aggregated decisions. It should be obvious that, on this interpretation at least, what is important about sovereignty is its link to democratic (or, at least, representative) politics, and not any ideas about nationalism or the mores of a particular *volk*—ideas which relate, on my reading, more to the sphere of our "sociability."

Exactly how each person is represented in the relations of sovereignty is something over which different political theorists quarrel. Rousseau amended Hobbes's earlier (and foundational) theory of sovereignty by insisting that the procedural rules constituting sovereignty must necessarily remain democratic, that is, guided by majority vote, because the people composing an initial sovereign cannot permanently alienate their sovereignty to a single person or a smaller group of individuals.[5] Without going further into the details of that argument, I will rely on this democratic conception of sovereignty throughout the book, understanding the relations of sovereignty as involving final recourse to majoritarian decision.

What is really valuable in relations of sovereignty, therefore, is that everyone is involved (directly or via political representation) in decisions about common outcomes, which grants both normative legitimacy and practical efficacy to these decisions. By contrast, activity that takes place only within the relations of sociability does not involve the prior construction of a political sphere. Instead, each individual decides whether and how to cooperate with others in a decentralized, voluntarist fashion. These two forms of decision-making thus illustrate two different ways in which we can conceive *consent*: either, as we see in relations of sociability, individual consent to individual circumstances which are, of course, determined by the choices of others, in the same way that one's own choices affect the circumstances that others will later face; or else, as we see in relations of sovereignty, collective consent to collective circumstances, from which then follow implications for the individuals constituting the sovereign. To put it succinctly, it is the difference between voluntarism and majority rule. It is also the difference between implicit consent to a social outcome that occurs as a (perhaps wholly unforeseen) by-product of individual actions, and explicit consent to that social outcome itself, as decided through a political procedure.

A final point worth noting is that the relations of sociability thus cohere only across time, with individuals following the prior choices of others in deciding whether to participate in any given networked activity. Sociability develops historically in a way that politics need not. Indeed, a unified political agency can be used to clear away the unwanted accretions of history—and perhaps, even, avert the occurrence of unwanted developments in the future. This is a fact that makes some people nervous about politics, but it needs to be weighed against the recognition that there are many different ways to be oppressed, and that many of them are private and relatively opaque, bound up in voluntaristic constructions against which only public power can provide effective relief.

Consider a concrete example to illustrate the difference between relations of sociability and those of sovereignty, taking up your position again as the head of Bolt Inc., the manufacturer of mechanical parts. There are two different ways in which the metric standard might become conventional in your industry. The first is via the dynamics of network power that I sketched in the last chapter: a standard might be proposed or promulgated by a private agent (or set of agents) such as the "Alliance for Rational Standards," and gradually come to dominance through the pull of network power. Assume that the Alliance—which is, in Rousseau's terms, a "partial association"—successfully initiates the industry-wide use of the metric standard of measurement, via dynamics of network power. This standard would then reflect the "will of all"—because the entire industry (and all consumers too) would have conformed to it. Indeed, the strategic adoption of the metric system by powerful companies in a major industry might even catapult it into more general use—perhaps even to universal acceptance. But the result would not represent the "general will" because the decision to adopt that set of standards was not taken by the whole people acting together in an instance of collective decision-making, but by each of them choosing individually to join up, following one another in turn.

Alternatively, the switch to the metric system could be achieved by a law being passed to that effect by the government. Bolt Inc. would then be obliged by a regulatory decision, backed by majority vote, to start using the metric system as part of an industry-wide switchover. Assuming that the state is functioning properly, this move would prove an expression of the general will, an example of sovereignty in action. Unlike the first case, Bolt Inc. would not get to decide by itself whether to conform to the Alliance's proposal; however, the people who work at Bolt Inc.—and its customers and suppliers—would all be part of the decision to switch, which would then be binding for all its competitors and clients, all at the same time.

Everyone switching to the metric system at once—in an instance of collective rather than aggregated decision-making—could come about only through political fiat, rather than through network power as we saw in the case of the Alliance for Rational Standards. I do not wish to seem to suggest that all of our standards only come into general use through network power dynamics: we can, and sometimes do, create or adopt standards as an act of political will. But many of the important standards that structure our relations of sociability (including those of globalization) are the products of network power dynamics—thus reflecting the power of sociability and not sovereignty.

THE GLOBALIZATION OF SOCIABILITY

I want to use this distinction between the relations of sociability and sovereignty to highlight what I take to be the central tension in contemporary globalization: that everything is being globalized *except politics*. We live in a world in which our relations of sociability—our commerce, culture, ideas, manners—are increasingly shared, coordinated by newly global conventions in these domains, but in which our politics remains inescapably national, centered in the nation-states that are the only loci of sovereign decision-making. We do, of course, have an international politics in the form of treaty organizations and U.N. agencies, but we do not have *sovereign* power operating at that level. After all, these quasi-political forums are ultimately the voluntary creations of nation-states—and thus the product of international sociability rather than supranational sovereignty. Even those theorists who take a relatively strong position in favor of what is sometimes called "cosmopolitan democracy"—the idea that democratic values (and possibly even procedures) can and should be reconstituted at a transnational or supranational level—usually argue that democratic norms should also be strengthened *within* national spaces, and that even a fairer or more egalitarian globalization would provide no straightforward analogue to national democratic sovereignty.[6]

Globalization works to extend and deepen relations of sociability at a global level, but without the concomitant construction of a global sovereignty—however much some national sovereigns may be able to influence particular aspects of this process. When we recast the process of globalization in this light, we can make better sense of the controversies that have figured in recent discussions of it. In the previous chapter, I claimed that the dynamics of globalization present nothing particularly novel or unprecedented, however new the scale on which they are occurring. A similar case can be made with regard to the *debate* over globalization: what is interesting or puzzling about globalization is nothing other than what we should already find interesting or puzzling about social relations more generally. What we find in the debate about globalization is the latest iteration of a longer-running dispute about the desirable and possible forms of human association in social and political life. At stake is our understanding of how power operates in different domains of human activity and what it means to give our consent to the circumstances of social organization that we create for ourselves.

A wide variety of "pro-globalization" positions can be interpreted as claims about the desirability of relations of sociability as against relations of sovereignty in constituting human affairs. For example, with very few alterations, the argument for the desirability of free trade among nations applies with equal force to the relations among individuals within any nation. The logical structure of the arguments for free trade is the same in either case. More generally, pro-globalization commentators generally have great confidence in the social structures that individuals form through voluntary contracting with one another, and little patience for the idea that "consenting adults" (as it is often put) should not be free to interact with each other individually, whether on a newly global stage or in the more familiar domains in which arguments about sociability and sovereignty have frequently been played out historically—for example, in debates about the desirability of private market activity. Arguing the specifics of "globalization" adds nothing new to what is, in fact, an old argument about whether and to what extent it is desirable for people to engage in social relations with one another as self-determining private individuals, or, by contrast, as citizens with an equal share in a collective decision-making power.

Critics of globalization are usually concerned about the impact that the predominance granted to relations of sociability will have on our capacity to exercise sovereignty, which is valued because of its link to democratic decision-making. They may also be concerned about the relatively obscure ways in which power inheres in relations of sociability, and hold up a model of transparent public decision-making as a contrast. Against the claim that the relations of sociability should be privileged because they occur between formally free individuals, these critics will direct our attention to the role that powerful interests have in shaping social outcomes whose consequences affect all of us, but over which we have little effective say, and to the importance of the background conditions against which our individual choices are made. They may further argue that within the relations of democratic sovereignty, every individual has a role in shaping collective outcomes, which is not true in networks of commerce and culture. But while these concerns are given new weight by globalization, which sets the global relations of sociability and the national systems of sovereignty in stark contrast, they apply as much *within* national settings as outside them. Globalization may have magnified a disjuncture between the powers of particular private agents and the collective decision-making power of sovereignty, but this mismatch recapitulates a longer-standing distinction between two different kinds of consent—that which we see in instances of voluntarism, and that in democratic politics—each with its particular virtues and problems, now brought into focus on a newly global stage.

AGENCY AND STRUCTURE

Understanding globalization as the extension and deepening of the relations of sociability at a global level requires considering the circumstances of contemporary social theory; the problems we face in analyzing globalization replay familiar controversies in social analysis in a new context. Twentieth-century social thought was distorted by a false dichotomy that still resounds in the globalization debate, and which makes it difficult to come to terms with the social dynamics driving globalization. The problem, pitched at the highest level of generality, is how to understand the relationship between human agency and the social structures in which people find themselves. To what extent and in what ways is human agency, both individual and collective, constrained and determined by these structures? Conversely, in what ways are these structures the products of our agency? A further refinement of this problem attempts to articulate the transformational potential of these structural constraints, for if we understand how social structures can change over time, we may be able to say something about the role of the agent in the historical process.

While these questions may sound somewhat abstract, they animate our thinking about social relations, including those constituting globalization. They are just below the surface when popular commentators tell us that, on the one hand, globalization radically increases individual freedom or, on the other, that globalization binds us in the "Golden Straitjacket" of international capital. (Of course, some popular commentators maintain both positions simultaneously with little apparent discomfort.[7]) Some idea of how people react to, make choices in, and alter their social contexts is central to any plausible account of a global economy and society. Likewise, some idea of how transnational structures shape individual lives and consciousness will be part of any coherent account of the process of globalization.

Unfortunately, however, a great deal of modern social thought has vacillated between two unproductive extremes—and current commentaries on globalization too often reproduce this division. The false dichotomy is between what might be called *agency-dominated* and *structure-dominated* accounts of social life. This agency/structure dichotomy repeats in certain respects a division between what have sometimes been called "atomism" (or "individualism") and "structuralism," but these labels can prove confusing because they are used differently in different disciplines, or because they invoke methodological controversies in the philosophy of science that map unevenly onto the structure/agency divide. Another set of labels puts the opposition in terms of "objectivist" and "subjectivist" social theories, but this, too, is an invitation to confusion since these terms have a relatively technical meaning in philosophy that does not correspond to the proposed typology of social theories.[8]

The *agency-dominated* view imagines individual agency against the backdrop of social conditions that are taken as fixed or else assumed, implicitly or explicitly, to be radically subject to individual will. Indeed, although human agency need not be individual agency, most agency-dominated accounts neglect forms of collective agency, supposing that they appear to the individual as a set of background conditions. Individuals are therefore considered apart from the interpersonal circumstances in which they find themselves, and the collective agency through which individual agency often operates is not properly understood. Thus agency-dominated social theories risk treating individuals as radically unconnected to the others who make up their social world; it is this aspect that leads some commentators to describe them as methodologically "atomistic," since the primitive elements (or atoms) in the analysis are individuals whose actions are seen as adding up relatively straightforwardly to produce the broader structures of social life.

Importantly, the problem here is not with the focus on individuals but with an inadequately developed understanding of the context in which individuals find themselves. A thoughtful methodological individualism can avoid the charge of atomism by situating social features of obvious relevance to individual choice and action within the purview of those individual choices and actions, as I attempt to do in developing the idea of network power.[9] But agency-dominated accounts cannot explain with any theoretical richness the ways in which individuals generate a social world that constantly returns to shape them. These accounts therefore verge toward the autistic, imagining that we are not only self-given but endowed with powers of reason and will more than adequate for any task we might face. Other people simply drop out of the analysis; their impact on our reason and will is assumed into the background.[10]

A great deal of contemporary American social science falls into the category of agency-dominated analysis, whether in the model of individual economic action against the backdrop of an abstract free market or in the strong form of "agential liberalism" common to some forms of political theory and formal ethics. For example, the neo-Kantian contractarianism now common in the American academy abstracts from the social particulars in which a person finds herself in order to think about what is owed to that person *as a person*. Although such thought experiments have been important in the development of recent ethical theory, they can present too narrowly agentialist an approach unless an attempt is made—as a second wave of Rawlsian moral and political philosophy is now doing—to set these arguments in relation to more fully elaborated empirical settings.[11] The problem is even more acute in neoclassical economics, in which the effort to abstract from background conditions in order to study bilateral exchange in its pure form can prevent a broader comprehension of other economic processes (such as production) and may verge on solipsism in its focus on individual choices outside their social context.[12]

By contrast, on the *structure-dominated* view, individual deliberation and action drop out of the picture altogether. The privileged site of analysis in structure-dominated theories is the social structure or system; these accounts hold that we can understand the important features of our social world apart from what we as agents believe ourselves to be doing with them or in them. Note that it is the vitiation of agency that makes these accounts unsatisfactory, and not the attention to social structure itself, which would be part of any adequate effort to engage in social explanation. Structure-dominated styles of reasoning are now in abeyance in the contemporary academy, at least in the Anglo-American world, but they flourished in many different disciplines throughout the twentieth century, including structuralist anthropology and theories of positive sociology in the mode of Durkheim.[13] Arguably, many postmodernist and poststructuralist social theories continue to leave little real scope for individual agency, despite some important analytic divergences from mid-twentieth century structuralism. (For this reason, although structure-dominated accounts are often referred to as "structuralist" the label can be misleading.[14])

Partisans on either side of the divide between agency-dominated and structure-dominated accounts have sometimes attempted to refute or simply to dismiss the other position. However, it may be that neither account is right, but that both accounts are *partial,* requiring elements of the other to complete an appropriate, synthetic position. That is, each puts forward in strong form a single insight about the way that the world is: in certain circumstances, and under certain conditions, the constraints of the social world may prove malleable for any individual agent, who can then act in a way of her own choosing. In those cases, a focus on individual deliberation and choice is an appropriate explanatory lens. In other circumstances, the pressure of the shared structures that train action and tame thought may be so great that individual agency can be safely set aside, and social explanation focused on impersonal entities, such as the laws under which people live or the social classes into which they are born or the myths they are brought up to believe. But accepting both positions as only partly right requires specifying some more general account beyond either, which can nevertheless accommodate both.

What social theory requires, then, is a theory of *structuration,* an integrated account of agency and structure. Although the term "structuration" is borrowed from the pioneering efforts of Anthony Giddens, I do not mean to privilege his particular account of it, but to indicate a type of social theory (of which his is one good example) that develops an integrated theory of social structure and individual agency together. It is this ambition that marks theories of structuration as a group, at least in the way that I use the term. The most interesting developments in social theory in the last fifty years—apparent in the work of such diverse thinkers as Giddens, Pierre Bourdieu, Jürgen Habermas and Roberto Mangabeira Unger, for example—share the ambition to grapple with agency and structure together, rather than to choose one element to set against the other.[15] Of course, theories of this kind are not unique to the last fifty years: much of what remains interesting and insightful about the work of Karl Marx or Max Weber is precisely this analysis of individual action and social structure considered together in the sweep of history.

All of these accounts focus in one way or another on what Giddens calls the "duality of structure," the fact that our social structures are both the product of our individual actions and their grounding—or, as Giddens puts it, that structure is "the medium and outcome of the conduct it recursively organizes."[16] When it is framed so broadly, it is hard to understand why any social theorist would propose anything other than a theory of structuration, given that both our intuition and our experience should lead us to affirm agency and structure as irreducible, at least in any simple way, to one another. Nevertheless, it has been difficult for many scholars to move beyond the dichotomy that supposes either that we are masters of our contexts or that our contexts must master us, even though it seems clear that either statement can, at different times, be true—and that the real work to be done is in understanding where, between these two extremes, any particular set of circumstances can be seen to lie. The mainstream perspective on social life in the Anglo-American world is now an agency-dominated one that discounts structure, tending to approach the problem of agency atomistically. In this context, perhaps the most interesting exercise that a theory of structuration might attempt is to show how a relatively coercive social structure can emerge from, and prove compatible with, a robust view of individual agency. (Under other conditions, our task might be the opposite: to articulate a place for individual agency and will in the circumstances of a social theory that denies it, as we saw in the work of some Marxist humanists writing in the former Eastern bloc.[17]) To show how structure emerges in relation to agency is not to deny viable agency, but to show its real capacities, by distinguishing between the necessary and the contingent in history—the scope of real constraint and possibility.

Showing how a form of entrapment can be generated through the accumulation of individual choices is one potent way to reveal the limits of agency in social structuration. Some social theories accomplish this move by making restrictive assumptions about people and their cognitive or reflective capacities. But a theory of structuration should be able to bring to light felt necessities or constraints without recourse to the idea of false consciousness and perhaps even without any assumption of direct coercion undertaken by any single person or set of persons against any others. The benefit of such a theory of structuration is that it can then illustrate, for example, how contemporary globalization can prove coercive or entrapping even if it is entirely driven by free, choosing people who create the conditions under which their agency gradually loses the power to alter their circumstances.

STRUCTURATION IN GLOBAL NETWORKS

Any plausible account of globalization must be a theory of structuration, considering agency and structure together in a more productive manner. It is perhaps unsurprising that many of the most interesting contemporary commentators on globalization are also social theorists who have advanced theories of structuration in their contributions to social thought.[18] Following their example, we must avoid falling into one of two extremes in our analysis of globalization. It is not adequate to claim simply, as many did in the celebratory 1990s—celebratory in the American context, to be specific—that globalization represents a clear advance in human freedom and individual autonomy, the birth of an era in which people are free to roam the world with their ideas, desires, and money, to remake themselves just as they will. To accept this view requires ignoring or dismissing the ways in which globalization generates—and perhaps even depends upon—forms of coercion or systematic injustice. On the other hand, it is not helpful to argue, as some anti-globalization critics have, that globalization works as an agentless process, a virus that infects, or a juggernaut that draws along unsuspecting and unconscious participants in its wake. To accept this view requires imagining people not as conscious, choosing, and deliberative agents, but as adjuncts to the real action, which remains invisible to them. For, in fact, both of these descriptions of globalization can hold true, at certain times and for certain people, but far more often the truth will lie somewhere between these two extremes. Both claims must be assessed in context, rather than derived from a view of social relations as either structure all the way up or agency all the way down. To make such an assessment, we must be able to articulate how people choose within a domain of choice that is itself determined by the prior and simultaneous choices of others. This requires a social theory that puts the rich relationship between agency and structure at the center of its analysis.

This kind of social theoretic framework will be useful not only for illuminating the convergences in today's globalization, but also for writing the history of past eras of globalization in the production of new "global histories." For example, the Cambridge historian Christopher A. Bayly's recent work on what is sometimes called the "long" nineteenth century, *The Birth of the Modern World, 1780–1914*, focuses on global connections and the multiple "motors of change" driving modernity in this period.[19] Bayly admirably brings out the way in which global networks operating at many levels and across many different domains contributed to a multi-faceted European hegemony during this period of empire. He argues that "a proper understanding of the global networks of politics, commerce, and ideology can illuminate both the exercise of dominance of Western imperial domination and the prefigurings of its fragmentation."[20]

Of course, writing such a global history necessarily broaches the question of how power is exercised in transnational networks. Indeed, Bayly argues: "It was the parasitic and 'networked' nature of Western domination and power which gave it such strength, binding together, and tapping into, a vast range of viable networks and aspirations."[21] However, this poses a difficulty for, as he notes, "one problem with a history which charts global interconnections and the multiple origins of change is that it may find it difficult to deal with power. . . . Interconnections and networks seem to speak of dialogue and accommodation, rather than of dominance."[22] But Bayly's study shows that "it is possible to describe the world in the nineteenth century as a complex of overlapping networks of global reach, while at the same time acknowledging the vast differentials of power which inhered in them." In fact, he suggests that it was, in part, the "capacity of European companies, administrators, and intellectual actors to co-opt and bend to their will existing global networks of commerce, faith, and power that explains their century-long dominance."[23]

In a sense, then, the problems that afflict discussions of contemporary globalization also afflict historical examinations of past periods of global integration, for while it is important and appropriate to write global history through discussions of transnational networks, it may be difficult to articulate how power inheres in those networks without simultaneously advancing an alternative account of power. The idea of network power offers a theory of structuration enabling us to see how power operates in today's global networks. Put in the service of new global histories, it might help to articulate the power at work in previous episodes of global sociability as well, offering a more precise account of how power is structured through networks of human agents, past and present.

CONVENTIONS

The idea of network power draws on ideas from a variety of scholarly literatures, any one of which can provide a starting point for a consideration of structure and agency together. The thread running through all of these

THE POWER OF SOCIABILITY 59

different accounts is a concern with the analysis of social *conventions*. The definition of a convention is itself part of the debate, but most theories of conventionality emphasize the elements of interdependent action and mutually reinforcing expectations in order to demonstrate how individual actions can produce social structures or patterns. On this view, a convention is a set of actions driven by consent, which depends on reciprocal expectations for joint coordination, and which achieves shared benefits.

The most famous theorist of conventions is David Hume, whom we may also consider the greatest philosopher of human sociability.[24] It is worth quoting Hume at some length here, since he inspired the later study of the convention in contemporary philosophy. In a famous passage, he writes,

> It has been asserted by some, that justice arises from HUMAN CONVENTIONS, and proceeds from the voluntary choice, consent, or combination of mankind. If by convention be here meant a *promise* (which is the most usual sense of the word) nothing can be more absurd than this position. . . . But if by convention be meant *a sense of common interest;* which sense each man feels in his own breast, which he remarks in his fellows, and which carries him, in concurrence with others, into a general plan or system of actions, which tends to public utility; it must be owned, that, in this sense, justice arises from human conventions.
>
> Two men pull the oars of a boat by common convention, for common interest, without any promise or contract: Thus gold and silver are made the measures of exchange; thus speech and words and language are fixed, by human convention and agreement. Whatever is advantageous to two or more persons, if all persons perform their part; but what loses all advantage, if only one person perform, can arise from no other principle. There would otherwise be no motive for any one of them to enter into that scheme of conduct.[25]

In the first paragraph, Hume equates a convention not with a promise, but with our more contemporary understanding of it, as a social routine or pattern driven by a set of common interests—something with which he also identifies the concept of justice.[26] In the second paragraph, he offers some examples of the phenomenon the general contours of which he has just described. In a famous analogy, he compares a convention to the synchrony of two oarsmen rowing; they are both engaged in a game of mutually coordinated expectation and interdependent action. Perhaps more interesting for our purposes here, he goes on to describe "measures of exchange" and the conventions of "speech and words and language" in a similar vein. (The conventional standards governing exchange and speech are the subject of the next chapter.)

The central dynamic in all these processes, Hume argues, is that everyone depends on mutual compliance with the convention for it to be of any benefit. A convention arises only in a social context: it "loses all advantage, if only one person perform." A single actor behaving in a given way may be rational in some circumstances, but not in conventional ones. Conventional actions require a context of social coordination to be worthwhile; pulling only one oar turns you in circles.

The contemporary study of the convention has focused on the idea of "coordination games" to describe situations like those Hume analyzed. While early game theorists such as John Nash and John von Neumann mostly studied games of pure conflict, scholars have also given attention to another kind of game, that of pure coordination.[27] Thomas Schelling was an important contributor to game theory; his notable work *The Strategy of Conflict* presented the problem with which I began this book, that of meeting a friend in New York City without having specified a rendezvous spot in advance. In this and other coordination problems, people typically make use of some prominent or conspicuous property or feature of one convention rather than another—relying on what Schelling sometimes calls "salience"—as a way of choosing a "focal point" for coordination in the absence of express prior agreement. He explains, "A prime characteristic of most of these 'solutions' to the problems, that is, of the clues or coordinators or focal points, is some kind of prominence or conspicuousness."[28] Focal points thus enable coordination by suggesting the selection of one possible solution rather than another. In Saussure's terms, these focal points are symbols, not arbitrary signs, because there may be intrinsic reasons for the initial selection of a particular focal point—which may then serve as a coordination mechanism for extrinsic reasons.

How focal points function as conventions is something that concerned the late philosopher David Lewis, who is credited with beginning the modern analytic study of the convention. Lewis drew on Schelling's work to elucidate the nature of language, understood as a social convention. In so doing, he argued that examples of pure coordination are but a special case of a more general social phenomenon: the establishment of conventions by common (that is, reciprocally determining) expectation of regularities. Conventions involve many different elements: interdependent action, reciprocal "higher-order" expectations conditional on expectations, and a pay-off structure that means the actors must coordinate or fail.[29] Lewis thus follows Hume in focusing on interdependence of action, recasting Hume's central problematic in terms of coordination games.

In Lewis's argument, conventions are, simply put, the solutions to coordination games: the fundamental aspect of a convention is the interdependence of action, the dependence of each agent on other agents' actions (or, indeed, expectations of their actions) in order to achieve a desired outcome. Lewis defines "a *coordination equilibrium* as a combination in which no one would have been better off had *any one* agent alone acted otherwise, either himself or someone else."[30] This equilibrium is not necessarily the best outcome for any individual agent that might have been counterfactually available, but it is the best outcome that any agent can achieve, given what other agents are also doing. Lewis explains, "In an equilibrium, it is entirely possible that some or all of the agents would have been better off if some or all of the agents had acted differently. What is not possible is that any one of the agents would have been better off if he alone had acted differently and all the rest had acted just as they did."[31] Lewis notes that the various conventions he examines are not all games of pure coordination but that like games of pure coordination, they give rise to coordination equilibria that define how agents behave. These coordination equilibria are thus determined, in the final analysis, for extrinsic, rather than intrinsic reasons—but why is one possible routine initially chosen over another? While Schelling emphasized the "salience" of a focal point for coordination, Lewis generalized this insight to consider the role of *precedent* in the formation of social conventions, including the convention of language, analyzing the role of reciprocally determining expectations in forming what he called "common knowledge." He argues that conventional solutions to the problem of coordination arise from preferences for a given action that are predicated on others' performances and from the knowledge that performance in a certain way is expected. This knowledge can arise from salience, as Schelling's examples show, but it can also arise from *precedent*, the fact that a solution has been achieved before in a particular way. (Of course, the fact of precedence may itself prove "salient" in many coordination games.) Lewis also focuses on the role of induction and how what we have reasons to believe (about ourselves and about others) can become decisive in determining one convention rather than another.[32]

The analysis of conventions, following Lewis's and Schelling's pioneering efforts, emphasizes that they may be arbitrary, and thus chosen for reasons of coordination based on their salience or the significance of precedent. Schelling reflects that "[coordination] solutions are, of course, arbitrary to this extent: any solution is 'correct' if enough people think so."[33] Jon Elster also notes that "Conventions may be equivalent: it is important to have one, but it does not matter which it is." Because the point of a convention is to achieve complementarities in action with other people, in a conventional equilibrium it is the case both that "no one can improve his outcome by unilaterally deviating from it," and that "no one would want anyone else to deviate from it either."[34] For, any individual deviation would diminish the value of using that convention for everyone else participating in it.

This discussion presents the convention in its purely coordinative aspect reflecting the arbitrariness that I emphasized in my discussion of signs in Chapter 1. To employ the language of sovereignty and sociability, we can say that, as conventions, focal points structure the relations of sociability in one way rather than another. (It is perhaps unsurprising that Schelling's original idea emerged from his reflections on war, since warfare is the quintessential example of social relations *outside* the order of sovereignty.) In many (perhaps all) cases, however, a political decision could reshape those social relations by selecting an alternative focal point around which people would coordinate their activity rather than allowing one to emerge from many decentralized actions. One reason that a political determination may sometimes be desirable is that some conventions may be intrinsically preferable to others but neglected on account of extrinsic considerations. In these cases the relations of sovereignty may be mobilized to affect a movement from one equilibrium to another.

NETWORK EXTERNALITIES

The analysis of conventions is obviously relevant to a discussion of standards, which are forms of conventional equilibria. However, the idea of network power focuses less on settled conventions than ones emerging due to a combination of extrinsic and intrinsic reasons. Therefore, it emphasizes the positive feedback dynamic central to the interdependent action that drives the adoption of one convention rather than another.

There is another academic literature that deals with the rise to dominance of shared standards, analyzing what might be considered the emergence of conventionality—even though it is not usually understood as a contribution to the theory of conventions. The literature on "network externalities" in economics makes the point that one standard may be chosen over another due to a difference in network size—owing, that is, to what I have here called network power. So far, however, the discussion of network externalities has been largely restricted to problems of technical coordination and the compatibility of different technology products, which can seem to limit its broader relevance. Nevertheless, the insights of this literature may have a more general application. In fact, the phenomenon identified in economics as "network effects" or "network externalities" is really nothing more than the common reliance by members of a network on a conventional standard, making its adoption advantageous and deviation from it costly.[35] In other words, these analyses are concerned with the structural emergence of conventions, albeit in a relatively narrow subject area.

In the language of economics, network effects are "positive externalities," extra, unpaid-for benefits which accrue to the user of a particular technology by the addition of a new user of that technology.[36] A common and much debated example of network effects is that of the VCR wars: the struggle for market dominance between the VHS and Beta videocassette recording systems. (Of course, with the more recent switch from VCRs to DVD players, this famous example of industrial rivalry has become rather dated.) Many economists—and some consumers old enough to remember—claim that Beta produced a "better product." If one accepts this claim, it might be argued that if intrinsic reason had been able to decide the use of the technology, consumers might still have been using Beta machines until fairly recently. However, this was not to be.

One explanation for this fact focuses on the role of network externalities.

Each VCR system used a videocassette that had incompatible dimensions with the videocassettes of its rival system: Beta tapes worked in Beta players only, and VHS tapes worked in VHS players only. Consumers, and the businesses that dealt with consumers by renting them tapes and selling them VCRs, had to choose one or the other. Of course, consumers could own both types of machines, and businesses could stock videos for both kinds—but that would not prove cheap. And perhaps even more significantly, the producers of videocassette tapes played a critical role, augmenting network effects by investing in the production of only one kind of VCR tape, which was determined by anticipating the number of potential buyers.

The network externalities argument is that an early lead by VHS in market share—a higher number of early VHS owners, whether due to advertising or low initial prices—meant that it was slightly better for a new consumer to choose VHS over Beta. We might say that the network of VHS users was larger and more attractive than Beta's, since it offered more friends from whom one could borrow movies, more stores from which they might be rented, and, most important, more videos produced for the VHS system, since producers focused on the larger VHS market early on. VHS won out because *extrinsic* reason swamped *intrinsic* reason. Beta's network of users was less appealing, even though Beta's technology might have been better. In the end, maintaining access to a greater network was more valuable than the superior technology. Network effects mattered to the outcome and probably even decided it.

The fact that network effects played such a critical role in determining which VCR system prevailed highlights an important aspect of this line of argument. Network effects are one reason for which we may see "path-dependence" in the economy. Path-dependence expresses the idea that one's current "path" is a function of where one has been—or, more simply put, that history matters. As it relates to network effects, the argument of path-dependence is that technologies that exhibit network effects may be "locked in" and resist being unseated, even by superior competitors. The sting in the idea of path-dependence is its assertion that history can deliver us into a suboptimal present—in which extrinsic, not intrinsic, merits decide what products we use or what lifestyles we adopt.[37] Other examples discussed in the debate over path-dependence range widely over various technological, institutional, and social issues, but the central questions in the debate remain fairly consistent.[38] The most well known example is the allegedly inferior QWERTY keyboard, optimal for nineteenth-century printing technology but decidedly suboptimal for today's electronic keyboard. But path-dependence has also informed discussions on subjects ranging from the dynamics of economic geography and the formation of industrial cores, to the extent to which institutions are the "carriers of history" and shape current market conditions.[39]

STANDARDS AS PUBLIC GOODS

Understanding how standards relate to network effects requires examining how different types of goods are consumed. If a given good exhibits network effects, then the value of that good to a user will increase as other people use it, and hence we will see economies of scale in the market for that good. A good that a person can use without diminishing another's utility from it—indeed, whose utility grows with additional users—cannot exhibit the "rivalry in consumption" that is usually assumed in economic theory. Only one person can consume a good that is "rival," like a sandwich, without sacrificing enjoyment. (If two people eat from the same sandwich, they both necessarily get less of it.) But multiple parties can enjoy a good that exhibits non-rivalry in consumption—for example, the *New York Times* web page or the galleries of the Metropolitan Museum of Art—without sacrificing any enjoyment. (Of course, many non-rival goods may nevertheless be "congestible," as when the Met is crowded with visitors on a Sunday afternoon or when the *New York Times'* server is overloaded with hits, and thus provide less enjoyment during busy moments.)

For a certain class of goods, not only *can* others use the good simultaneously without decreasing the enjoyment that any users receive, but others *must* use the good simultaneously for it to be of value to anyone. These goods are not just non-rival, they are—as one scholar has called them in describing software code—"anti-rival."[40] To borrow from Hume's definition of a convention, anti-rival goods lose all value if only one person consumes them. These goods are conventional goods that require common use because they coordinate a social function, and otherwise serve no other purpose. It really does take two to tango.

Here, once again, we arrive at an idea that we have seen emerging in several distinct areas of academic interest: in the argument concerning the arbitrary nature of the sign; in theories of convention and games of pure coordination; in theories of network externalities and path dependence; and now in discussions of "anti-rival" goods. Of course, the term "goods" may be somewhat misleading here. For it is not so much "goods" that exhibit network effects, as the particular kinds of social relations that govern the production and distribution of goods. Indeed, in the case of technical goods with network externalities, it is usually not the final product that is anti-rival (say, the particular terminal at which the Internet is accessed), but the standard underlying that product. Standards that govern access to other people—in this domain, as in others—generate positive externalities, since the more people who use a particular standard, the more attractive it will seem to non-users.

Understanding standards as conventional allows us to interpret the idea of network effects much more broadly than the economics literature in which this concept originated has done, and thus to identify in its core insight a logic that applies well beyond the relatively narrow confines of technical goods with increasing returns from interrelatedness or coordination. More generally, we can understand network effects as the positive externalities that are generated in the interdependence of action, the positive feedback that results from the use of a standard. Where we can identify a pattern of consistent social behavior that operates like a standard—regulating access to others by providing a framework for social coordination through conventionality—we should expect to see a positive feedback dynamic that makes it increasingly attractive for outsiders to adopt the same behavior. Not only technical coordination, but social structuration itself may be considered a process of this sort.

THE REASSERTION OF CONTEXT

The idea of network power draws on diverse theoretical resources from different academic fields, each of which exemplifies what we might call "the reassertion of context," of the interdependent and interpersonal setting of individual choice-making. Above, I explored contemporary arguments about conventions, coordination games, network externalities, and anti-rival goods that have recently been made in the fields of philosophy, economics, and social science generally. Each of these ideas introduces considerations of extrinsic reason into theories that formerly described individual action according to an agency-dominated model. Thinking about the extrinsic reasons that may apply when agents decide to join a network serves as an effective way of reintroducing the context of choice into social theoretic models from which it has been missing.

This reassertion of context has often occurred in response to the later philosophical work of Ludwig Wittgenstein. In one interpretation of his argument—and there are of course many to be reckoned with—Wittgenstein exposed the shortcomings of positivistic accounts of language by reasserting the overall context in which communication occurs. For example, if we assume that languages arise through agreements established among individuals who assign names to external objects, we may be taken aback when asked what language these individuals themselves relied upon when coming to their initial agreement about the meanings of words, or how they came to use gestures that refer to something other than an external object, such as a feeling. In criticizing positivistic theories (including aspects of his own earlier work) Wittgenstein initiated a broader philosophical shift in the way that we understand social relations, particularly the convention of language, which has had a powerful effect on philosophy and the social sciences ever since.[41]

As we saw above, thinkers in disciplines other than linguistic philosophy have made analogous moves to Wittgenstein's (without necessarily realizing it) by bringing the obviously neglected domain of social life back into arguments about how people behave. This move to incorporate the background conditions of individual action provides a powerful rebuff to agency-dominated social theories. For example, if we assume that all market exchanges are undertaken by self-interested agents, we may forget that the social and legal foundations of the market emerge from and are maintained by different dynamics, including the complex ethical and epistemic commitments of those same agents. Or if we begin with a social theory that takes as its basis too strict an idea of rational action, we may end up advancing an account of rationality rather far removed from what reasonable people actually do in concrete social settings in which their choices are conditional on the choices of other agents.

This reassertion of context is undeniable, and can prove transforming. It is undeniable because it generates a more plausible and realistic account of how agency actually operates in social life, which is always in a context of interdependent choice. It is transforming because when the principal extrinsic reason for joining a network—the pull of network power—diverges from the intrinsic reasons for doing so, we can end up "choosing" something that appears undesirable, which serves to repudiate the attitude underlying many agent-dominated accounts and invites a critical reassessment of many social practices. The reassertion of context can be a repeated intellectual "innovation" because it is, in the end, an obvious one—following as it does on the prior evacuation of structure from the consideration of agency. In other words, we should not be surprised that different scholarly conversations may resemble one another in reasserting context, since the evisceration of the setting of social action suggests its later reintroduction.

In the development of network power, extrinsic reasons for joining networks are compelling because standards are cooperative regimes that allow users to coordinate their activities. Any adequate social theory must count such coordination as a basic fact of social life, and therefore admit that individual agents find themselves situated on a continuum between the extremes of genuinely free choice and structural coercion based on circumstances they did not themselves establish. Simply posing the issue in this way suggests a different set of questions and concerns from those pursued in a great deal of contemporary political theory or economics.

The reassertion of context also invites a controversy about the role of methodological individualism in social explanation. In my argument so far, I have been keen to distinguish an overly reductive "atomism" from a thoughtful methodological individualism, which I have assumed will be capacious enough to account for the wide range of social practices that are the backdrop to individual action. If we stay within a broadly individualistic methodology—for example, following the philosopher David Lewis's theory of convention in which social practices can emerge from a sufficiently nuanced account of individual behavior—can we explain our social life adequately? Or, rather, as the philosopher Charles Taylor suggests, are many of our practices "irreducibly social," such that their very existence should call into question some rather deep intellectual commitments?[42] Put differently, does any theory that supposes the social world to be constructed by individuals run the risk of the kind of error to which Wittgenstein drew our attention in his transformative approach to the philosophy of language?

These questions involve a level of philosophical argument deeper than I have taken up in this chapter, in which I have been focused on overcoming the structure/agency dichotomy with recourse to a theory of structuration. They concern, rather, the issue of descriptive or explanatory *emergence* and, in particular, whether a reductionist strategy that understands wholes by decomposing them into their parts misses properties that emerge only in the ordered whole—for example, because the whole interacts with its constituents, altering the entire system in the process.[43] The problems of emergence raise complex philosophical issues debated in the philosophy of natural and social science which are relatively removed from my concerns here.

I have introduced the idea of network power to articulate some overlooked aspects of interdependent choice-making from a perspective that imagines everything in the social world as constructed by individuals. How we should ultimately understand that process of construction—that is, whether a nuanced methodological individualism can escape the pitfalls of atomism—is an issue that I cannot take up here. The idea of network power is not intended to reveal anything about the deeper problems inherent in understanding the possible "preformational" origins of human sociality, even while it is meant to generalize the reassertion of context in considerations of individual decision-making. If even this very limited project runs the risk of perpetuating a narrow atomism in social theory, it is a risk that any theory of structuration entails. I must assume that for the critic of methodological individualism, a theory of structuration that risks reducing structure to agency is still preferable to one that simply ignores it altogether. After all, if we wish to understand important dimensions of our social life—including what we call globalization—we surely cannot credit any approach that does not involve some ultimate recourse to our self-conception as agents.

CHAPTER THREE

English and Gold

THE UNIVERSAL STANDARD DESCRIBED in the first chapter is not merely hypothetical. Over the last century, we have seen such universal standards come and go during various episodes of globalization. In this chapter, I focus on two of the most well known, the English language and the gold standard, in order to explore how such standards originate, become universal (or near-universal), and crowd out alternatives.

Nowhere are the dynamics of network power clearer than in the domains of language and money. Within a single linguistic or monetary community, we take these systems of exchange for granted. Language and money are inescapable: they are the standards facilitating everyday communication and commerce, and thus also the stock examples of sociability in the history of political and social thought. As communication and commerce have gone global, so too have the tokens that mediate these relations. When one language or one currency gains great network power, the disruption it generates focuses attention on an otherwise obscure process.

At the end of the nineteenth and the beginning of the twentieth century, at the height of what some commentators rather naively call the "first globalization," international commerce was ruled by a gold standard to which all important currencies were fixed. At the beginning of the twenty-first century, in our episode of accelerated globalization (which these same commentators call the "second" globalization), international communication is dominated by the English language. Gold and English present interesting examples of universal standards: one now defunct and one still on the rise. Exploring these universal standards in language and money can give us insight into the way that standardization develops, and falters, in globalization.

LANGUAGES AS STANDARDS

Language is the medium and ground of almost all human interaction, the system of signs that we use for social coordination. More than that, though, language presents an example of a system of pure coordination, and one that does not—perhaps even could not—exist outside the social intercourse that it enables. Saussure points to this inescapably social aspect of language: "in order to have a language, there must be a *community of speakers*. Contrary to what might appear to be the case, a language never exists even for a moment except as a social fact, for it is a semiological phenomenon."[1] For that reason, language has motivated the philosophical analysis of conventions in many different fields.

The purely conventional nature of language means that linguistic coordination exhibits the economies of scale we see in the use of standards: the greater the number of people who use certain words or speak a certain language, the more attractive those words or that language will be for others to learn. If everyone in my community means something relatively fixed by "chair," or "danger," or "love"—of course, just how fixed will vary—I must know what those words mean to them and use the words similarly. Likewise, if the boundaries of my community have changed in some relevant way to include others who speak a different language—as we see in episodes of regional economic or political integration—then it will benefit me to speak that other language if I want to gain access to the population of its speakers. For example, the French Canadians in Quebec are under pressure to learn English in order to benefit from national economic and political life, which occurs in predominantly Anglophone settings. If we consider this problem of coordination on a multilateral and not just a bilateral level, the point becomes clearer: the need for communication among multiple parties is most easily solved if everyone agrees to speak a single language, or to share a common second language. Of course, we are never in a position to decide such a thing, and instead we inherit a world of many languages—at present, probably between 5,000 and 6,700 in total. But the network power of language nevertheless pushes us in fits and starts toward linguistic consolidation.

This linguistic consolidation can be understood as we understand other conventions—an insight that Saussure urged early on: "The propagation of linguistic features is subject to the same laws as any other habit, such as fashion. In any community, there are always two forces simultaneously pulling in opposite directions: particularism or parochialism on the one hand, and on the other the force of 'intercourse,' which establishes communication between men." What is this "force of 'intercourse'" to which Saussure refers? He continues, explaining that: "If parochialism makes men keep to themselves, intercourse forces them to communicate with others. Intercourse brings a village visitors from elsewhere, brings together people from all around on the occasion of a celebration or a fair, unites men from different provinces under the same flag. In short, intercourse is a principle of unification, which counteracts the disuniting influence of parochialism."[2]

Saussure clarifies later that parochialism is not a separate force from unification, but indicates rather the extent to which unification has proceeded in any given context: it is "the negative aspect of the force of unification." Thus, it is variation in the force of intercourse in particular areas that is responsible, on Saussure's account, for the geographic diversity of language seen around the world. He argues, "If the force of unification is powerful enough, it will establish uniformity over the whole area."[3]

Saussure does not go on to examine at any length the different factors contributing to the force of unification, but he does provide an early analysis that we should welcome in this more accelerated age of global integration. Indeed, his theory of linguistic waves—the way in which an element of one language will diffuse across linguistic boundaries depending on geographic and historic contexts—provides an undeveloped but highly suggestive account of something like the power of linguistic conventions.[4] Finally, we might argue that globalization compresses not just space but *time*: for it is time, in Saussure's analysis, and not geographic distance that is ultimately responsible for linguistic differentiation. The force of unification varies across time based on contingent historical factors.

THE GLOBAL DOMINANCE OF ENGLISH

The remarkable rise of English in the twentieth century offers a dramatic example of how the "force of intercourse" can lead to the emergence of a universal standard. Like any natural language, English is a standard in the first sense I discussed, a *mediating standard,* a system of signs that inherently governs communication with others who use it. It is a Germanic language (with significant amounts of French thrown in, thanks to the Norman Conquest) whose modern form emerged in the British Isles around 1475 from Middle English. From England, it spread throughout Britain and Ireland by conquest, trade, and cultural exchange. Then British imperialism carried it across the globe: in 1900, the British Empire encompassed one quarter of the world's population, which explains why English is an official or dominant language in over 60 countries, including the United States, Canada, Australia, India, South Africa, and indeed all the countries of the British Commonwealth.[5] English offers a dramatic example of the linguist's quip that "a language is a dialect with an army and navy." However, the current global position of English is the result of more than a few centuries of outright conquest. In the past few decades in particular, it has grown rapidly in importance as the language of international commerce, governance, and technology, alongside the increasing power of the United States in these and other areas.

Yet despite much discussion of English as a "global language," it is important to recognize that its population of speakers is still rather limited in absolute numbers. While English has perhaps 300 to 450 million native speakers, both Mandarin Chinese and Spanish can claim more. Of course, English is undoubtedly the world's most common second language: the numbers on non-native speakers of English range widely from 100 million to well over a billion, depending on the level of proficiency specified—and it is this widespread international presence that makes it a "global language," as the linguist David Crystal explains. By the most generous estimates, some English is spoken by as many as one in three humans—a great number, but still far from making English a global common medium. It is, at present, a universal standard only in particular domains, with the promise of greater popular penetration in the future.[6]

What these numbers fail to reflect, however, is the special significance of English in these particular domains, especially in elite global circles. It is *the* foreign language to learn for an ambitious young person, allowing communication with other English speakers, both native and non-native: the *lingua franca* for high-level work in international business, law, science, and other important fields. The late French president Georges Pompidou urged his countrymen, "we must not let the idea take hold that English is the only possible instrument for industrial, economic and scientific communication."[7] Even in the early 1970s, his warning probably came too late.

The position of English as the global second language is especially clear in those domains of international coordination in which the participants are mainly (or even entirely) non-native speakers. For example, in the 1950s, English was settled upon as the mandatory language for air traffic control, creating a common standard for international travel today. It is also the official language of the European Central Bank, though not the native language in any of the countries in the European Monetary Union. It is the working language of ASEAN, allowing non-native speakers from a variety of Southeast Asian nations to communicate with each other. It is the most common language on the Internet, with a large amount (perhaps 80 percent) of the information stored in the world's computers in English.[8] The late Japanese prime minister Keizo Obuchi endorsed the idea of making English Japan's official second language as part of a broader package of political and economic reform in the country. In all these cases, what is particularly striking is that non-native speakers are using English to communicate with other non-native speakers.

In a few quick generations, English has gone from the language of the colonial elite abroad to the global second language of choice.[9] Any number of telling (but variable) statistics could be paraded out to support this fact: the number of English-language daily newspapers in major developing world cities, the percentage of business deals conducted in English, the proportion of multinational scientific research teams communicating in English. But none of these figures would reveal the crucial dynamic element in the process of language transmission. As the late Peter Strevens, a linguist at Cambridge University, argued, even within our lifetimes, "English will be taught mostly by non-native speakers of the language, to non-native speakers, in order to communicate mainly with non-native speakers."[10] On this reckoning, English will indeed become the first truly global language, whatever its current status.

The German philologist Jakob Grimm wrote presciently about English in 1852: "Of all modern languages, not one has acquired such great strength and vigour as the English . . . [it] may be called justly a LANGUAGE OF THE WORLD: and seems, like the English nation, to be destined to reign in [the] future with still more extensive sway over all parts of the globe."[11] A little more than one hundred and fifty years later, we are seeing half of his prediction borne out: even as the English nation has retreated from world ascendancy, the language it left behind has consolidated its grip.

THE NETWORK POWER OF ENGLISH

English is a standard that possesses great network power, regulating access to a significant and growing network—perhaps the most important linguistic network in the history of humanity, and certainly the most far-flung. English reigns, not only in English-speaking countries, but also increasingly as a general rule of global linguistic coordination, in both domestic and foreign cities and in mixed-ethnicity households. Accounts of the rise of English often focus on the wrong variables, failing to see it as a phenomenon driven by different factors at different times in its ascendance and now as mainly a means of reaching an increasingly Anglophone global population. For example, some analyses go so far as to claim that English is particularly suited to become a global language, as if the citizens of the world had been casting about for a means of communication and had settled rationally on English (rather than, say, Esperanto). According to this view, English is uniquely appropriate as the medium of pop music, advertising slogans, and cinema. (Obviously, one might argue just as convincingly that the causation runs in the opposite direction: that these popular forms are adapted to the language of the countries in which they first arose.) But even granting its suitability for commercial jingles, the widespread use of English cannot be explained as the result of any *intrinsic* superiority. In fact, the "efficiency" of English seems very doubtful indeed, given its irregular patterns of spelling, and the complex residues of its French, Greco-Latin, and Anglo-Saxon inheritances. It has great lexical diversity, but a varied and difficult graphology, or, more simply, lots of words and an unusual grammar.[12]

To understand the global emergence of English we cannot suppose that it has spread due to its intrinsic properties. Indeed, the attempt to understand the dominance of English in this way reads almost like an effort to use the analytics of sovereignty to understand the relations of sociability—an error that many early theorists of language committed. But we never took a vote on whether to have a global tongue (and if so, which one); there has been no common decision made by us together. Rather, we are becoming an Anglophone world due to the accretion of decisions made by all of us individually, each one of us factoring in the interdependent choices made by billions of others. The politics of sovereignty did not give us English as a global language; the history of sociability did. It comes to us as the result of a particular history, the accretion of past choices that structure our current options, and is unrelated to anything special about English itself. As David Crystal puts it, "A language does not become a global language because of its intrinsic structural properties, or because of the size of its vocabulary, or because it has been a vehicle of a great literature in the past, or because it was once associated with a great culture or religion."[13] Rather, a language becomes a global language because of its network power.

THE TRAJECTORY OF ENGLISH

A network power analysis examines how a standard gains prominence at different points in its trajectory, surpassing critical thresholds in its movement to universality. In the movement of the English language to global dominance, we see both *force* and *chance* in its early history, and a merger of *reason* and *force* in its current position. Perhaps as with any standard lacking a decisive early advantage over competitors, the survival and spread of English was as much a matter of historical contingency as anything else. By some accounts, at least, Old English would never have survived had Alfred the Great, the king of Wessex, not beaten the Danes at the Battle of Ethandun in May 878, checking the Viking advance into the Anglo-Saxon heartland. Alfred also contributed to the future of English by vigorously promoting it as part of a broader political project, arranging for important translations from Latin into his dialect, West Saxon.[14]

A few centuries later, we see direct force in the spread of English, as it expanded by conquest within the British Isles, to Ireland, Wales, and Cornwall.[15] David Crystal writes: "The history of a global language can be traced through the successful expeditions of its soldier/sailor speakers. And English . . . has been no exception."[16] The main burst of its expansion came with the growth of the British Empire abroad. The journalist and wit H. L. Mencken wrote in 1935: "The English-speaking peoples . . .

have dragged their language with them, and forced it upon the human race." English imperial policy certainly fits this description. The education of Indians in English was a mainstay of nineteenth-century imperial policy with the explicit aim of creating an Anglophone elite—sometimes called "Macaulay's children" after the historian and colonial administrator Thomas Macaulay, who pushed for native education in English—that would serve as an intermediary class between the British rulers and their subcontinental subjects.[17]

As is often the case, what was born in war is later maintained by necessity. Within the British colonies, English provided the means to gain access to colonial authorities, and, subsequently, to other colonial and postcolonial subjects for whom the English language offered a shared standard. As citizens in countries like India and Nigeria now find, the colonizer's language has become an international standard that they ambivalently embrace, a "neutral" option in an otherwise contentious choice among regional languages. Thus, the spread of English continues, but due to extrinsic reason rather than direct force.

The postwar ascent of English is undoubtedly tied to American power in commerce and technology. David Crystal summarizes, "when new technologies brought new linguistic opportunities, English emerged as a first-rank language in industries which affected all aspects of society—the press, advertising, broadcasting, motion pictures, sound recording, transport and communications." He also points to the American origins of many of these communication technologies. But this postwar ascendance draws on the earlier British expansion: the empire on which the sun never set handed its world market over to Mickey Mouse and Coca-Cola. Hollywood would not have its current reach without having inherited a global pool of English speakers—or at least populations habituated to looking to the English-speaking world for their next dose of modernity. Thus, American pop culture benefited from fortuitous timing and a bloody inheritance, arriving at a moment when technology could bring people together both physically and imaginatively in ways that would previously have been inconceivable. And many of those people were already accustomed to speaking English because of an imperial past—a past they cannot disown since it integrates them into their postcolonial nations and, increasingly, the broader Anglophone world.[18] In short, as Crystal puts it, English was in "the right place at the right time."[19]

What combination of causes drives the network power of English currently? English is now propelled largely by network power, the desire to speak it as a way of communicating with others, the majority of whom are also non-native speakers. In this power, we see *the merger of reason and force,* of extrinsic reasons and indirect force. For any non-native speaker, the desire to speak English is both a reasonable and a forced choice—reasonable because it is the best option for communicating with others, forced because, given the global dominance of English, this option may be the only practicable one available, especially as the increasing prominence of English erodes the viability of other languages as a possible global second language.[20]

As a general matter, after a standard possesses considerable network power, it structures the choices of non-users so that they rationally adopt it, even though they may also feel compelled to do so. We see in the early history of a standard many different causes contributing to its expanding network—and to its growing network power. But late in a standard's ascendance, network power grows by itself, such that, past the threshold of inevitability, the standard's dominance structures the choices of users and non-users alike as reason and force merge to bring about its adoption. The English language has surpassed the threshold of inevitability in many domains of communication—from aviation to scientific research and international business—and looks on course to become the world's first truly global language. Assuming that the "force of unification" remains strong in the coming centuries, the critical question—which I examine at greater length in Chapter 5—is whether English will do so as a global *second* language, co-existing with a rich abundance of other languages, or whether it will coordinate a much less diverse (perhaps even monolingual) globe.

Past the threshold of inevitability, users rationally adopt a standard that they would not choose except because of its network power. Many people now learning English do so because of this felt necessity. And yet, they are undeniably *choosing* to do so. Unlike the direct coercion which drove the adoption of English in the past—when schoolchildren in British India were drilled in the rote memorization of passages from English literature or Native American children were barred from speaking their language in reservation schools[21]—current learners do so out of formally free choice under the influence of network power. Thus in the early genesis of the network power of the English language, we see both chance and force, but late in the curve of network power, reason and force combine to compel the adoption of a standard. Even this highly simplified account of the network power of English should undermine the claim that any choice we make expresses our freedom and depends on reason alone. Such a claim denies the more complex dynamics in which choice occurs under conditions that may seem both coercive and perfectly reasonable given the consequences. How we should interpret these complex social dynamics, and whether we should understand them as *power,* is the focus of my discussion in Chapter 4.

LINGUISTIC CHANGE AND NETWORK POWER

Of course, the global spread of English is not the only impact that globalization is having on language. Broadly, five related linguistic phenomena are occurring in the contemporary world. We see that (1) English is emerging as a global standard, at least in particular spheres; (2) regional languages are gaining in importance; (3) local languages and dialects are dying off; (4) many languages are increasingly hybridized; and (5) some languages are being revived or renewed as part of the assertion of national or ethnic identities.[22] Popular writing on language and globalization rarely addresses all of these developments, and tends to draw from those it does address relatively unsophisticated conclusions: that English will be the sole language for the entire world, or else that Chinese will soon replace it, and so on. However, all five of these linguistic developments are consistent with the emerging pattern of global network power. Understanding why a desire for linguistic coordination elevates the role of (1) English and (2) many regional languages also allows us to understand (3), the loss of local languages, (4), the hybridization of language, and (5) efforts at deliberate linguistic revival, which must make use of and contend with network power dynamics. Or, put differently, all these developments emerge from the much greater "force of unification" produced by the technological and social changes that we see in contemporary globalization.

These changes, considered together, portend a very different future for language than that we have known. Globalization is radically altering this domain of human interaction with intimate connections to community and identity, a theme to which I return in Chapter 5. Crystal summarizes these disparate impacts of globalization on language: "The current situation is without precedent: the world has never had so many people in it; globalization processes have never been so marked; communication and transport technologies have never been so omnipresent; there has never been so much language contact; and no language has ever exercised so much international influence as English."[23]

Languages are complicated standards, systems of signification that grow and evolve in complex ways. Analyzing them in the context of network power, we must ask who it is that wants to communicate with whom, and by what means—which languages—such access can be had. Audiences vary: sometimes we want to talk to our grandmothers, sometimes we want to negotiate with business partners, and sometimes we want to follow dialogue in a film. If one language could allow us to do all these things we would feel very little need—other than for personal edification or curiosity—to learn new ones. It is regrettable but unsurprising, then, that so few Americans learn foreign languages, given that most of them can conduct all of their personal and public affairs in English. Indeed, the stereotype of the oafishly monolingual English-speaker need not be confined to the United States, for the lack of fluency in a second language seems endemic in Anglophone countries. In Great Britain, for example, the power and convenience of English has also sapped much of the impetus to learn other tongues: the rate of foreign language qualification is already low and declining still further in British secondary schools, with approximately two-thirds of Britons unable to speak a second language. Of course, in continental Europe, the situation is vastly different. About half of Europeans claim to be able to speak at least one foreign language (usually English), and sometimes many more.[24]

Languages have network properties that affect the kinds of networks that form around them. (I discuss these properties at length in Chapter 6.) They are open to newcomers—almost anyone can learn an additional one—but it is not costless to do so. Learning a second language usually takes time and energy. They are largely compatible with other languages; this is what makes it possible to learn a foreign language in the first place. People can learn multiple languages and express similar ideas in different language systems. Translation may be difficult—particularly for expressing complex ideas or emotions—but simple communication is almost always possible in translation. Therefore, in our multilingual world, we either learn new languages or rely upon translation, depending on the relative ease with which we learn them, the efficacy of translation, and the magnitude of our desired access to foreign-language speakers. Finally, languages are malleable: in the sweep of history—and even on a much shorter time span—languages can and do borrow liberally from one another.[25]

With these properties in mind, we can make sense of the predicament of language in this age of globalization. As I discussed above, (1) English is emerging as a global standard, particularly in areas of social life where the benefits of speaking it are clearest. This rise to universality is perfectly comprehensible given network power dynamics. For the same reasons that in a global sphere of elite activities English has become universal, so too (2) particular languages are gaining regional ascendancy. As with the spread of any standard, the critical variable to consider is the network, the relevant community with which one wants to be able to communicate. The rise of Hindi, Indonesian, Spanish, Portuguese, Arabic, and other regional languages mirrors that of English, at a different scale and for different audiences. Just as a middle-class resident of New Delhi sees English as a gateway to success abroad in New York or London or Toronto, a dialect-speaking villager from Bihar may need to know Hindi in order to advance as a rural migrant in New Delhi.

LANGUAGE DEATH

The other side of the rise of English and regional languages due to network power is "language death," the rapid and dramatic loss of the world's linguistic diversity.[26] The claim that the world's linguistic diversity is threatened—that minority languages are dying at a rapid rate—is an empirical one that necessarily involves claims about what divides one language from another and how few speakers a language must have to be threatened. Despite some controversy about measurement, linguists have settled on rough estimates that indicate something of the magnitude of the problem. In his book *Language Death*, David Crystal, reviewing the evidence and studies, puts the number of languages in the world today at 6,000, with a reasonable range of 5,000–7,000, which corroborates a number of respected studies, including an oft-cited survey from *Ethnologue*, which counted 6,703 languages.[27] It is more difficult to determine whether a given language is threatened with losing all its living speakers: that is, with language death. Crystal is cautious about attempting to conclude too much about the future of a language from the size of its population alone, but it is clear that the size of a language's speaking population—and its context, whether rural or urban, isolated, and so on—usually indicates something of its prospects. Crystal notes that "a quarter of the world's languages are spoken by less than 1000 people; and well over half by less than 10,000."[28] He argues that a "total of 10,000 suggests safety in the short term, but not in the medium term."

Scholars Daniel Nettle and Suzanne Romaine, in their sobering book *Vanishing Voices,* also cite the 10,000-speaker threshold as a "crude generalization," but nevertheless find it "useful as a first approximation" in determining the level of threat to a language.[29] Using this number gives us a rough estimate—a middle estimate, according to Crystal—that about half the world's languages are endangered. However, even this middle estimate may be overly sanguine: a more sobering statistic is that "96% of the world's languages are spoken by just 4% of the population."[30] It is entirely plausible, then, that higher estimates of the number of languages at risk will prove more accurate. One figure that Nettle and Romaine propose is that 95 percent of the world's languages may vanish in the next century.

Nettle and Romaine distinguish between what they call "sudden" and "gradual" language death.[31] Sudden death is, as it sounds, the result of the rapid destruction of a linguistic community or its forced dispersal. Gradual death is the linguistic loss that occurs under conditions of unequal power and resources driving the gradual abandonment of a minority language, usually over several generations. The dynamics of network power are exemplified in the *gradual* loss of languages, the creeping destruction of linguistic diversity as members of a minority group abandon their native language (for a variety of possible reasons) to speak a more dominant tongue.

A thought experiment reveals the network power dynamics of gradual death clearly. Imagine a polyglot genie in a magic lamp with the power to endow effortless knowledge of any language. Now suppose that you did not already speak any language at all—but knew which languages everyone else in the world spoke—and were offered three wishes by this polyglot genie. (Or imagine that the genie would offer each newborn, or presumably the newborn's parents, the effortless knowledge of three, and only three languages.) Which three languages would you choose?

Given three languages, you would probably choose your local language or dialect—the idiom of the people and family with whom you live immediately. In addition, you would probably choose English, as the global second language, and, for a third choice, the most important regional language with which you will come into contact. Of course, some of us might choose ancient Greek or Latin or Sanskrit, but probably not very many. Most of us would prefer to read these languages in translation, and to maximize the access we have to people currently alive.

If you were born into an English-speaking family, the three wishes would seem a luxury. I suspect that many of us would name English, Mandarin Chinese, and Spanish as the three choices, based on the numbers of speakers and the perceived importance of these languages today. Those of us with ties of ancestry or imagination to various European countries might choose German or Italian or French, but for personal rather than pragmatic reasons. By contrast, if you were born into a family in rural Punjab, you would almost certainly choose Punjabi, Hindi (or Urdu), and English, thereby gaining access to the local, regional, and global languages of choice. If you were born into a Yanomami family in Brazil, you might choose Yanomami, Brazilian Portuguese, and Spanish, depending on how close you lived to the Venezuelan border. (Or you might choose the language of neighboring indigenous groups, depending on whom you expected to meet more regularly.) The details may change but the underlying logic is the same: the choices that people would make correspond to their best guesses about which languages will be spoken by the people they will come to know. Just as the lost friends in New York City will take a gamble on Grand Central Station for an unplanned rendezvous, so too would most of us gamble on languages that we suspect others will choose, in order to maximize the number of people with whom we might speak. Given the selection of three languages, our choices would converge to cement the position of English and the regional or national languages, but would also keep local languages alive, as forms of personal and familial communication.

Now, suppose that the genie finds it possible only to grant *two* linguistic wishes to each person. The situation suddenly becomes more difficult. Perhaps the regional languages will get squeezed, as more people lock onto English for extra-local communication, but choose to be able to speak to their grandmothers in a local tongue. Or perhaps the regional languages will seem more necessary in a world of increasing regional integration, which pushes for the adoption of English and the important regional languages. Then, given just two wishes, our grandmothers will be left out.

And what would happen in the case of a weak genie willing to offer only *one* language? Everyone who knew that English was the global convention would ask to speak it, and the few who did not would be left to regional or local languages, effectively shut off from the great majority of the world. Why would English be chosen? Because even in the absence of explicit agreement, everyone will expect that everyone else will expect that they will choose English—and will choose accordingly.

Although there is no genie in a magic lamp to grant our wishes, the example does illustrate some of the predicaments of language in a globalizing world.[32] We can all learn multiple languages, and some of us do—hence the rise of English as a global second or third language, alongside the rise of regional or national languages. But languages are difficult to learn, and learning three of them is a feat for many people, particularly given the expense (or outright lack) of structured language courses and the rarity of bilingual childhood education. This fact alone will put a squeeze on languages and force us to make hard choices. These choices are particularly hard at the institutional level given the importance of structured language study in schools to the survival of vernacular literature and the preservation of a language's grammatical structure.[33] Further, as more of us learn second or third languages for reasons of business, academic research, entertainment, conversation, or religion, these languages become solidified as the ones to learn in order to participate in these activities. The less common mother tongues may begin to seem useful only for talking with our grandmothers. The distribution of our spoken languages will change with these priorities and possibilities of access.

THE THREE-GENERATION SHIFT

Consider a stylized example of social change and linguistic loss that corresponds to what Nettle and Romaine call the "classic three-generation shift" or what Crystal calls the "three-stage shift" by which a language dies a gradual death.[34] Imagine a young couple who speak only a local language—either today or earlier this century—with possibly a few foreign words imported from the outside to signify specific objects, practices, or ideas: this first generation is monolingual and may be geographically and socially isolated. Now their children, the second generation, grow up with more penetration of language from the outside for a variety of reasons, often emigration to cities or foreign countries, but perhaps too the emergence of new media and mass education. Learning a more dominant regional language to the level of fluency allows these children access to new opportunities, professional and social. Since these opportunities are available in the regional language, more of their energies are used to build a life structured around a language other than their mother tongue, which becomes a language of personal and local intimacies. Using the regional language, this second generation can gain access to others in their peer group—who are perhaps fellow citizens of the same recently independent nation and who may come from other linguistic backgrounds, but who also use the more widespread language for access. This second generation exhibits "diglossic" bilingualism: a dominant language is used outside of the home for official functions, high culture, and access to the broader market and polity. In the twentieth century, both radio and television played an increasingly significant role in cementing the position of dominant languages.

Given the choices that this second generation made—and the world that they thereby formed—their children, the third generation, grow up with facility in the dominant language, and only a passing acquaintance with the language of their grandparents. The local language will not be a language of activity and vibrancy: what few words they know will seem suited only for talking to the elderly. As Crystal writes, "Within a generation—sometimes even within a decade—a healthy bilingualism within a family can slip into a self-conscious semilingualism and thence into a monolingualism which places that language one step closer to extinction."[35] This third generation may learn English as the global *lingua franca*, if a prior generation has not beaten them to it.

This stylized pattern of linguistic change applies both to migrants from a village to a metropolitan area and to villagers living in a world in which once-distant regions have come to seem less foreign. With every generation, social, technological and political changes allow us to reach greater or different parts of the "outside." Local languages then decline in a multigenerational shift, given the network power of those regional or global languages that facilitate access to the outside. Globalization increases the rate at which these changes occur, by jumbling together different communities of speakers and offering new opportunities in foreign languages. Nettle and Romaine write that "Globalization has increasingly led to layers of diglossia on an international scale."[36] These bilingual populations are vulnerable to linguistic shifts—but they may also be the best hope we have if minority languages are to be preserved at all.

On this note, it is important to recognize that the social standing and resources that different linguistic communities can command affect both the rate at which this shift occurs, and whether a diglossic relationship—minority language at home, dominant language in public—will prove sustainable. A community that is proud of its minority language will much more easily maintain it, alongside a second or third language for outside interaction. The question of whether language death is inevitable—and indeed, whether dying or dead languages can be revived—turns on whether this diglossic relationship can be managed by small linguistic communities. Like Crystal, Nettle and Romaine argue that fostering a healthy bilingualism is essential for the maintenance of linguistic diversity—and that whether we lose about half or almost all of the world's languages over the next century will depend on the political choices we make now. The most urgent need is remedying economic disparities between different groups, whether by the provision of land rights for indigenous peoples or in the fairer distribution of the costs of asymmetric bilingualism, a subject to which I turn below.

HYBRIDIZATION AND REVIVAL

The network power of languages can account for the rise of a global second language, the rise of large regional languages, and the disappearance or endangerment of smaller languages. It can also account for the greater hybridization of language today, as new forms of coordination bring speakers of many different tongues together, often in new settings and contexts. Unsurprisingly, the languages that are spoken in this linguistic upheaval bear some of the marks of this process in the importation and blending of words from one language to another. This hybridization is the result of people having greater access to one another and needing new words to express shared experiences in speech. While much is made of the creation of hybridized languages, we should not be surprised that words and core concepts are diffusing as rapidly across the globe as the people who speak them.

The hybridization of language is related to the endangerment of minority languages both positively and negatively. Words borrowed from the outside may increase the status of that outside language, and make the minority language appear outdated or isolated to its speakers. Crystal writes, "Endangered languages come to be used progressively less and less throughout the community, with some of the functions they originally performed either dying out or gradually being supplanted by other languages."[37] On the other hand, importing words to signify new experiences and adapting them can breathe vitality into a threatened language, since all languages must change with the experiences of their speakers, if they are to remain relevant and dynamic. (Japanese presents an interesting and complicated example of such importation alongside historical continuity and preservation, with a separate alphabet, *kakatana,* used for imported foreign words, while *hiragana* is used for words of Japanese origin.)

Through these examples, we see how developments (1), (2), (3), and (4) come about. The final development that globalization has brought is (5), the deliberate revival of languages, often linked to a communal or national reassertion.[38] Here too, the dynamics of network power are at work, but it is *against* them (at least initially) that projects of national reassertion must struggle, in that such projects contend against the force of unification present in newly globalized relations of sociability. In the recovery of threatened or national languages, what we see is the attempt to use the power of sovereignty to countervail the power of sociability, the pushback of politics against globalization in the specific domain of language. To be more concrete, we see efforts by groups of people who recognize that the alternative to individually resigning themselves to the gradual disintegration of their language (as each of them individually decides—for extrinsic reasons—to abandon it) is a constructive moment of collective reassertion.

However, even this reassertion takes advantage, prospectively at least, of network power dynamics. A project of national or communal reassertion often involves a large initial cost for the first generation of speakers—consider the project of reviving modern Hebrew or Gaelic or Basque—after which succeeding generations will more readily adopt the language, and the communal identity that is thereby reinforced. It takes effort to reverse the gradual linguistic loss illustrated by the three-generation shift, but the initial investment in the revived language establishes it as conventional, aiding a form of social coordination that cements bonds among members of that network and distinguishes them from outsiders. Catapulting a dying or dead language back over the threshold of visibility is the important first step in this process, and there the resources of a state or organized community often prove critical. Without such resources—without mobilizing the power of collective decision-making or sovereignty—it is difficult to save local languages (or revive dead ones) given the pressures of global network power. This is why a lack of state support can prove decisive when social and economic inequalities map onto linguistic difference, as is the case with many Native American groups, but not, say, with the prosperous Catalunians of Spain. More generally, minority languages have a chance where the relations of sovereignty can be mobilized to reverse the choice scenario presented by sociability: the one-by-one (rational) defection to a dominant network.

A BRIEF HISTORY OF MONEY

Money is the other commonly discussed standard that exhibits network power, due to its role in the coordination of economic exchange.[39] As we saw in the last chapter, Hume mentions gold and silver as conventional "measures of exchange." In the history of the development of money, we see the rise of particular commodities to conventionality as money-forms. Money stands in for value in economic exchange. Many commodities have been effectively monetized in the past, at least for limited periods: shells, cattle, grain, whiskey, and even tobacco. Of course, the best known monetary tokens in modern times, before our era of paper currency, were coins made of precious metals: gold, silver, and copper. As John Kenneth Galbraith writes in his history of money: "The historical association between money and metal is more than close; for all practical purposes, for most of time, money has been a more or less precious metal."[40] In Europe, at least, it is true that metal and money have been indistinguishable; precious metals became so closely associated with money that, even today, the words for money and for precious metals are often the same in many European languages (for example, *argent* in French).

But money was not everywhere only metal, which reveals the interesting *social* dynamics behind the elevation of a particular token to the status of money. For example, the medieval Indian Ocean trade used "money cowries" in addition to gold and silver. In fact, as the economist Glyn Davies explains, "of all forms of money, including even the precious metals, the cowry was current over a far greater space and for a far greater length of time than any other."[41] Cowries are attractive as a medium of exchange because they are "durable, easily cleaned and counted, and defy imitation or counterfeiting." Indeed, the money cowry continued into nearly the present day as a medium of exchange for small-value items; the first professor of banking and finance in Nigeria, later an executive director at the Central Bank of Nigeria, recalls using them in his childhood village.[42] It is hard now to imagine these small seashells as the unifying currency of a vast international system, but our surprise only draws our attention to the fact that these shells—like all monetary tokens to one degree or another—were merely placeholders of value in a game of social coordination. Shell money was used similarly across western North America in the form of ten-inch long, tubular *dentalia* shells, which had a limited supply (and thus relatively fixed value) as tokens of monetary coordination.[43]

Perhaps the most unusual kind of money is the stone currency called *rai* used on the islands of Yap, a group of four small islands in the central Pacific.[44] These disc-shaped pieces of limestone were quarried on Palau, an island 260 miles distant; the largest have a hole in the middle. Like many kinds of money—perhaps all, depending on how we are to view the psychology of money today—Yap stones have a ceremonial or religious function in addition to being a storehouse of value and medium of exchange. They were used to buy houses, brides, and land, while shell currency was employed for smaller purchases. The largest stones were not always even moved as they acquired new owners in exchange—in much the same way that the 700,000 gold bars stored in the New York branch of the Federal Reserve Bank stay put even while legal title to them fluctuates with the transactions of different parties.

The stones of Yap are still locally valuable but U.S. dollars have replaced them as legal tender. Their end began with the Japanese invasion of Yap, in which the largest of them were hauled off for use in the construction of roads and seawalls. The *rai* show the coordinative aspect of money clearly, in that these stones have no functional use in ordinary social intercourse, unlike, say, gold and precious metals. Thus their value depends entirely on the *extrinsic* reasons generated for their use, as determined by the convention of a particular community. Under a foreign occupation, the *rai* proved more valuable, intrinsically, as building material.

The cowry and the *rai* are now relics of monetary history, and it is easy to see them as mere tokens used extrinsically for monetary coordination. But monetary tokens based on precious metals are more familiar, at least in the modern West, and continue to command our attention: precious metals continue to be among the most important commodities in international trade and finance, even as they have lost their privileged status as legal tender. It may be that gold will one day share the inglorious fate of the *rai*, used only by industry, or of the money cowrie, treated now as a bauble and plaything. Indeed, Thomas More envisioned such a fate on his imaginary island, Utopia, where slaves wear chains of gold and children use precious gems as toys, but that possibility seems distant at the moment.[45]

Gold is probably the first metal that early humans came across, and its malleability and striking color ensured its significance in almost every culture that has existed in a gold-bearing region. It had value as a commodity before it became money—for use in the production of jewelry, ceremonial objects, and so on—just as it has today, now that it is no longer money. The use of precious metals as money goes back at least 4,000 years. The Greek historian Herodotus claims that the first place to coin metals of determined weight was the ancient kingdom of Lydia.[46] Archaeological evidence shows the use of gold in ceremonial vessels in Central and Eastern Europe by 4000 BC. By 3100 BC, Egypt had set a ratio for the exchange of gold and silver. (The gold/silver exchange ratio was important in the bimetallic economy that flourished throughout the Old World.) Gold jewelry was found in southern Iraq, in the famous city of Ur, around 3000 BC, and by 1500 BC, the rich mines of Nubia had made Egypt a world power, the source of the commodity that had become an international standard of value. The *sheckel*, a coin used throughout the ancient Middle East, was made of electrum, a gold and silver alloy containing about eleven grams of gold. Gold possessed value throughout the world, not just in the Middle East. Squares of gold were declared legal tender in China by 1091 BC, even though China was later to use mainly silver. And in the ancient New World, we find evidence of gold jewelry in Peru as early as 1200 BC.

How and why gold (along with silver) became money is difficult to determine precisely. Obviously, a number of factors made the elevation of this commodity to the status of money a reasonable choice. Precious metals are striking, divisible, malleable, and everywhere the same. The *intrinsic* merits of this choice of standard seem better than those of other commodities that have functioned as money—say, cattle, grain, or the stones of Yap—at least for any kind of long-distance trade. However, basing the standard of value on the restricted supplies of a natural metal is by no means an obvious choice, and it brings with it its own problems. Indeed, such international monetary arrangements were long prey to cycles of expansion and contraction based on the supply of gold and silver coming from new trade routes and new mines. Nevertheless, for a great deal of our history, the familiarity and universality of gold as money obscured the fact that its value came ultimately from *extrinsic* coordination and not its intrinsic qualities.

THEORIZING MONEY

Theories of money advance arguments about how and why one commodity becomes the general measure of exchange—why gold or *rai* or cowry shells. In the beginning of the first volume of *Capital,* Marx presents a theory of the development of money as the process by which one commodity gradually replaces others in a system of barter exchange.[47] In brief, Marx argues that money emerges from the circulation and exchange of commodities, which are goods that are traded and therefore have an exchange-value and not merely personal "use-value." In simple trade such as barter, one commodity is expressed in terms of another: one good becomes the "equivalent" of another. In this process, one good can emerge as the "universal equivalent" or general equivalent through which all other commodities become commensurable. Marx writes, "the progressive development of a society of commodity-producers stamps one privileged commodity with the character of money."[48] He sometimes calls the money-form the "commodity of commodities" to illustrate its function as a universal mediating token.

In the Near East—and thereafter the rest of the world—gold played this role. "Gold, as we saw, became ideal money, or a measure of values, in consequence of all commodities measuring their values by it."[49] And having that form, commodities become comparable by their money equivalents, their prices: "one commodity infects another through this common value-relation, so that their prices, expressed in gold or silver, gradually settle down into the proportions determined by their comparative values, until finally the values of all commodities are estimated in terms of the new value of the metal that constitutes money."[50] In this analysis, we see the network power of a successful monetary standard rising to prominence over other standards, so that it becomes the convention, the universal equivalent. Thus, the money-form emerges in the transition from a world of multiple commodities, each expressible in terms of the rest, to a world with a single, general equivalent such as precious metal.

Why should gold take this role? Marx mentions its imperishability and its divisibility into small units as possible reasons for its initial prominence. But while these properties of precious metals make them useful for exchange, Marx notes the use of paper money as a substitute for actual metal.[51] His analysis of money thus focuses attention on what I have called the extrinsic reasons for the adoption of a standard, even while he understands the rise of any particular form of money as depending, initially at least, upon the value of that commodity in exchange. (This is not to say that Marx thinks it is money that makes all things commensurable; rather, it is because commodities are already commensurable in terms of the labor-value embodied in them that they can be expressed in terms of a conventional standard of value.) Marx thus synthesizes and completes earlier accounts, including Aristotle's argument that money takes its value by convention, by recasting the money-form as a social artifact with a historical trajectory.[52]

To appreciate Marx's account, it is helpful to consider the earlier theories of money presented by John Locke and Adam Smith. Locke emphasizes the conventional element in the development of the money-form. He writes in *The Second Treatise* that money arose when men "*agreed, that a little piece of yellow Metal, which would keep without wasting or decay, should be worth a great piece of Flesh, or a whole heap of Corn.*"[53] This is a point that he reiterates at a few different places: "Gold, Silver, and Diamonds, are things, that Fancy or Agreement hath put the Value on, more than real Use, and the necessary Support of Life."[54] These precious things prove useful as a way to preserve the value, achieved through exchange, of perishable items that last only a short while: "And thus *came in the use of Money,* some lasting thing that Men might keep without spoiling, and that by mutual consent Men would take in exchange for the truly useful, but perishable Supports of Life."[55] Except for a few instances where Locke vacillates—for example, arguing that precious metals have some inherent worth, "so valuable to be hoarded up" or because they are a "Fancy" in addition to an agreement[56]—he maintains throughout a consistent view that the value of money comes from its conventionality, for what we might call extrinsic rather than intrinsic reasons.

Importantly, Locke argues that the agreement to use gold as money brings with it the possibility of economic and social development, even before the emergence of a properly political order. He writes, "But since Gold and Silver, being little useful to the Life of Man in proportion to Food, Rayment, and Carriage, has its *value* only from the consent of Men, whereof Labour yet makes, in great part, *the measure*, it is plain that Men have agreed to disproportionate and unequal Possession of the Earth."[57] Thus does one agreement bring with it subsidiary changes that can themselves be considered "agreed" upon, if only tacitly. From limited, interpersonal exchange, Locke supposes that we move to divide the world into private property and inaugurate full-fledged commercial society. However, we should not understand this agreement to use precious metals for money as a deliberate, collective one—as, say, in the decision of a government either to monetize or to demonetize gold. Rather, it emerges through the relations of sociability, by informal agreement. Locke makes this clear by emphasizing the pre-political stage in which money may emerge: "This partage of things, in an inequality of private possessions, men have made practicable out of the bounds of Societie and without compact, only by putting a value on gold and silver and tacitly agreeing in the use of Money."[58] This scenario contrasts with the way in which the allocation of property resources and the organization of production might occur within a properly political society, in which, Locke argues, the economy would be regulated by positive law, not merely tacit consent to a convention of pre-political sociability.

Adam Smith, by contrast, emphasized the intrinsic value of gold as part of his explanation for its use as money, considered both as a "measure of values" and "medium of exchange."[59] Smith argues: "At first when men dealt in a few species of goods, any species might be the common measure of the value of the rest." He does not mean that any commodity will serve as the general equivalent, but only that commodities can be traded for others based on their relative values. But as the number of possible commodities increases, keeping the relative values in one's memory proves difficult, so we want to fix "on some particular commodity as the common standard." Smith explains: "This common measure has always been that with which they [the people in an area] were best acquainted," and tells us that in Greece, this meant oxen, while in Italy, because of local conditions, sheep. "Hence every wise man when he had dealt some time in merchandise would attempt to form a better measure."[60] Smith argues that the precious metals, in particular gold and silver, proved "a more certain and accurate measure of value than cattle could be" because "equall quantities [of a monetary measure] should have equall values."[61] Precious metals are divisible, and their alloy content is easily ascertained, so they make, according to Smith, an intrinsically better measure of value than the alternatives.

Interestingly, Smith compares the process of fixing on a monetary standard to that of establishing a system of measurement, arguing that the "artificiall" measures of precious metals came to replace cattle just as a standardized system of lengths replaced the reliance of each man on his own foot as a "naturall" measure.[62] But while such an account emphasizes the conventional aspect of money, Smith argues against Locke's view that money arose out of social agreement. Instead, he holds that gold is first a measure of value, because it is intrinsically valuable in itself, and then later becomes used as a medium of exchange because of properties that make it suited for exchange—its light weight, its divisibility and so on.[63] Thus he holds that the value of gold is not something determined by a tacit agreement to use it as money, but that gold is already valuable and consequently serves as money. Among other virtues he claims for precious metals is that "their beauty is undoubtedly superior to that of the other metals; gold takes a finer polish than any other, and silver next to it." He also insists (however implausibly) that "all houshold utensils . . . plates, spoons, kettles" would "with a few exceptions be the better if made of gold or silver." Thus, the precious metals already had a "naturall" price because of their utility and scarcity; their value derives not so much from extrinsic coordination (though they serve as useful media of exchange) as from intrinsic worth.[64]

Drawing these different theories together, we can understand the dynamic emergence of the money-form as Marx did: as the generation of a universal commodity-equivalent that takes its value because of extrinsic coordination but which developed historically from an intrinsically valued commodity. Thus, as he argues—and as the last century has shown—a gold standard can give way entirely to paper money, the monetary equivalent of a purely arbitrary sign. But gold was not only, or not merely, an arbitrary sign, even though it did emerge through exchange as Locke describes, constituting a perhaps informal agreement on a basic form of sociability. It is something like a *symbol* in Saussure's typology, for the gold standard retains a connection to the intrinsic value of bullion; thus gold was able to represent value as money precisely because it was valuable intrinsically in a way that our paper currency is not.[65] But while that intrinsic value may have been important at early stages of monetary integration (particularly in a relatively unconsolidated but far-flung monetary network), it could later be dispensed with once a general equivalent of whatever kind came to coordinate value in exchange.

Finally, it should be noted that the seeming naturalness of any particular standard may be linked to rather deep features of our psychology at least once it is in widespread use. The gold standard is no exception. Indeed, the psychological attachment to gold—independent of its intrinsic or extrinsic merits—exemplifies the manner in which standards of value in particular can become the objects of fetishistic attachment. Consider that even paper money without any intrinsic value is nevertheless hoarded and used in elaborate religious rituals and private fantasies: commercial societies suffer peculiar idolatries.

John Maynard Keynes brings out this psychological element in his analysis of the gold standard. He acknowledges that "the choice of gold as a standard of value is chiefly based on tradition. In the days before the evolution of Representative Money, it was natural, for reasons which have been many times told, to choose one or more of the metals as the most suitable commodity for holding a store of value or a command of purchasing power."[66] But the reasons for which it was "natural" may not exhaust our attraction to gold. Keynes continues in a more provocative and playful vein: "Dr. Freud relates that there are peculiar reasons deep in our subconsciousness why gold in particular should satisfy strong instincts and serve as a symbol. The magical properties, with which Egyptian priestcraft anciently imbued the yellow metal, it has never altogether lost."[67]

THE RISE OF THE GOLD STANDARD

Whatever the reasons—conscious and unconscious—for gold's special place, the fact that it has held such a place in recent times is indisputable.

The historical record of monetary arrangements shows us the development of gold as a universal standard for international commerce in the modern world. Its global reach in international commerce is as old as the European trade networks it underpinned. But while gold has been a precious commodity and *numeraire* for millennia, the international monetary system that was based almost solely on gold lasted for only fifty years or so, beginning around 1870 and ending in the economic and political chaos of the Great Depression, from which the gold standard was never to recover fully.[68] During this brief period of deepening international integration—the so-called first globalization—gold occupied an undisputed position as the commodity of commodities, a universal standard of value. The rise of the gold standard, its universal adoption, and its subsequent fall reveal both the network power at the heart of international commercial relations, and one of the drawbacks of the power of standards.

In his history of the modern international monetary system, *Globalizing Capital,* Barry Eichengreen examines the rise of the gold standard at the end of the nineteenth century.[69] Before it was demonetized in this period, silver was legal tender along with gold, and was the most common precious metal used in bimetallic systems, in which silver and gold were both minted into currency and convertible into each other. Usually between fourteen and sixteen ounces of silver traded for every ounce of gold. Fixing this exchange rate for one metal at too high a level would drive the other metal out of the country, because it would be better for people to convert their money into the first metal. As Eichengreen explains, "Only if the mint and market ratios remained sufficiently close would both gold and silver circulate."[70]

At the beginning of the nineteenth century, only Britain used a gold standard. Most other European nations were bimetallic, and some whole regions, including China and significant parts of Eastern Asia, were monometallic users of silver. Keynes writes: "whilst gold as a store of value has always had devoted patrons, it is, as the sole standard of purchasing power, almost a parvenu. . . . For except during rather brief intervals gold has been too scarce to serve the needs of the world's principal medium of exchange."[71]

Such a scarce metal proved an unlikely vehicle for an expanding commercial empire. Indeed, Britain lost its bimetallic standard due to a historical accident: in setting the rate at which silver bullion could be exchanged for gold in 1717 (following large imports of Brazilian gold to be minted in England), Isaac Newton allowed the price for gold to remain too high, thus driving silver coinage out of circulation in England. (In his defense, Newton proposed monitoring the ratio to see if it required further adjustment, but he did not remain master of the mint long enough to change the policy and preserve bimetallism in England.) Acknowledging the absence of circulating silver, England switched off the bimetallic standard informally in 1774, by disallowing its use for purchases larger than £25, and formally in 1821, when it was demonetized even for small transactions.

By the middle of the nineteenth century, the bimetallic economies were having an increasingly difficult time managing their dual systems, due to large fluctuations in the supply of gold and silver arising from new discoveries and mines in the western United States. Yet Eichengreen argues persuasively that these fluctuations did not push the bimetallic systems onto the gold standard, as some accounts claim. He examines and rejects other arguments for a monometallic gold standard as well, including ones based on technological superiority. Ultimately, he argues, it was England's accidental switch onto the gold standard that led other countries to abandon bimetallism too. The gold standard gained network power as a means of gaining access to the British imperial economy, and gradually displaced the rival bimetallic standard. In discussing the emergence of an international monetary regime, Eichengreen cautions: "To portray the evolution of international monetary arrangements as many individual countries responding to a common set of circumstances would be misleading." Instead, he explains, "Each national decision was not, in fact, independent of the others. The source of their interdependence was the *network externalities* that characterize international monetary arrangements. . . . the international monetary arrangement that a country prefers will be influenced by arrangements in other countries."[72]

These network externalities led gradually to the adoption of the British gold standard rather than bimetallism. The use of gold was required for access to the British market, which was the most significant and often the fastest growing market at the time, and to British capital. As Eichengreen writes, "a chance event like Britain's 'accidental' adoption of the gold standard in the eighteenth century could place the system on a trajectory where virtually the entire world had adopted that same standard within a century and a half."[73] Britain controlled a great deal of international commerce, commanded a vast empire, pioneered the industrial revolution, and exported capital and technology to the rest of the world. Its gold standard thus possessed great network power, just like its language, English. It was therefore the increasingly obvious solution to the problem of international monetary coordination.

Eichengreen was not the first to make this argument in general terms. Max Weber (who lived through some of this monetary transition) explained of the gold standard at the time: "While England probably still came into the gold standard somewhat reluctantly, because silver, which was desired as the official standard, was undervalued by the official ratio, all the other states in the modern world with a modern form of organization have chosen their monetary standard with a view to the most stable possible exchange relation with the English gold standard."[74] For although the British gold standard was formally compatible with the use of silver elsewhere, it was not always easy for Britain's trading partners to manage the practical requirements of bimetallism. The tipping point came in the middle of the nineteenth century, when the new united Germany demonetized silver. At that moment, we might say that the gold standard crossed the threshold of inevitability: with the two largest economies of Europe on the gold standard, the rest of the world quickly fell in line. In just a few decades, only isolated Central American republics continued to circulate silver coin. The nineteenth century saw the sudden end of a monetary convention that had been already established by the time of the ancient Greeks.

THE COLLAPSE OF THE GOLD STANDARD

The gold standard then reigned undisturbed for approximately fifty years, despite the deflationary pressures it generated in the late nineteenth-century economy. (The demonetization of silver restricted the overall money supply.) Having locked on to the gold standard, no country was prepared to isolate itself by switching back onto silver without the support of the rest of the international monetary system. The crisis of the First World War did push governments off the gold standard temporarily; however, a gold standard (or gold-backed standard) returned in the 1920s, and along with it, deflationary pressures in the economy.

This universalization of the gold standard came at a cost. It secured an international monetary standard underlying international trade and capital flows, but at the price of restricting the money supply. Compared to paper money, a strict monetary standard also hindered national governments in the range of policies they could pursue in response to cyclical downturns —a problem that would become especially clear during the Great Depression. Eichengreen argues that the gold standard was nevertheless kept in place because of the lack of enfranchisement or political power of the working classes, which would later come to demand greater protection from macroeconomic fluctuations, even at the cost of abandoning a strict monetary regime: "In a sense, limits on the extent of democracy [in the pre–World War I world] substituted for limits on the extent of capital mobility as a source of insulation."[75] Eichengreen's argument is close to that of a famous contemporary observer of these events, John Maynard Keynes, who in his inimitable style dissected the problems associated with an international standard of value.

Keynes was, of course, not just a commentator on the gold standard, but a central figure in the construction of an alternative global monetary regime after the gold standard was finally abandoned during the economic crisis of the 1930s. Keynes located the beginning of the end of the gold standard in the First World War, when national governments accumulated gold reserves in a period of crisis and expanded the supply of money using paper currency, observing that "when severe stress comes, the gold standard is usually suspended."[76] And he wrote, before the final end of the gold standard:

> One great change, nevertheless—probably, in the end, a fatal
> change—has been effected by our generation. . . . war concen-
> trated gold in the vaults of the Central Banks; and these Banks
> have not released it. Thus almost throughout the world, gold
> has been withdrawn from circulation. It no longer passes from
> hand to hand, and the touch of the metal has been taken away
> from men's greedy palms. . . . Gold is out of sight—gone back
> into the soil. But when gods are no longer seen in a yellow pan-
> oply walking the earth, we begin to rationalise them; and it is
> not long before there is nothing left.[77]

Gold, now no longer "commodity money," becomes merely a way by which central banks coordinate their activities: "It has become a much more abstract thing—just a standard of value." As such, "It is not a far step from this to the beginning of arrangements between Central Banks by which, without ever formally renouncing the rule of gold, the quantity of metal actually buried in their vaults may come to stand, by a modern alchemy, for what they please, and its value for what they choose."[78]

But even an abstract standard of value based on gold—such as appeared in the 1920s—does not enable real management of the money supply: "It limits the discretion and fetters the independent action of the Government or Central Bank of any country which has bound itself to the international gold standard." Some commentators argued at the time that this lack of national discretion was beneficial because many countries would, in the absence of an international standard, prove inept at managing their economic affairs. As Keynes summarizes their position, these defenders of the gold standard claimed that "it may not be the ideal system, but . . . it maintains a certain standard of efficiency and avoids violent disturbances and gross aberrations of policy."[79] This line of argument is repeated today in debates over domestic monetary arrangements in developing world countries.

Against this conservative view, Keynes argued that it is just as difficult (and maybe even more so) to maintain the gold standard as it is to handle a national currency.[80] He argued instead that governments should have the ability to manage monetary policy without locking it on to a rigid international standard of value. The tensions in the use of such an international standard are glaring given the restrictions it imposes. Achieving a balance between international coordination and domestic autonomy could be achieved, he argued, only by pulling back from the gold standard, withdrawing from the highest level of international integration. An international monetary system must provide stability in the exchange of domestic currencies for an international standard of value but needs also to preserve "adequate local autonomy" for each country.[81]

Once local autonomy had been experienced in the exigencies of wartime monetary policy, the demand for its continuance could not be kept in check. Keynes believed that advocates of a full return to the gold standard after the First World War "did not fully foresee how great the urge would be towards local autonomy and independent action" and instead "conceived that a sort of automatic stability would be attained by everyone voluntarily agreeing, or being practically compelled, to govern his behaviour in conformity with the average behaviour of the system as a whole." This conformity would require that every central bank "surrender its right of independent action," favoring international integration against local autonomy.[82] But while the world continued to use gold as a mechanism of inter-bank coordination, it did not return to a system of metal currency for everyday use.

UNIVERSAL STANDARDS

Keynes's main concern about the gold standard (or even a gold-backed standard managed by central banks) was that it may not be sensible to have an "ideal standard of value" that is "of an international character," given the tensions between international coordination and local autonomy. A universal standard is not, in this case at least, the solution to all local problems; instead it may itself introduce new difficulties that make it inappropriate for the purposes for which it is proposed. Here Keynes was arguing against the grain of his times, which supported the very highest degree of international economic integration. He noted, "The lack of an international standard of value is assumed to be just one more of these foolish hindrances to international mobility, such as tariffs, which can only serve to impoverish the whole world in the misguided attempt to benefit some separate part of it."[83] But he saw the task of conforming to an international standard as itself generating a number of new problems for national economies; it was not a straightforward solution. His argument in this vein is similar in significant respects to his more general argument in favor of insulating national economies from a global system, not only at the level of currency but even for trade in goods and capital. I will return to this theme in later chapters on economic globalization.

The tensions in the use of a universal standard are seldom clear to those in a dominant position with regard to it for they do not need to suppress local innovation in order to participate in a universal network. Keynes recognized this in relation to Britain's position in the world credit market. It is worth detailing his argument at some length here, for the parallels that emerge in relation to the contemporary debate over economic globalization are striking.[84]

Keynes argued that the power of the British economy, especially given its massive exports of capital, was so great during the last half of the nineteenth century that the British could determine credit conditions around the world by varying the country's internal holdings of gold. "This power to call the tune, coupled with certain other characteristics of the period . . . put Great Britain in a position to afford a degree of *laissez-faire* towards foreign lending which other countries could not imitate." Thus British policy-makers (and British economists) tended to overlook the problems that a rigid international standard of value posed for economic development. Keynes explained that economists and policy-makers "attributed the actual success of [Britain's] *laissez-faire* policy, not to the transitory peculiarities of her position, but to the sovereign virtues of *laissez-faire* as such. That other countries did not follow her example was deemed—like their bias towards protective tariffs—to be an indication of their inferior political wisdom." However, by the time of his writing, the situation had changed and Britain had been forced to recognize the central dilemma that Keynes articulated: "adherence to an international standard tends to limit unduly the power of a Central Bank to deal with its own domestic situation so as to maintain internal stability and the optimum of employment."[85] Britain could no longer avoid the macroeconomic question confronting all nations: "it is a question just how international it wants to be—just how sensitive to every international change."

Interestingly, Britain was losing the power to overlook this tension inherent in a universal standard of value just as the United States was gaining the power to be blithe about it. Keynes again sounds eerily contemporary: "Owing to her immensely large holdings of gold, the United States is able to obtain, to a great extent, the combined advantages of a local and of an international standard; and she is, besides, exceedingly jealous of surrendering any of her own autonomous powers to an international body."[86] Today, of course, it is not the vastness of U.S. gold holdings that makes its local standard an international one, but its ability to "debt-finance" its consumption by issuing dollar-denominated bonds to be purchased by foreigners—a situation of much greater ambiguity and vulnerability as it is based only on the network power of American paper currency, which is used as a means of gaining access to dollar-denominated commodities in the United States and elsewhere.

To mitigate the problems of a universal standard, Keynes suggested a particular way of destabilizing the ease of international capital flows by creating uncertainties, adding what today might be called "transaction costs" to the flow of money across borders.[87] He suggested that a small extra cost to capital mobility—via an increased "distance between the gold points"—would arrest volatile short-term movements while allowing long-term compatibility with an international gold standard. (His argument looks like a precursor to that now advanced by advocates of a "Tobin tax" scheme.) Keynes recognized the obvious objection that such devices may hurt international finance. But he argued, "it is a question of how high a price in the shape of domestic instability it is worth while to pay in order to secure international banking business."[88]

As an alternative arrangement, he suggested a uniform international banking system governed by a "Supernational Bank" to manage exchange rate volatility—a proposal that spurred the creation of the International Monetary Fund after the Second World War. Keynes made this proposal in light of the fact that an international standard—the gold standard—already existed and actually governed the global commerce of his day. As such, he wanted to transform it into a different international system: one that was less sensitive to the available quantities of a particular metal rather than the needs of entire domestic economies. But theoretically, for him the broadest question remained: "should standards of value be international?"[89] Comparing the problems of international capital mobility with its advantages, he argued that it is "a serious question whether it is right to adopt an international standard, which will allow an extreme mobility and sensitiveness of foreign lending, whilst the remaining elements of the economic complex remain exceedingly rigid."[90] This question would later be answered in the negative in the midst of the worldwide economic and political crisis of the 1930s. The abandonment of the gold standard accompanied the rapid dissolution of the international system altogether. But events might have gone differently if Keynes's earlier advice had been heeded, and a better balance struck between the demand for national autonomy and the advantages of international cooperation.

SOVEREIGN CONTROL OF MONEY

The crisis-driven switch from the gold standard to a politically (rather than historically) determined monetary standard, as occurred in the Great Depression, provides a dramatic example of the use of sovereignty to command and reengineer the relations of sociability on behalf of a democratic polity. In the domain of money—just as in that of language—the power to countervail a global standard requires the reassertion of politics against sociability, an effort to capture global social relations and tame them to the needs of a domestic political majority. This tension is obvious in any widely used convention: a standard that has become universal enables the widest sphere of cooperation but usually at the expense of local variation and system-wide heterogeneity. I will argue in Chapters 8 and 9 that this tension between international economic cooperation and local autonomy continues to play itself out in the politics of contemporary economic and monetary arrangements—a politics that replicates many of the problems that engaged Keynes's attention.

The political control of the money supply may prove useful not only for managing macroeconomic stability, but even for transforming the domestic regime of production, enabling all the economic activities that money coordinates to come under democratic control. In the final chapter of his landmark *General Theory* Keynes suggested as much, offering his thoughts on the "social philosophy towards which the General Theory might lead," in which he argued the relevance of his new brand of monetary economics not only for the achievement of full employment but for the redress of the "arbitrary and inequitable distribution of wealth and incomes."[91] In the first section, he argued that there was some reason to maintain an inequality in income and wealth, but not at such a high level as then existed. But in the second section, he argued a more subtle and important point: that using the political control over money, it is possible to promote aggregate investment through a low rate of interest—the opposite position from that of classical political economy—and that such a low rate of interest would, in effect, eliminate any returns to capital beyond the cost of replacement and management.[92] He did not shy away from articulating what such a macroeconomic strategy would bring about: it would mean "the euthanasia of the rentier, and, consequently, the euthanasia of the cumulative oppressive power of the capitalist to exploit the scarcity-value of capital."[93]

What Keynes was proposing here was nothing less than the gradual and non-revolutionary overthrow of the capitalist class, though he was quick to note a "moderately conservative" implication of the General Theory, which is that no comprehensive scheme of state ownership of the means of production would be required, only state control over the money supply and associated instruments of fiscal policy. No wonder then that Keynes's opponents on the right, such as Friedrich von Hayek and Ludwig

von Mises, argued for a return to the gold standard even after the Second
World War, preferring to have economic output determined by the scarcity
of a metal rather than the relations of sovereignty.[94] But what proved a
more successful strategy than a revival of the gold standard was to attack
Keynesianism at the level of economic theory, while sequestering practical
control over interest rates beyond the reaches of democratic politics in the
hands of independent central banks with formal or informal mandates to
maintain a margin of unemployment as a buffer against inflation. Hence,
the experiment with sovereign control over money in the postwar period
has shown that it is just as possible to manage its supply in order to *uphold*
the scarcity-value of capital, as it would be to undermine it.

CHAPTER FOUR

Power and Choice in Networks

IN PREVIOUS CHAPTERS, I have examined the way in which convergence on a dominant standard can occur through choices that can be viewed as both free and forced, and I called the dynamics driving this convergence "network power." What does it mean for these network dynamics to constitute a form or relation of power? In this chapter, I take up this question, first examining in more detail the conditions of choice that are generated given great inequalities of network power. Choices made in such conditions can become more and more constrained by the lack of acceptable alternatives until they prove formally free but substantively coerced.

Understanding the coercion that may be present in such circumstances of "free" choice leads into a broader argument about the meaning of power and its relation to social contexts. In the second half of the chapter, I explore the characterization of network power *as* power. By contrast with the usual view of power defined as the command of a political superior—a model of power that is connected to our idea of sovereignty—network power presents a model of power working through the structure of social relations. Some familiar heterodox theories of power, such as those of Michel Foucault or Antonio Gramsci, share this approach to power, but they can have trouble locating or articulating the role of agency in social structuration. I argue that the idea of network power presents a heterodox theory of power that escapes from some of these problems.

CHOICE UNDER NETWORK POWER

Two features are relevant for the consideration of choice in situations of network power. First, the consequences of an individual's choice are determined in coordination with the expectations of others who face similar, interdependent choices. Second, since network power grows through the operation of choice, as individuals must choose to join networks, it must always involve consent of a formal kind, at least. I ignore here cases in which networks move to ascendancy through the forced conversion of outsiders because the more interesting case is not when direct force brings about conformity to a dominant standard, but when the structural conditions of formally free, interdependent choice drive communities to that point. I have already discussed at length the first of these features—the crucial role played by interdependent expectations in the dynamic growth of networks and the power of their standards—and I will now turn to the second. The concept of network power reveals complexities in the connection between the idea of consent and the idea of freedom. Beyond what I earlier called the threshold of inevitability, a standard is pushed toward universality, and its network becomes poised to merge with the population itself. It is "pushed" by the activity of people evaluating consequences and, ultimately, choosing to adopt a dominant standard because of the access it allows them to forms of cooperation with others. Can we say that someone has chosen freely simply because she has actually made a choice, even when the consequences of that choice—and thus the reasons for it—are conditional on the choices of countless other people facing similar consequences?

As a dominant network moves toward universality, the costs of deviation from the to-be-universal standard increase until not being a member of the universal network is equivalent to social exclusion in the domain governed by that standard. This escalation of costs is the indirect force that drives network power: reason merges with force in a network's ascendance, since it is rational to adopt a dominant standard (given the extrinsic benefits it offers) but this decision is also forced by the threat of lost access to any viable network in which the activity in question may be pursued. Beyond the threshold of inevitability, reason and force merge to drive a standard to universality. We may describe the decision to conform to the dominant standard in these circumstances—in which it is rational, given the imposition of overwhelming costs, for all individuals to converge on that standard—as the result of either indirect force or extrinsic reason. The choice to adopt a dominant standard is in fact *both* a "forced" choice in which the only alternative is social exclusion, and, given these alternatives, a choice rationally made.

FREEDOM AND COERCION

How are we to evaluate these free but involuntary choices made under conditions of greatly unequal network power? For those who identify freedom with the mere act of choosing, the choice among unacceptable alternatives may not be considered "unfree." Such people might argue that the consequences of one standard's rise to dominance cannot be considered coercive so long as network power is driven by the individual consent of those in lesser networks who opt to join the dominant network. This claim resembles that of libertarian philosophers such as Robert Nozick to the effect that social outcomes generated by private market actions are always legitimate, so long as they emerge from an exercise of rights allocated in initially free conditions.[1] Such claims can be expected from theorists keen to defend the relations of sociability—even when they become manifestly oppressive—on the simple grounds that an individual's having made a choice indicates individual consent.

But how best to gauge individual consent to circumstances that have been *collectively* determined is a very complicated matter. Should we consider consent to be present in all—or any—individual choices made in the context of social structuration that restricts the alternatives from which an individual may choose? Or does the consent manifested in the domain of sovereignty—that is, collective consent to collective circumstances that then determine individual circumstances—seem a more plausible approximation of our understanding of what consent should mean in the setting of interdependent choice?

In liberal political thought, particularly of a libertarian bent, freedom is often identified with an individual's freedom to make choices for herself. In this identification lies a truth and a danger. The truth is that freedom may sometimes be manifested in the choices a person makes. The danger is that the simple act of choosing does not signify anything until we specify the domain of options over which someone chooses. Indeed, the libertarian argument may prove merely circular, first identifying freedom with the act of choosing and then simply denying the possibility that individual choice-making could coexist with unfreedom. But the act of formally making a choice, without having a set of viable alternatives from which to choose, is not a real choice at all. Such a scenario is sometimes called a *Hobson's Choice,* named for the sixteenth-century livery stable owner Thomas Hobson, who offered students at Cambridge University any horse they wanted, so long as it was the one stabled next to the door. If it is not to lapse into a version of Hobson's Choice, free choice must be defined not merely by the fact of someone's having chosen something, but by the existence of viable alternatives available to her at the time when she made her choice.

The most important line of philosophical criticism against the libertarian view of these matters correctly emphasizes the significance of the presence or absence of acceptable alternatives, thus factoring a consideration of the conditions of choice and not merely the act of choosing into the concept of freedom in choice-making. Against Nozick's claim, the philosopher Gerald Cohen offers the argument that "a person is not forced to do A if he has a reasonable or acceptable alternative course."[2] Conversely, he argues that without an acceptable alternative, the "choice" of A should be considered a forced, not a free, choice.

Building on Cohen's work, Serena Olsaretti provides an important, sustained examination of the nature of choice and criticizes simplistic ideas of liberty that conflate "freedom"—by which she means the mere freedom or ability to choose—with what she calls "voluntariness." On Olsaretti's definition, "a choice is voluntary if and only if it is not made *because* there is no acceptable alternative to it."[3] Olsaretti explains: "What I want to emphasize here is the distinction between claims of freedom, which are claims about the options an individual faces, and claims of voluntariness, which are claims about how the nature of those options affect an individual's will."[4]

Olsaretti brings out this distinction—and the poverty of theorizations of choice that fail to make it—through a contrast between two imagined cities, which she describes as follows:

> *The Desert City.* Daisy is the inhabitant of a city, located in the middle of a desert, which she is free to leave. However Daisy, who would wish to leave, knows with absolute certainty that if she leaves the city, she will not be able to survive the hardship

of the desert and she will die. Her choice to remain in the city is not a voluntary one.

The Wired City. Wendy is the inhabitant of a city fenced with electrifying wire, which she is unfree to leave. However, her city has all that anyone could ever ask for, and Wendy, who is perfectly happy with her life there, has no wish of leaving it. She voluntarily remains in her city.[5]

Olsaretti explains the difference: "In the first example, freedom does not suffice for voluntariness; in the second, unfreedom (that is, lack of the freedom to not perform the action one does perform) does not undermine voluntariness." Freedom and voluntariness thus come apart in these two examples: Wendy's lack of freedom to leave the Wired City does not indicate that her choice is non-voluntary—in fact, it conforms to her wishes—while even though Daisy is "free" to leave the Desert City, she is nevertheless "forced" to stay put.

The way in which Daisy makes a "free" but non-voluntary choice to stay in the Desert City highlights the connection between a lack of acceptable alternatives and substantive unfreedom (or what Olsaretti calls non-voluntariness). As Olsaretti points out, Cohen's original argument relies not so much on the abrogation of freedom (conceived simply as the freedom to act in one way rather than another) as on the abrogation of voluntariness: "According to Cohen, someone is forced to do something if she has no reasonable or acceptable alternative to doing something, which is compatible with saying that she is free to do that thing." But the point is that even if one is formally able (or free) to do something, it does not make the doing of that thing *voluntary* simply because it was done. Referring to Cohen's example of workers who "choose" hazardous jobs, Olsaretti interprets it as showing that "the fact that workers are free to sell their labour does not imply that, when they sell their labour, they sell it voluntarily"—that is, under conditions in which they may choose other, acceptable options.[6]

Olsaretti helps us to see how even freely made choices may be non-voluntary if made in the context of unacceptable alternatives: "What makes choices carried out under coercion non-voluntary is exactly what also makes other types of limited choices non-voluntary. The alternative faced by the man who hands over the money when threatened with a gun is to be killed; the alternative of a worker who sells his labour power for whatever price is to remain unemployed and suffer severe hardship. The relevant condition which undermines voluntariness in the first case is also present in the second, namely, the absence of an acceptable alternative."[7] How we are to judge the acceptability of the alternatives from among which an individual chooses is a complicated question. Olsaretti suggests that "the voluntariness of choice is a function of *both* the individual's preferences and the acceptability or unacceptability of the options, where the criterion for the acceptability of options is an objective one."[8] Her proposal seems a sensible one if we want to respect individual desires while also avoiding problems of false consciousness or an unreasonable choosiness that may attend any individual's subjective preferences. Olsaretti suggests that a theory of basic needs might buttress the claims she would wish to make about certain options being objectively bad, since it seems reasonable to assert that being denied a basic need must make an option unacceptable, even if it happened to conform to an agent's subjective choice.

Differentiating between free and voluntary choice-making allows us to avoid making two mistakes, as Olsaretti makes clear. The first mistake, she explains, "is to conflate questions of voluntariness with questions of freedom, to suppose that, *given* that the agent whose voluntary choice is under discussion is free to act as he does, and does what he does, it follows that he acts voluntarily." This seems straightforward enough. However, if Olsaretti is right and it is the case that merely having made a choice is not sufficient to indicate its conformity with our real wishes, then it follows that we must examine anew the question of how we are to judge the real voluntariness of our choices. This brings us to the question of structural coercion, which—as Olsaretti argues—it is a mistake to try to divorce from the analysis of individual choice: "The second mistake that is sometimes made consists in (rightly) separating questions of freedom and questions of voluntariness, and in then (wrongly) suggesting that there are no structural features of an individual's 'choice considerations' which are of moral interest."[9]

COERCION UNDER NETWORK POWER

Olsaretti's distinction between freedom and voluntariness in choice-making helps us to specify the conditions under which network power may be considered coercive, since network power describes a circumstance of social structuration that can prove limiting but which can nevertheless accommodate—indeed, requires—the formal freedom of the agents to choose among networks. In choice situations structured by a great inequality of network power, the decision we make to adopt one standard rather than another may be a non-voluntary choice: that is, in some sense coerced even while being formally free. Indeed, as Olsaretti shows, *direct force* (for example, being robbed at gunpoint) may be considered equivalent to *indirect force* (for example, the compulsion felt by people in certain classes to sell their labor-power for a wage in conditions of capitalism) in the sense that in both cases, an individual agent makes a choice that can be considered "forced" due to the lack of acceptable options. But these instances of coercion are generated differently: in the first case, by an individual act of violence; in the second, by structural determinations beyond the capacity of any one individual to alter.

This second kind of systemic coercion is the kind that large discrepancies in the network power of different networks may generate. As a standard gains greater numbers of users, it passes the threshold of visibility and begins to exert network power. Given the existence of multiple powerful networks, the act of choosing one rather than another may indeed be wholly voluntary. But once we see the rise of a single dominant network—particularly if the threshold of inevitability has been passed or is on the collective horizon of expectations—the voluntariness of individual choice-making is increasingly eviscerated until all that remains is the individual's ability to actively take up the one viable option that she faces. These circumstances of network power may be described as a version of Hobson's Choice: an individual must either choose to use the dominant standard, or else choose not to conform, suffering social isolation and the loss of access to everyone pursuing the activity in question. As one standard overtakes another, the option to take up the dominant standard gradually becomes an offer that cannot be refused.

This effective lack of choice results from a great disproportion in network power between two networks, which renders the less dominant network progressively less viable. Beyond the threshold of inevitability, the extinction of smaller networks seems assured and the only viable option for its members will be to adopt the dominant standard. In fact, even before the threshold of inevitability has been passed, the rise of a dominant standard will structure incentives so that people will be choosing—even when relatively uncoerced by the threat of social isolation—not just for the sake of cooperating with members of a dominant network but also because their own network is being destroyed by the departure of its members. Users of a less dominant standard may resent the felt necessity of switching onto the dominant one in order to maintain access to others, but they will nevertheless feel compelled to do so.

To return to Olsaretti's example, there is no direct force employed to keep Daisy in the Desert City; she stays because of a lack of acceptable alternatives. This situation is analogous to a universal standard chosen because the alternative—social isolation—is deemed unacceptable, either by the agent herself or because social cooperation with others in the sphere of activity which that standard mediates could be considered an objective need. It corresponds to the case in which only *extrinsic* reasons—the various benefits of social coordination—militate in favor of a standard that would otherwise seem undesirable (or at least, less desirable than alternatives rendered non-viable by its rise). How to assess the different contributions made by extrinsic and intrinsic reasons in a standard's rise to universality is difficult without a better specification of the acceptability of alternative courses of action. But it seems clear that although it is always extrinsically reasonable to choose a universal standard, the question as to whether that standard also possesses any intrinsic desirability is difficult to answer through the observation of individual choice-making alone. As Olsaretti emphasizes, "it is not always necessary that two acceptable options be present for a choice to be voluntary"—as we see in the scenario of the Wired City, or in the case of a universal standard that is intrinsically preferable to any alternative (in addition to already being a form of social coordination). But it is certainly the case that the greater the number of acceptable options from among which we can choose, the more confident we can be that the choices we make among them are really voluntary ones. As Olsaretti explains, "It is possible, then, for someone to choose voluntarily, even in the absence of acceptable alternatives. However, we must note that the presence of at least two acceptable options from which to choose reassures us that no adaptive preference is at stake and solves an epistemic problem: if someone has two acceptable options to choose from, then *we have more reason to be sure that,* whichever one she chooses, she chooses it voluntarily. The existence of two acceptable options, in other words, is a necessary condition for us to *know* that a choice is voluntary."[10]

FORCED CHOICE

Up to now, I have discussed the voluntariness of choice in relation to the presence or absence of acceptable alternatives. This argument may be presented in terms of the "costs" of choosing one way rather than another. Indeed, we can understand the end point of network power, following the rise of a universal standard, as a condition in which the costs of choosing anything other than the dominant standard are so high as to induce compliance, whether or not that compliance may be conceived of as voluntary. This compliance is mandated by a structure of choice that may be entrapping and yet arises from the interplay of free decisions taken by reasonable people. Of course, after what I have called the merger of indirect force and extrinsic reasons at the threshold of inevitability, the costs of failing to conform to the dominant standard will be based on structural conditions rather than derived from the agency of any particular individual or group.

The idea of coercion as the imposition of costs requires a brief discussion and clarification. We can translate coercion into the language of costs: any given choice—even an extreme one such as the command "Obey or die!"—can be understood as imposing costs to a particular course of action. Perhaps we might say that the refusal to adopt a dominant standard imposes costs not of one's own choosing, just as the refusal to follow the command "Obey or die!" imposes costs not of one's own choosing. However, there is a problem with using this kind of language. Beyond some limit, however vague, we must accept that a quantitative change will become qualitative, and the point will no longer be about the overwhelming nature of the costs of one option as opposed to another, but about the absence of any real choice at all. Bearing this in mind, perhaps we should simply consider the imposition of enormous costs to choosing B over A simply as amounting to coercion to choose A, a kind of non-choice (as if B were not actually in the domain of choice) or what Olsaretti would call a non-voluntary choice. In this way, what we might call the Sovereign's Choice ("Obey or die!") resembles Hobson's Choice ("Choose this or nothing!") because they are both forms of substantive unfreedom masquerading as choice. The first results from *direct* force and the latter from *indirect* force, but in both situations, the force applied denies the chooser the ability to make a real decision for herself based on the costs and benefits of selecting one alternative against another. In either case, the choice is, as it were, already made.

Thus, beyond the threshold of inevitability we find a paradox, a marriage of freedom and unfreedom in which each individual may seem to have been in control of her fate—and yet have had no other fate to choose. When we lock onto a dominant standard, we have all, formally speaking, made a choice—and we have all chosen the only real option, since the incentives structured by network power will have driven us toward this single choice. We may all consent to our common destiny: the acceptance of a network poised to become a universal standard. But simply because our reason and our consent have a role to play here, we should not conclude that we have been liberated from coercion. Instead, reason and consent are part of the same landscape of causes and effects that determines our decisions in the first place.

This self-reinforcing structure of choice is common in many social processes. That it consists in a form of unfreedom (or what Olsaretti would call non-voluntariness) is not a new insight: Saussure spotted this basic problem in relation to language, which we might take as a model for the relations of sociability more generally. He wrote:

> The signal, in relation to the idea it represents, may seem to be freely chosen. However, from the point of view of the linguistic community, the signal is imposed rather than freely chosen. Speakers are not consulted about its choice. Once the language has selected a signal, it cannot be freely replaced by any other. There appears to be something rather contradictory about this. It is a kind of linguistic Hobson's choice. What can be chosen is already determined in advance. No individual is able, even if he wished, to modify in any way a choice already established in the language. Nor can the linguistic community exercise its authority to change even a single word. The community, as much as the individual, is bound to its language.[11]

As Saussure explains, "A language can therefore be treated simply as a form of contract, and the linguistic sign is a particularly interesting phenomenon to study for this reason. For if we wish to demonstrate that the rules a community accepts are imposed upon it, and not freely agreed to, it is a language which offers the most striking proof."[12] The lack of freedom that arises in circumstances of social structuration (like the inheritance of a language) may at first be hard to grasp since—unlike natural constraints—the circumstances of social life are artifacts of human will and agency, and may even be arbitrary. "Since the linguistic sign is arbitrary, a language as so far defined would appear to be an adaptable system, which can be organized in any way one likes, and is based solely upon a principle of rationality." But Saussure argues that once the impact of historical change and the requirements of social integration are considered in relation to language, the naïve view that holds that languages are governed by rationality and easily adaptable cannot be maintained: "the language is no longer free from constraints, because the passage of time allows social forces to be brought to bear upon it. One is left with a principle of continuity that precludes freedom of choice."[13]

DOMINATION AS A MODEL OF POWER

Network power describes choice under conditions that we can consider nonvoluntary, albeit formally free. Can we claim that the imposition of unfreedom under such conditions involves an exercise of *power*? Our consideration of systemic coercion leads naturally into a consideration of systemic power.

One common notion of power owes much to the definition of *domination* put forward by Max Weber in the early twentieth century. (Weber distinguished "power" from "domination," arguing that the "concept of power is sociologically amorphous" but that the "sociological concept of domination"—which he defined as "the probability that a *command* will be obeyed"—is more precise and thus better suited to social analysis.[14]) Weber argued that domination takes the form of a command by a political superior, or what he called the "authoritarian power of command." This idea has obvious attractions and can be a useful starting point for a great many social analyses, including Weber's own impressive undertaking in *Economy and Society*. But relying on this definition as basic to *all* ideas of power may make it difficult to understand power when it does not resemble a command but inheres in social relations. For example, it makes it hard to analyze the role of power in instances of systematic group oppression, as under patriarchy or racial apartheid. It may also make it difficult to understand the power that is manifested in the case of the "class compulsion" to work under capitalism, because labor extracted under the impersonal threat of deprivation does not resemble the bilateral master-slave relationship, in which one person commands the labor of another by threatening violence.

Importantly, however, Weber did not restrict himself to this particular definition of domination, and thus his analysis proves more capacious than those presented by many of the scholars who have followed him. He prefaces his definition of domination as "authoritarian power of command" with an admission that domination exists in many other forms as well: "Without exception every sphere of social action is profoundly influenced by structures of dominancy."[15] After this broad acknowledgment, Weber discusses in detail two different, paradigmatic types of domination, contrasting "domination by virtue of authority" with "domination by virtue of a constellation of interests." He argues that other forms of domination may also exist, but restricts his comparison to these "two diametrically contrasting types of domination."

The first form of domination, that which exists "by virtue of authority, i.e., power to command and duty to obey," Weber identified as being found in "patriarchal, magisterial, or princely power," while the second form of domination, that which exists "by virtue of a constellation of interests," he considered to be exemplified in its "purest type" in examples of "monopolistic domination in the market."[16] It was the first formulation that he went on to develop more extensively, and which is now commonly referred to as the "Weberian" idea of power. But the second type of domination he specified is important for the characterization of network power as power—or indeed, for any of the heterodox theories of power that assert (against the more limited "Weberian" notion) that power need not always resemble authoritarian command. Weber clearly recognized that there was a distinction between these two forms of domination, although he also noted that this distinction was one that admitted of gradations and transitions in actual social settings. But he cautioned against failing to recognize the difference, at least theoretically: "we must not overlook the clear-cut antithesis between factual power which arises completely out of possession and by way of interest compromises in the market, and, on the other hand, the authoritarian power of a patriarch or monarch with its appeal to the duty of obedience simply as such."[17]

Weber wrote that domination through a structure of interests is "based upon influence derived exclusively from the possession of goods or marketable skills guaranteed in some way and acting upon the conduct of those dominated, who remain, however, formally free and are motivated simply by the pursuit of their own interests."[18] The clearest examples of this situation are economic ones that involve a monopoly (or near monopoly) position in a market. For example, Weber argued that the position of a "large central bank or credit institution" represents this type of domination, for large banks dominate those to whom they lend money by requiring debtors to bend to their demands regarding conduct. Importantly, this arrangement is seldom seen by the bank—or even by the debtors—as a form of domination: "The credit banks do not, however, pretend that they exercise 'authority,' i.e., that they claim 'submission' on the part of the dominated without regard to the latters' own interests; they simply pursue their own interests and realize them best when the dominated persons, acting with formal freedom, rationally pursue their own interests as they are forced upon them by objective circumstances." More generally, a monopolist "can impose upon [other businesses] a way of conduct according to his own interests, without, however, imposing on them the slightest 'obligation' to submit to this domination."[19] He cites as examples of such domination not only the position of large banks and industry cartels in relation to other market participants, but also the relation of the Standard Oil Company to gasoline retailers, and that of German breweries to tavern owners.

Market relations offer obvious examples of this domination of formally free persons obligated not by direct authority but by interest. Indeed, Weber's analysis brings to mind another famous example, Marx's earlier study of wage-labor under capitalism. Weber took up this issue briefly as an example of domination according to interest, claiming that "the worker in the office or plant . . . is subject to a discipline no longer different in its nature from that of the civil service or the army, although it has been created by a contract concluded in the labor market by formally 'equal' parties through the 'voluntary' acceptance of the terms offered by the employer."[20] But although Weber emphasized relations in the market as the paradigm case of this second form of domination, he did not limit its scope to market activity or economic power alone. "Domination in the broader sense can be produced not only by the exchange relationships of the market but also by those of 'society,'" for which he cited examples drawn from other kinds of social interaction including the dictates of fashion or conversation. Furthermore, he argued that "such situations of domination can be found also outside the sphere of private markets and relationships." He explained: "Even without any formal power of command an 'empire state' or, more correctly, those individuals who are the decisive ones within it either through authority or through the market, can exercise a far-reaching and occasionally even a despotic hegemony." As evidence, he cited the position of New York within the United States and that of Prussia within early proto-national German associations such as the German Customs Union and later the German Reich itself.[21] The parallels here with later concerns, including current ones about American-led globalization, are striking; indeed, it is particularly interesting to note that in the course of his discussion Weber drew a distinction between an imperial position that we might call "hegemonic," and one in which there is direct political domination of a subordinate society such as through military occupation.

Weber did not deal at great length with the idea of domination by a constellation of interests, instead moving on to develop his idea of domination as command, explaining that he would "use the term domination exclusively in that narrower sense which excludes from its scope those situations in which power has its source in a formally free interplay of interested parties such as occurs in the market but also in other groups of interests." He made it clear that in his sociological terminology, "*domination shall be identical with authoritarian power of command.*"[22] Too many scholars following Weber's lead have gone further still, identifying domination not just terminologically but also philosophically with what Weber called the "authoritarian power of command." However, we should recognize that the author of this original definition fully appreciated the existence of a range of ideas of power that went considerably beyond the one he ultimately chose to concentrate on, including types of domination that arise due to one's position in a structure of interests in which the dominated remain formally free, consenting to the power exercised over them.

NETWORK POWER AS DOMINATION

We can map the distinction that Weber drew between the "authoritarian power of command" and the power that originates in "the formally free interplay of interested parties" onto the contrast we have already identified between sovereignty and sociability in the history of political thought. The idea of power as authoritarian command locates power in an act of sovereignty; the idea of power as emerging out of a "constellation of interests" looks instead to the power at work in relations of sociability. While the analytics of power as sovereignty are the subject of much research and debate—with concerns about "the state," majority rule, minority interests, and so on part of the familiar lexicon not just of political theory but of popular discourse—the analytics of the power at work in sociability are comparatively undeveloped. Although Weber himself flagged the issue —and was keenly aware of the forms of unfreedom present in markets and other social structures—later scholars have neglected to develop the distinction he put at the heart of his analysis of domination. Indeed, while the power manifested in sovereignty has been the focus of great critical attention, the power operative in the private spheres of market, family, and community or in social systems of language and ideology has largely escaped similar scrutiny until relatively recently. But Weber recognized it, and even argued that the more obscure power operating in the relations of sociability can be "much more oppressive" than the relatively transparent power in sovereignty.[23]

The idea of network power takes as its starting point this relatively undeveloped argument about "domination by virtue of a constellation of interests" and attempts to work out an elaborated conception of this second kind of power, the power at work in relations of sociability. An instance of network power represents a case of domination "by virtue of a constellation of interests," for a standard provides the "good or marketable skill guaranteed in some way" that acts "upon the conduct of the dominated." It is a "good" in the sense that it offers the benefits of cooperation with other users, and it acts upon the conduct of the dominated by structuring the incentives of choice so as to eliminate genuinely free or voluntary choice-making. Network power "has its source in a formally free interplay of interested parties," as Weber defined this second type of domination. The adoption of a standard, even after the threshold of inevitability, always comports with rationality, in the sense that it will always reflect a frank appraisal of the settled consequences of that choice, even if the adoption of the option in question has essentially been forced by the lack of viable alternatives. Because of this structure of choice, the members of a dominant network do not need to coerce others into joining them by using the power of command. Rather, as Weber writes of the large banks: "they simply pursue their own interests and realize them best when the dominated persons, acting with formal freedom, rationally pursue their own interests as they are forced upon them by objective circumstances."

These objective circumstances are structured by the aggregation of individual choices given the economies of scale in the adoption of a standard. Thus, after the threshold of inevitability, at least, the interests of those who use a lesser standard coincide with the interests of those who use the dominant standard. In fact, as with the large banks and monopolists, we can consider a universal standard as a monopoly over competing modes of cooperation. "Domination" is in this sense in the interest of the dominated—since the use of a monopoly standard remains preferable to social isolation—and it is through self-interested action that such domination comes about. Nonetheless, this domination benefits the dominated only because of the lack of acceptable alternatives to the dominant standard, as is the case with any monopoly.

Understanding network power as a theory of power requires placing it in the category of the second type of domination that Weber identified. Two aspects of this model of domination need to be further elaborated in relation to network power. First, Weber develops what I earlier called a theory of structuration, an account that links agency and structure together in a way that allows us to make sense of both. On this account, even with a commitment to a broad form of methodological individualism, we can see the emergence of structures of domination from the interplay of formally free choices based on self-interest. Second, in such a model, outright coercion need not prove the main indication of power. One straightforward view of power associated with the "authoritarian power of command" model understands power as the ability to accomplish one's aims against the resistance of others, usually in a situation of conflict.[24] Of course, where other people are an impediment to the achievement of one's aims, the use of coercion may be necessary—and, where it succeeds, ample proof of the effective use of power. But in a situation of extreme inequality in network power, direct coercion as such is not necessary. The ability to induce others to act in a certain way—to influence the "conduct of the dominated"—comes, in the first instance, from the objective circumstances that shape the interests of the dominated. In such cases, where the source of the "force" is systemic and impersonal rather than direct and conflicting, there may well be no resistance to be overcome.

If we drop the insistence that power always means the ability to accomplish one's will against the resistance of others, then the strategy of accomplishing one's ends by co-opting others seems at least as attractive as outright coercion. The social theorist Talcott Parsons famously divided the different ways in which people can get others to do things for them into four varieties: "activation of commitments," "persuasion," "inducement," and "coercion." Parsons's quadripartite division shows the poverty of an equation of power with coercion alone—it misses three of the four broad ways in which we use others to accomplish our goals. The philosopher Brian Barry, reviewing Parsons's analysis, conceives of power as the ability to get others to do things for you, based on changing their incentives with promises or threats or some combination thereof.[25] As I indicated above, I think this analysis can be taken too far: not every form of power can be interpreted as a change in costs and benefits, since the subjective experience of power may be far removed from such calculations. However, in circumstances of network power—in the merger of indirect force and extrinsic reasons in the adoption of a particular standard—this view may help us to understand the power of a dominant standard in shaping the consequences (and thus the incentives) of individual choice. Although, in Barry's presentation, power is conceived as manifested in cases where one individual gets others to do something for him—which is not an exact analogy with network power—we can nonetheless usefully broaden the concept of power which he and Parsons use to help us say more about network power. Network power works through the simultaneous promise of belonging to a dominant network and the threat of social exclusion, which together give a network influence over the actions of individuals. The change of incentives comes from the increasing loss of real choice under conditions of growing network power: as the incentives to switch onto a dominant network become greater, the alternatives, even if freely available, become even less attractive.

THREE VIEWS OF POWER

Of course, Weber is not alone in identifying a kind of power located in the structure of interests. The philosopher Steven Lukes, in his influential book *Power*, discusses different conceptualizations of power, examining what he calls the "one-dimensional," "two-dimensional," and "three-dimensional" views, including accounts of hegemonic or systemic power.[26] Central to all three conceptualizations of power that Lukes examines is the understanding that power can be identified because its exercise affects someone else: "The absolutely basic common core to, or primitive notion lying behind, all talk of power is the notion that A in some way affects B."[27] For Lukes, the exercise of power is also always detrimental to the person over whom power is exercised. As he explains, "The three views . . . can be seen as alternative interpretations and applications of one and the same underlying concept of power, according to which A exercises power over B when A affects B in a manner contrary to B's interests."[28] But these views differ in their ability to explain the varieties of power operating in society, and Lukes argues that each successive view solves problems found in the previous one.

The one-dimensional view is associated with the political scientist Robert Dahl and theorists of interest group conflict. The view is not confined to these theorists, however, but tallies with the standard "Weberian" account of power, holding that A has power over B to the extent that he can get B to do something that B otherwise would not do.[29] This understanding sees power as a force that overcomes resistance. It looks at who wins in processes of community decision-making when there is conflict among different preferences, which are understood to express different interests.

To illustrate the one-dimensional view of power, consider a City Council meeting in which there is a debate over whether to build a new school. Suppose that some citizens feel the community desperately needs a new educational facility while other citizens oppose it because it will raise their tax burden. In this situation, we can say that the group that prevails has power understood in the "one-dimensional" sense because it prevailed in the conflict. For example, if the citizens who desire the school bring the issue to a vote and garner a majority, then we can say that this group has political power. This example shows the affinity between the one-dimensional view of power and the idea of sovereignty from which it takes its cue.

The two-dimensional view is associated with the sociologists Peter Bachrach and Morton S. Baratz, who criticize Dahl's conceptualization of power.[30] Bachrach and Baratz examine both decision-making and "nondecision-making," by which they mean the ability of powerful groups to keep certain issues off the table of collective deliberation and decision altogether. On this view, power is seen not only in which interest group wins out in a situation of conflict, but in which group has control of the agenda of politics and determines how issues are even brought into consideration and open conflict in the first place. Lukes finds this view more persuasive than the first because it can include the power that groups have to influence others by deciding that something is not going to be decided upon.

In the City Council example, it is safe to say that the citizens who vote for the school possess political power if they win. However, imagine the scenario in which these citizens call for a vote on the new school but the head of the City Council stands up and announces that the school issue is simply "not on the agenda" at this time and moves the deliberation on to the next item, perhaps preparations for an upcoming city parade. In the two-dimensional view of power, we can say that the head of the City Council has made a "nondecision" by making a decision about which items will be on the table for collective deliberation and determination and which will not be. He, too, has power: not the power to overcome resistance in a situation of conflict, but a kind that operates at one level of remove from the outright clash of interests.

The three-dimensional view of power focuses on collective influences and the way in which social structures shape individual preferences.[31] It is associated with more radical thinkers, such as Antonio Gramsci (whom I discuss at greater length below). Lukes identifies two different cases in which collectivities exercise power in the three-dimensional view: first, the "phenomenon of collective action, where the policy or action of a collectivity (whether a group, e.g. a class, or an institution, e.g. a political party or an industrial corporation) is manifest, but not attributable to particular individuals' decisions or behaviour," and, second, the "phenomenon of 'systemic' or organisational effects, where the mobilisation of bias results . . . from the form of an organisation." Lukes notes that while these collectivities are composed of individuals, "the power they exercise cannot be simply conceptualised in terms of individuals' decisions or behaviour."[32]

In the three-dimensional view, power is no longer assumed to produce observable conflict as in the one-dimensional view, or even suppressed conflict kept off the political agenda, as in the two-dimensional view. Lukes thinks that this conceptualization of power is more persuasive than the two-dimensional view, since it has the potential to resolve certain key issues left ambiguous in the idea of "nondecision-making." Chief among these is the problem of identifying when a nondecision has been made, since it may be hard to locate a decision that produces a nondecision.[33] This problem is particularly acute when a single, observable actor is not in charge, but in which group preferences and social structures work to produce a nondecision. As Lukes explains, "the power to control the agenda of politics and exclude potential issues cannot be adequately analyzed unless it is seen as a function of collective forces and social arrangements."[34] Of course, understanding power in this way produces certain difficulties, even as it solves others. Ideally, any three-dimensional view should have as its basis a theory of structuration that articulates the scope of human agency within social structures.

In the City Council hypothetical, how are we to tell when an issue has been kept off the table, if we cannot observe the head of the City Council announcing that (like the new school) some other decision is "not on the agenda"? For example, the communities that demand the new school may also be in need of new medical facilities, better roads, and safer streets. If these needs are never voiced, how are we to say whether power has been exercised in keeping these items off the agenda too? In this case, we do not just have an impaired or distorted act of sovereignty—as when a "nondecision" is taken by a single actor or set of actors within the ordinary political process—but the possibility that the relations of sociability have a stranglehold on sovereignty from the get-go.

Wherever such a stranglehold exists, it would seem likely that certain issues will not even have the chance to become "political": they will simply never be raised. Lukes views this possibility as the consequence of systemic bias: "the bias of the system is not sustained simply by a series of individually chosen acts, but also, most importantly, by the socially structured and culturally patterned behaviour of groups, and practices of institutions, which may indeed be manifested by individuals' inaction."[35] In this three-dimensional view of power, the bias may operate by affecting peoples' subjectivities, their senses of themselves. Thus the theorist of three-dimensional power will often want to identify a gap between the real and perceived interests of those over whom power is being exercised in order to show how power operates through collective arrangements. The controversial idea of "false consciousness"—the notion that people act against their own interests because they systematically fail to identify them—frequently has a role to play in three-dimensional views of power because it can offer an account of how such a gap might be generated and sustained.

To continue with the City Council example, suppose that the city objectively does need a new school facility in one district—that is, that the existing facilities are actually inadequate in some relevant way—but that the citizens do not work to pass the legislation necessary to raise taxes and build a new one. This problem may not even be brought to the attention of the City Council as a concern. Why not? Those affected by the inadequate school may have a view of themselves and their needs that does not allow them to conceptualize the lack of adequate schooling as a problem that could or should be solved. For example, they may not believe that they need or require a new school facility, perhaps because they do not feel that they deserve a better one, or because the existing one seems adequate despite all evidence to the contrary. They may even believe it unfair to tax any richer citizens to provide it, perhaps because they believe that they, too, will someday be richer, and thus identify in anticipation with the interests of the wealthy. If questioned about the school explicitly, they may argue that "everyone should look out for himself" or that "the government never gets it right."

Such beliefs may be part of a larger system of three-dimensional power that has shaped these opinions and allows richer citizens to keep their taxes low without having to engage in either decision-making or explicit nondecision-making. As Lukes writes, "the most effective and insidious use of power is to prevent such conflict from arising in the first place."[36] The new school issue never even makes it to the City Council meeting because those who lack a decent school cannot conceive its lack as a problem. Perhaps even to recognize that their community has an inadequate school would provoke anxiety about their relative class position—and so it is easier to concentrate on the upcoming city parade.

It is important to note that in this three-dimensional view of power, the citizens involved give their *consent* to the power that affects them, and are acting freely in accepting this disadvantageous—and perhaps even unjust—situation. Of course, to claim that the refusal of these citizens to recognize their lack of a decent school as a problem emerges as the result of an exercise of power may require the observer to believe that these citizens do not fully understand their own "interests." Many scholars are reluctant to make these kinds of assumptions, for obvious reasons, although not every three-dimensional theory of power will require such an account. For example, a more nuanced theory of recognition that views interests almost as proxies and situates them in a broader context of self-understanding might escape the need for the assumption of false consciousness, and in the next chapter I will outline such an account.

Just as it solves certain problems, a three-dimensional view of power introduces others, such as the question of how best to conceive of the exercise of power of this kind—and indeed, how we might even go about identifying it. Lukes admits the difficulties of maintaining a three-dimensional view because of this problem.[37] He argues that to identify its exercise requires a relevant *counterfactual*—what agent B would have done absent A's power—and also an account of the *mechanism* of power, showing how A got B to act. (A counterfactual is a statement about what *would* have happened if some antecedent condition had been different— for example, what B would have done if A had not had power over her.)[38] Lukes discusses the difficulty of meeting these two criteria in the case of three-dimensional theories of power. In part, this is because of the role that collectivities and other social units greater than the individual play in such three-dimensional theories, since many theorists would prefer to attribute all relevant causation to identifiable individuals and their actions alone.[39] On a three-dimensional view power, however, it may at times seem entirely plausible to identify the power of A, in the example given above, with that of a group of people, such as a network—or even, loosely speaking, the medium through which they are united, such as a standard—as I will discuss in greater detail below.

NETWORK POWER AND SOCIAL STRUCTURE

Against naively individualistic accounts of power, the temptation is to claim that power is to be found in social structures, and not in the actions of individuals, who may themselves be subject to a power of which they are unaware. And while this argument may sometimes prove compelling, it risks sliding from the discussion of specific examples of power into a general description of social processes. It may be more helpful to develop an account of the kind that Weber proposed in his discussion of the sort of power that operates through relations of private interest. Such a three-dimensional account would need to be set in the context of a theory of structuration, enabling us to describe the capacities of agents *within* social structures, and would thereby prove capable of differentiating between ongoing social processes in which power does not have a relevant role, and more specific exercises of power.

The idea of network power may be understood as a theory of three-dimensional power, in which collective or systemic conditions are seen as affecting the preferences of individual agents. Consider the two criteria of three-dimensional theories that Lukes suggests: to maintain that a dominant Network A has exercised power over someone in a smaller Network B, we require a relevant *counterfactual* and a *mechanism* of power. The counterfactual is clear: except for the inequality in network power, the member of Network B would stay a member of Network B. The mechanism of power may be somewhat less clear because it is not the case that anyone in Network A has to *do* anything directly to a member of Network B to make him switch networks.[40] Certainly, it may be the case that some people in Network A do something, for example, design or support standards incompatible with alternatives or use ordinary pressure or coercion to gain a larger network for the standard. But these forms of power are preliminary to the actual exercise of network power, even though they might be undertaken with the goal of gaining network power in mind. Rather, the exercise of network power is systemic and network-wide: faced with expectations of collective convergence to Network A, members of Network B will feel "compelled" by the incentive structure to switch networks. Members of Network B are thus trapped in a game of rational expectations, along with all others similarly situated, which may in time result in the universality of Network A.

Two points should be made about the characterization of network power as three-dimensional. First, the idea of network power identifies the exercise of power without referencing "false consciousness" or denying individual rationality. Members of Network B need not suffer from false consciousness, or even ignorance of any hidden costs of their choosing to join Network A (even though it is clear that people often do). Frequently they will be able to see all too clearly both the benefits and the costs of joining the dominant network, and recognize that they will have no choice but to join it in the end, given a certain configuration of network power.

Second, the idea of network power requires no attribution of *agency* to units greater than the individual, even though it recognizes that networks, conceived as groups of individuals, can possess *power* due to the accretion of many past individual choices.[41] The idea of network power highlights the influence of these past choices on the structures in which we act, but does not require that we imagine any acting agents to exist other than the individuals who are constrained by the structures that they themselves (or other people) have built. Distinguishing the identification of the power possessed by networks from the conceptualization of power presented in structurally deterministic theories of social action is important for the accurate characterization of network power as power. It is possible to articulate a systemic condition of power *without* attributing ultimate agency to anything other than interdependent human choices and actions. This means that while we may speak of a network manifesting power, the source of that power can always be traced back to the actions of the individuals composing that network. Some may find it awkward at first to discuss the "exercise" of power at the group or network level, but as Lukes argues, this difficulty may prove to be linguistic rather than conceptual. The agency involved can ultimately be assigned to individuals acting together, who become part of a collectivity through which we can then identify the "exercise" of power in social relations. Such an exercise need not be conscious or deliberate, and it need not be undertaken by any specific individual.

The idea of network power may hold certain advantages over other three-dimensional theories of power, which run into difficulties when it comes to distinguishing social structure in general from specific examples of the exercise of power. Lukes recognizes the nature of this problem, asking: "when can social causation be characterized as an exercise of power, or, more precisely, how and where is the line to be drawn between structural determination, on the one hand, and an exercise of power, on the other?" The failure to make this distinction has plagued, for example, certain strains of Marxist thought, especially the work of the postwar structuralist Marxists such as Louis Althusser and his followers.[42] The problem of distinguishing social causation or structural determination from an exercise of power is a complicated issue, as we will see below in the discussion of Gramsci and Foucault, and I am sympathetic to the thought that there may be no final or definitive theoretical resolution to the problem, but merely a series of partial and contingent steps. That said, many structuralist accounts of social relations will be unable to make this distinction properly because of the limited role they accord to human agency.

One way that we can be sure that, in identifying the power possessed by groups or institutions, we do not slide into conflating the exercise of power with the structure of society itself is by providing evidence that people within the group or institution in question could have acted differently. Only given the reality of counterfactual considerations—that someone exercising the power we believe we have detected was able at some point to *not* exercise it, and that outcomes would have been different had he *not* done so—can we be confident, first that human agency has had a part to play, and concomitantly, that what we are examining really is an exercise of power, since power cannot exist absent human agency (although it may be the case that agency can exist in the absence of power). Of course, in circumstances of the collective exercise of power, the relevant action may have occurred in the past and contributed to the initial establishment of institutions that now channel power. Lukes argues that "to identify a given process as an 'exercise of power,' rather than a case of structural determination, is to assume that it is *in the exerciser's or exercisers' power* to act differently. In the case of a collective exercise of power, on the part of a group, or institution, etc., this is to imply that the members of the group or institution could have combined or organised to act differently."[43] In the next chapter, I will argue that not only the assertion of an exercise of power, but also the normative evaluation of that exercise requires such a counterfactual assessment. Indeed, it may be that any account of power as inhering in social relations needs to adopt such a stance in order to identify power and then judge it.

Importantly, this claim about counterfactual assessment is not the same as the claim that a coherent theory of power must be able to locate a single agent with the power to alter collective circumstances. (To claim this would make us again unable to account for the power at work in circumstances of group oppression, class compulsion, and the like.) Given that network power operates through a social network, we do not need to be able to identify any individual Person A able to affect the actions of Person B by exploiting network power dynamics. Rather, as in "a collective exercise of power," the requirement is only that a given configuration of networks might have been ordered differently if some people had *not* acted in a way that led to an inequality in network power. We can say that a network has power in this three-dimensional view given that the networks might have formed differently, with different consequences for members of less dominant ones. Lukes puts the matter well: "To use the vocabulary of power in the context of social relationships is to speak of human agents, separately or together, in groups or organisations, through action or inaction, significantly affecting the thoughts or actions of others (specifically, in a manner contrary to their interests). In speaking thus, one assumes that, although the agents operate within structurally determined limits, they none the less have a certain relative autonomy and could have acted differently."[44] In fact, without the assumption that some agents could have acted differently at some point, it is not clear that we can ever speak of power. Lukes argues that "within a system characterised by total structural determinism, there would be no place for power,"[45] though it may be more precise to say that in such a system, there would be no real place for *agency*, and thus no place for the power that stems from agency.

HEGEMONY AND DOMINATION

Many of the interesting heterodox theories of power that emerged in the twentieth century were attempts to formulate "three-dimensional" views of power, in order to make sense of power as it works through social relations. Each of these views must contend with the problems of theorizing power in such a way that the ultimate agency of individuals within social relations is not obscured. This problem threatens two of the most celebrated three-dimensional views, those of social theorists Antonio Gramsci and Michel Foucault. To demonstrate how the idea of network power can be considered a "three-dimensional" view of power, I consider it alongside the Gramscian concept of hegemony and the Foucauldian idea of disciplinary power, situating it in a broader debate about power, subjectivity, and social structures.

Antonio Gramsci offered his arguments about hegemony and domination against the backdrop of traditional Italian political thought, which saw force and consent as opposed.[46] It thus took its model of power from the relations of sovereignty and not sociability, but Gramsci could not do the same, since he was concerned with demonstrating the ways in which power was at work in social relations outside the formal domain of the state. In view of capitalism's surprising durability, Gramsci undertook an investigation into the modes of acceptance and consent, theorizing "hegemony" alongside "domination" as an important instance of social power. In the idea of hegemony, Gramsci sought to *combine* force and consent, to describe a form of power in which force is exercised through a system to the dictates of which the dominated willingly submit. Gramsci argued that analyzing the history of political institutions reveals two modes of class control: "domination" (*dominazione*), which is coercion or force, and usually arises out of the state's monopoly on violence, and "hegemony" (*egemonia*) or "intellectual and moral leadership," (*direzione intelletuale e morale*), which emerges from consent and which is usually spread through the ideological and cultural institutions of civil society.[47] Gramsci argues: "the supremacy of a social group manifests itself in two ways, as 'domination' and as 'intellectual and moral leadership.'"[48] He does not mean to oppose these strategies; indeed, he claims that hegemony usually accompanies domination, or even precedes it, in political maneuvers.[49] The ruling classes almost always rely on both hegemony and domination in any given circumstance, for domination alone is a crude form of control and difficult to sustain (especially in liberal democracies, where the state is at least formally under democratic control of some kind).

Hegemony represents the consensual aspect of control, the shaping of the consciousness of a dominated class in order to secure its willing submission. It has meant different things at different times—not only to theorists following him but also to Gramsci himself.[50] He used it to counter an older Marxist argument that saw capitalism developing into a mode of open conflict between the proletariat and the bourgeoisie, and which viewed power as outright coercion exercised against the proletariat by the (bourgeois-controlled) authorities—corresponding roughly to the one-dimensional view of power described above. Gramsci argued instead that conflict is more effectively quelled by linking force and consent, offering a prototypical three-dimensional view. As the Gramsci scholar Joseph Femia explains, "Gramsci came to view hegemony as the most important face of power, the 'normal' form of control in any post-feudal society, and, in particular, the strength of bourgeois rule in advanced capitalist society, where material force is resorted to on a large scale only in periods of exceptional crisis."[51]

This control rests, at least in part, on the production of consent through a "contradictory consciousness" on the part of workers. Gramsci explains, "The active man-in-the-mass has a practical activity, but has no clear theoretical consciousness of this activity. . . . One might almost say that he has two theoretical consciousnesses (or one contradictory consciousness): one which is implicit in his activity and which truly unites him with all his fellow-workers in the practical transformation of reality; and one, superficially explicit or verbal, which he has inherited from the past and uncritically accepted."[52] This latter consciousness has serious consequences and "produces a condition of moral and political passivity." Femia elaborates Gramsci's position: "Gramsci seems to be saying [that the masses] are confined within the boundaries of the dominant world-view, a divergent, loosely adjusted patchwork of ideas and outlooks, which, despite its heterogeneity, unambiguously serves the interests of the powerful, by mystifying power relations, by justifying various forms of sacrifice and deprivation, by inducing fatalism and passivity, and by narrowing mental horizons."[53] Thus, when "Gramsci speaks of consent, he refers to a *psychological* state, involving some kind of acceptance—not necessarily explicit—of the socio-political order or of certain vital aspects of that order."[54]

Viewed from the perspective of network power, Gramsci's idea of hegemony usefully unites consent and power, but—on a common interpretation, at least—it does so by using false consciousness arguments that, however valid in some circumstances, are not necessary to understand the power of many dominant standards. Network power does involve "hegemony"—its formations are hegemonic formations in which people consent to the switch to a dominant standard, which they may both accept and yet keenly resent. However, this hegemony is not necessarily produced through the creation of "contradictory consciousness": we can assume that people understand fully the choices they are making. It is important to maintain this explanatory tack, as one of the interesting things about globalization is the extent to which people consent to structures that are consciously and explicitly viewed as undesirable. By contrast, the acceptance of exploitative domestic regimes of production—in both Gramsci's time and our own—may be hard to explain *without* recourse to an argument about contradictory consciousness underlying a three-dimensional view of power.

However, one way in which false consciousness arguments might be usefully deployed in relation to the idea of network power would be to describe how some members of a smaller network view a larger one. In many contexts, we might find a systematic overvaluation of dominant standards, which hastens convergence on them. But we need not suppose such an erroneous evaluation—and further, it need not arise from false consciousness but might result from simple asymmetry of information. We should not be surprised that members of one network might have less information, or less reliable information, about the standard used by another. Such asymmetry might, even when we are acting reasonably, lead to choices we regret. However we do not even need to assume any asymmetry of information to recognize the central dynamic in network power—the fact that a dominant network will be preferred purely on account of the access it provides to greater numbers of people (or more influential ones)—in contrast with theories of hegemony that identify a gap between real and perceived interests.

Gramsci sought to explain contentment—or at least acquiescence— and the failure of revolutionary prophecy. In so doing, he adjusted the terms of Marxist theory to explain a missing discontent whose absence was perplexing. The idea of network power attempts to readjust the terms of globalization theory to explain how an open and insistent discontent is compatible with acquiescence and individual consent. However, the idea of network power can suppose that both the contented and the discontented possess exquisite self-awareness—and that it is only contemporary theorists who fail to recognize the paradox of force and freedom at the heart of the social relations of globalization.

FOUCAULT ON POWER

Other than Antonio Gramsci, no modern social theorist has generated as much interest in heterodox theories of power as the late Michel Foucault.[55] Throughout his work, but especially in the first volume of *The History of Sexuality* and in his lectures in 1978 at the Collège de France, *"Il Faut Défendre la Société,"* Foucault argued against a model of "juridico-political power," which represents power as the law, based on the sword of the sovereign and carrying with it the sanction of death.[56] He felt that this conception was increasingly inadequate as a model for the power operative in modern society. "We must construct an analytics of power that no longer takes law as a model and a code,"[57] he wrote, claiming that "we have been involved for centuries in a type of society in which the juridical is increasingly incapable of coding power, of serving as its system of representation."[58] Foucault opposed to this "juridico-political" model a conception of power as immanent in the relations of force pervading society at all levels. He explained that the "analysis, made in terms of power, must not assume that the sovereignty of the state, the form of the law, or the over-all unity of a domination are given at the outset."[59] Foucault's idea of power thus shares much with the first type of domination that Weber outlined, even down to the sweeping claim that "power is everywhere," which mirrors Weber's argument that "without exception, every sphere of social action is profoundly influenced by structures of dominancy." Both present a contrast with power conceived as "the authoritarian power of command," or, as Foucault puts it, the "juridico-political model." Foucault's varied historical and social theoretic works all rely upon and develop this alternative view of power, which brings us back (albeit in a more elaborate form) to the distinction between the power of sovereignty and the power of sociability that has been familiar in political theoretic discourse since the early modern period.

In formulating his alternative concept, Foucault argues that "power is not an institution, and not a structure; neither is it a certain strength we are endowed with; it is the name that one attributes to a complex strategical situation in a particular society."[60] Power cannot be imagined on its own, as an autonomous force, but is our description of tactics and strategies used in social relations generally. "Power is everywhere; not because it embraces everything, but because it comes from everywhere."[61] Along these lines, Foucault articulated a number of "propositions" on power. He argues: "power is exercised from innumerable points, in the interplay of nonegalitarian and mobile relations." And he elaborates: "Relations of power are not in a position of exteriority with respect to other types of relationships (economic processes, knowledge relationships, sexual relations), but are immanent in the latter."[62] Implicit in this proposition is the essentially two-sided character of power, which means that "resistance is never in a position of exteriority in relation to power."[63] The parallels to Weber's "domination by virtue of a constellation of interests" are again notable.

The idea of network power shares many features of Foucault's account. Calling network power "power" is not an attempt to imagine it as an isolable force, but rather to describe a social structuring and its effects on individuals whose choices derive from and contribute to it. The French philosopher Gilles Deleuze explains that in the Foucauldian idea, "power is not homogenous but can be defined only through the particular points through which it passes."[64] Similarly, network power only makes sense relationally; it cannot be abstracted from the social contexts it seeks to describe and their "relations of force"—that is, the elimination of choice and the generation of unfreedom. As Foucault writes, "Power invests [the dominated], passes through them and with the help of them [*sic*], relying on them just as they, in their struggle against power, rely on the hold it exerts on them."[65]

Foucault is right to struggle against an understanding of power that looks to the relations of sovereignty as the model—for with such an understanding we miss the power at work elsewhere in society, in forms of social regulation, elite or expert discourses of all kinds, and even forms of consciousness. The philosopher Charles Taylor comments on this reinterpretation: "Foucault's thesis is that, while we have not ceased talking and thinking in terms of this model [the 'juridico-political'], we actually live in relations of power that are quite different and that cannot be described properly in its terms."[66] As a corrective to many liberal conceptions of power, Foucault's project is a welcome one, redirecting our attention to the power at work in relations of sociability that operate on different lines from those of sovereignty.

Indeed, Foucault's vision of power is probably the most familiar three-dimensional view in contemporary social thought. It has been widely influential, including in the analysis of globalization. For example, one of the most ambitious accounts of globalization from the standpoint of left social theory, Michael Hardt and Antonio Negri's *Empire*, draws on and expands the Foucauldian idea of power to help explain contemporary globalization. For many theorists who see globalization as a new "empire," it represents a complex form of social organization constituted by relations of power scaled at the planetary level. To understand these relations of power requires a heterodox account that goes beyond the standard "Weberian" intuition, precisely as Foucault attempts.

POWER WITHOUT AGENCY?

Foucault's project is not, however, without its problems. Charles Taylor identifies three significant features of Foucault's account of power, not all of which prove helpful. First, Taylor explains that "it is not concerned with law but normalization," and hence it "is above all concerned with bringing about a certain result" rather than setting up restraints. Second, "the new power is productive" and "brings about a new kind of subject and new kinds of desire and behavior that belong to him." Finally, "this power is not wielded by a subject," unlike the old model of power "that presupposes a location of the source of command." As against the Weberian, or what Taylor calls the "Hobbesian" conception, "the new kind of power is not wielded by specific people against others," but "is rather a complex form of organization in which we are all involved."[67] (Again, the distinction between sovereignty and sociability should jump out at us as a clue to what is being proposed.)

Taylor focuses his criticism on the last element of Foucault's theory, the idea of power without a subject. He is not alone in his disagreement with this aspect of Foucault's account, though I think he puts the matter very clearly. Anthony Giddens has also criticized Foucault for his "subjectless history" in which "human social affairs are determined by forces of which those involved are wholly unaware" and Jean Piaget complains that "Foucault's ouster of the subject is more radical than any hitherto."[68] The problem is the failure to connect clearly the social strategies through which power is manifested to the agents who make and resist them—though even the claim that these strategies are ultimately made by agents (rather than the reverse) is controversial on some interpretations of Foucault's philosophy.

In laying out the grounds for his disagreement, Taylor identifies a number of theses that Foucault advances about power. First, that "the power Foucault is interested in is internal to, intrinsic to these other relations. One could say that it is constitutive of them, that built in to the very understanding of the common activity, or goods sought, or whatever forms the substance of the microrelation, are forms of domination."[69] This fact explains why "the dominated cooperate in their subordination. They often come to interiorize the norms of the common activity; they go willingly." Foucault's second thesis is "that we cannot hope to explain the local 'rapports de force' in terms of some global relation of dominators and dominated," but rather must look at the effects that "the microcontexts of domination produce on each other and with each other." Taylor explains that "More than saying that power comes from the bottom, we should say that there is an endless relation of reciprocal conditioning between global and microcontexts."[70] Finally, that "aside from the particular conscious purpose that agents pursue in their given context, there is discernable a strategic logic of the context itself, but this cannot be attributed to anyone as their plan, as their conscious purpose."[71] While Taylor accepts the possibility of some version of the first two theses, he rejects this last proposition, because it fails to connect purposeful human action to the creation and maintenance of the historical contexts that exhibit this strategic logic.

Taylor's complaint is an important charge against all heterodox visions of power alleged to operate without a subject. Such accounts fail to show how we can be simultaneously the conscious agents we believe ourselves to be *and* enmeshed in structures of power in which we are acted upon.[72] The complaint reveals the same difficulties with three-dimensional views of power that Lukes articulated: the problem of identifying a mechanism of power and a counterfactual situation absent that power. As I argued earlier, absent the connection to some plausible account of structuration, three-dimensional views of power will routinely encounter problems analyzing agency and, therefore, analyzing power itself in a coherent way.

Taylor offers a few examples of theories that do incorporate human agency within accounts of systemic power, such as ideas of unconscious motivation or false consciousness and of unintended but systematic consequences, as in theories of the "invisible hand" or the "cunning of reason in history." However, he cannot identify any such analysis in Foucault's account. Taylor argues persuasively that in order to maintain the third thesis, "the undesigned systematicity has to be related to the purposeful action of agents in a way that we can understand."[73] That is, we must identify a mechanism or link by which individuals' actions aggregate to produce the systems of power that Foucault identifies, even if they did not intend to produce them. As Taylor writes, "It is certainly not the case that all patterns *issue* from conscious action, but all patterns have to be made *intelligible* in relation to conscious action." Hence, in order to maintain Foucault's theses on the idea of power without a subject, "we would need some systematic account . . . where microreactions concatenate in this systematic way." Taylor admits that he does not know how to develop such a framework: "I do not say something like this cannot be found, but I am at a loss to say even where one should start looking for it. And Foucault does not even feel the need to start looking."[74]

The idea of network power attempts precisely this task: to articulate clearly one way in which "microreactions concatenate" systematically, generating a relation of power in which agency can be identified, at least retrospectively, but need not be located in an ongoing individual exercise of power as command. In contrast to the Foucauldian conception, then, the idea of network power leaves no doubt as to the role that subjects play in the formation and maintenance of structures of power. Nor, as I argue in the next chapter, does the idea of network power leave ambiguous the possibility of resistance to power. Network power is systemic but it is not totalizing simply because of its systematicity.

On my interpretation of Foucault, then, his notion of power without a subject is suggestive but ultimately fails to address individual agency in an adequate manner. In the end, Foucault lacks a microanalytics of power, which is surprising given that his precise aim was to develop not a theory, but an "analytics" of power (and at the "microlevel" too). We may understand Foucault's project as an attempt to escape the identification of power with sovereign relations—and to grasp it instead in its social dimension, but made with such eagerness that even the ordinary idea of the subject was discarded under the apprehension that any suggestion of agency would necessarily replicate the problems associated with *political* agency. However, the problem is not with agency as such. If we cease to rely solely on a "juridico-political conception" of power, we can see how agency is at work in relations of power that do not resemble the political. The analytics of network power show how aggregated individual choices can come to constitute a form of decentralized power immanent in social relations—and all without the command of a central authority. Moving beyond the "juridico-political" requires broadening our conception of power, not abandoning our idea of agency.

NETWORK POWER AS POWER

Steven Lukes argues that power is an "essentially contested concept," which means it is "one of those concepts which 'inevitably involve endless disputes about their proper uses on the part of their users.'" The argument about what we mean by power is itself part of a broader series of normative commitments and background assumptions which are themselves debatable and cannot be precisely worked out; our idea of power plays a role in the very relations of power it seeks to represent. Therefore, it makes no sense to seek an ultimate definition or factual determination of what power *is*—as if power were an object we could describe precisely. Rather, we discuss it and debate it as a way of gaining insight into social relations more generally and, Lukes suggests, "to engage in such disputes is itself to engage in politics."[75]

From this perspective, the identification of network power *as power* is simply an effort to articulate features of the contemporary world that are experienced as coercive, entrapping, or unfree in some significant way. It is an attempt to recover, within the broad confines of a methodologically individualistic account of human agency, some sense of the power at work in relations of sociability, and to contrast that form of power with the kind more usually described (and scrutinized), the power in relations of sovereignty. The concept of network power should be able to lend credence to ideas of hegemony and other three-dimensional views, helping to develop them by specifying an underlying mechanism of consent-based power which operates at a systemic level. As to our immediate concern, it can help us to understand better the experience of globalization by giving an account of the kind of power at work in the construction of a new world order. It does so while still comporting with our commonsense notion that we are active, deliberative, choosing agents who are relatively reasonable and unconfused.

Network power shares with other heterodox theories of power the rejection of coercion as a defining characteristic. It focuses instead on power as a systemic property, but it does so without losing sight of individual agency. It is multidirectional: network power exists in all the ways people are drawn to each other, wanting to gain access to cooperative activities with other people. It is relational: we cannot even talk about this power outside the multiple networks of individuals whose choices are shaped by allegiance to a common standard. It is immanent: not an abstract force, but inherent in our mediating social institutions.

The idea of network power argues that we are pulled by our choices along avenues smoothed by the prior choices of others. In an age of accelerating globalization, these social dynamics are ever more central and ever more apparent. It is our very sociability that draws us out of ourselves and into conventions that regulate our access to others—access based on standards that at once free us and entrap us, binding us in ongoing histories only partly of our own creation. Or, as Marx put the matter famously and succinctly: "Men make their own history but they do not make it as they please; they do not make it under circumstances chosen by themselves, but under circumstances directly encountered, given and transmitted from the past."[76]

CHAPTER FIVE

Evaluating Network Power

IN THE LAST CHAPTER, we explored the characterization of network power as power in the light of theories in which consent and coercion are viewed as running together. However, claiming that the dynamics of network formation should be understood as a form of power tells us nothing about the instances in which its exercise may be unjust, needing to be countered if at all possible. While the concept of network power enables us to see how the dynamics of network formation constitute part of the dynamics of social structuration more generally, and thus constitute a relation of power, nothing in our analysis so far helps us to decide if and when such power may be normatively justified. For that, we require a different mode of assessment. Of course, this assessment will depend on the particulars of the normative framework that we adopt. An obvious starting point for any such assessment is the impact of network power on the "interests" of the parties at stake. However, such an analysis can miss the identity concerns that should also be part of our evaluation of the network power operating in globalization. Exploring these identity concerns requires a different normative framework from one in which the parties know their interests and are concerned with the distribution of costs and benefits. It requires looking at the intersubjective prerequisites of identity-formation, which I explore in my discussion of the contemporary literature on recognition.

INTERESTS AND IDENTITIES

How are we to evaluate the coercion at work in network power? Or, put differently, why should it matter that lock-in to a dominant standard eliminates the viability of alternative standards? If we find the *power* in network power objectionable, why should that be?

Two broad classes of concerns motivate our anxiety about the coercion in network power, and which set of concerns appears more immediately troubling will depend on the context in which a dominant standard develops. The first class might be called *distributional concerns,* which are worries about the unfair or unjust imposition of costs on different parties. This could mean either relative disparities among a comparatively homogeneous group, or the problem of some parties existing at an absolute level of deprivation. These concerns have to do with the *interests* that different people have and the extent to which they can or cannot realize them under circumstances of network power. The second class might be called *identity concerns,* which are worries about the way in which the rise of a standard to universality affects the cultural or historical identities that people value. Of course, these two classes of concerns are not necessarily easy to distinguish, a point to which I will return later in this chapter.

Viewed in a distributional framework, network power presents a problem because it can entail the unequal imposition of costs on some parties, which affects their interests. From this perspective, the network power of a dominant standard can be evaluated by using criteria belonging to any of several different theories of justice. I want to consider concerns about the justice or fairness of the distribution of relative advantages and disadvantages generated by the adoption and use of standards by different agents in a very general manner. My ultimate concern is with the extent to which individuals are able to realize their interests, and I therefore presuppose reasonable individuals with reasonable knowledge of what they want out of their interactions with others, although this may seem, on some accounts, implausible. I also recognize that any evaluation of the consequences of network power must depend upon the particular theory of justice one adopts, and that the reason for focusing on some particular set of interests rather than another may also reflect differences in an underlying foundational account of morality. However, I want to put these considerations to one side; despite their importance in many debates in contemporary philosophy, these foundational issues are less relevant to my analysis here.

Of course, the extent to which different people get to realize their interests is not the only ethical concern we have, at least if we do not adopt an overly encompassing idea of "interests." We also worry about the extent to which people lose their culture, identity, or sense of place under certain circumstances, and it is unclear how we could convert these identity concerns into just another variety of interests without a great deal of conceptual and normative distortion.[1] This second set of concerns requires examining the non-instrumental value of standards. By value here I do not mean the power of a standard to *do* something for its users, since that benefit is addressed by our concern with the proper distribution of the costs and benefits arising from the use of a standard. Rather, I want to consider the contribution that the use of a standard can make to a person's sense of identity and place in the world.

Much of the contemporary criticism directed against globalization takes this second class of concerns as its starting point, arguing that globalization destroys cultural and institutional diversity. An obvious caution about embracing a concern for identity is that identity claims are often advanced by reactionary elites threatened by change or by people possessed by a sense of solidarity that rests on oppression and false consciousness. But to claim that this is always or necessarily the case is to miss the heart of the ethical issue here, however true that account of it may sometimes be. As I will argue below, many identity concerns do and should have a legitimate place among our moral intuitions. For example, when we are confronted with the loss of minority languages or cultures, we are not primarily worried that people from these communities will have to pay a disproportionate share of the costs of language classes or of cultural assimilation, although this unfairness at the level of interests may also trouble us. Mainly, we feel anxious and ambivalent about that assimilation itself, and what it may entail subjectively for the persons whose identities are at stake. And we feel this anxiety without supposing that those people who feel their identities are at stake are only or merely in the sway of powerful, parochial interests within their own insular communities.

Questions about identity are notoriously tricky ones to parse. The meanings and value of cultural identities have received a great deal of attention in the last few decades from political philosophers and historians concerned with multiculturalism, cultural pluralism, and postcolonial history.[2] Although this body of work provides many helpful frameworks in which we can address the question of identity, I place my examination of these concerns within the framework of theories of *recognition*. Such theories enable a simultaneous engagement with both distributional and identity concerns, since they view both of these domains as relevant to the process by which we come to be who we are and get what we want. In this perspective, one way of understanding the importance or worth of cultural identities is to suppose that solidarity within a particular community constitutes a critical dimension of the intersubjective process of recognition that enables someone to become an effective and responsible individual. However, independent of whether identity concerns can best be understood within a theory of recognition, it seems to me that an appropriate evaluation of network power must engage such concerns at some level. Without considering issues of both interests and identity, we will be unable to evaluate network power properly, and we will fail to generate an adequately rich psychological rendering of the controversy over globalization.

Both distributional and identity concerns also feature in an earlier discussion of universal standards. Keynes drew attention to both these classes of concern, and one aspect of the difference between them, in the following way:

> Everyone agrees that there are many fields of human activity
> in which it is only common-sense to establish international
> standards. If there are arguments to the contrary, they are gen-
> erally of a non-economic character. We may dislike the idea of
> adopting the metric system or a universal language; but, if so,
> our objections are not likely to depend on economic advantage.
> Now, in the case of a currency system, it is obvious that advan-
> tages of variety, idiosyncrasy or tradition, which might be held
> of overwhelming force in the case of a language, can scarcely
> weigh against economic well-being. In determining our cur-
> rency system, therefore, we need be influenced by nothing
> but economic benefit—including in this political expediency
> and justice.[3]

Keynes saw that questions of globalization may not all be answered within a single evaluative framework; rather, some issues are better addressed by one kind of assessment rather than another. A concern with interests, or as he puts it, "economic well-being" and "political expediency and justice," may be an appropriate lens through which to examine some ethical questions about global standardization, but not others. Reasons of a "non-economic character"—what he calls the "advantages of variety, idiosyncrasy or tradition"—require a different analysis, which I undertake here in relation to questions of identity.

THE ROLE OF COUNTERFACTUAL IMAGINATION

Before examining distributional and identity concerns in greater detail, I want to argue that our consideration of them should employ counterfactual reasoning or imagination. Since the emergence of a standard represents a new form of social cooperation and a new relation of power, we must evaluate it not only with regard to the status quo—asking whether the users of a standard are better off with it or without it given their present circumstances—but also with regard to alternative possibilities.[4] We should not simply compare our current arrangements to the ones preceding it as if no other routes had been possible in history, but must instead ask what arrangements might have been established otherwise, with what subsequent effects. Thus, when examining distributional or identity concerns, it is not enough to evaluate them with regard to historical precedent without also casting an eye on unrealized historical possibility. This is particularly important in the light of the way that universal standards become accepted as social facts, and are hence easy to mistake as inevitable or invariable.

The need for applying counterfactual thinking when considering contemporary globalization is all the clearer because many people in the world tend to feel the weight of unrealized possibilities strongly and judge the adequacy of current arrangements in relation to them. Accordingly, the ethical assessment of globalization requires imagining systemic counterfactuals rather than holding to the assumption that our current conditions are historically inevitable. We should not consider such counterfactual imaginings to be either fantastic or delusional, for, at an individual level at least, we routinely evaluate our current circumstances in this way when we wonder about the kind of persons we might have become had things gone differently for us. Such an exercise of the imagination is a critical part of the processes of social learning and institutional reform. Of course, any investigation that relies on the possibility of alternative worlds risks embarrassment, since counterfactuals always have less of a hold on us than the reality we know. However, this risk does not make the task any less necessary.

In fact, counterfactual imaginings may be required for an even deeper reason: that an adequate understanding of our social world may depend upon it. On this account, we understand any state of affairs, whether social or natural, by understanding the states of affairs that preceded it, the states of affairs that could follow, and the mechanisms involved in these transformations. But beyond this rather general similarity, the analogy between the social and the natural quickly breaks down. In the natural world, we comprehend something by understanding what it will change into—that is, what it will become through the operation of natural processes. In the social world, by contrast, we comprehend something by grasping how *we* might transform it. The exercise of counterfactual imagination is thus central to social analysis, not so much because it allows us to imagine the future, but because it is only by imagining possible futures that we really come to understand the present.[5]

DISTRIBUTIONAL CONSIDERATIONS

There are two broad ways in which, at the level of interests, we may judge the rise of a dominant standard to constitute an injustice to non-users: by considering the absolute level of deprivation that any user or non-user may confront, and by considering the relative distribution of benefits and costs among the different users and non-users. Recall Serena Olsaretti's argument that a choice is *voluntary* only if the option that an agent chooses—even if it is the sole option on offer—is an *acceptable* one, where the acceptableness of an option is to be understood in relation both to the agent's own subjective desires and to a set of objectively determined basic needs. So the first way in which the rise of a dominant standard may constitute an injustice is if it creates conditions under which someone is deprived of the resources necessary to satisfy her basic needs. This form of injustice is of particular concern where a standard mediates an activity that is integral to the well-being of its users. One possible way to interpret basic needs that makes sense in the context of standards is to focus on the demand for recognition, to which I return in the second part of this chapter. In most cases, however, because standards are conventions that mediate cooperative activity, the injustice we will be concerned about will lie primarily with the maldistribution of the costs and benefits of that activity.

The distribution of the benefits that emerge from the cooperation that a standard enables must be considered in addition to the costs that different parties incur in switching to that standard, or that are sustained in using that standard rather than another. Broadly, three types of costs attend the process of convergence on a dominant network: the difficulty of adapting to a new standard; the difficulty of leaving a prior standard, if necessary; and the difficulty of using the new standard, if one is at a disadvantage compared to other users of that standard. These costs will often be unequally distributed in a fashion that privileges insiders and early defectors against outsiders and latecomers. For example, as long as there are advantages to positioning oneself in a dominant network earlier rather than later, we will see an unequal division of the benefits of network membership laid out chronologically. We can define *first-comer benefits* as the advantages derived from the early adoption of a standard, and *late-comer penalties* as the disadvantages derived from switching onto a dominant standard late in its ascendance.

Such benefits and costs exist in a wide array of actual networks for any number of specific reasons, but they all arise from two general advantages to early membership in a network. First, early network membership allows the early establishment of cooperative relations with others using the same standard, with the benefits that such positioning brings, as in trade or business relations, for example. Second, early membership allows greater familiarity with the standard, making its use easier. That is, early exposure to the standard facilitates its use, whether in straightforward ways, such as with an inflexible measurement system, or in adaptive ways, such as with a language. Late-comer penalties usually involve the loss of these early advantages, as well as, perhaps, other context-specific disadvantages.

Whether any given distribution of benefits and costs is normatively desirable remains unclear unless we specify the extent to which these arrangements approximate a particular ideal of distributive justice—that is, the extent to which they fail to manifest the requisite level of concern for one agent's well-being as against another's. It may also be the case that the costs and benefits under consideration are in some way incommensurable—that is, involving losses that cannot really be compensated for by the benefits for which they are exchanged. But even without examining the variation among competing theories of justice or well-being, we can question whether these advantages or penalties *should* accrue in the way that they do. (It would be a rather extraordinary piece of luck if they simply did happen to conform to a robust ideal of justice.) For example, it is not clear why a late-comer to a dominant network should deserve a penalty, especially if the rise of that network was a matter of chance or force. In general, we will want to examine whether the reasons that led someone to join a standard later than others proves morally relevant to our assessment of whether she should take proportionally fewer of the gains from shared cooperation with others.

To consider a relatively innocuous example, consider the British adoption of the metric system. When the British switched from the imperial system, they incurred the significant difficulty of learning the metric system, internalizing new weights and measures and leaving behind familiar ones. Indeed, many British citizens, particularly older ones, have yet to make this switch fully. Once they have begun to use the metric system, many British citizens continue to be at a disadvantage compared to a Frenchman who has been calculating in centimeters and kilos from childhood.[6] Moreover, importantly, all of the costs of the British switch to metric were borne by the British alone, while there were no costs, only benefits, to their neighbors and trading partners. Note also that these costs were not only practical and instrumental, for the difficulty of dealing in kilos and not pounds is not only one of habituation and calculation, but impinges on one's sense of national identity. To the extent that the use of the imperial standard is symbolically meaningful, the cost of leaving it behind may be significant.

A few questions should frame our evaluation of the fairness or unfairness of this particular distribution of benefits and costs. Were the British at fault because they did not adopt the metric system early, and if so, why? What costs might we consider they ought to bear, given our answer to the previous question? Might the failure of the British government, or of past generations of British citizens, to adopt the metric standard justify the penalties faced by this generation of Britons? Are the individuals now encountering the high costs involved in using the metric system particularly vulnerable in some way, such that we might think that the common benefits of a shared standard should accrue to them disproportionately as part of a broader agenda of distributive justice? In a normative evaluation of network power, we will want to consider the *reasons* for which agents face costs that are, at present, higher than they might have been, and the moral relevance or irrelevance of those reasons; the *structure* of choice in which those agents find themselves, and the extent to which they are or are not morally responsible for it; and the *capacity* of these agents to bear such disproportionately higher costs.

Probably most instances of network power in globalization are less innocuous than the British adoption of the metric system. Consider the question of who should bear the costs of the linguistic assimilation of immigrants in the United States. Should the immigrants themselves bear the cost or should the receiving nation subsidize programs in English as a second language? Is it morally relevant that a newly arrived immigrant was born into a household that spoke a language other than English? Is it more important to focus on the fact that she *chose* to immigrate or that she *did not choose* the distribution of opportunities that makes that immigration desirable? Does she have more or less capacity than other citizens to bear the costs of assimilation, and is that relevant to our assessment?

STANDARDS AND BARGAINING PROBLEMS

As a general matter, the distribution of benefits from the adoption of a single standard may be crucial to assessing the justice of convergence. Standards enable cooperative, interdependent action such that everyone is better off using a common standard—but the question is how much better off?

In cooperative situations, it is bargaining that generally proves decisive to the outcome. As there are no benefits to defecting, parties always face the problem of distributing the benefits that accrue to their cooperation, as the mathematician John Nash identified in his essay "The Bargaining Problem" more than fifty years ago.[7] Explaining Nash's findings, the economist Amartya Sen has written: "the central issue in general is not whether a particular arrangement is better for everyone than no cooperation at all would be, but whether that is a fair division of the benefits. One cannot rebut the criticism that a distributional arrangement is unfair simply by noting that all parties are better off than they would be in the absence of cooperation; the real exercise is the choice *between* these alternatives."[8]

For example, to return to the adoption of the metric system by the British, the British (as a whole, at least) were obviously "better off" having switched to metric than they would have been had they remained with the imperial system—for exactly the sorts of reasons of "economic benefit" that Keynes discussed above. Indeed, it was surely the advantages of conformity with the globally dominant measurement system that provided the incentive for this switch in the first place. But the French, Dutch, Germans, Thai, and so on were *also* better off once the British had decided to switch. Everyone benefited, including Britain—and yet Britain alone bore the costs of the transition.

Consider another example of the harmonization of existing standards conceived as a bargaining problem: that of the "determination of a currency system," to borrow Keynes's words. Without the gold standard, we operate in a world of paper currencies established by particular national governments. Recently, a trend has emerged in which governments in the developing world have adopted the currency of another country, known as the "anchor," as legal tender—as we see in examples of "currency boards" or "dollarization." In these cases, one country switches to the monetary token of another, thus harmonizing its standard of value and creating what is sometimes called a "currency union." Of course, the most dramatic currency union in recent years was the arrival of the Euro, a European-wide currency that emerged not from the harmonization of existing standards but from standardization, the creation of a new single standard of value for the Euro monetary bloc.

The reason that a government adopts an anchor currency is either because it has had trouble managing its own monetary policy and wants to have its rate of inflation controlled by a foreign Central Bank (thus achieving the partial reinstatement of the "sound money" policy which existed under the gold standard) or else because two countries share a great deal of trade with one another. (In the unusual case of the Euro, the hope that tighter monetary union would foster deeper political, social, and cultural ties played the most significant role.) In the latter case, the benefits are shared by the countries involved, as the economists Alberto Alesina and Robert Barro explain: "By sharing the same currency, two countries economize on trading costs, and the larger the currency union, the larger the benefit. Money is like language—the more people speak the same language, the easier it is to communicate; the larger the number of people sharing the same currency, the easier it is to trade." Alesina and Barro do note, however, that the capacity to gain "seignorage revenue" (the revenue made by printing more money) is transferred from the "client state" to the state providing the anchor currency. They suggest compensating for this loss on the part of the client state—which we can interpret as a way of sharing the costs that arise from the common use of a single standard. Of course, the most significant cost of establishing a currency union is that the client state loses the ability to use monetary policy for countercyclical purposes. "A country that dollarizes loses its ability to target its monetary policy to its own disturbances—instead, the country has to accept the policy chosen by the anchor." This does not concern Alesina and Barrow, for they argue: "it is unclear that many small, open, and developing countries actually have the ability to use independent monetary policies effectively for stabilization purposes."[9]

More generally, the argument about the "efficient" size of currency unions, associated with economist Robert Mundell's work, is that an effective currency union unites areas that share the same macroeconomic cycle; therefore, they can depend on a single countercyclical monetary policy determined by a single Central Bank. (This argument assumes, of course, that inflation is a purely technical problem without political significance, such that one Central Bank can manage a currency for multiple polities.[10]) As Alesina and Barro explain: "The size of the currency union is determined by a trade-off between scale and heterogeneity. As the size of the union increases with new entrants, more and more transaction costs of trade are saved. However, as the size of the union increases, the less the monetary policy of the anchor can be tailored to each member."[11]

This basic trade-off resembles that between the force of "unification" and the force of "parochialism" that Saussure identified in his analysis of linguistic convergence, where the extent of unification is determined by the degree of intercourse between linguistic (or, in this case, monetary) zones. Indeed, perhaps unsurprisingly, the use of a language presents a parallel problem of coordination and bargaining to that of currency. The philosopher Philippe van Parijs has recently discussed what he calls "Linguistic Justice," investigating the justice of the costs incurred by different groups that are generated in attempts to solve problems of linguistic coordination in pluralistic societies.[12] Consider a country with majority and minority language groups, such as Canada, which is predominantly Anglophone, but which includes a Francophone province, Quebec. It is to the advantage of both English-speaking Canadians and Quebecois to have some way to communicate. There are three different strategies for solving this problem: total bilingualism (all Canadians would speak both French and English); total monolingualism (all Canadians would speak only French or English) and asymmetric bilingualism (one entire group would learn the language of the other). Among these three strategies, total bilingualism is the most demanding, given that everyone in Canada would then face the difficulty of acquiring a second language. As English is the majority language in Canada, total monolingualism would effectively mean that the Quebecois converged on the use of English and abandoned French. (The opposite scenario, in which all Canadians adopted French as a substitute for English, seems even less plausible.) The final option, asymmetric bilingualism, can mean one of two scenarios: that the minority Quebecois learn English or, less likely, that all Anglo-Canadians make the effort to learn French. Asymmetric bilingualism will in fact almost always amount to the former case, in which a bilingual minority group ends up speaking the dominant language to a largely monolingual majority—a situation that Van Parijs diagnoses as unjust in the absence of any scheme of cost-sharing. Unsurprisingly, the pressures of network power in Canada are slowly generating this pattern, despite resistance from some Quebecois leaders and some efforts outside Quebec (and within its Anglophone minority) to increase French language training throughout Canada.

Is it fair that the burden of linguistic coordination in Canada should fall on the shoulders of the Quebecois disproportionately? Again, asymmetric bilingualism means that everyone benefits from easier coordination, but the minority language group alone bears the costs of this coordination. Who should bear the costs of achieving linguistic coordination? Consider that minority groups may be the most ill-equipped to bear the costs of assimilation if, as is frequently the case, minority status translates into an array of other social disadvantages. Does the fact of having been born into a family that speaks a minority language possess any moral relevance? And, if not, what practical accommodation with the intransigence of monolingual majorities is it justifiable to make?

At least the Quebecois need not abandon their language altogether, given the feasibility of learning and using multiple languages. Because the dominance of English in Canada is compatible (however costly) with the continued survival of Francophone communities, the rise of one convention to universal status need not lead to the loss of all alternatives. But consider a more difficult situation in which the resources available for language instruction are limited, and students belonging to a linguistic minority never have the opportunity to learn even their own language beyond a minimum level. Here, the costs of using the dominant standard might include the loss, or effective loss, of their original language altogether. In this case, because the costs of compatibility have increased, the standards in question prove incompatible to a greater degree, and thus the elevation of one standard entails the attenuation of lesser networks. Where the minority language is not French, say, but one of Canada's many indigenous languages, the costs to the minority language group are dramatically higher—and can mean the loss of an entire way of speaking and living, as we saw in the discussion of language death in Chapter 3.

IDENTITY CONCERNS

This possibility brings us to the second set of concerns we might have about greatly unequal network power: concerns about identity. For it is not simply that the "costs" of speaking the dominant language, rather than their native tongue, are higher for speakers of an indigenous language than they are for Quebecois who have to learn English. Rather, it is that many of the costs of achieving linguistic coordination are not exactly costs in the way that we tend to think of them, at least in cases where greatly disparate levels of network power raise the possibility of language death. This is because the loss of a language is not something that can be compensated for in any clear way—which puts pressure on the idea that it constitutes a "cost" in any ordinary sense. It relates, rather, to what Keynes described as the "advantages of variety, idiosyncrasy or tradition," or what I here call identity concerns, as distinct from the "economic benefits" that appear to be primary when considering the advantages of a particular currency union.

The concern with identity is not one that fits easily into a great deal of contemporary liberal political theory, as it involves long-standing and deeply felt attachments to forms of life through which particular groups of people are connected. The network power of dominant standards can undermine these forms of life whenever great inequalities in network power lead to the loss of members from smaller networks. Network power can therefore prove coercive not only in the unjust distribution of costs that Van Parijs identifies, but in another way too. Languages are connected to identity in a way that makes linguistic justice a much broader issue than one of appropriate cost-sharing under circumstances of asymmetric bilingualism. At stake in network power can be our self-understanding and the character of the relations we have with others, whether equal or dependent, respectful or humiliating.

Consider the historical injustice of France's language policies throughout the nineteenth and twentieth centuries, in which the speakers of the country's many dialects were forced to learn French and forbidden to use their mother tongues. For example, Occitan (also known as Provençal) was once the dominant language in cities like Marseille, where signs hanging in the windows of tourist shops at the turn of the century would read "Français parlé ici" to alert tourists from Paris that the shopkeeper could speak French. In less than a century, due to outright force and network power, the number of Occitan speakers has dwindled to perhaps half a million, mainly in rural and isolated areas of France, Italy, and Spain.

How are we to judge the suffering of the former speakers of Occitan? From one perspective, their knowledge of French no doubt opened up new opportunities: the ability to take part in a Francophone national government, easier economic intercourse with the rest of the French nation, better job opportunities in Paris and overseas in the colonies of the French empire. Of course, even with such benefits, the costs of linguistic assimilation may still have been unfairly distributed. But it seems a mistake to imagine that the hurt consists only, or even mainly, in the unequal distribution of political or economic rights and opportunities, ignoring the obvious cultural wounding. After all, the promotion (rather than rejection) of bilingual education among Occitan speakers might have allowed them to participate in French national institutions at the same time as preserving their local language.

The situation is made more complicated because network power works by altering the circumstances of individual choice, dividing people against themselves and turning them into the agents of their own ambivalent assimilation. What compensation can be offered for the half-hearted abandonment of one's historical identity? The language of costs and compensation, however appropriate it may be in some instances, does not seem the right moral lexicon for thinking about this problem.

Of course, not all inequalities in network power impinge so crucially on identity; many may strike us as generating a relatively benign (even entirely beneficial) convergence. For example, we may accept that lock-in to a dominant technical standard is inevitable and disproportionately costly for members of small networks, even while denying that any special accommodation should be granted those members. If the international metric system gains a foothold in the United States, Americans will find the standard difficult to use at first. A European might claim that despite this hardship, the adoption of the metric system will be better for Americans —or at least just as good for them—as the imperial system. Implicit in this claim is the argument that some developments in the direction of unified standards should not be contested, for they do not represent oppression. There may be distributional concerns that need to be addressed, such as transfer payments to those learning a new system, but this assessment surely requires examining the relative positions of the parties involved with respect to more than just the use of a minority standard.

The situation seems different when we consider languages. Few will unreservedly claim that it is "better" for members of minority cultures to switch to English or to a dominant regional language. Many will reasonably claim that having access to a global "second language" such as English or an important regional language might benefit members of vulnerable linguistic groups, supporting a "healthy bilingualism" and a sustainable diglossic relationship, as many linguists recommend for the preservation of linguistic diversity. David Crystal writes, "A world in which everyone speaks at least two languages—their own ethnic language and an international lingua franca—is perfectly possible," but he recognizes that "persuading individual governments to work towards a bilingual (or multilingual) world is by no means easy, not least because of the costs involved."[13]

However, the opportunity of learning a global second language *as* a second language is relatively uncommon among the most vulnerable or impoverished populations, members of which usually adopt a more dominant regional language instead, in some version of the "three-generation shift." We should not be surprised that this is the case: members of vulnerable linguistic groups are not, as a general rule, trying to gain access to the English-speaking global elite, but to locally dominant populations with whom they come into regular contact. And they must usually do so without the resources to acquire a second language while maintaining their own tongue, or without the social standing or status to make a point of carefully attending to their own language. So lacking a global second language that might help to preserve the linguistic diversity of the world, we are confronted with the loss of local languages and dialects.

Most of us find this linguistic erosion sad, and not on the abstract grounds that linguistic diversity is valuable for anthropological reasons, but because we do not feel that anyone should have to be separated from such an important constituent of their identity as their native language.[14] Why do we see a difference in the evaluation of the network power wielded by these two standards, one technical and one linguistic? Obviously, in the case of a measurement system, we feel that little is "at stake" for users of a lesser standard in terms of their identities and communities. Even while the switch to metric may impose costs on the holdouts in the United States, the switch will not mean that the new users cease to be "American" in any salient respect—and they will rapidly develop decent, if not equal facility with the new standard. This may be because a measurement standard allows us to gain access to objects—to weigh, cut, and parcel them—before entering them into the social world as goods, and it is arguable that little of importance is at stake in the different ways that we deal with goods. (Of course, people who work intimately with certain goods—sculptors, carpenters, butchers—may object to this characterization.) By contrast, it seems that an enormous amount is at stake in the way that we deal with other people, and make our lives with them in communities.

THE POLITICS OF RECOGNITION

While these concerns about identity clearly have some hold on us, it is hard to specify what precisely is at stake in them—*why* identities matter. One promising way to understand these concerns is with a theory of *recognition*, which provides an argument about how people develop a sense of themselves through social recognition by others. A common claim in any theory of recognition is that our identities are formed intersubjectively and that social recognition is an essential aspect of human well-being. Such theories take as their starting point the idea that people come to develop a healthy sense of self only through social relations of recognition and that a sense of self is a good that people deserve or, on a different rendering, something that people have reason to value. To put the argument negatively, the *denial* of recognition results in a distorted or wounded sense of one's self.

Many contemporary social movements, including feminism, multiculturalism, gay rights, *dalit* empowerment, and other identity-based movements, share this demand for recognition, and together these movements brought a politics of recognition to the center of many social struggles in the late twentieth century. The philosopher Charles Taylor, among others, has analyzed these new social movements. He writes:

> The demand for recognition . . . is given urgency by the supposed links between recognition and identity, where this latter term designates something like a person's understanding of who they are, of their fundamental defining characteristics as a human being. The thesis is that our identity is partly shaped by recognition or its absence, often by the *mis*recognition of others, and so a person or group of people can suffer real damage, real distortion, if the people or society around them mirror back to them a confining or demeaning or contemptible picture of themselves. Nonrecognition or misrecognition can inflict harm, can be a form of oppression, imprisoning someone in a false, distorted, and reduced mode of being.[15]

Taylor is concerned to trace the path that this demand for recognition took in the breakdown of a feudal order driven by honor and based on caste—how, that is, the politics of recognition emerged with modern forms of social relations. He is therefore concerned with the history and politics of recognition and its place in modern, pluralistic societies. He explores how we should regard and conceive this demand and argues how some version of equal recognition might be achieved in liberal political settings.

A similar concern motivates Jürgen Habermas's discussion of the crisis of the modern welfare state, which can provide material redistribution but which is increasingly called upon to provide moral recognition too. Habermas writes in his famous work, *A Theory of Communicative Action*:

In the past decade or two, conflicts have developed in advanced Western societies that deviate in various ways from the welfare-state pattern of institutionalized conflict over distribution. They no longer flare up in domains of material reproduction; they are no longer channeled through parties and associations; and they can no longer be allayed by compensations. Rather, these new conflicts arise in domains of cultural reproduction, social integration, and socialization; they are carried out in sub-institutional—or at least extraparliamentary—forms of protest; and the underlying deficits reflect a reification of communicatively structured domains of action that will not respond to the media of money and power. The issue is not primarily one of compensations that the welfare state can provide, but of defending and restoring endangered ways of life. In short, the new conflicts are not ignited by distribution problems but by questions having to do with the grammar of forms of life.[16]

Habermas recognizes that these conflicts over what he calls the "grammar of forms of life" involve substantially different issues (or, at least, are mediated differently) from the straightforward concern over distribution of material needs. He argues that the emergence of these protest movements vindicates his thesis that systems of abstract media (of money and power) are colonizing what he calls the "lifeworld"—the domains of communicatively structured action—and that the lifeworld is striking back. Furthermore, while he notes that these movements often take a defensive rather than an emancipatory form, he distinguishes further the different reactions to lifeworld colonization that he sees taking place in late modernity.

However, it is Habermas's student and successor as the director of the Institute for Social Research in Frankfurt, Axel Honneth, who has developed the most helpful contemporary account of recognition.[17] Honneth's theory has a more explicitly psychodynamic element than Taylor's, enabling us to articulate precisely how and why recognition is central to the formation of identity, and it is more developed than that of Habermas, and does not require any account of "lifeworld" and "system" in modernity.

THE MORAL GRAMMAR OF RECOGNITION

Honneth posits a tripartite structure of the social relations of recognition and offers an account of how the struggle for recognition provides the "moral grammar" in which social conflicts are played out. He starts with an idea that he finds in embryonic form in the early writings of Hegel (but which was abandoned by the time Hegel wrote *The Phenomenology of Spirit*), which is that history is driven by a struggle for recognition among individuals in three related but distinct domains of social life. Drawing on the later insights of George Herbert Mead, Honneth develops an account of these three domains, placing these structures of recognition at the center of a normative account of social struggle. This account differs from other theories of social conflict that analyze social struggle as resulting from a conflict over interests, which Honneth traces (somewhat inaptly on my reading) to a tradition of social thought originating with Machiavelli and Hobbes.[18] As an alternative, he wants to develop the fragmented and incomplete account of a moral grammar of social struggle that he finds in the early Hegel and in Mead, and which he believes is further refined (albeit distortedly or only partially) in the writings of Marx, Sorel, and Sartre.[19]

In his conception of the tripartite structure of the relations of recognition, Honneth distinguishes among three forms of mutual recognition: "the emotional concern familiar from relationships of love and friendship," "legal recognition," and the "approval associated with solidarity," which are all "particular ways of granting recognition." A distinction among these three ways of relating to others is found in a variety of social theories, which Honneth canvasses: "It is evidently quite natural to distinguish forms of social integration according to whether they occur via emotional bonds, the granting of rights, or a shared orientation to values."[20] What Honneth finds in Hegel and Mead is the idea of a connection between these different arenas of social interaction and a theory of intersubjective recognition from which he can analyze the motivation for social conflicts in terms of a failure of recognition.

Recognition comes in different forms in these different domains; hence, any theory of recognition that does not attempt to distinguish among the structures of these relations will encounter difficulties in parsing the ways in which the demand for recognition sometimes pulls us together and sometimes pulls us apart. Honneth's account is nuanced enough to avoid these difficulties. The first relation of recognition comes when we are loved and valued by intimates, by a circle of family and friends with whom we develop our basic capacities and trust in ourselves. The second is a domain of legal relations, of universal validation rooted in respect for our autonomy. The final relation is one that is social, but not universal, and takes place when others recognize us for our contributions to a particular "community of value." Unlike the demand for equal recognition before the law—which constitutes recognition of the second kind—the third relation of recognition is based on solidarity with some other people, but not everyone. When we receive social recognition in these three different ways—that is, when we are given love, rights, and solidarity—we receive what we need in order to develop and flourish as individuals. When we experience a failure of recognition in one of these domains, we are impaired in our ability to participate in the social world as fully-fledged members, whether because of emotional wounding or disconnect, a lack of legal rights guaranteeing protection and participation, or the absence of a community of shared values in which we can come to appreciate our uniqueness.

NETWORK POWER AND THE STRUGGLE FOR RECOGNITION

A framework of recognition such as Honneth's helps to guide our concern about identity by directing our attention to the social requirements that underpin human flourishing. The loss of a standard in a circumstance of extremely unequal network power can amount to a failure of recognition and bring with it the wounding that Honneth and others describe. In contrast to the distributional concerns discussed earlier, it is not simply that some people are denied the realization of some interest that they want (and should properly get), but that they are denied the intersubjective recognition necessary to develop a robust sense of self. We can understand a concern for recognition in terms of Olsaretti's distinction between voluntariness and freedom in choice-making, if we understand some minimal form of recognition as constituting a basic human need. An option that results in the denial of such recognition may be thought of as an "unacceptable" one and thus would be chosen only non-voluntarily, however "freely."

For our discussion of the impact of network power on identity, it may be helpful to restrict our focus to the latter two relations of recognition that

Honneth describes: those mediating legal status and social solidarity. This is because at first glance, at least, the intimate relations of love developed in personal life seem relatively immune to network power dynamics (at least as they may be considered in the context of globalization).[21] The second two relations of recognition are more obvious candidates for inquiry, as both address broader forms of social belonging.

Since the social contexts in which different standards come into conflict are varied, it is important to be able to articulate the different ways in which a relation of recognition might be dependent upon membership in a given network. In contemporary globalization, we see two broad patterns of the demand for recognition, which pull in opposite directions. Both struggles involve standards and network power, but one seeks the conditions of its realization and the other of its suppression. Without a single framework in which these seemingly different trends can be understood together, these demands can seem confusing.

On the one hand, in relation to participation in a community under law, the demand is for equal recognition, unbiased with regard to any particular characteristics. In many liberal democracies, this aspiration finds articulation in the demand for equal civil rights for members of minority groups. Internationally, it can be seen in the rapid rise of the human rights movement, demanding equal and humane treatment around the globe, irrespective of national, religious, or ethnic identity. We have also seen it more recently in the legalization of gay marriage in a great many countries, which offers the extension of social recognition that heterosexual couples take for granted to gays and lesbians.[22] The status that is conferred in marriage derives from citizenship generally and is not a mark of solidarity with a particular community.

In these instances, network power may augment what is a desirable broadening of the relations of recognition. For example, if forms of legal status enable equal participation in a community under law, the network power dynamics that push in the direction of universalizing this legal status also help to satisfy demands of recognition. It is not implausible that some intersubjective relations of recognition based on legal status have some of the properties of a standard. In fact, lacking such status can limit the potential of otherwise capable partners in cooperation, which will create pressure for an expansion of that legal status. The case for gay marriage is an obvious contemporary instance, given that legal matrimony provides access to a range of social benefits and privileges. Even where the relation of recognition does not operate like a standard in a network, but where it can be linked to one, we will see a struggle for recognition that focuses in part on network power dynamics. For example, the demand that human rights or labor standards be "linked" to the commercial standards of the World Trade Organization comes from the hope that social relations we *want* to be universal might more easily become so if they were linked to standards possessing great network power.

On the other hand, the struggle for recognition is also seen in a demand that pulls in the opposite direction: not for universal human rights, but for the recognition of distinctness, uniqueness, or particularity— for solidarity with the other members of what Honneth calls a "community of value." Here, network power represents a potential obstacle, at least where it undergirds a globalizing social formation that threatens to undermine differences. We see this concern in worries about cultural homogenization. National and local cultural autonomy or authenticity can seem threatened by the network power of dominant standards in cultural commerce. Here, the push to become like everyone else is not an achievement of recognition, but its denial.

This third relation of recognition does not demand the universalization of a standard but its restriction. For example, the Quebecois do not want to lose their language, through which they enjoy a particular kind of solidarity and a different kind of recognition from the universality they demand and expect under Canadian law. Because they understand themselves to be members of a different culture, it is not the embrace of mainstream Canadian culture that they want, but a degree of insulation from it, in order that their local relations of solidarity may survive. The politics here is very different from the universalizing impulse that animated, for example, the politics of recognition in the civil rights movement, in which African-Americans sought equal rights and respect owed to them *as American citizens*.

The distinction between the demand for recognition in these two domains allows us to make sense of what Taylor calls the politics of equal dignity and the politics of difference: "With the politics of equal dignity, what is established is meant to be universally the same, an identical basket of rights and immunities; with the politics of difference, what we are asked to recognize is the unique identity of this individual or group, their distinctness from everyone else."[23] What Taylor calls the "politics of difference" emerges in response to a threat to what Honneth calls solidarity. It may not be the case that members of minority cultures want a set of special privileges accorded them by majority cultures, as much as it is that they want an ability to live in solidarity with others who are recognized for the same distinctness. On an account of intersubjective recognition, this solidarity is not so much a special privilege as the fulfillment of a social need. Understanding this issue, however, requires a sophisticated account of the way in which the recognition of one's particularity works in our psychosocial development, and of the myriad ways in which it can be blocked or denied.

RECOGNITION AND AMERICAN IDENTITY

Despite the politics of multiculturalism in the United States, many Americans remain wary of this third relation of recognition, regarding the desire to draw away from the grasp of universality for the sake of a particular social solidarity as regressive, primitive, or dangerous. By contrast, the politics of recognition based on a demand for inclusion—the second relation of recognition—is more familiar and widely comprehensible. But the idea that the requirements of universality and solidarity might pull apart appears strange, since the proudest moments in the history of the United States have been when the two progressed together, as in the Civil Rights era.

Additionally, it may be easier for Americans especially to overlook their particularity—and thus to discount the struggle for recognition based on solidarity—because their standards are currently globalizing. The United States is frequently presented as a "universal nation," as Jedediah Purdy puts it; American national solidarity thus appears not as a *particular* identity but as an incipient *universal*. This was true even before the twentieth-century ascent of the United States, but it is all the clearer now. Purdy argues, "At the same time that we disclaim imperial ambitions, we Americans suspect that we are the world's universal nation."[24] Americans can suspect this because of a combination of domestic parochialism and enormous overseas power, which means that, when they do look abroad, they discover a world that in substantial chunks looks as though it is poised to become just like theirs—exactly as they had expected. Purdy explains, "We are parochial and universalist without inconsistency, because being universal defines our parochialism."[25]

Perhaps only the citizens of a country with so many domestic standards poised to become global commonplaces could adopt such a stance. By contrast, if the brightest students in the United States needed to pass examinations in Mandarin as a condition of success in a Chinese-dominated global economy, we would probably hear loud insistence on the beauty and uniqueness of the English language and of the "American way of life." The particular—denied its universal pretensions—would then be revealed for what it is. Indeed, it is worth noting how loud the cries on behalf of the English language and the American way of life have already become in the United States, under the very modest provocation of increased Hispanic immigration and only medium-term threats to American dominance abroad.

THE STANDPOINT OF FREEDOM

A comprehensive normative assessment of network power should address both identity concerns and distributional concerns. As they are less familiar, I have spent more time discussing identity concerns in the light of theories of recognition. I do not want to imply, however, that these concerns are necessarily (or even usually) distinct. We care about distributive justice because we care about human flourishing—which is also why we worry about the loss of identity.

Moving toward a more integrated view of distributive justice and recognition is possible from either direction. A capacious theory of distributive justice will reference those goods that people require, as John Rawls put it, "to have a lively sense of their worth as persons and to be able to advance their ends with self-confidence."[26] It may be that further reflection on these "social bases of self-respect" will lead to questions about identity-formation and socialization, beyond the stance that assumes rational, uniform agents in an anonymous bargaining position. While that stance may prove helpful for specifying some of the relatively general conditions of egalitarianism (such as respect under the law), it seems less appropriate if we wish to address concerns about identity. Of course, there are obvious and familiar difficulties in developing a robust theory of recognition from the standpoint of distribution. Any theory of distributive justice involves a few common elements: something to be distributed, some rules according to which a distribution is judged just or unjust, and the identification of the people to whom the relevant resources are to be distributed.[27] To the extent that the social bases of self-respect are grounded in the intersubjective dynamics of recognition, it is not clear that they are amenable to this kind of framework. But it is clear that we can capture at least some of the insights of a theory of recognition from a standpoint mainly concerned with justice. One of the most promising ethical accounts along these lines is the "capabilities" approach advanced by Amartya Sen and Martha Nussbaum, which directs us to consider the extent to which different people have the freedom to achieve valuable elements of well-being.[28]

We can also orient the discussion from the other side, viewing distributive concerns from the standpoint of identity. In many cases of cultural conflict, in fact, this vantage seems more appropriate, for it is not just that groups fight over their interests but that they fight over these interests *as proxies* for concerns about social standing and recognition.[29] It does not take much reflection on the difference between *relative* and *absolute* levels of consumption to see that a demand for recognition may often lie behind material concerns, where the goods that are sought are "positional."[30] Indeed, a theory like Honneth's is capacious enough to incorporate within it many distributional concerns, understood as mattering to a group's relative social standing in the structure of the relations of recognition.

Perhaps one way to bring theories of distributive justice and of recognition together is to understand both concerns about interests and concerns about identity from a standpoint focused on freedom and its practical realization.[31] This standpoint seems a particularly appropriate one to adopt for an analysis of network power, which involves the structure-driven abrogation of freedom. It understands distributive justice as the freedom to get what you need. It understands recognition as the freedom to become who you are. Of course these two freedoms are interconnected. We only know what we need once we come to know who we are, but we only become who we are by managing to get what we need.

CHAPTER SIX

Countering Network Power

IN THE PREVIOUS CHAPTER, I suggested different ways in which our concerns about distributive justice and identity might motivate the normative evaluation of network power. Once we have decided that a particular network configuration is abusive or unjust, we may wish to change it. However, how best to counter network power—which is driven by consent rather than direct coercion—is difficult to determine. A strategy based on negative rights that demarcate a zone of autonomy will prove of limited use against a kind of power driven by our desire to connect with one another. Neither can the provision of positive rights be very helpful, except inasmuch as it leads us into a nuanced institutional examination of the properties of any given network. Pursuing that examination leads us to specify particular "network properties" that govern the movement between networks in order to determine how best to defuse network power.

THEORIES OF RIGHTS

Modern rights theorists sometimes distinguish between "positive" and "negative" rights, although on any sophisticated account, the opposition is usually understood as imperfect at best. Negative rights are rights as we most commonly understand them: rights to non-interference in some particular domain.[1] A negative right guarantees the right-holder a zone of autonomy and freedom that neither the state nor (depending on the right) private parties can invade. Familiar negative rights include the right to freedom of association, the right to freedom of speech, and the right to the free exercise of religion. These rights carve out particular zones of non-interference, setting limits to what the government can require of or impose on its citizens in these areas. Negative rights can thus be thought of as functioning as trumps against the power of sovereignty, efforts to check state power. (Whether they would therefore prove self-defeating or self-undermining in situations of full *democratic* sovereignty is a question I leave for another discussion.)

We also speak of rights in a different manner, for example when we argue that citizens should have a "right" to public education or health care. These "positive rights" are sometimes called entitlement or welfare rights, and are understood as guarantees for the positive provision of something by others, usually the government. This provision enables the right-holder to do things that private action alone would not necessarily enable. For example, the right to food, shelter, or medical care guarantees an entitlement to some minimum level of these goods to those people who would otherwise lack them, or who would have to forgo other basic necessities in order to purchase them. Cultural, economic, and social rights are also increasingly being asserted, advancing a demand for states to guarantee baseline cultural, economic, and social outcomes for their citizens. We can understand such positive rights as efforts (whether successful or not) to use the power of the organized state to correct inequalities or abuses in the domain of "civil society," particularly in the economy. This is obvious from the fact that welfare rights are not ordinarily thought of as *political*, as trumps against state power, but rather as entitlements that perhaps only the state can guarantee. However, we can understand them to be political rights if we see them as an effort to enable effective political or social participation by those who otherwise would lack the means to participate.

On this view, welfare rights represent the same effort to enable people to determine their politics, whether through negative rights against tyranny or positive rights enabling the freedom to participate effectively in self-government.[2] Negative and positive rights require different responses by the state or the relevant authority. Positive rights usually require the state to do something affirmatively for the right-holder, while negative rights prohibit the state from doing something to the right-holder. When we say that we have a "right" to freedom of speech, what we mean, mainly, is that we have a guarantee that the state will not interfere with our exercise of speech. (Whether it should mean any more—for example, guaranteeing anyone an equal hearing as against the socially and economically more powerful—is a question of ongoing philosophical and jurisprudential controversy.) When we say that we demand a "right" to housing, what we mean is that we want a guarantee that the state will provide us with a minimally acceptable level of housing, should we ever lack it.

However, even though this rough distinction between negative and positive rights may prove a useful starting point for a discussion, it does not hold up to closer philosophical scrutiny. For example, some negative rights, like the "right to a fair trial," actively require the state to provide something to its citizens. Indeed, all negative rights require some kind of enforcement when we speak of them in a legal context, some affirmative response from government to a private individual's situation of powerlessness, without which the right would amount to nothing. On this view, the distance between positive and negative rights shrinks markedly. Indeed, some political theorists have dropped the distinction altogether, criticizing the original formulation and arguing instead that we should think about all rights *relationally*.

To understand a right relationally, we should ask: "*who* is free, *from* what restraint (or *because of* what enabling condition), *to* perform which action?"[3] Both positive and negative rights can be treated within this relational view without requiring a strong positive/negative distinction. A relational view focuses our attention on the important interests that rights are meant to serve—for example, the maintenance of certain forms of liberty—and away from relatively sterile typological controversies. Indeed, we may also reconstruct the distinction relationally with reference to the difference between sociability and sovereignty. Negative rights function as trumps against sovereign power, usually on behalf of particular individuals. Positive rights use sovereign power to transform the relations of sociability, protecting against the abuse or indifference of private actors. Of course, what an insistence on the *language* of rights does for us once we have come to understand rights in this way is an important question beyond the scope of this book.

NETWORK POWER AND RIGHTS

An inequality in network power is undesirable when it threatens valued aspects of identity or imposes distributional injustice or unfairness. How might rights help in such circumstances of coercive network power? The guarantees provided by "negative rights" will prove unhelpful in combating convergence onto a dominant standard because what they promise is (at its most essential) the right to be left alone. Network power, however, is driven by the opposite impulse: the desire to gain access to others for the sake of cooperation with them. Network power results in a Hobson's Choice in which such access to others is offered on fixed and not necessarily favorable terms. So negative rights that allow one to opt out of engagement do not change the composition of the choice set, and thus do not affect the inequality in network power. They cannot enable new alternatives; they simply guarantee the prospective hirer of Hobson's horses the right to walk away without interference. It would not seem appropriate, therefore, to attempt to use a tool designed to check the relations of sovereignty—as we might view rights understood as "trumps" on state power—to constrain the relations of sociability.

The difficulty of using negative rights to counter network power proves important for contemporary debates about multiculturalism and group rights.[4] Some advocates for cultural minorities argue that collective or group rights should be accorded to vulnerable groups. This strategy will work only insofar as the cultural loss sustained by these groups has been caused by state interference or the predations of certain private parties that the state can (and will) control. For example, cultural rights may prove very important where members of minority cultures are being forced to abandon their languages, customs, or religious practices by the state or by organized interests. But while such interference remains a pervasive problem, it is not the only threat facing members of minority cultures, particularly in liberal societies in which basic rights to expression are generally respected—and yet where cultural loss due to network power in the sphere of sociability may remain acute. For, when cultural loss is based on network power, coercion and consent are merged, and the zone of autonomy that negative rights guarantee will not be able to abolish the network power driving convergence onto a dominant standard. Threats to minority cultures from "globalization" usually come from the emergence of global standards with network power, against which the strategy of negative rights will likewise prove of little use. The linguist John McWhorter makes this point vividly in relation to threatened minority languages: "It is not difficult to make the case that people must not have their languages forcibly taken from them or beaten out of them. But in reality, just as often the reason groups abandon their traditional languages is ultimately a desire for resources that their native communities do not offer."[5] Negative rights will protect against only the former cause of language death, and not the latter.

Positive rights, by contrast, can be interpreted as efforts to enable new choices or to guarantee new outcomes, equipping the right-holder with the capacity to engage in some social activity without embarrassment or undue risk, by altering the distribution of resources. However, it is unclear that a strategy of positive rights will prove any more effective in combating the coercive features of network power because it is unclear in the abstract what such a strategy should or could entail. The ability to cooperate with others is different from goods like food or housing because it is largely unavailable for centralized provision or redistribution. In fact, without changing the institutional conditions of network power it is not clear that the state *could* ensure the preservation of non-dominant standards for those who would like to use them, even if we believe that it should. It is unclear whether the state can provide straightforward access to a "good," when the good in question is a form of social relations. What would it mean, for example, to guarantee the speakers of Occitan a viable linguistic community, and how could it be achieved practicably?

Certainly, I do not want to deny that the survival prospects of minority standards can be improved where access to critical resources is ensured —a point that many linguists make, for example, in relation to minority languages spoken in impoverished communities. But guaranteeing land rights or other welfare provisions is a rather indirect route to preserving cultural inheritance, even while it may often be the most effective and appropriate response. My argument is rather that we cannot imagine a *direct* guarantee providing for the continued use of a threatened standard, which is the sort of thing one would expect from a strategy of positive provision. To do so would require keeping some minimum level of membership in the networks that use threatened standards, which might be accomplished by subsidizing the users of non-dominant standards or by penalizing those users who want to switch to a dominant standard. For example, a government might pay speakers of a minority language to continue speaking their mother tongue, though this payment would probably have to be enforced through monitoring linguistic use in the minority community. Alternatively, it might attempt to halt the attrition of members from a lesser network by denying members of a lesser network the ability to adopt a new standard or by increasing the costs of such a switch through various penalties. In this case, the government might deny speakers of a minority language the right to learn the majority language or penalize them financially if they do.

However, our regard for important kinds of individual freedom and our recognition of the fluidity of social relations militate against this kind of approach. The fact that people are not goods to be allocated will make us question most attempts to use positive rights to counter network power, if these attempts are made through guarantees of a right to some minimum viable network based on a non-dominant standard. The state action required to enforce such a right could result in a strange and misguided attempt to freeze people into a status quo. For the members of a less dominant network may often want to be able to cooperate with others, but not on terms that lead to social dislocation or an unjust imposition of costs. They do not want to be kept as subsidized museum pieces; however, increased funding for the preservation of minority cultures and languages is crucially important. And they do not want to be denied the ability to cooperate with others on the grounds that this cooperation will erode cultural diversity. They know already—perhaps far better than members of a dominant network—how much is at stake in the transition to a dominant standard.

What users of a minority standard would like is to have access to members of the dominant network without being forced to give up their original standard. It is reasonable to ask what roles the state might play in providing this freedom, but it does not seem to me that a strategy based on either negative or positive rights offers any straightforward solution to the problem. Conceiving a strategy of rights *relationally* leads us to investigate who is free, because of which network configurations, to cooperate with whom, and on what terms. But in this relational framework, the simple idea of a "right" must then cede the analytic ground to a more institutionally detailed set of investigations and remedies. Thinking about the relations we are trying to enable takes us beyond rights as they are commonly understood, and demands that we focus instead on what network configurations people have good reasons to want and how they might achieve them institutionally.

If the driving force behind an inequality in network power is the desire to cooperate with others, then we need to investigate whether alternative forms of cooperation might be facilitated without the need to switch networks. Following this reasoning, the most effective way to defuse network power is to provide alternative and multiple channels for such access, thereby refusing to privilege just one. Any remedy for network power must be predicated on such alternative forms of social mediation—on new modes of access to desired cooperation—rather than on attempts to withdraw or disconnect from expanding networks. As network power is driven by the desire to gain access to forms of cooperation with others, any institutional alternative to the power of a dominant network must prove operative at the same level of generality. So, in short, to counter the power of a dominant standard, we need to open up access to its network in a way that does not require outsiders to abandon their standards. The extent to which this will prove possible is ultimately dependent on the particular institutional configurations in question.

THREE NETWORK PROPERTIES

Investigating these institutional configurations requires us to examine what I call *network properties*. Changes to these network properties might open up new possibilities for users of threatened standards, disabling network power by altering the structural conditions of choice. What I mean by network properties are the features of networks that differ according to how the standards underlying them differ in their configurations, and that govern the movement between one network and another. The extent of network power depends upon the configuration of these network properties, so it is in these actual configurations that we must search for strategies to defuse network power through directed institutional change. Note that network properties do not "cause" network power, but that they represent configurations of network structure that mean a dominant network will attract new members from other networks.

In some discussions of globalization, commentators have distinguished between "open" and "closed" architectures, arguing that the age of globalization is one of "open" architecture in which social forms spread rapidly across geographic space.[6] While this idea is evocative, it does not helpfully distinguish the range of possible meanings of closed and open network architectures. My analysis of network properties subdivides this general idea of "openness" into three different aspects: the acceptance of parallel systems, of new entrants, and of revision. I call these network properties *compatibility, availability,* and *malleability.*

The first property, *compatibility,* has played a central role in the discussion so far. Indeed, I have been relying on a critical assumption that I made in the very first chapter: the incompatibility of standards, meaning that someone can use either Standard A or Standard B, but not both at the same time. Given incompatibility, Network A can exert power over Network B, since users must adopt either Standard A or Standard B to gain access to their respective networks. This assumption of incompatibility has been crucial to my presentation of the idea of network power, for it pits two networks against each other and makes access available to each only through a single standard. Therefore, the gain of a member by one network is necessarily the loss of a member to the other; incompatibility turns network competition into a zero-sum game, which is why the universalization of a dominant standard leads to the loss of alternatives.

However, the actual extent of incompatibility between or among different standards is ultimately an empirical question, and in practice many degrees of compatibility may be seen to exist among different networks. Relaxing the assumption of incompatibility now will allow us to explore network properties, because it introduces the possibility of overlapping or simultaneous network membership. For example, I argued in Chapter 3 that the English language has (at least in several significant domains) passed the "threshold of inevitability." However, since multilingualism is possible—whatever the distribution of costs—English could become a global second language, compatible with alternatives at the local level. But, where a universal standard is strictly incompatible with alternatives —as in the example of the legal monetization of gold but not, say, cowry shells—incompatibility will augment the network power of the dominant standard.

More formally, this first network property, *compatibility,* can be seen as *the acceptance of parallel or simultaneous standards* to gain access to a given network. Networks that exhibit compatibility are accessible by more than one standard. This accessibility comes in one of two forms:

either a network is accessible by multiple standards, as in the case of a bilingual population that may be accessed through either of two different languages, or it is accessible to members of a different network through translation. This first case is what we might call *parallel compatibility*, or *costless compatibility*, while the second we might call *translatability*, or *compatibility with costs*.

Consider the difference between these two kinds of compatibility: suppose a tourist shop on the U.S.-Canadian border accepts either U.S. or Canadian dollars from its customers. This parallel or costless compatibility means that a tourist from New York, wanting to pick up a Canadian souvenir on her way home, can simply pull out U.S. dollars and make the purchase—or else use up her remaining Canadian dollars on the way out of the country. There are no costs to the use of either standard; both are equally acceptable. Or, take the example of a bilingual population, such as U.N. officials, who are supposed to have a working knowledge of both French and English. These workers should be equally accessible to both French and English speakers.

Now, consider the case of translatability or compatibility *with* costs. In this case, the tourist shop on the U.S.-Canadian border accepts only Canadian dollars, and the U.N. official speaks only English (or else her French is too poor to be comprehensible to French speakers). Unlike the case of *in*compatibility—the case we assumed in the development of the idea of network power—compatibility is still possible in both these instances, but it is more difficult. That is, the tourist shop and the U.N. worker are still accessible to users of other standards—to the New York tourist with U.S. dollars or the Francophone diplomat—but in both cases some level of translation will be required. The tourist must run to a currency exchange shop down the street and buy Canadian dollars with her U.S. ones and the diplomat must arrange for the services of an English-French translator during his conversations with the U.N. official. The difficulty of that translation will determine just how compatible these two networks are in practice, how costly it will be to operate across both while using just one of the standards.

Strict incompatibility must be understood as the situation in which a network is accessible only through a single standard and does not admit the use of parallel standards or translation. Effectively incompatible standards are ones that are very costly to translate—so costly that it is easier for the user of one standard to adopt a different one rather than to translate between the two. We can imagine a continuum of compatibility, moving from total compatibility (parallel or costless compatibility) through ever more costly levels of compatibility up to outright incompatibility, in which translation is either unavailable or else so difficult that the adoption of a different standard is preferable as a way of accessing its network. The degree of compatibility, then, proves to be a question of the difficulty of translation between the standards of two different networks.[7]

Consider the example of an anthropologist studying a group of people whose language is not known by any outsiders. No translation is possible between these two languages because no translator exists yet. To communicate, one party (the anthropologist or someone from the minority language group) will have to learn the other's language. In this case, translation is unavailable (or, if you prefer, "extremely costly") but the solution of parallel compatibility remains possible given bilingualism. Now, if translation were available—perhaps if someone in the minority language group had already learned another language—then the anthropologist might have employed his services as a translator instead.[8]

Where translation is available, it offers compatibility at a cost. Of course, using translation to achieve compatibility may be more costly than adopting a single standard for both networks, but because it allows the members of both networks to cooperate with each other, it reduces some of the pressure to converge on a single, universal standard. For example, measurement systems are entirely compatible through translation given the ratios that make one measurement system intelligible in terms of another. But using these ratios takes time and effort—it "costs" something. If the United States were to adopt the metric system, it would eliminate some of the costs that its use of the imperial system imposes on its citizens and on foreigners wanting to cooperate with them. But given that the United States does not have to adopt the metric system (since it is possible to translate between the imperial and metric systems) the incentive to do so is lessened. Still, where the need for translation is frequent and enduring—as in the case of commerce between two countries using different measurement systems—the joint adoption of a single system will prove advantageous to both in the long run. It is testament to the size and insularity of the U.S. domestic market that the imperial system remains in use. A smaller country with more foreign trade with metricized neighbors would have probably adopted the metric system some time ago, just as the United Kingdom did.

Thus incompatibility is central to the concept of network power since it forces individuals to adopt a single standard if they wish to gain access to a dominant network, resulting in the progressive augmentation of that network's size. Incompatibility, or compatibility with very high costs, forces the adoption of just one standard, leading to the decline of lesser standards. Parallel compatibility—where it is possible—preserves the diversity of standards without denying the sought-after benefits of cooperation with other people. For example, the linguist David Crystal speculates that easily available automatic machine translation between languages—what we might consider costless compatibility—would eliminate the drive to adopt English as a universal language.[9] But even if compatibility is not costless, many users of a non-dominant standard might still prefer achieving compatibility at a cost rather than switching outright to a dominant network.

The second network property that I wish to discuss, *availability*, indicates the *ease with which a network accepts new entrants* desiring to adopt its standard. A newcomer to a given network may experience more or less difficulty in adopting a given standard and becoming part of the network of users of that standard. A network is available to the extent that it is accessible to all new entrants willing to accept its standard. Obviously, all things being equal, *greater availability should translate into greater network power,* since availability means that potential entrants face lower costs of adopting a new standard and switching into a new network. As new entrants join, the network grows, and exerts more pull on non-members. Note that these costs of switching may include both the difficulty of learning the new standard, and, where newcomers are distinguishable from prior users of the standard in question, the speed with which new users gain acceptance from other users.

Consider a few common examples of standards exhibiting availability. Of the two broad types of standards introduced in the first chapter—mediating standards and membership standards—consider first the case of mediating standards. Since mediating standards allow their users to cooperate by providing shared forms of coordination, they are almost always available for adoption by outsiders. For example, when the British began the adoption of the metric system in 1965, no country using the metric standard registered a complaint or could in any way block its adoption of that standard. If anything, most users of the metric standard welcomed the change as it expanded the effective reach of the metric system in the world. Now, for a Parisian tourist visiting London, mundane activities no longer required calculations in the awkward weights and measures that they once did. More importantly, global trade inched closer to becoming fully metricized. And if the United States were ever to succeed in adopting the metric system, it too would be welcomed into the community of nations already using it. In fact, as the United States is the main holdout against metricization, the metric system would then become the global standard of measurement. (Only a few small countries—mainly ones dependent upon the U.S. economy, such as Caribbean island nations—have not officially adopted the metric or so-called international system of measurement.)

By contrast, the second type of standard, what we called a membership standard, is not always available for outsiders to adopt unless the network for which it regulates entry is itself open to new members. For example, many private clubs have entry requirements that operate as standards that are closed to new members in order to maintain a small and exclusive membership. By contrast, consider the standards set forth in international treaties, such as the instruments establishing the World Trade Organization, or certain U.N. conventions, such as the United Nations Convention on Human Rights. These treaty organizations do have entry requirements that operate as standards, but they are not designed to maintain exclusivity so much as to promote multilateral agreement on baseline free trade or human rights commitments.

The third property, *malleability*, indicates the extent to which a standard underlying a given network is *open to (piecemeal) revision*. A network is malleable if the underlying standard—the norm or institution by which members gain access to one another—can be revised without disrupting the ongoing social relations it supports. The revision that malleability enables should be understood as more or less piecemeal and gradual, since radical divergence may be better conceptualized as a switch to an entirely new standard. Although standards may change over time through unconscious or unplanned processes, what I mean by malleability is openness to deliberate change on a noticeable if incremental scale.

A standard's malleability may prove attractive to members of competing networks, regardless of the central content of that standard. Usually, a moderate amount of malleability leads to greater network power. A degree of malleability helps because networks can then incorporate aspects of other standards that are either useful in themselves or come as the necessary price of drawing new members away from a competing network. Too much malleability however, and a standard begins to lose coherence —and its network power with it—although the amount of permissible malleability will depend upon the coordination problem that the standard solves. For example, many forms of coordination require relatively precise expectations: to successfully meet a friend beneath the clock in the center of Grand Central Station, we must mean that place and that place exactly and not, say, a coffee shop across the street. Likewise, too much malleability destroys the value of mediating standards, such as measurement systems. A meter must represent the same length of distance everywhere, which is why such care has been taken to express its length in terms of the speed of light, the universal constant.[10] Similarly, too much variation in the way a language is spoken locally will render that version of the language less intelligible to others, as we see in the many different versions of English now spoken around the world or, historically, in the shift from the Latin Vulgate to distinct Romance languages following the collapse of the western Roman empire. Standards will differ, therefore, in how malleable they can be without losing coherence. It is *possible* to change the way English is spoken if English speakers in some community accept particular lexical changes.[11] But it is *not* possible to change the amount of distance captured in the concept of a meter without abandoning what we have meant by the "meter" ever since the distance was first formulated in 1793. The first standard, the English language, is malleable in a way the second, the metric system, can never be.

In my analysis of the gold standard, I discussed the tension, inherent in the use of all standards, which exists between the coordination that standards provide and their flexibility to adapt to changing circumstances. Gold offered a precise and universal standard on which to coordinate exchange, but without the flexibility of overall supply that paper currencies provide. Consider in a similar vein the case of a language that is poised to become regionally or globally dominant, such as Spanish or English. The intelligibility of the language to all its speakers requires a relatively low degree of malleability. On the other hand, because language is central to group identity, its speakers will express their own history and culture through alterations in it, which will generate dialects within the language and inhibit the ease of global communication. How these two opposing demands made on language will play out remains unclear in the case of English. With the proliferation of different Englishes—sometimes called the "New Englishes"—comes the possibility of a global multidialectalism, locally nuanced varieties of English used alongside the version favored in elite international circles.[12]

CONFIGURATIONS OF NETWORK PROPERTIES

Examining these three network properties reveals how the institutional configuration of a network influences network power. The network properties are related in complex ways. To some extent, availability and compatibility are opposed. Compatible networks can be accessed by multiple standards rather than by the adoption of a single dominant one. Thus the costless (or just relatively easy) compatibility of one standard with another diminishes the attraction of the second standard's availability. Assuming that there are some costs to switching to a new standard, this compatibility will enable the same access that the availability of the second standard would provide but without the need to give up the original standard. Likewise, a significant degree of availability may defuse the demand for generating new forms of compatibility if the creation of such compatibility would require costly change. Therefore, compatibility will be desired over availability where the use of translation on an ongoing basis is less costly than switching onto a dominant network. (These costs of switching over include the loss of access to members of the original network.) If a standard is both available and compatible with others, the relative cost of its compatibility will be central to determining whether members of a dominant network will be reached through translation or through the adoption of their standard.

Malleability and availability also exist in some tension, in that a standard cannot be both malleable and available to too great an extent without losing its coherence. A network that is both open to everyone and whose core is totally revisable will sustain neither a settled in-group nor a settled standard. It is not clear that such a network could support ongoing, settled social relations, allowing people to gain access to each other in predictable, regular ways. On the other hand, a standard that is available to newcomers will be more attractive if it is also somewhat malleable. We can imagine malleability without availability—a standard revisable by all existing members of a closed network—and availability without malleability, a network open to newcomers who must strictly accept its standard. Finally, malleability and compatibility can co-exist, but the evolution of malleable and compatible standards is indeterminate. It may be that, given relatively high costs of using translation to render two highly malleable standards intelligible, one or both standards will change to resemble the other, reducing the need for translation.

What combination of network properties would maximize network power, generating the greatest attraction to a dominant standard? The precise configuration will depend on the position of a standard on the trajectory of network power. Certainly, along the entire trajectory, availability increases network power as it welcomes new entrants that augment the network's size. Early in the growth of a network, allowing compatibility and some malleability may help in attracting new entrants or establishing the benefits of access to the network. Beyond a certain point, however, compatibility will serve not to attract new members to a network but to allow them access via translation, thereby reducing network power. Near the threshold of inevitability, compatibility will defuse network power by allowing users of non-dominant standards the benefits of cooperation with members of the dominant network without the need to use that network's standard.

So for a strong network with an already sizable membership, the optimal properties for the augmentation of network power are maximal availability, maximal incompatibility, and a low (or perhaps zero) degree of malleability. Incompatibility or compatibility with very high costs will mean that the only route of access to the members of a dominant network will be through the adoption of its standard, on settled terms. A low level of malleability is important, not least so that potential entrants may be provided with a predictable standard through which they can easily come into conformity with the other users of that standard. This configuration of network properties seems to occur in two very different but equally dominant standards that I explore in the following chapters: the Microsoft Windows operating system and the rules governing the World Trade Organization.

Of course, not every standard can be configured in this way. Consider two examples of mediating standards, languages and measurement systems, which cannot be made incompatible with competing standards.

Languages cannot be made incompatible because translation between them almost always remains possible, if sometimes difficult, and because people can learn to speak multiple languages. Furthermore, languages are malleable, at least in terms of their vocabularies. Measurement systems, too, can be translated by using ratios at any level of network power, while remaining fully non-malleable. However, with languages and measurement systems, the need for frequent translation can become quite costly, which is why it may be preferable to adopt a new standard outright on occasion. Consider, too, in this vein, the "efficiency" argument for adopting a single currency union in order to economize on trading costs.

By contrast, the network properties of membership standards may often be configured specifically with network power considerations in mind. Imagine a standard that determines eligibility for membership in a desirable private club or association. Suppose further that this club would become more attractive if it had a larger membership (implausible though this may seem to current club members). Early in the club's history, it may establish reciprocity agreements with several other clubs, accepting their standards for membership equally with its own. But as it gains new members, and hence becomes more attractive, it may choose to discontinue that reciprocity (ending compatibility), after which point its network is open only to those who meet its own selective admission criteria. As I argue in Chapter 8, the World Trade Organization seems to have had a rather similar history of institutional configurations, beginning as the General Agreement on Trade and Tariffs—a fairly ineffectual and highly compatible treaty organization—but evolving over time into perhaps the most powerful international organization there has ever been, through the exploitation of network power dynamics.

MAPPING NETWORK STRUCTURES

This analysis of network properties is meant to suggest ways in which the question of remedying or escaping from network power may be answered by providing a framework for the detailed examination of particular social networks. What has been missing from the discussion so far is the role that particular actors in a network have in configuring networks to serve their own interests. For example, some members of a network may have more or less power in deciding how malleability will work, or whether a network will maintain a high or low degree of availability. The discussion of network properties also highlights the diversity of types of networks. In any actual setting, examining general properties like availability, compatibility, or malleability will require delving into rather precise configurations of networks, and in so doing we will want to look at which actors are privileged in the arrangement of a network and how. Such an analysis may also indicate points of weakness that could be exploited, should we at any point wish to transform an existing network, augmenting compatibility, for example, in order to defuse an instance of abusive network power.

In thinking through such issues, it may be useful to draw on a set of concepts that have been elaborated in a particular branch of contemporary sociology called "social network analysis." Social network analysis is a formal methodology used in sociology, anthropology, and organization theory to map configurations of "networks," which are understood as sets of actors, depicted as single points, or "nodes," which are connected by "ties."[13] Any social group can be mapped in such a way, represented as a formal structure that can be analyzed using topological and graphological methods taken from advanced algebra. This allows different possible network patterns to be analyzed abstractly.

Social network analysis has identified a few common characteristics that distinguish one network from another, which may be useful in understanding the actual structure of any given transnational network exhibiting network power. First, and most obvious, is the *size* of a network, which is described by the number of nodes it possesses: that is to say, the number of participants it has. Second is the *type of tie*, whether it is reciprocal or one-way, and whether these ties are *strong* or *weak*.[14] Third, the *density* of the network, which is the proportion of ties present out of all possible ties. For example, given five nodes, imagine two different network arrangements: one in which the five points are arranged in a straight line, with ties linking them horizontally in a railroad fashion, one node to the next, and the other in which the five nodes are arranged as a five-pointed star drawn so that each node is connected to two others. The second network is denser, as it realizes more of the possible (though not all possible) ties in a five-node network. Different characteristics emerge given different kinds of network structures.

Consider a few of the common network structures, the basic topologies or shapes of which many large and complex networks are composed. A *chain* or line network is a series of points arranged in a single line, each node connected to the next. Networks of gossipers may resemble chain networks, each passing some information on to the next person in the chain. A *hub* or star or wheel network consists of a central node that is connected to other nodes surrounding it, which are not themselves connected to each other except through the central point. Real-world examples of such networks include telephone companies or commercial airlines that route all calls or flights through a central hub. Finally, imagine a field of scattered points in which every node is connected to every other. This *clique* or full matrix network may resemble a community in which everyone speaks the same language or uses the same currency. Each member of the community—every node—is tied to every other by the shared convention. Of course, there are many variants on these basic shapes, and hybrid networks can be composed of several of them. Imagine, for example, the network of parents and teachers brought together in a "Parent-Teacher Association." Not every parent or every teacher will be part of the PTA, but the two groups, which may resemble two different clique networks, will be united via a few members common to both groups who participate in the PTA.

Social network analysis can help to identify the way in which holding a particular position in a network—perhaps especially a central one—may be related to power over flows of information and other resources within the network. In the abstract, social network analysis argues that the more central a node, the more power it exerts in a network. For example, it is a powerful position to be a node at the center of an otherwise unconnected set of nodes in a hub network. Of course, arguing that this is always so in real-world settings requires a bit of interpretation. It may often be so—as with networks of information or resources that flow through a central and privileged position—but if the network is linked by some onerous activity, such as managing the paperwork for a committee, it is less clear that the central node is important in a way that also proves desirable. Thinking about how certain positions facilitate connectivity in a network also helps us to imagine which changes to a network might prove beneficial. Where two networks come into contact, as yet unconnected but with the potential to connect, there may be an opportunity—what is sometimes called a "structural hole"[15]—that will offer advantages to any agent who succeeds in establishing ties between the two unconnected networks, forging a larger structure.

Beyond these basic topologies, we can identify broadly different axes along which we may distinguish more complicated network forms. For example, networks vary from being uniformly densely connected, what is sometimes called *reticulated*, to being *segmented*, or more cellularly organized, with groups of dense connection linked weakly to other groups. Networks also vary in the extent of their centralization, from highly centralized hub networks to decentralized clique networks with no central, privileged node connecting otherwise unconnected nodes. A four-fold typology of networks emerges from combining these two variables: reticulated or segmented on the one hand and centralized or decentralized on the other.

Analyzing these different categories of networks may help us think about the importance of a few central players linking parts of a network, or about the danger of relying on those central nodes in times of disruption or crisis. Social network analysis may thus be useful for examining any number of social phenomena in which we can specify the role that particular agents play in a field of relations. This way of analyzing network structure can suggest concrete questions to pursue with regard to any actual social network. For example, studying the density of ties may indicate something about the direction or extent of resource flows between members on a periphery and those in the core of a segmented network, or about the strength of interpersonal bonds in a reticulated one. Of course, any lessons we may wish to draw from the analysis of abstract network structures must be cautiously elaborated, given the difficulties attending any analogy between formal structures and the real-world settings they are meant to model.

Consider one example of social network analysis with real-world import: security experts at the RAND Corporation have argued that the dynamics of what they call "netwar" are different from those of conventional warfare, and that security from terrorist attack requires scrutinizing the structures of "SPINs"—segmented, polycentric, ideologically integrated networks. Some analysts claim that the "Al-Quaeda" terrorist network is best understood as a SPIN, which confers on it certain advantages of flexibility and coordination in fighting against an enemy with overwhelming military superiority. Of course, thinking about "netwar" did not begin following the terrorist attacks of September 11, 2001, although it is gaining prominence given the new geopolitics of the so-called global war on terror. RAND researchers previously analyzed the Zapatista rebellion in

Mexico along similar lines; indeed, the first formulation of the concept of SPIN came from sociological research into the structure of American social movements in the 1960s.[16]

SOCIAL NETWORK ANALYSIS

Social network analysis was first developed in the 1950s by structuralist anthropologists interested in mapping the social relations of particular communities.[17] It has been employed in anthropology ever since, though its use has been subject to controversy. It has also moved into other areas, particularly sociology. More recently, it has become very popular in the study of transnational networks, which has given it a new lease of life in the literature on globalization.[18]

It is important to distinguish between the abstract methodology of social network analysis and the empirical study of social networks: the two stand in relation to each other as formal economic theory does to empirical descriptions of the economy. As with any formal analysis, the difficulty with analytic mappings lies in their translation of details, first from "real-world" settings into abstract mathematical objects susceptible of formal manipulation, and then back again into real-world details with new insights gained from the analytical exercise.[19] Gaining insights from the translation into topology and back requires a broader theoretical or conceptual strategy guiding the use of this formal method. Lacking it, social network analysis has sometimes been accused of being a methodology in search of a question, a graphic redescription or recasting of fields of social relations without regard to their actual content. Where it has been most useful is in studies of computer-mediated communication systems and of epidemiology, because the relations tying nodes together in networks in these areas are uniform and relatively straightforward by comparison with the more complex social relations that social network analysis has the ambition to explain.[20]

For our purposes here, social network analysis may be useful if we regard it as an attempt to think rigorously about the structure of networks. As an exercise in mapping, social network analysis may prove a helpful supplement to a broader inquiry, offering a way to reflect on certain kinds of social phenomena via a formal description of the structure of the field of social relations at a particular point in time and with regard to a particular kind of interaction under scrutiny. It can generate specific insights about a given network structure, which can help us bring an idea of structure back into our social analyses as a contribution to—but not a substitute for—the broader traditions of social theory.

One serious problem with the effort to use social network analysis as a social theory is that the formal study of network relations can distort our ideas of agency. Because social network analysis focuses on ties between nodes, a theory of social life that derives from the kind of mappings it provides will fail to fully recognize human agency and will offer instead, through this abstract methodological scaffolding, a new structure-dominated account of social relations. Indeed, we see this sort of theory developed in a branch of social theory called "actor-network theory," which shares with social network analysis a focus on the overall network, including its "non-human actors," as the prime explanatory variable.[21]

A more limited role for social network analysis would examine the control of a given node over ties in a network, and map out secondary relations accordingly. This may not be a philosophically ambitious enterprise, but it may prove helpful with relational studies that are part of a larger project. For example, when linked to theories of elite decision-making, social network analysis can help us to identify the ways in which positions of centrality in a network constitute elite status, by enabling control over decision-making.[22] Mapping the relations among organizations offers an even clearer example of social network analysis because it is more straightforward to chart the formal relations among organizations with specific purposes, missions, and resources than the informal relations that may exist among scattered individuals.

Thus, the tools of social network analysis may be helpful in a concrete analysis of an instance of network power, suitably supplemented with philosophical and empirical analysis. This combination would resemble more closely the network theory now practiced in some branches of sociology, which focuses less on formal methodology than on network analysis in concrete social settings. However, it seems to me that this literature still lacks a systematic philosophical framework and, especially, a concept of power.[23] Such a concept cannot be derived from sources internal to social network analysis, but must be brought in from the outside—for example, from the idea of network power. Social network analysis cannot provide such an understanding by itself, for formal methods cannot generate an interpretation of the problems they may be used to analyze.

DESTABILIZING SOCIABILITY

I began this chapter by questioning how far the idea of rights may have something to contribute toward remedying network power in those instances in which we judge it to be abusive. Conceived as zones of privacy sheltered from state intrusion, rights, I argued, will not be able to contribute much to moves made against a form of power that emerges through our desire to gain access to other people, rather than to be protected from them. Conceived as guarantees for the minimum maintenance of some socially necessary good, a rights framework seems equally unhelpful, because membership in a network is not a uniform good, such as housing, concerning which we may easily specify a particular allocation we wish to see guaranteed. Even in the clearest cases of goods constituted by social relations—for example, gender equality or racial tolerance—the state can intervene to correct egregious abuses, but it cannot mandate tolerant attitudes or egalitarian social relationships with any efficacy.

Thinking about network properties and the power of standards offers a different way to proceed, and suggests a different way to think about rights. Where a dominant standard exerts a monopoly-like influence over members of other networks, the search for new forms of compatibility or malleability—the attempt to open up new forms of access on different terms—might be seen as amounting to an unworking of an existing pattern of social relations, the destabilization of the structures of sociability that lead to "domination by virtue of a constellation of interests." An inquiry into what I call network properties, supplemented by the selective use of the tools of social network analysis, may prove helpful in formulating strategies for this destabilization.

The relation of destabilization to the idea of rights requires further elucidation, as our general idea of a right seems the opposite of destabilization: the instantiation and maintenance of some zone of guaranteed protection or privilege. Can we imagine the idea of a right—a social guarantee—pressed into service on behalf of an agenda of unworking or destabilization? One scholar who has argued along these lines is the social and legal theorist Roberto Mangabeira Unger, who advances the idea of *destabilization rights* as part of his broader effort to revise contemporary social thought and to emphasize the role of "structure-revising structures" in contemporary societies.[24] He argues for destabilization rights that work at a systemic level: "Destabilization rights protect the citizen's interest in breaking open the large-scale organizations or the extended areas of social practice that remain closed to the destabilizing effects of ordinary conflict and thereby sustain insulated hierarchies of power and advantage."[25] Unger's argument is that when we think about undoing a system of social relations that we find objectionable—not an objectionable *instance,* but an objectionable *system,* like that of racial segregation—we appeal to rights that modern courts have interpreted broadly as permitting or requiring a reworking of social relations generally (and not merely the provision of individual redress). In the United States, the end of a legal apartheid regime in schooling and social life provides an obvious and dramatic instance. But some scholars following Unger's lead have argued that public law litigation more generally has evolved over the last three decades to resemble a partial regime of such "destabilization rights."[26]

The idea of destabilization rights draws on and attempts to generalize lessons from the experience of governmental action to redress systematic exclusion or humiliation in the social life of advanced democracies. This would seem one way in which we can use the relations of sovereignty—the forms of organized political power—to countervail the power of sociability when it is oppressive. Unger argues: "Governmental action to disrupt and reconstruct the overprotected and subjugation-producing arrangements may be needed not only because the people in charge of the organizations or practices at issue may be the biggest beneficiaries of the insulated hierarchies but because there may be no people visibly in charge." Hence, he envisions destabilization as directed not only against particular organizations and institutions, but also taking in broader areas of social life, as "when the claimant seeks to disrupt an area of social practice rather than a discrete organization."[27]

Instances of abusive network power resemble social practices in which it may seem that there are "no people visibly in charge" and in which the worry is how to "prevent recurrent, institutionalized relationships" from generating "closure and subjugation." In relation to such abuses, the *ideal* of destabilization must be central. But what is added to this ideal by imagining it embodied as a *right?* The attempt to translate successful governmental action against social exploitation into a new set of rights may prove helpful in specific institutional settings and under particular historical circumstances—and it is within this setting that Unger and other legal scholars advance their argument. But advocating destabilization within a program of "rights" seems to do little analytic or practical work, other than justifying such public action as a defense of individual liberty. That defense may play an important role as part of an overall ideological strategy, especially in public law litigation in societies in which an appeal to rights is a compulsory trope of political rhetoric. Philosophically, however, that defense can be made more simply and pointedly: there are many different ways to be oppressed, and collective public action is a prerequisite for re-establishing most, if not all, forms of individual freedom which are otherwise threatened by private power. Proliferating new rights—or even interpretations of existing law dependent on a framework of right—may or may not prove an effective specific articulation of this more general concern.

For example, even if the idea of a destabilization right is the best way to justify domestic public action against systematic private power, it will prove ineffective against forms of *global* sociability that are not subject to direct governmental intervention. Unlike the national circumstances in which Unger and other legal scholars suggest the remedy of destabilization rights, globalization presents us with social relations of power that operate at a level above specific governments, where there may be no transnational actor or set of actors with the authority or ability to upend them. Where the relations of sociability have "flown the coop" and are instantiated in *global* networks of actors, the power of sovereignty may be inadequate to the task of destabilizing transformation. To put it differently, the suggestion that we offer destabilization rights to citizens as part of their repertory of legal protections and privileges may not be enough to countervail power at the global level, even while the coercive aspects of globalization reach ever more deeply into national and individual space. The question of whether the power of national sovereigns is sufficient to mitigate those coercive aspects is not a question about the extent of legal rights so much as it is about the practical limits of alternative forms of globalization.[28]

ALTERNATIVE GLOBALIZATIONS

The structural gap between political procedures designed to work at a national level, and the development of social relations in which problems increasingly occur at a transnational level, reveals the central tension in contemporary globalization. Everything has been globalized, except for politics—which remains tied to national sovereignties without an easy or attractive analogue to national sovereignty available at the global level.[29] With this tension in mind, one possible ambition would be to progress toward a regime in which global *alliances* could destabilize oppressive social relations, for example to maintain a diversity of standards against monopolistic coercion. These alliances—of state agencies, civil society organizations, and multilateral institutions—might coordinate their actions so as to effect the destabilization of existing or incipient global standards whose network power is judged objectionable. In doing so, however, they would not be bringing the power of sovereignty to bear on the relations of sociability but rather constituting a new form of "international society" to advance an alternative form of globalization.

This brings us to an important distinction between two ways in which we might imagine the construction of "alternative globalizations." The first option corresponds to the strategy expressed above—the formation of new global alliances to destabilize oppressive networks. It imagines transforming the relations of sociability through new transnational and international alliances oriented to a different set of ethical evaluations or political aims. In this strategy, we counter the problems of sociability by forging a new and better kind of sociability—a new international society, with more egalitarian norms and new institutions for channeling our cooperation with one another in a fairer fashion. Consider the concrete efforts currently being made to move along this path: new treaty regimes attempting to generalize norms of conduct internationally, for example the International Labor Organization's compacts on child labor; new nongovernmental organizations attempting to directly rework global sociability, such as those promoting Fair Trade products that give consumers a different way to engage with developing world producers; and corporations or industry groups promulgating "corporate codes of conduct" for their overseas manufacturing. All of these efforts depend upon forms of *voluntarism*, new networks of people choosing to participate in new institutions for civil society or new alliances of states deciding to join international regimes. Each of them rests, in the end, on a *coalition of the willing*.

There is a second route to the reconstruction of global society: the reengagement of politics at the national level with the intent of influencing the possible forms of international society. This route does not so much attempt to transform global society directly through new (and arguably better) global networks, as to transform the political regime for domestic agents, who, through their activities, then construct a different global civil society. Consider, for example, the two responses to globalization that I discussed in Chapter 3: the reassertion of national languages against language loss and the reassertion of national monetary regimes in the context of the "Keynesian revolution" in macroeconomics. Both of these efforts transformed the options that citizens had under the private circumstances of sociability by using state power to reshape national networks.

Either route may prove a desirable or practicable one to take up under particular circumstances. In a country such as the United States, which possesses only a fragmented and fractured form of sovereignty—that is, one in which all of the different branches of the central government and a supermajority of individual state governments must align in order to achieve political change of any significance—the search for alternative globalizations usually focuses on reworking global sociability, through consumer boycotts, NGO movements, and other forms of social voluntarism. Yet there are good reasons to be skeptical about the effectiveness and legitimacy of many forms of voluntarism, however well motivated or admirable the individuals who participate in them. First, their effectiveness depends on successfully mobilizing large numbers of people to contest the power of a few powerful private actors—but with only private persuasion rather than public power to assist them. This is related to the obvious problem of holdouts, who will often be the beneficiaries of the existing system and thus predictably reluctant to participate in the construction of an alternative. The second is that the legitimacy of voluntarism may itself be called into question even when it succeeds—that is, when a new network of sociability replaces an old one—because the legitimacy which public action brings to a movement was never there in the first place. Both the worry about effectiveness and the worry about legitimacy come from the failure to engage politics in the contest against network power. However worthy the motivations of many people who find no other practicable choice than to engage global sociability directly—in daily purchases, choices, and activities, lacking any effective recourse to politics—their effectiveness against powerful private actors and the legitimacy of civil society movements that express only a "coalition of the willing" remain unclear. These issues will recur in the debates over specific elements of globalization that I discuss in succeeding chapters.

A final point on the construction of alternative globalizations bears mention. Whether or not the strategy of reworking the relations of sociability directly seems preferable to operating through those of sovereignty in any particular setting, it should be clear that it is the construction of alternative global regimes and not the rejection of globalization *in toto* that motivates the so-called anti-globalization movement today. Most critics of contemporary globalization want a world order that is fairer, more equal, and more respectful of cultural diversity than the one that is now emerging. Their commitment to achieving such an alternative within a broadly multilateral framework is not at question; the struggle for an alternative is not the fantasy of autarky. Indeed, it is less from the critics than from the supporters of contemporary globalization that we hear the simple-minded declamation that it must be *this* globalization or nothing at all.

CHAPTER SEVEN

Network Power in Technology

THE DYNAMICS OF NETWORK POWER outlined in the previous chapters are clearly evident in the domain of high technology, the globalization of which is a defining feature of our age. New technologies of communication and media have helped to establish a world of global commerce, culture, and consciousness. These technologies solve practical problems of coordination, facilitating interactions across great distances and building on the great eighteenth- and nineteenth-century advances that mark the modern age off from those preceding it. The Internet and the airplane, in our day, have furthered the compression of distance begun by the sailing ship, the railroad, and the telegraph.

Communications technologies in particular are based on underlying protocols or technical standards which can "spread" very quickly across borders to emerge as universal conventions. The relation between technology and standards is one that deserves scrutiny because competition over the control of technical standards is pervasive in the political economy of high technology. In this chapter, I discuss the network power of some of these standards, focusing on relatively familiar technical advances such as Internet browsers and operating systems, but also examining a few more obscure but nevertheless powerful ones, such as the ISO 9000, an international quality control standard. In all of these cases, what may look like an unproblematic process of technical coordination is shown to involve an ongoing contestation over standards that take their value from their common usage, but which are not for the most part under common control.

INTERNATIONAL TECHNICAL STANDARDS

The creation and diffusion of standards underlying new technologies is a driving element of contemporary globalization. Business consortia, governmental bodies, and international organizations all promulgate their own technical standards, and consulting enterprises have sprung up to help businesses and consumers navigate their way through them. But international technical standards are not new: they have been around since at least the late nineteenth century in most major industries. Early industrial consortia often made great efforts to harmonize production, adopting common protocols to reduce the cost of adapting new designs, measurements, and quality levels when switching between suppliers in international chains of production. This process of standardization played an important part in what James Beninger has called the "control revolution," which followed from prior industrial advances and enabled the globalization of industrial production and mass consumption.[1]

Currently, international bodies responsible for promulgating technical standards exist in every area of industrial activity or commercial enterprise. We should not think of these standards as restricted to the high technology sector, although we may read about them most often in that context. For example, there is even a "Global Cement Information System" dedicated to disseminating international standards in cement production—a product critically important for all infrastructure projects, but far removed from the glitter of Silicon Valley.[2] Of course, standards do play an extremely important role in high technology, whether in telecommunications, media, or Internet applications.

The harmonization of potentially diverse standards is of critical significance for technological progress in these fields. It is also a critical element of business strategy: the fortunes of companies rise and fall with their control of technical standards. In their efforts to further such coordination, standards bodies—and even dominant companies—undertake standardization or harmonization (and often both). We should distinguish *standardization*, the creation of a new standard, from *harmonization*, the convergence on an existing standard by users of alternative ones. When two networks using different standards come into competition, harmonization may offer a strategy for reducing the costs of exchange.

The harmonization of existing technical standards, and standardization in emerging fields, are essential for the spread of compatible technologies and products—in short, for "technological progress." These standards resemble measurement systems in that, without a common denominator, it becomes impossible to measure and compare products. However, they can be even more critical since products or processes operating according to divergent standards may prove incompatible, lacking the capacity for translation of the kind that we see in measurement ratios. (This problem is particularly acute when technologies are used to aid social coordination, for example in information and communication technologies as opposed to, say, the production of stainless steel, in which more easily "translatable" material processes prove central.) Technologies of coordination must often literally build a standard into the mechanics of the product, so that it becomes not just a means of external measurement and comparison, but an integral element of the product itself. Given the possibility of building machines or designing technical processes around any one of a number of technical standards, the need for compatible machinery and the harmonization of underlying standards has been clear from the beginning of the industrial age and is even clearer today, in the "New Economy" of networked high technology.

STANDARDS IN THE NEW ECONOMY

The new high tech economy depends upon the efforts of an immense number of international standards bodies. They include the Institute of Electrical and Electronics Engineers (IEEE), which has 800 active standards and another 700 under development, and is responsible for most cabling and networking standards in the United States, many of which subsequently spread abroad; the National Committee for Information Technology Standards (NCITS), which focuses on information processing standardization and has created important standards such as MPEG and JPEG formats for multimedia files, SCUSI-2 for interfacing computer components, and the C++ programming language; and the World Wide Web Consortium, a collection of international academic institutions (which offers what it calls "recommendations" rather than "standards") which created the HTML and XML mark-up languages. These standards, even when not formed by an explicitly international body, quickly gain an international presence through harmonization driven by global commerce. That these standards rapidly develop a worldwide reach is unsurprising. When designing a law or national policy, it may be appropriate to think of a limited space and a particular context. By contrast, when devising a standard for multimedia applications, the widest possible use is not only desirable but will often prove necessary if the standard is to be attractive to its users, who will want to be able to reach as many potential co-users as possible. Perhaps like any form of cooperative activity, these standards tend to universality within their domain—which, in the case of high technology, can mean universality in networks with a literally worldwide expanse.

While international standardization is not new to contemporary high technology, it is nevertheless a relatively modern phenomenon, with mass industrial standards dating only from the late nineteenth and early twentieth centuries. In 1906, the first international body for the promulgation of technical standards was born, the International Electrotechnical Commission (IEC), which is today made up of 49 national committees and cooperates with other standards bodies and international organizations to coordinate international standardization in electrical and electronic engineering.[3] It publishes standards for electronics, so that manufacturers can make products that are compatible with other products throughout the international chain of manufacture and distribution. The American National Standards Institute, founded in 1918, is an umbrella organization for American standards development bodies, and often represents the United States in international standards negotiations. ANSI does not create standards, but advises on the development of new ones and attempts to help in the harmonization of existing standards. It publishes catalogs of standards, including over 8,000 different ones in its recent issue.[4]

In the United States, electronics standards are promulgated by the Electronics Industry Alliance (EIA), which began in 1924 as the Radio Manufacturers' Association.[5] The EIA is the main trade organization for the $381 billion U.S. electronics industry, covering all major sectors of electronics, including telecommunications. It has 200 staff members providing services, lobbying, and creating standards for the electronics and computer industry. Within the EIA, the Telecommunications Industry Association (TIA) is one of the most prominent standards bodies, with over

1,000 high tech companies as members and 70 current standards on offer covering all major telecommunications technologies.[6] (Founded in 1924 as a trade association dedicated to organizing exhibitions, it led an independent life until its recent incorporation under the umbrella organization, the EIA.) The TIA's international counterpart is the International Telecommunications Union (ITU), formerly the CCITT, which is dedicated to ensuring compatibility in international telecommunications through the promulgation of global telecom standards. It is "an international organization within the United Nations System where governments and the private sector coordinate global telecom networks and services."[7] Perhaps its most familiar standard is that governing Group III telefacsimile machines, which makes possible the international transmission of faxes.

All of these bodies exist in complicated public-private partnerships in areas in which setting the standard means creating the market (at least to some significant degree) through forms of public-private partnership and in regimes of ongoing "cooperative competition."[8] The creation of standards is not merely a way to provide a solution to a coordination problem; it may be equally an act of business strategy. Consider an example from automobile manufacturing, which might appear less susceptible to network power dynamics than the electronic technologies discussed above. In 1995 and 1996, the three largest car companies in America—Daimler-Chrysler Corporation, Ford Motor Company, and General Motors Corporation—formed the Auto/Steel Partnership along with their suppliers to create standards in auto manufacturing. These standards, the NAAMS Global Standard Components, are now widespread in the industry.[9] The Auto/Steel Partnership aims to "describe and define the components that have been adopted as standard by those companies when designing and constructing stamping dies and body assembly tools for sheet steel body components." The standards for stamping were first published in 1995, while those for assembly came out in 1996, and were placed on the World Wide Web in order "to keep pace with the rapid rate of revision and expansion" and to make access to the "standards available to all users at no cost." Of course, the motivation behind the standardization of auto manufacture is clear: so long as the Auto/Steel Partnership has enough market share, the standards it promulgates will dominate in the industry, benefiting its member firms.

MICROSOFT: THE NETWORK POWER OF TECHNOLOGY?

International standardization is a widespread and long-standing phenomenon; only recently, however, have the full implications of the possible *monopoly* power produced by standardization become of general concern. The case that brought this feature of standardization to public attention is *United States vs. Microsoft,* in which the Microsoft Corporation was accused of anticompetitive practices stemming from its near-total dominance of the operating systems (OS) market. (The concern about Microsoft's control of the OS market had been pervasive in the high tech world long before it came to public attention.)

Microsoft's flagship product, the Windows OS, controls approximately 90 percent of the market in operating systems—with some variation depending on the year. An operating system is the platform on which other software applications run, the basic interface between the user of a computer and its machine code. There are clear network power reasons for this dominance: operating systems exhibit a variety of network effects that will work to cement the position of a leading standard once a sufficient number of other users have accepted it. However, it is not Microsoft's control of the OS market that spawned the anti-trust litigation, but the way in which the corporation allegedly made use of its market dominance.

Since almost everyone uses the Windows OS, Microsoft can promote an array of other applications simply by *bundling* them with Windows—so that dominance in this key area can translate into dominance in many other areas. For example, by bundling its web browser, Internet Explorer, with the Windows OS, Microsoft was able to take the market over from its rival (and the former industry leader) Netscape. Whether or not this practice constituted a legally actionable anti-trust violation, it is clear that it succeeded as a matter of business strategy by exploiting the network power of one product to push others. As Robert Reich explains, "Windows is used so widely that other producers of computers, browsers, and other software have to license it from Microsoft if they want to connect their gadgets and codes to most other gadgets and codes in the market. This gives Microsoft power to thwart competition and discourage innovation."[10]

The federal investigation into and prosecution of Microsoft lasted over a decade, during which time the case—and the dynamics of innovation and control in computing more generally—gradually came into public focus. In 1991, the Federal Trade Commission set up an investigation into

Microsoft's practice of "tie-in" sales, in which it linked its applications, such as its Internet browser, to Windows. The FTC investigation reached an impasse and was closed in 1993. Later that same year, the Department of Justice began its own investigation, which eventually led to a federal government lawsuit against Microsoft beginning in 1998. In the five years between 1993 and 1998, Microsoft first consented to, and then violated, an agreement not to use tie-in sales to promote its products. When it launched its web browser, Internet Explorer, it bundled it with Windows, arguing that the browser was not a separate product but an inbuilt and inextricable feature of the Windows OS itself. This move enabled it to quickly overtake its main competitor, Netscape Navigator, but it also led to the federal lawsuit against it.

The lawsuit was led by the Clinton-appointed U.S. Attorney General Janet Reno and joined by 20 U.S. states. It charged Microsoft with anti-competitive practices such as locking out the applications of competitors by leveraging its market dominance in the operating system market. The original trial lasted 23 months and ended with a verdict by Judge Thomas Penfield Jackson against Microsoft, which was to be broken into two separate companies, one that would make the Windows OS and the other that would make applications to run on it. Though this original court case would later be reversed and remanded, it did reveal how Microsoft used its operating system monopoly to undermine competitors' applications. It became very clear that Microsoft's monopoly was based on more than network effects alone, but included more predatory and anti-competitive tactics.

Microsoft denounced the decision and appealed. On appeal, the district court decision to divide Microsoft was overturned because of errors (such as speaking to the press) alleged to have been committed by Judge Jackson. The case was sent to a new judge, Colleen Kollar-Kotelly, who was chosen at random by a computer. Less than two weeks later, in September 2001, the Department of Justice—now under the administration of President Bush, to whose election campaign in 2000 Microsoft had donated generously[11]—reversed course and dropped the effort to have Microsoft split in two. Two months later, the Bush administration announced a new settlement with Microsoft in what most analysts and commentators took to be a strong (that is to say, cheap) victory for the company. (Microsoft stock price jumped 7 percent in after-hours trading following the announcement that Judge Kollar-Kotelly had approved the settlement.) Kollar-Kotelly announced sanguinely: "Promises have been made that the company will change its predatory practices, which have been part of its competitive strategy."[12]

The settlement demanded very little of a company that had been facing a radical restructuring just two years earlier. Microsoft was not broken up, or obliged to open its code to competitors; it simply had to release some technical data to allow other software companies to write programs for Windows, and it promised to refrain from retaliating against computer manufacturers that use rival products. For Microsoft's rivals, these promises amounted to very little, and several parties continued to press private lawsuits against the corporation. Nine of the suing states and the city of Washington, D.C., refused to settle on terms so favorable to Microsoft, and continued their own separate cases against the company. In 2004, the original settlement was finally approved on appeal, and the case *U.S. v. Microsoft* came to a close.

Microsoft's legal woes, however, were far from over. It settled the nine state cases against it for damages totaling $1.5 billion, including a $1.1 billion settlement with the State of California. (According to some observers, Microsoft has managed to turn many of these state settlements to its advantage by donating computers—and its software—to schools, in lieu of cash payouts and with the probable expectation that it will thereby gain future customers.) The civil lawsuits brought by its competitors also cost Microsoft dearly, since they went forward with the benefit of the original trial court's findings of fact, which revealed the company's anti-competitive behavior. In 2003, it paid out $750 million to AOL-Time Warner (which had bought Netscape) to settle an anti-trust suit. In 2004, it settled patent disputes with Sun Microsystems for $1.6 billion and with InterTrust for $440 million. In 2005, it paid Real Networks $761 million and settled IBM's claims of discriminatory pricing and overcharging for another $775 million (and that does not even exhaust IBM's pending litigation against Microsoft).

Most significantly, in March 2004, the European Commission, which had begun an anti-trust investigation of Microsoft in the 1990s, fined the company €497 million, approximately $600 million in 2004 dollars, the largest single anti-trust fine against a company that the EU had ever lodged up to that point. Importantly, the Commission forced Microsoft to make a version of Windows without its media player bundled with it, and has demanded an end to bundling and more transparency in the Windows OS code.[13] Microsoft has now twice appealed the ruling, and it is unlikely that the matter will be settled for another few years—but the contrast with the Bush administration's approach to the company is striking.

NETWORK POWER AND ANTI-TRUST

However the European Commission case is finally resolved, it is clear that Microsoft's dominance will continue in several areas, particularly in the operating systems market (and also that of word processing software, since Microsoft Word controls 95 percent of that market). Given this dominance, it seems unlikely that Microsoft will abstain from further bundling practices; even the large cash pay-outs to competitors that it was forced to make following civil suits brought against it have not dented the company's generous $50 billion cash reserves. The more critical issue is what public control, if any, governments may try to exert over the network power of the technical standards at the heart of Microsoft's lucrative monopoly position.

Microsoft contends that the dynamics of the high tech industry alone spurred its rise to dominance, given the supply-side economies of scale in digital production—a point which it claims Judge Jackson failed to understand. While its opponents have argued that Microsoft's anti-competitive practices are as ruthless as that of any monopolist, it is also true that network power alone would have had the capacity to establish convergence on shared operating systems and word processing programs. Significantly, therefore, the implications of the Microsoft case go beyond the OS market and even the high technology sector, and illustrate broader problem posed by network power in modern economic and industrial life. Indeed, the reason that I introduced above the many other areas in which industrial standardization occurs was to situate the Microsoft trial within the context not just of high technology networks, but of the imperatives of industrial standardization more generally. For Microsoft's dominance provides a dramatic example of the monopolistic tendencies of network power in areas where technological standardization is a necessary industrial practice—that is, in most (if not all) of modern industry. Indeed, the network power of technical standards is a general feature of industrial production. Many other industrial standards could also quite feasibly support monopolies if ever they happened to fall under the control of a single corporation. Significantly, this fact alone would not necessarily put them in violation of U.S. anti-trust laws, since these monopolies could plausibly come about as unprejudiced market outcomes, rather than be sustained by any explicitly anti-competitive practices.

In a network power framework, this fact is easy to understand: where a technology embodies a successful standard, economies of scale will drive the adoption of that standard by increasing numbers of users, leading to the establishment of a single, universal standard of coordination, all else being equal. This solution is efficient at one level, but, as with any successful standard, it threatens to undermine innovation and local flexibility. It also threatens to give too much control to a single private actor, if the standard is privately owned or controlled. An interesting literature on "flexible production" has studied this problem of achieving economies of scale within regimes of relatively decentralized ownership and production in which innovation and autonomy are less at risk.[14]

In extreme cases, network power will propel successful standards to positions of complete monopoly (in the domain of high technology as well as elsewhere), giving a single private actor enormous power over the relations of sociability where those relations are based on a proprietary (that is, privately owned) standard. In the specific case of Microsoft, it seems that these relations of sociability swamped the countervailing power of sovereignty through the functional equivalent of a "pay-off" to the Bush administration, however legal its campaign contributions may have been under U.S. electoral law. In an economic system committed to competitive markets—and, wherever necessary, sustained by government intervention to support competitive conditions—perhaps the only real solution to this problem is to address the network power of technology not at the level of business regulation, but at the level of intellectual property. The problem may not be that one standard will overtake others given our desire to cooperate in as large a network as possible, but rather that any private company (or, more generally, any single actor) should own or control that standard itself.

In fact, Microsoft faces its greatest challenge from a social movement that contests the idea of private ownership of information standards altogether: the free software movement, sometimes called—though I will distinguish the two below—the "open-source" movement. Individuals, companies, and even countries looking to escape dependence on Microsoft's products have been turning to open-source or free software programs in large numbers. Of particular interest to a range of companies and even countries—including China, Brazil, India, and many in the EU—is the free software operating system *Linux,* which poses a possible long-term challenge to the dominance of Windows.

FREE SOFTWARE

The phenomenon of shared, collaborative production in software and other industries has become increasingly visible in recent years, with a wide variety of legal, sociological, and economic works examining some aspect of this new movement. In many of these discussions, the term "open source" is used interchangeably with that of "free software." Understanding the difference between the two and the politics of standardization in software production requires a brief historical excursus into the development of modern computing and the new networks of production and distribution that it enables.[15]

The story begins with the creation of the "Unix" operating system, which was developed in the early 1970s by scientists working at Bell Labs, the research arm of the then-monopoly AT&T. As Eben Moglen, a law professor and founder of the Software Freedom Law Center, explains, "The idea of Unix was to create a single, scalable operating system to exist on all the computers, from small to large, that the telephone monopoly made for itself."[16] Unix was written in a computer language called "C" which was also a creation of Bell Labs. As the C language "became common, even dominant, for many kinds of programming tasks," by the late 1970s, "the Unix operating system written in that language had been transferred (or "ported," in professional jargon) to computers made by many manufacturers and of many designs."

Initially, AT&T distributed Unix widely, in both academic and industry circles. But it maintained commercial control of the Unix standard and required licensees to pay fees, which were too high for individual computer users to afford. In the course of the 1980s, during the revolution in personal computing, Unix or Unix-like systems became the center of commercial battles in which various companies and industrial consortia backed a particular proprietary version of the operating system. Indeed, although the proprietary operating systems of Microsoft run on a different platform from Unix (called DOS or MS-DOS), Microsoft even marketed an early Unix-like system known as Xenix.

Outside this commercial competition, a researcher at MIT named Richard Stallman—or "RMS" as he is known—developed a version of a Unix-like operating system that he called GNU (a recursive acronym for "GNU's Not Unix"), which he distributed for free. The method of his free distribution is the crucial part of this story, for unlike the earlier developers of Unix (or other operating systems), RMS did not simply distribute the code to any who wanted to use it, for whatever purpose (including the development of proprietary software). Rather, he distributed it under a new form of copyright license that he invented, the GNU General Public License (GPL). Any program that uses free software obtained under the GPL must in turn license itself under the GPL, making its source code available for any computer programmer to adopt, adapt, borrow, give away, or sell, so long as she does not exclude others from doing the same. As Moglen explains, this meant that "anyone could freely modify and redistribute such software, or sell it, subject only to the restriction that he not try to reduce the rights of others to whom he passed it along." The underlying idea is that no person or group of people should be able to control source code, and that everyone should have the ability to see code, work with it, and transform it. The GPL thus uses copyright law to *undo* the usual limitations and proprietary emphasis for which authors turn to copyright—which is why movement adherents have dubbed it "Copyleft." Copyleft stems from a commitment to intellectual freedom and egalitarian or non-dominating social relations of production and sharing—or what RMS called in his famous *GNU Manifesto*, "friendship" among programmers.[17] The third version of the GPL—"GPL v. 3"—is now being drafted online in a participatory manner, to guard against more recent threats to free software.

The initial gift of code that RMS provided under the GPL has since been incorporated into many later innovations, which have been released for others to use and adapt. The most significant of these later contributions to free software was the development of the "Linux" operating kernel for use on personal computers by Linus Torvalds, who released it under the GPL in 1991. The subsequent GNU/Linux development has been a major focus of collaborative development in the free software movement (although other free software programs have also been successful). Moglen explains:

Because Torvalds chose to release the Linux kernel under the
Free Software Foundation's General Public License . . . the hundreds and eventually thousands of programmers around the
world who chose to contribute their effort towards the further
development of the kernel could be sure that their efforts
would result in permanently free software that no one could
turn into a proprietary product. Everyone knew that everyone
else would be able to test, improve, and redistribute their im-
provements. Torvalds accepted contributions freely, and with
a genially effective style maintained overall direction without
dampening enthusiasm. The development of the Linux kernel
proved that the Internet made it possible to aggregate collections of programmers far larger than any commercial manufacturer could afford, joined almost non-hierarchically in a
development project ultimately involving more than one million lines of computer code—a scale of collaboration among
geographically dispersed unpaid volunteers previously un-
imaginable in human history.

Due to the ongoing development of the Linux operating system, Torvalds's
original contribution now represents only a fraction of the kernel, which
has grown substantially as a result of the contributions of others.

This model of free software development is now often called open-source
production. However, the term "open source" was deliberately adopted
in 1998 by programmers building off the success of GNU/Linux who
wanted to avoid what they felt were the undesirable political connotations
of the word "free" in "free software," and who had a variety of personal and
ideological disputes with RMS and his Free Software Foundation. The idea
of "open source" has since then attracted increasing press coverage and commercial attention. As the Open Source Initiative (OSI) admits, "This termi-
nological debate is understood by all parties to be a proxy for wider issues
about the community's relationship to the business world."[18] The term
"open source" as a depoliticized alternative to "free software" has also been
promoted by Eric Raymond, a libertarian computer programmer, celebrity
hacker, and self-described "anarcho-capitalist," who has expressed a variety
of controversial public positions supporting unrestricted access to firearms
and an intensification of American military campaigns overseas.[19]

"Open-source" software may sound as though it is simply "free software" rebranded for marketing purposes, built on the base that RMS established with the GPL—but in reality the two forms of software may differ considerably, depending on which particular "open software license" is used, and there are now dozens of licenses that the OSI has certified. The divergences between "open-source" software and free software may continue to grow as the third version of the GPL is produced (under the direction of the Software Freedom Law Center and the Free Software Foundation) to reverse recent developments in "digital rights management" and state-level software patents, both of which threaten to erode the full control that users have over programs licensed under the second version of the GPL.[20] However, this revision poses a threat (so it is argued) to companies using "open-source" software—for example, working off the GNU/Linux kernel—but which do not want to be forced to open all their code as would be required under the GPL v. 3. Whether these companies are trying to privatize a common resource in a way that contravenes the spirit of "free software" is a point of controversy among programmers.

The importance of free software can be understood in terms of its network properties. A proprietary standard like Microsoft's Windows operating system can come to occupy a monopolistic position, like any universal standard, exhibiting what Max Weber called "dominancy by virtue of a structure of interests," or what I have described here as "network power." A proprietary standard of that kind is *available,* in that it is open for new users to adopt (usually contingent on payment of some kind), but it is not necessarily either *compatible* or *malleable.* Indeed, the incompatibility of Microsoft standards with other programs has proved a serious source of friction for the company, provoking ongoing litigation against it. But this combination of network properties—availability, incompatibility, and non-malleability—is a "winning" combination for a universal standard, as I described in Chapter 6.

By contrast, free software is available, compatible, and malleable. Its difference from proprietary standards lies not in the code itself, but in the forms of intellectual property underlying it. As Eben Moglen explains, "This use of intellectual property rules to create a commons in cyberspace is the central institutional structure enabling the anarchist triumph." The triumph lies not only in the superior productivity that comes from mobilizing large numbers of people to collaborate in a non-hierarchical manner on a common endeavor—as we see in the case of GNU/Linux—but in the creativity and personal freedom that has flourished thereby. This triumph, it should also be said, subsists despite not being reflected in market share (at least in the operating system market), since most consumers do not use free software or open-source programs. Why they do not is, in part, because of a problem we have seen before: the lock-in to a dominant standard that provides social coordination.

GLOBAL QUALITY MANAGEMENT: THE ISO 9000
To illustrate these dynamics using a less familiar (and less controversial) example, consider the rise to global prominence of the ISO 9000, a set of codified principles for quality control in production that is still largely unknown outside the organizations that use it. The ISO 9000 is neither high tech nor politically contentious, and so it is well suited to being analyzed for our purposes. It is a standard that provides a solution to a global coordination problem: how quality control should be assessed up and down the chains of global production and commerce. It specifies a set of principles for quality control assessments promulgated by the primary international standards body, the International Organization for Standardization (ISO). The various standards promulgated by this body are numbered and use the title, "ISO," a name whose origin is a matter of some speculation, with some assuming that it is an acronym for International Standards Organization and others arguing that it is a word derived from the Greek "isos," which means equal. (In this latter formulation, ISO is used because it is through ISO standardization that companies are rendered "equal.") The ISO creates standards for almost every area of technical and industrial work, with the exception of electronics, which remains within the purview of the International Electrotechnical Commission (IEC). Most ISO standards suggest ideals and targets in technical and other fields: they are, for the most part, product standards.

The ISO 9000, by contrast, is essentially a management standard, a process-oriented scheme for disclosure of assessment rather than one for product quality. It is by far the most widely known management standard, with the ISO having certified almost 900,000 organizations in 161 different countries as conforming to it at the time of this writing.[21] According to some scholars, the ISO 9000 seems to be losing some of its luster in the advanced industrial world as problems with the standard emerge.

Nevertheless, particularly in developing world economies without reputations for consistent product quality, ISO 9000 certification provides entry into global markets linking disparate and distant contributors in a chain of production, without which smaller suppliers without an international reputation might be left out. Notably, its impact is even felt outside the world of private business, as some law courts and government bodies have also begun seeking ISO 9000 certification.[22] How effective this set of quality control standards will prove in certifying bureaucratic rather than commercial operations remains to be seen.

The ISO 9000 is a standard in the second sense that I discussed in Chapter 1, a *membership standard*. It does not inherently govern any social relations—as English does in structuring speech, for example, or as code governs computing—but provides a target for compliant companies and organizations, useful as a signal to others. It specifies what aspects a business must review, how to conduct internal audits, and procedures for disclosing which quality control assessments were made. Consisting of five distinct but related standards, the ISO 9000 ensures formalization of documentation so that a company can see what kinds of assessments a supplier has performed, and will understand the results of those assessments. Certification by private, and usually commercial, third-party auditors is the common way that a company demonstrates conformity with the standard. Importantly, while the standard provides a way to document quality assessment, it does not specify any particular quality control systems for adoption. What it offers is a standard by which a company can make sense of the quality assessment procedures that were performed by the company from which it receives supplies.

This may seem a step removed from what is of most interest to consumers—the level of product quality—but what it enables is something more basic: a way of talking about what kinds of quality assessments have been done without yet specifying a particular target level. A client company that demands ISO 9000 certification from its suppliers can rely upon a single comprehensive and comprehensible standard rather than needing to navigate the divergent standards of many different possible suppliers or to enforce its own assessment procedures on them. Thus, the ISO 9000 encourages conformity not at the level of actual production—or even in the assessment of that production—but in the way that such assessments are disclosed and communicated. It represents the standardization of the international language of business management, offering a system that makes internal audits accessible to outsiders, providing needed clarity as a business attempts to understand what a supplier wants to communicate about its production process. Seen in this light, as a mechanism for enhancing communication and disclosure, its widespread use becomes more understandable. It is a form of recognition and signaling in the complex global marketplace. Indeed, while the benefits of ISO 9000 certification remain hotly contested, one recent study has concluded that certification is a benefit to compliant firms, not because of any operational changes it brings about but because certification reduces "informational asymmetries" in the market.[23]

THE NETWORK POWER OF THE ISO 9000

As with any global network, the ISO 9000 has a history that explains its current dominance.[24] It emerged out of earlier standards—a number of them, in fact. Its immediate predecessor was the British Standard BS 5750, published by the British Standards Institute in 1979 for use in the military and public utility sectors. In 1987, the BS 5750 had its scope expanded to include service-providers, and in 1988, the International Standards Organization adopted it without any revisions and renamed it the ISO 9000.

Interestingly, the British Standard BS 5750 was itself the earlier product of Cold War–era military integration: the British Standards Institute adapted British military quality control standards for use in civilian manufacture. These military standards came from earlier NATO versions, but the original standard was the U.S. Department of Defense standard for quality control (MIL STD 9858A), which was developed during and following World War II, and on which the later NATO standard was based.

Thus, the ISO 9000 standards derive from military methods for the control and monitoring of suppliers, which is no surprise given that warfare in an industrialized and global world necessarily unites many local suppliers in a worldwide network. But the ISO 9000 is even more deeply linked to government patronage. It gained considerable prominence when the European Commission began promoting it as a way of integrating management practices across the diverse member states of the European Common Market. In fact, owing to this early European support, more European manufacturers are ISO 9000–compliant than American firms. However, American firms are increasingly becoming certified, largely in response to client demand—whether from European subsidiaries in the United States or U.S. government agencies. (Ironically, some American businessmen see the ISO 9000 certification as a costly process necessary to satisfy European customers—as an onerous European "import"—unaware that it was first designed by the United States military and exported to Europe in the context of World War II and the Cold War, from where it is only now being re-imported as a civilian standard.) Many European and American regulatory agencies require ISO 9000 certification—or that of ISO 9001, a similar standard for medical suppliers—as part of regulatory compliance. Further, U.S. and European military purchasers, both within NATO and in national militaries, require ISO 9000 certification from suppliers. U.S. and EU non-military government purchasers are also increasingly coming to insist on certification, where it is not already required.

With important government agencies and their suppliers requiring ISO 9000 certification, private parties face increasing pressure to become compliant as a way of accessing this significant market share. The network of industries using the earlier BS 5750 series of the British Standards Institute grew because military suppliers and government agencies required it, thus providing a large and relatively stable market. The standard thus surpassed the threshold of visibility owing to the support of government patrons willing to develop and promulgate it, which in turn led to its adoption by the International Standards Organization.

While we might suppose that *intrinsic* reasons drove its initial creation and adoption by the military, the proliferation of ISO 9000–compliant businesses and other organizations would seem to suggest that *extrinsic* reasons have recently been playing a more significant role. (Indeed, the growth of the ISO 9000 appears to be client-driven: according to numerous management studies, certification has become an aspect of contract negotiations and is adopted mainly in response to customer demand.) The prominence of the ISO 9000 is owed in large part to its support from the state. The standards underlying the ISO 9000 gained prominence because of their establishment by and link to state actors, after which other government agencies linked back to it, piggybacking on the standard in the construction or revision of regulatory schemes. Once it gained followers in the world of private business by virtue of this co-evolution with the state, the ISO 9000 began to spread by what we might consider *the merger of force and reason*, similar to the recent trajectory of the network power of the English language. The ISO 9000 is now a standard that many businesses feel they "must" adopt, or else face losing customers.

Thus, in any given market sector in which this demand becomes sufficiently widespread, reason and force merge, and the ISO 9000 passes the threshold of inevitability. To be active in that sector, then, ISO 9000 certification becomes a requirement, as it is now in aeronautics, auto manufacture, and defense contracting, for example. Clearly, the ISO 9000 functions as a market signal in the global coordination of production, as is evidenced by the fact that executives complain it does not help their businesses run more efficiently but is nevertheless required by customers. In fact, they indicate the opposite: that certification is costly and time-consuming, and often a barrier to achieving product quality that cannot be documented according to ISO 9000 rules.[25] Nevertheless, they rationally choose to certify as ISO 9000–compliant given the demands of commercial coordination.

PUBLIC CONTROL OF TECHNICAL STANDARDS

I introduced the ISO 9000 to make four related points about the control and promulgation of technical standards in globalization, which pertain to the fight over operating systems too. First, given its widespread and increasing use worldwide, manufacturers with a broad base of clients overseas feel under increasing pressure to become ISO 9000–compliant, even where the clientele demanding certification does not yet exist. Expecting that potential clients either want or will want certification, many firms are adopting the ISO 9000 as preemptive strategy to gain access a larger number of potential clients. Managers choose to become certified because it provides a signal to possible customers, even though they often feel simultaneously that the certification is a waste of resources and accomplishes little internally.

Second, the role of the state in the early life of a standard—in its design and initial propagation—may be critical to its emergence and internationalization, even though these standards may be essentially private rather than public, spreading through voluntary choice rather than legislation or regulation. In fact, a standard may gain prominence by its early link to the state (in one form or another), but once established also provide a convenient benchmark that unrelated state agencies (and other governments) may use as a reference point in turn.

Third, as the ISO 9000 becomes seen as the international industry standard, its content is increasingly the site of political contestation. Environmental and labor groups want to link various corporate-responsibility standards to ISO 9000 certification, so that the core function of market signaling which the standard provides would be tied to these other objectives, for example, fair labor practices as articulated by the International Labor Organization (ILO). It is interesting to note that the demand for linkage here is to a private standard exhibiting network power, not to a multilateral treaty organization like the World Trade Organization, which depends on government participation.

Finally, within companies, too, the standard has a political edge—one of the main benefits that executives report having come from ISO 9000 certification is the establishment of new routines of worker supervision, self-monitoring, and continual internal auditing which employees would otherwise resist. If these changes are represented as integral to ISO 9000 certification, which is perceived as a common and non-negotiable need for company survival, they are accepted more easily. The standard may thus serve as an alibi for a set of other purposes, which are themselves frequently left obscure or unstated.[26]

Currently, the ISO 9000 functions like an open-source quality control standard, owned by no one but usable by any number of parties, public or private. Now imagine instead that a single, multibillion-dollar corporation owned (or otherwise took control of) the ISO 9000. Suppose that in 1988, instead of the International Standardization Organization adopting it, the BS 5750 was bought by an American multinational that licensed it for a fee to users. Assume further that the same process currently driving the globalization of the ISO 9000 would lead companies to use the privately owned ISO 9000, pushing it to a monopoly position. (Of course, the corporation might help this along with anti-competitive practices that undermined competing quality control standards in their initial stages and by buying out and assimilating more advanced competitors.) Given the four points just discussed about the ISO 9000—its history of public use and links to state support, the politics of its adoption internally and externally, and its emerging universality—we might feel very uncomfortable with a single business controlling the widely used standard as if it were just any form of private property. (We are leaving aside specific anti-trust legal violations or the economic effects of monopoly ownership that we might also consider.) For the truth is that the ISO 9000 is not a form of private property in the same way that someone's backyard may be. Its value comes entirely from its common, social use as a coordinating mechanism, as a signaling device. The form of private property here resembles not the ownership of a car, but the private control of a language—not a rival good but a conventional one or an "anti-rival" good, in that the more people who use it, the more valuable it is for others to use in turn. In the case of a privately owned ISO 9000, one strategy the government might employ to neutralize some of the anti-competitive effects would be to refuse to privilege any single owner with final control over the standard—which might be especially important given that the "good" in question takes its value from (and in turn mediates) social relations. However, to keep the standard open would require a different kind of legal regime than one resembling private possession; it would require, in effect, de-privatizing the standard.

To return (with the example of the ISO 9000 in mind) to the Microsoft case and the battle over operating system standards, an analogous remedy—and one that was considered originally along with the breakup of the company—would require Microsoft to open its code to competitors so that all of its rivals could claim equal property in it. While this remedy was not imposed in the end, the question of intellectual property proves unavoidable, since New Economy monopolies rely on such property rights over standards. Even the rather modest requirement that Microsoft separate its web browser from its desktop still broaches the status of intellectual property—that is, the extent of Microsoft's copyright over Windows and whether it can use that right to require computer manufacturers to bundle Microsoft's other applications with it.

The extent to which we should grant and protect private control of widely used standards is a question that will continue to plague us in an age of network power, regardless of how any particular court case proceeds.[27] Whether a standard in common use is more like a language or more like someone's backyard is analytically clear: it is obviously more like a language than a discrete object or piece of land. Furthermore, it is more like a language than even a particular expression in language, such as someone's novel. But this analytic distinction does not settle the matter: we could still permit private control of common standards if it were beneficial. Deciding whether it is beneficial or not requires entering into a much broader series of debates about politics and production than we have so far allowed ourselves. Part of the problem, of course, is that powerful private interests often have a great deal at stake in our deciding that widely used standards—like Microsoft's Windows—should be granted the same kind of legal status that we accord to someone's backyard, even if (unlike someone's backyard) they are indispensable to our productive and creative relations with one another.

The nineteenth-century complaint that private ownership represents a form of theft will surely be substantiated ever more dramatically in the twenty-first century, whether or not we choose to make that charge explicitly. For consider the point: the value that a particular standard has is only partly a function of its intrinsic properties; more often, I have argued, it is the *community of users* that makes a standard valuable, for extrinsic reasons. In other words, *we* through our social coordination provide the value which successful private actors—first-movers in the relations of sociability—then skillfully cash in on. It could be otherwise, if we decided to use the power of sovereignty to reshape the private relations of sociability. For example, we could have voted to have Microsoft Windows (or an alternative) serve as a universal standard or to regulate access to it in a manner that would encourage a diverse range of compatible alternatives. Instead, we waited to see what the aggregation of our individual, decentralized, and interdependent choices would deliver to us—and now we protect the result as "private property."

It may be true that the benefits of scale make sharing a single standard desirable in many instances. In these cases, if we can build properties of malleability into that single shared standard, we will be able to alter and revise it more easily later—an attractive feature of free software that is not available with closed proprietary standards. If we can build properties of compatibility into it, the pressure to abandon less dominant standards will decrease, preserving a richer variety of alternatives. But even where these ameliorations are not possible and we must adopt a universal standard, we are not required to give possession of it over to any private agent—and there may be many good reasons, including those concerning creativity, workplace autonomy, and system-level efficiency, for refusing to do so. In the case of Microsoft Windows, however, the universalization of one particular operating standard came about via the private relations of sociability rather than through public deliberation and collective choice.

TECHNOLOGICAL UTOPIANISM

One reason that we do not arrive at shared standards through public deliberation and collective choice is that many opponents of proprietary standards remain ambivalent (or outrightly hostile) toward the public agency that such collective choice-making involves. Indeed, how best to counter the power that private actors have over technical standards remains the subject of a debate that reveals the "technological utopianism" of the open-source movement. Many movement adherents partake of a libertarian or anarchistic temperament, expressing a skepticism or hostility to organized politics, deriding the "state" or the "government." But it is one thing to claim that a particular government is corrupt or inefficacious —witness the U.S. decision to settle with Microsoft—and quite another to miss the ways in which the relations of sovereignty can be used to tackle problems which emerge as a result of the untrammeled dominance of the relations of sociability. Indeed, the skepticism that many open-source adherents express in relation to public agency borders on a more general failure to appreciate the essential role of politics in fashioning and maintaining emancipated and egalitarian social relations in digital production.

Technological utopians are right to praise the new forms of "peer production" and the new electronic "share economy" that have emerged in the networked information economy, and which are prominently associated with open-source collaboration. The fantastic or "utopian" element that I want to identify is emphatically *not* the idea that there can be non-dominated, relatively egalitarian, or emancipated forms of productive activity, but rather that these relations of sociability can survive without the mobilization of a broader democratic politics of sovereignty on their behalf. My contention is that, like the right-wing anarchism of "libertarianism," today's left-wing anarcho-syndicalist movements—including the new forms of "technological utopianism"—fail to recognize adequately that only the organized power of sovereignty can counter powerful private agents.[28]

As an example of this kind of argument, I could choose any number of anti-government screeds posted online but will take as my starting point a sophisticated contribution, *The Wealth of Networks,* recently published by law professor Yochai Benkler. I want to state at the outset that Benkler's analysis of these issues is elegant and insightful, and that what I want to scrutinize critically is not his commitment to a free networked information economy, but the strategies that he supposes will be effective in defending it. Benkler examines in great detail the success of collaborative, networked production, offering an analysis of the subject that exhibits the combination of skepticism toward organized politics and concomitant hope for non-dominated, voluntaristic relations of sociability that characterizes technological utopianism. Benkler signals this skepticism about sovereignty and his support for voluntarism at the beginning of his book, writing that his "approach heavily emphasizes individual action in non-market relations," and adding that "the state plays no role, or is perceived as playing a primarily negative role" in most of his argument. His admits that his argument, therefore, "seems more of a libertarian or anarchistic thesis than a liberal one," and suggests that this is because "what is special about our moment is the rising efficacy of individuals and loose, non-market affiliations as agents of political economy."[29] He then narrows his position further, arguing that his thesis is less a "libertarian" one—since he wants to deny or curtail claims to intellectual property—than it is "anarchist, focused on the role of mutual aid and highly skeptical of the state."[30] Indeed, Benkler's assessment of state action is nowhere positive: "the state in both the United States and Europe has played a role in supporting the market-based industrial incumbents of the twentieth-century information production system at the expense of the individuals who make up the emerging networked information economy." He is quick to qualify that this hostility comes less from a commitment to an anti-statist philosophy than from his conclusion that "there is more freedom to be found through opening up institutional spaces for voluntary individual and cooperative action than there is in intentional public action through the state."[31]

Against the alliance of the state and powerful market actors, Benkler argues in favor of non-dominated relations of sociability. He believes that it is in new technological networks—signal instances of the constructive force of voluntarism—that real freedom (and wealth) is to be found. The state should facilitate these constructions and otherwise attempt to do no harm: "Once the networked information economy has stabilized and we come to understand the relative importance of voluntary private action outside of markets, the state can begin to adjust its policies to facilitate nonmarket action and to take advantage of its outputs to improve its own support for core liberal commitments."[32] Thus the relations of sovereignty function in Benkler's thought primarily in the form of an antagonist, "the state," which is largely ignored or else held suspect. Actual politics, on this account, bears an obscure relation, at best, to "the state." For example, Benkler notes that "How we shall live in this new [technological] environment will in some significant measure depend on policy choices that we make over the next decade or so," and he argues further that "we must recognize that [these choices] are part of what is fundamentally a social and political choice."[33] But the political will motivating such choices remains curiously distinct from the organized, coercive power of "the state," as if the sovereign were not, at least in a democratic system, *we ourselves*, but someone else entirely: someone to be held at arm's length, to be bargained with cautiously, to be watched attentively. It is hard to see, on such an account, how the policies that Benkler rightly suggests that we need—such as limitations on intellectual property rights, a rolling back of copyright extensions, and support for public open-source platforms in a variety of different technical settings—could ever be enacted given the gulf he envisions between the non-dominated, solidaristic setting of the relations of sociability and the essentially unaccountable and unresponsive relations of sovereignty.

PROPERTY AND PRODUCTION

The problem with failing to appreciate the role of sovereignty—and imagining that flourishing relations of sociability can somehow endure independently of it—is not just that it distorts our understanding of politics but that it limits what we can grasp about the relations of sociability too. For example, if we consider why these new possibilities for a non-dominated sociability have arisen, Benkler directs us to new *technological* possibilities: the contours of the new network technologies that distribute access to the means of production widely and inclusively, allowing for new forms of "peer production" based on collaborative sharing in non-market contexts.[34] New technologies are no doubt part of the issue, but his argument takes us to the heart of a longer-running debate about the nature of property and its role in production. Benkler explains: "the primary raw materials in the information economy, unlike the industrial economy, are public goods—existing information, knowledge, and culture. Their actual marginal social cost is zero. Unless regulatory policy makes them purposefully expensive in order to sustain the proprietary business models, acquiring raw materials also requires no financial capital outlay."[35] This is an argument that Benkler repeats at several points, drawing a contrast with the "industrial" mode of production that came before the new "information" economy. For example, he writes: "The capital cost of effective economic action in the industrial economy shunted sharing to its economic peripheries. . . . The emerging restructuring of capital investment in digital networks . . . [is] at least partly reversing that effect."[36]

Here and elsewhere, Benkler assumes that there is, straightforwardly, a "capital cost" that falls out (as it were) of the basic terms of the neoclassical production function in economic theory. But this assumes that the return to capital is independent of the social struggles that Benkler diagnoses in the current fight over control of the information economy. The truth is much more complex—as the so-called capital controversies of the 1950s revealed.[37] Indeed, the cost of capital is a function of a broader set of property relations, in the industrial as much as in the information economy. After all, property ownership mediates access to something, whether material or immaterial, in a *social* setting; it is purely a social relation, a relation among people, not between people and things. The complaint of left anarchists to the effect that "property is theft" (as Proudhon famously put it) was intended to suggest precisely this claim: that it is *labor* that is productive, and that the relations between labor and capital are neither natural nor necessary, but depend instead on background conditions of power operating through property.

Thus, instead of seeing the emergence of the networked information economy as linked in some critical way to the earlier efforts of the free software movement—for example, in the initial gifts of code by politically motivated actors like RMS which led to alternative regimes of shared property—Benkler emphasizes an allegedly natural "cost of capital" that happens now to be distributed in an arrangement more favorable to nondominated work relations. He argues: "The current networked stage of the information economy emerged when the barrier of high capital costs was removed. The total capital cost of communication and creation did not necessarily decline. Capital investment, however, became widely distributed in small dollops, owned by individuals connected in a network."[38] On this view, not only was the rise of the industrial economy a function of capital costs, considered naturalistically and thus as outside the social relations of contestation or struggle, but the information economy, too, emerges necessarily from the structure of objective costs: "The rise of peer production is neither mysterious nor fickle when viewed through this lens. It is as rational and efficient given the objectives and material conditions of information production at the turn of the twenty-first century as the assembly line was for the conditions at the turn of the twentieth."[39]

This naively functionalist economic history is not intended ironically. Strikingly for someone concerned with the social relations of production, Benkler seems to have missed (or else is content to neglect for some other reason) the vigorous and lively debates that occurred in early industrialism over the justice and efficiency of capitalist production. Those debates matter today because their participants took positions that were in fact very similar to the sort of arguments now appearing in the open-source movement. Indeed, the fate of these earlier movements asserting a producerist ethic of workplace solidarity may very well be repeated, without a more sophisticated understanding of the complex interplay of politics and production in history.

The workers involved in those earlier struggles would not have accepted that there was a natural, non-exploitative "cost of capital" that determines one set of workplace relations rather than another—the assembly line then and shared digital platforms now. From their perspective, what Benkler calls the "capital cost of effective economic action" could not be considered a natural fact; rather, it emerged from a series of social and political struggles that these workers fought and lost. Indeed, they lost them in part because of the "predatory regulatory policy" that Benkler warns might artificially raise the cost of working together today, but that he does not acknowledge has lain behind every claim ever made regarding the ownership of the means of production, whether of code now or physical machines then. However, the claim of the laborers who took over their factories—and of the anarchist and socialist landlords and factory-owners who gave up their inheritances to found new cooperatives in fits of conscience and social experiment (rather like RMS and the GNU)—was that the allocation of property rights under law obscured the real nature of production. Like Benkler, they argued for greater freedom in workplace relations and for a new kind of share economy, but unlike Benkler they thought this was a realistic possibility in their time. Indeed, for the utopian radicals, Lockean socialists, producerists, anarcho-syndicalists and others who featured in the varied and dramatic world of early labor radicalism seen in novel cults of production and science, free-labor communes, and unions, the industrial age promised a new form of production in which the constraints of the past might give way to the solidarity of laboring men. This new age of industrial technology (that Benkler claims was fixed within given economic parameters) seemed as promising to them then as the information economy does to us today.[40] These men had all they needed—so their story went, much as Benkler's goes now—to realize a new world of *social* production: they had their labor. Only their labor was creative, producing not just commodities but even the machines they worked on. Everything else—the alleged dictates of capital, the property claims of the factory owners, the proclamations of the paid politicians to respect "the system"—was just a cover for theft after one manner or another.[41]

ANARCHISM REVISITED

The reason for this brief excursus into labor history is that it supports a more general contention: that every new phase of production—for example, industrial at the end of the nineteenth century, "informational" today—has always begun with a temporary loosening of existing controls over labor, and thus of our settled ideas about the organization of production and the prerogatives of ownership, profit, and capital that attend it. People with the practical skills to participate in the vanguard form of production of their age, whether industrial laborers in the past or computer programmers in the present, often feel empowered and deeply involved in what they experience as a new age of emancipated work—at least, that is, until this kind of work, too, becomes routinized and alienated. The role of their labor in production is clear to them, as is the role of abstract claims to property in imposing obstacles to their work. The claim by free software guru RMS in 1979 that "all software should be free and charging money for software was a crime against humanity"[42] was thus but the latest iteration of Proudhon's argument that "property is theft." RMS's radical claim against property rested on the idea that control over social resources (the "means of production") unjustly and inefficiently privileges some people over others. He made this point succinctly in relation to intellectual property: "'Control over the use of one's ideas' really constitutes control over other people's lives; and it is usually used to make their lives more difficult."[43]

A struggle often follows the development of new productive capacities when powerful parties attempt to take control of them for private profit by asserting special prerogatives or privileges of property. There are usually two responses made by those keen to defend what they see as emancipated forms of production against efforts to appropriate or privatize them. The first is to argue that only the organized politics of democratic sovereignty can preserve the productive, free relations of sociability made (temporarily) possible by the emergence of a new way of working together—a claim associated with Marxists as well as, in a different way, some socialists and liberals. The second, which has been argued by anarcho-syndicalists in the past and by techno-utopians now, is to imagine that we can do without sovereignty (corrupted in the past, as it is now) and focus instead on deepening and strengthening our solidarity in sociability. Every attempt to privately enclose productive resources—whether land, capital, or information —has always generated these two broad responses, in various guises and combinations.

The anarchist response is hostile to the state and hopeful that egalitarian forms of voluntarism will be able to hold out against private power, perhaps in part because they are more productive. For example, Benkler recognizes that current efforts to control free software and enclose the "digital commons" come from legal maneuvers by powerful private parties: "The political and judicial pressures to form an institutional ecology that is decidedly tilted in favor of proprietary business models are running head-on into the emerging social practices [of the open-source movement]."[44] However, his faith is not so much in reforming the relations of sovereignty such that they will be able to tilt the "institutional ecology" in the other direction (away from the corporations and in favor of peer production and a non-market, share economy) but in collections of diffuse social movements and NGOs: thus, more sociability to counter sociability. "There is already a more significant social movement than existed in the 1990s in the United States, in Europe, and around the world that is resisting current efforts to further enclose the information environment."[45] Yet how these movements—these forms of beneficent voluntarism in civil society—will counter private power without engaging organized politics is unclear.

This anarchist position seems committed to two beliefs about the state and its relation to individual agency. First, there is usually some version of the claim that, as Marx put it polemically, the state is but "the executive committee of the bourgeoisie," or, as a techno-utopian might argue today (without necessarily grasping Marx's deeper structural argument), the government has been bought by Microsoft lobbyists. Marx didn't stop at that description, of course, but the anarcho-syndicalists do, moving from that assessment to a second, more dubious claim that private agency operating through virtuous or egalitarian relations of sociability is an appropriate and adequate response to the corruption of state power. This is the extraordinary thought that provoked some of Marx's frustration with Proudhon and fueled the later ideological battles between Marxists and their anarchist rivals on the left: that it is somehow easier or better to elude the state than to claim it for ourselves.

On the Marxist reading, however, the anarchist position is not so much a strategy as an error. For the relations of sovereignty do not exist beyond or outside us such that we can part ways with them, the better to take control of our immediate lives and circumstances. (Indeed, the anarchist response replicates the theoretical division between state and civil society that Marx put in a great deal of intellectual effort to overcome.) We cannot ever disengage from a corrupt state, since we cannot ever do without politics—at least not for very long and not for very many of us. We can only take it back, restoring the proper relations of sovereignty under which, subsequently, a set of subsidiary rules governing sociability can be put into effect. If there is a reason to form voluntary coalitions, such as the movements of NGOs that Benkler applauds, it must be as part of an effort to capture the power of sovereignty and put it to use in this way. On this view, organized political power is to be seen as the prize at the end of social struggle, because ultimately only centralized power can halt the enclosure of common resources by private parties and defend a robustly egalitarian vision of human flourishing. By contrast, on the anarchist view, organized politics appears as the threat against which, in a Sisyphean task, we are perpetually defending ourselves.

It would be a shame if we lost the evident advances that the new network technologies promise because of a conceptual confusion about politics and its role in production, both historically and currently. For even if the new digital economy offers an objectively more promising terrain for arrangements that favor non-dominated work relations than did, say, the nineteenth-century factory, it is also more distant to most people and, at least as the situation now stands, far from being a site of visibly organized resistance. The open-source movement should not suppose that it can forever counter private economic power with private virtuous action —whether in the egalitarian social relations of online collaboration or through loosely coordinated attacks by hackers on monopolistic corporations—lest it end up, like anarcho-syndicalism in the early twentieth century, ceding the organized power of the state to its capitalist opponents. Then all that would remain of this latest producerist initiative would be to reflect nostalgically on the free Internet of the 1990s in the way that anarchists once looked back to the Barcelona of 1936: there, once and briefly, we ran things ourselves.

THE POLITICS OF FREE STANDARDS

Not all open-source or free software advocates imagine that the free relations of sociability could survive outside or beyond the state. Indeed, the original free software pioneers that started the whole movement with their gifts of labor, political commitment, and legal innovation have long recognized the importance of democratic politics in fostering the practical conditions for non-dominated relations of production. RMS in his *GNU Manifesto* and Eben Moglen in his amusingly titled *dotCommunist Manifesto* make it clear that the practical conditions for enduring anarchist production depend upon a favorable political background.[46]

The lawyers and law professors who, like Benkler, work to support these networked forms of production and distribution are also, on the whole, keenly aware of the necessity of politics. The inescapability of politics has become all the more clear as new and powerful forms of digital "enclosure" have been enacted in recent legislation, such as in the Digital Millennium Copyright Act of 1998. In this context, law professor Lawrence Lessig argues: "We will not reclaim a free culture by individual action alone. It will also take important reforms of laws. We have a long way to go before the politicians will listen to these ideas and implement these reforms."[47] Lessig recognizes that the maintenance of a free culture by private action alone is impossible. It requires collective political will—not just the virtuous actions of individuals—to preserve a free culture.

Another law professor who has written critically on these issues, James Boyle, argues that real freedom in the creation and distribution of intellectual property "must be taken through collective action and imagination, through the postulation of a fictive 'we' that becomes real only in the context of a practice which presupposes the very community it calls into being." Boyle offers here a succinct and elegant definition of democratic sovereignty, of the "we" defined through politics capable of keeping a free culture unenclosed. Boyle continues, making the point even more explicit: "The intellectual land grab I have described here can be halted, and even pushed into reverse," but he recognizes that doing so will require that a general will be constituted through an organized politics.[48] Indeed, it seems unclear how much progress the free software movement can make today against the process of digital enclosure—enabled now by the sort of looser "open-source" licensing against which the GPL v. 3 is directed— without a public *political* commitment to egalitarian modes of production.

Once we see that the ultimate aim of the movement for "free software" is the autonomy that we have in our work relations with each other, and that this autonomy requires common, rather than private, control of the standards that we use in production, then our focus should shift to considering the kind of politics that can ensure public control of the digital means of production that we currently use, as well as any that may come to exist in the future. Importantly, a mobilized political will capable of defending a free networked information economy would not, naturally, have to be restricted to that purpose alone. It could be put into the service of unalienated and autonomous work relations elsewhere in the economy too—not only in the domain of high technology (where it might be relatively "less costly" to do so) but throughout the industrial economy, the whole of which is similarly governed by standards, proprietary and otherwise, that determine the ways in which we work together. Using sovereignty in this way would require serious political engagement and an effort to build support outside the programming community, in order to preserve and extend the non-dominated relations of production that currently exist within that domain. However, the alternative now being pursued is just the opposite: a retreat to the defense of particular networking platforms in a sort of digital last stand. Whether this will suffice remains to be seen. But it is hard not to suspect that the free networked information economy will not be able to survive in the long run unless today's techno-utopians abandon the errors of their anarchist forebears and fight for non-dominated forms of production in all sectors of the economy, as part of a broadly *political* program.

CHAPTER EIGHT

Global Trade and Network Power

BESIDES THE GLOBALIZATION of technology, the globalization of commerce is one of the most significant features of our age. Here, too, the idea of network power can help us to make sense of how global networks of sociability have been remaking our world—and why the standards on which they depend have the power that they do.

Although there are many different ways in which global trade is managed, the most important—and the most visible—is through the World Trade Organization (WTO), an institution that represents the culmination of several centuries of uneven advance toward a global free trade regime. The series of international agreements that make up the WTO now function as a universal standard, coordinating the trading policies of the vast majority of the world's countries. Unlike many standards that reshape global activity in relatively obscure ways, the WTO is highly visible, and perhaps for this reason it has become the most controversial standards body of the present-day international system. Exploring the way that the WTO has come to structure global trade provides insight into the way that standards for international governance move to universality. Placing it within the more general debate on the desirability of free trade helps us to understand the tensions between sociability and sovereignty in the current global order.

TRADE UNDER THE WTO

The WTO is an international organization based in Geneva, Switzerland, with the objective of helping trade "flow smoothly, freely, fairly, and predictably."[1] As of July 2007, it had 151 member states, with a few dozen more in negotiations to join. The approximately 30 WTO agreements (written up in 30,000 pages of rules) now govern virtually the whole of global trade, with the exception of some significant sectors such as agriculture, finance, and labor. The most important of these agreements regulate the international trade in goods, services, and intellectual property. The WTO administers these agreements, acts as a forum for further negotiations about current and proposed agreements, settles trade disputes, and reviews national policies to judge their compliance with WTO obligations. A series of contentious negotiations to craft new agreements liberalizing trade in agriculture, services, and international investment—the "Doha Round" of trade negotiations—collapsed in the summer of 2006, for reasons I discuss below.

Membership in the WTO requires the ratification of all its existing agreements by a member state's legislature, which often means the overhaul of extensive parts of a nation's regulatory and legal regime. In addition, unless a state was part of the WTO when the organization was first established, admission is predicated on *all* existing members ratifying the state's membership. Despite these strict requirements, almost every country that is not yet a member of the WTO is currently applying to become one, and the WTO's membership has swelled from an original 76 members to nearly double that number. China became a member in December 2001, and the Russian Federation is, at the time of writing, in the final stages of its accession to membership. In 2004, even Iraq and Afghanistan asked to begin talks to join the WTO. American occupation is not always the spur for late arrivals, however; in fact, Iran was able to begin accession talks only after the United States dropped its repeated objections. (The U.S. had blocked Iranian accession in the past on 22 different occasions.) With the accession of these final members, the WTO will have become the organizing framework for all trade among the world's countries, excepting pariah nations and microstates.

The most important objective of the WTO is the liberalization of trade in goods, services, and ideas across national borders. Such free trade requires the elimination of quantitative restrictions and tariffs, but also of policies that constitute "unreasonable" trade barriers. The WTO has built into the multilateral trading system the principle of "non-discrimination," under which goods from a foreign country must be treated in the same manner as domestic goods. (Developing countries are given some support in adopting these measures—mainly in the form of technical assistance and extra time to meet their obligations.) Non-discrimination amounts to awarding most-favored-nation status to all other WTO members, and to receiving it in return. The principle of non-discrimination on the basis of national origin would require, for example, that computers from Taiwan exported to the United States be treated as if they were computers from the United States. Likewise, computers from the United States exported to Taiwan will receive the same treatment as domestic Taiwanese computers. The justification for this principle is that the differences that affect the price of a good should be determined by the value of the good itself—to the qualities that make consumers want to buy it, and not to the prejudices of customs officials or the arbitrariness of national borders. The fact that some computers come from Taiwan—or from Japan or Germany or Malaysia—should be irrelevant to their sale as computers.

Non-discrimination seems straightforward when we consider a tariff regime in which different tariff rates reveal discriminatory trade practice —for example, national prejudices expressed through custom duties. But when looked at from the perspective of divergent national regulatory regimes, violations of this principle are much harder to determine. For example, suppose that the United States subsidizes its computer manufacturers, making it cheaper for them to bring their products to market. Would this policy violate the idea of non-discrimination, in that these subsidies are not available to Taiwanese computer manufacturers and will make American computers cheaper? Under WTO rules, this policy would almost surely be considered an unfair subsidy to U.S. domestic industry, acting as a discriminatory customs regime in disguise. But compare a regulation that requires products sold in the United States to be produced according certain methods, perhaps in order to uphold domestic environmental or labor standards. Such a regulation might run afoul of WTO rules eliminating restrictions based on "process or production methods," which are seen as separate from the final product itself. Increasingly, such domestic economic and industrial policies are coming under scrutiny as "informal" or "indirect" barriers to trade.

THE NETWORK POWER OF THE WTO

The WTO represents the victory of the ideal of global free trade. Its institutional success, however, is probably overdetermined: that is, whatever the intrinsic reasons for which a country might wish to join a free trade organization, it can be made to do so by extrinsic reasons alone, because of its desire to coordinate its commercial policies with those of its trading partners and the world's major economies. The thought here is that a multilateral regime for international trade might have many different objectives and designs, any one of which, if accepted by the world's powerful economies, would quickly become the trading standard to use—independent of the persuasiveness of the specific trade policies it advances.

Indeed, while the WTO's main accomplishment has been to lower trade barriers in certain sectors, we should recognize that it promotes a specific trade regime, governed by formal rules encoded in the agreements which the organization administers and applicable only to certain parts of the global economy, with the notable absence of sectors such as agriculture, foreign investment, and labor. It does not just call for the elimination of trade barriers, but also serves to coordinate the kind of trade—and the kinds of trade-related policy measures—that its member states pursue in particular domains. Taken altogether, then, the WTO agreements can be considered a kind of standard, albeit a complex and multifaceted one, and we should not be surprised to see the WTO exert network power as the coordinator of the multilateral trading system.[2]

Membership in the WTO is predicated on accepting every one of its agreements, which together constitute what I described in Chapter 1 as a membership standard. These agreements establish broad principles in the governance of multilateral trade, for example, the principle of "non-discrimination." It may be that these principles are ones that all member states, including new ones, would have wished to adopt anyway, for intrinsic reasons. Such a possibility cannot be ruled out without a detailed investigation into the particular circumstances of each nation's accession. However, it is clear that whatever the intrinsic reasons, there exist ample extrinsic reasons to join the WTO. The network power of the WTO produces, simultaneously, freer international trade according to its specific rules, and an increasing loss of the freedom to trade in a manner apart from that proscribed by WTO rules. (Whether this is beneficial is a complex empirical question.) Certainly, a country could refuse to join the WTO and attempt individually to negotiate bilateral trade pacts with its current and potential trading partners. But given the difficulty of doing so, and the globally dominant position of the WTO, membership is the easiest option, perhaps even the only credible option for almost every country. WTO advocates often fail to acknowledge—or at least claim not to see—that membership in the organization cannot be reduced to a simple notion of choosing whether or not to join its agreements, given its near total control of world trade.

What are the network properties of the WTO that guarantee its network power? The current WTO is open, non-compatible, and non-malleable, though, importantly, this configuration of network properties has shifted in the course of its development, as I discuss in the following section. It is open in that any nation that will abide by its rules, signing onto the agreements that constitute membership in the organization, is welcome to join it (provided that current member states do not reject it for other reasons). It is non-compatible in that a country cannot trade according to any other standards and remain a member of the WTO in good standing. For example, a country cannot be a member of the WTO and maintain discriminatory trade practices—whether through the outright manipulation of tariff rates or government support for critical industries. WTO standards are thus incompatible with alternative trade or industrial policies; they require strict compatibility of national regimes. It is true that entry into the WTO has been softened by extended grace periods for developing countries unable to jettison their incompatible economic policies all at once. But after these adjustment periods are over, the true incompatibility of the WTO with a diversity of national regulatory regimes will become even more apparent.

Finally, the WTO is relatively non-malleable. Decisions are made by the consensus of national representatives present at any given meeting of the WTO Ministerial Conference, the highest body in the trade organization. Where consensus cannot be reached, WTO procedures allow the decision to be made by a vote. But there has never yet been such a vote, and consensus remains the informal modus operandi. Additionally, some WTO agreements require formal consensus in order to be amended. Besides operating according to consensus decision-making, it should be noted that the WTO operates in relative secrecy. Trade policy negotiations are completed behind closed doors. When public interest groups call on the WTO to be transparent, WTO national representatives respond that trade negotiations would be difficult to finalize if scrutinized during the bargaining process. (Of course, one might very well ask on whose authority these representatives act in private if public scrutiny would indeed undermine any trade negotiations conducted in the open.)

These aspects of WTO decision-making all contribute to the difficulty of revising its core terms. To change any element of the WTO is beyond the ability of any one member, or even a majority or supermajority of members. WTO agreements are revised only by consensus of all members; hence, the standards are malleable only if every member agrees. As discussed in Chapter 6, this configuration of network properties—availability, non-compatibility, and non-malleability—is the ideal combination to maintain and augment network power, at least once the network in question has reached a sufficiently large size.

THE EMERGENCE OF THE WTO

The emergence of the WTO reveals the way in which this combination of network properties came into being over time, effectively augmenting the power of the trading organization. In fact, the real shift in international trade does not come with the WTO, which is only the latest and most successful multilateral trading arrangement. It comes with the move from bilateral, country-to-country trade treaties to a collective, multilateral trading regime capable of coordinating global commerce. Historically, this movement occurred following World War II, during a series of conferences held to establish a new international trading structure. Out of these meetings came a draft charter for an institution called the International Trade Organization (ITO), which was to be the counterpart of the IMF and to set the rules for international trade much as the IMF was designed to set the rules for foreign exchange and serve as the guarantor of the world financial system. However, the U.S. Congress blocked the ITO, for various reasons.[3] Negotiations for a multilateral trading structure finally succeeded in 1947, with the conclusion of negotiations in Geneva that established the General Agreement on Trade and Tariffs (GATT).

Before the establishment of the WTO in 1995, the GATT governed the postwar multilateral trading system. As with the WTO, the GATT comprised both a set of agreements and the organization that oversaw the process of their formation, revision, and maintenance. However, its character as an international organization was much less pronounced than is that of the WTO, and the GATT treaties themselves possessed very little network power. The WTO later incorporated all of the GATT agreements, but also took on the permanent institutional features of an international organization with member states. The GATT also had a much more limited role than the WTO has today: it dealt only with trade in goods across borders, and while it was successful in lowering tariff rates on the international trade in many goods, its overall effectiveness was considered uneven. Throughout several successive "rounds" of GATT negotiations, many powerful nations, including the United States, pushed for a yet deeper liberalization of trade. This pressure resulted in the transformation of the GATT into the current WTO.

The final series of GATT negotiations, the "Uruguay Round" which lasted from 1986 to 1994, laid the foundations for an expanded and updated multilateral trading system, resulting in the creation of the WTO on January 1, 1995. All "contracting parties" to the GATT became "members" of the WTO, which incorporates the GATT, plus a good deal more. It includes a revised General Agreement on Trade and Tariffs covering the trade in goods, and, in addition, two other general trade agreements: a General Agreement on Trade in Services (GATS), which regulates the trade in banking, transport, travel, telecommunications, and other service industries, and the Trade-Related Aspects of Intellectual Property Rights (TRIPS), which covers intellectual property protection. The WTO also includes many specific agreements, such as those governing trade in textiles and clothing, trade-related investment measures, and "Sanitary and Phytosanitary Measures," dealing with regulations for health and safety.

Besides a broadened mandate to cover the trade in ideas and services in addition to goods, the other important change seen in the transition from the GATT to the WTO was the way in which trade disputes are settled. The WTO's *Understanding on Rules and Procedures Governing the Settlement of Disputes* (the Dispute Settlement Understanding or "DSU") updated the GATT dispute resolution system that preceded it.[4] Under the GATT, the implementation of any judgment (called a "panel report") required a *positive* consensus of all contracting parties to adopt it. Therefore, it could be rejected by a single dissent by any country, even the losing party. Hence, judgments were rarely enforced and trade disputes usually remained unresolved. Furthermore, since the GATT intruded less deeply into national regimes, it generated fewer controversies in the first place—though critics charged that this apparent lack of disputes resulted from a lack of any effective forum for the resolution of conflicts in the first place. By contrast, the DSU panel reports of the WTO must be adopted unless there is a *negative* consensus against them. So every member— including the winning party—must vote against a WTO judgment or else it is automatically accepted. Of course, this negative consensus rule leads to decisions that are far more enforceable than those made under the GATT. WTO dispute resolution panels have ruled on many different cases, ranging from the legality of United States regulations requiring turtle-excluder devices (TEDs) to European Union standards for the importation of bananas.

THE GATT AND THE WTO

In the institutional development of the WTO, we have a revealing case of how network properties can evolve with an emerging standard to increase its network power. While the WTO is currently structured to be available, relatively non-compatible, and relatively non-malleable, this configuration of network properties is a recent one. The GATT was very different. In the literature on the history of international trade, the GATT is often characterized as "weak" while the WTO is depicted as "strong." There is more than the relative power of the dispute resolution system at the heart of this picture. What is also implied is the extent to which the GATT and the WTO manage to bring countries into—and keep them abiding by—an enforceable system of international trade.

This difference results from a change in the configuration of network properties. Like the WTO, the GATT was available: countries accepting the General Agreement were welcome to join it. But unlike the WTO, it was compatible with pre-existing national development and industrial policies, because it provided no enforcement mechanism by which countries could be compelled to alter policies at variance with GATT objectives. Membership in the GATT—to the great frustration of free trade partisans—allowed countries to maintain a role in the multilateral trading system without abiding fully by the principle of non-discrimination. It was also what we might consider malleable: since no country was required to accept any ruling against its trade policies, the GATT proved effectively revisable by each country, allowing loose and ongoing participation in world trade without strict conformity to any particular ideal of free trade.

At one level, these network properties made the GATT a relatively toothless institution for advancing free trade ideals, much to the chagrin of advocates of a more liberal postwar trading regime. But the GATT's configuration of network properties worked very well to draw countries into the organization, since formal acceptance of the GATT imposed few real changes to existing domestic economic agendas. For an emerging standard, this combination of network properties is ideal for attracting the largest initial membership, for the obvious reason that membership does not present any real costs. Then, with the support and backing of a large number of adherents, including many of the largest economies, the GATT was transformed into something with more "strength," which looked rather more like the original ITO that free trade advocates had desired: the WTO.

At its peak in 1994, the GATT had 128 contracting parties; the WTO now has 151 members, including significant additions such as China, and the rest of the world's nations largely clamoring to join.[5] Why would a country like China join the WTO but not the GATT? Obviously, the answer involves a significant shift in the stance of the Chinese Communist Party toward integration into a market-driven world economy. But part of the answer must also be found in the network power that the WTO wields but which the GATT did not. Thus, the GATT proved a useful predecessor to the WTO, drawing in countries through its availability, compatibility, and malleability, and then reducing the compatibility and malleability as the share of global trade to which it guaranteed access became significant enough to command conformity on more settled terms.

A UNIVERSAL STANDARD

The current configuration of network properties makes the WTO a "take-it-or leave-it" institution, a standard offering access to lucrative international markets on non-discriminatory terms to any country willing to abide by its dictates. The network power of the WTO is controversial because these dictates prove incompatible with a wide array of domestic policies, many of which are arguably unrelated to foreign trade as it is commonly understood. As the WTO is non-malleable, it is difficult to alter or adapt these dictates to local circumstances. Further, these rules are not restricted to the regulation of tariff regimes alone, mandating non-discrimination in the multilateral trading system. They have begun to dig deep into domestic economic space and internal social regulation, making them not simply "free trade," but "free trade plus," in the opinion of many critics. As with any standard, the WTO exhibits a tension between the cooperation that it provides and the autonomy and experimentation it thereby suppresses.

But note that any such charges against the WTO and the many suggestions as to how best to improve the organization do not function in the way that we expect protest and criticism to function in ordinary politics, for they have little hope of achieving anything. Important as criticism of the WTO is, its actual effect on the organization may prove negligible, since it is already in place and possessed of great network power. To disestablish parts of the WTO or to reestablish the entire organization on different principles—by adopting any of the many reforms offered up for its redesign—will prove difficult given the entrenched institutional positions of various international actors. Unlike some global standards, which are only now beginning to become dominant, the WTO represents a successfully globalized standard, exhibiting all the tensions between international compatibility and local autonomy that, for example, Keynes analyzed in his study of the gold standard, discussed in Chapter 3. These empirical and normative controversies now give way before a universal standard that has, to a large extent, become settled fact.

The WTO offers us an example of a universal standard, a form of sociability with literally global reach, driven forward by network power dynamics. Despite concerns about the particular structure of the WTO, and in spite of broader and more general worries about trade liberalization, the world's nations, driven by extrinsic reasons (if nothing else) now conduct their commercial intercourse according to its conventions. Thus, understood in the language of sociability and sovereignty, the WTO represents a highly developed form of global sociability that now performs some of the functions—and thus holds some of the power—that were formerly in the control of national sovereignties. National sovereignty has thus been fractured, with what formerly constituted its full power now divided among many bodies, only some of which are national representative bodies, such as parliaments. This does not make the WTO a global sovereign (as some of the more radical anti-WTO critics have suggested), but it does mean that some aspects of domestic policy that were formerly under popular (or at least national) control have been transferred to a transnational body of experts.[6]

Against this complaint, the defenders of the WTO often allege that giving up national sovereignty over international trade policy means nothing more than taking away a power that governments can only ever use deleteriously. This defense of the WTO rests, in the main, on a defense of the ideal of free trade. As free trade works to the benefit of all parties— so classical trade theory tells us—then the fact that the WTO usurps the prerogatives of national governments is fine, for those prerogatives could only be exercised, on this account, in one of two ways: according to economic rationality, and therefore in line with what the WTO would require of its members, or against economic rationality, in which case, it is argued, national governments are impoverishing not only their own citizens but the citizens of other countries as well.

WHAT'S WRONG WITH FREE TRADE?

Any deep complaint against the WTO must accordingly contend with the *ideal* of free trade that it embodies. Consider the most general case for trade liberalization usually put forward. Why do nations pursue economic integration, for example, by joining the WTO or negotiating bilateral trade treaties? Obviously, free trade proponents argue, they do so because trade works to the advantage of both parties, enabling each to exploit the comparative advantage the other possesses, just as classical trade theory suggests. Free trade is desirable because it allows each country to concentrate its productive efforts in ways that will give it the most return (and, reciprocally, ensure the same maximum return to its trading partners). The theory of comparative advantage, which underlies trade theory, and indeed all commonsensical arguments in favor of liberalization, is a formal or analytic proposition that adapts the standard defense of the economic division of labor to the context of international trade among different countries.[7] To argue against this theoretical defense of free trade can look like arguing in favor of waste or trying to justify an accounting error.

But, importantly, this theoretical defense of free trade assumes that policy-makers are concerned with *absolute* gains—the increased welfare that trade brings, irrespective of its benefits to the trading partner—and not *relative* ones. If we are concerned only with our absolute level of material welfare, then we may indeed wish for freer trade for all the reasons that classical trade theory tells us we should. If, however, we are worried not just about absolute levels of welfare but also about the relative positions of different countries (including, presumably, our own), then the situation becomes much more complicated.

The most important and obvious arena of relative comparison is military advantage. An absolute level of military capability means nothing, for a country's army is great or small only in comparison to those of its rivals. To the extent that free trade works, it undermines a nation's relative advantage over its rivals by producing economic convergence. Particularly on today's high technology battlefield, economic power can rather easily be converted into military power. Therefore, a country concerned exclusively with economic welfare may support free trade, but a country worried about both welfare and security will have a more ambivalent stance.

This insight quickly brings us to an interesting and neglected fact: that periods of international economic integration have tended to correspond to periods of international hegemonic stability. Great Britain's hegemony underwrote the so-called first globalization, starting in the 1870s through to the Great War, just as it was the unrivaled power of the United States from the early 1990s that resulted in the adoption of the North American Free Trade Act (NAFTA) and its expansion into the Free Trade Area of the Americas (FTAA) and the transformation of the weak GATT into the strong WTO. We should expect the call to free trade to come from the international hegemon, the country (or perhaps bloc of countries) that need not fear the quicker economic growth that trade brings to underdeveloped rivals. But as industrial rivals develop, the cries for free trade become weaker, both from the hegemon, now willing to forgo additional material welfare in return for greater relative security, and among its rivals, who may seek a strategic disengagement from the world economy in order to protect infant industries and support a mature industrial and military policy. In a period of great power rivalry without clear hegemony, we should expect free trade to fall low on the agenda. The call to arms is always stronger than the call to trade; perhaps only a national security expert can trump an economist.

Theorists of *doux commerce*, whether eighteenth-century writers, such as Montesquieu, or early-twenty-first-century popularizers of the same concept, such as Thomas Friedman, are right to spot that freer trade has some kind of relation with more peaceful politics. But they may have misunderstood the nature of the causal relationship between these phenomena. It may be the case not that trade pacifies international relations but that pacific relations are a prerequisite of economic integration. Periods of rapid globalization go hand in hand with periods of international peace, during which countries can worry less about relative and more about absolute levels of welfare. And given that international peace remains (so far at least) a consequence of hegemonic stability and mutual exhaustion, periods of globalization and periods of hegemony come together in waves. The world's leading power can always afford to think about the welfare gains that accrue from trade, and to ignore—for a time—the unsettling thought that economic power translates sooner or later into military might.

In the eighteenth century, at the beginning of Britain's maritime supremacy, David Hume argued for free trade as boldly as anyone ever has: "as a British subject, I pray for the flourishing commerce of Germany, Spain, Italy, and even France itself."[8] A century earlier, amid warring national rivalries, the mercantilists did not share Hume's optimism but instead adopted a protectionist and zero-sum approach to international trade —an approach derided by economists today but perhaps comprehensible given a concern with both national security and economic gain.[9] And a century and a half following Hume, many Britons maintained his optimism despite the rise of their military rival and second largest trading partner, Germany. Sir Norman Angell famously claimed, on the very eve of the First World War, that Germany would never attack Britain, given the interconnections between the two economies.[10] But Britain's free trade regime had provided shelter for the development of its military rival, and the liberal trading order that British hegemony had underpinned came to a violent end. On one reading of history, free trade appears less a formula for global peace than an effective means of amassing wealth for the next war. Certainly, John Maynard Keynes came to think that this was so, despite an earlier commitment to free trade—and for reasons that today's more sanguine commentators would do well to reflect upon.[11]

TRADE AND MULTIPLE EQUILIBRIA

Military power is not the only relative comparison of importance, of course. Even within a purely economic analysis, the consideration of relative and not absolute gains changes our calculations—and even our understanding of the consequences of free trade. Indeed, classical trade theory, with its emphasis on comparative advantage, is being called into question in a world of commerce based not on wool and wine but on semiconductors, biotechnology, and blockbuster films.[12] In a modern economy, comparative advantage is the product of national development strategies rather than fixed natural resources. Therefore, the relative differences between nations that determine the control of emerging and existing markets can generate broader economic outcomes as the product of strategic interaction with similarly situated rivals.

The mathematician Ralph Gomory and economist William Baumol recently argued for a revision of classical trade theory along these lines in a book-length treatment.[13] They contend that classical trade theory fails to take into account dynamics that generate multiple trading equilibria rather than a unique one—a point previously made by John Stuart Mill and others, but to which Gomory and Baumol have now given precise analytic expression. Given the many different possible outcomes, the question becomes not how a country should pursue its comparative advantage (understood statically) but how a country can move toward producing one outcome rather than another—how a South Korea can move from agriculture and labor-intensive production a few decades ago to standing at the forefront of advanced industries such as semiconductors today. The answer is not the invisible hand of free trade—which can generate many different results, according to Gomory and Baumol—but politics: it makes a great difference which policies governments choose to pursue. In competition for emerging industries that exhibit properties like economies of scale—an inconvenience for economic theory routinely encountered in the real world—national policies and national rivalries matter enormously.

One of the interesting insights that Gomory and Baumol present is that trade between nations at a similar level of development (and thus in competition in the same sectors) is most likely to deviate from the conclusions of classical trade theory: "Among developed nations changes that benefit one of them may well come at the expense of the other."[14] For example, the control of new markets or new technologies may disproportionately benefit one country or group of countries over and against its rivals, such that free trade consolidates (or undermines) existing advantages rather than working to the benefit of both countries. This strategic competition may be particularly important between developed countries and their emerging industrial rivals. Trade between such countries may work mainly to the benefit of the more developed country, which can thereby maintain existing advantages and lock in new dominance in new industries.

By contrast, it is trade between a developed and an underdeveloped nation that is most likely to be mutually beneficial and conform to classical economic theory, as these economies are not competing for dominance in the same industries. A more nuanced ethical assessment of globalization would need to account for these dynamics, since free trade may sometimes work to raise living standards, but at other times the benefits of trade liberalization may be missing. On this account, then, economic rivalry alone may be enough to undermine a liberal trading order—and not because of any self-defeating blanket protectionism, but entirely in the pursuit of economic self-interest, according to which free trade might be recommended between certain agents at certain times, but not at others. This theoretical amendment comports better, too, with the limited and very mixed empirical data that we have on the connection between trade liberalization and economic growth or poverty reduction, which offers a picture much murkier and more ambiguous than classical trade theory (and its contemporary proponents) would suggest.[15]

TRADE AND SOVEREIGNTY

On this account, we should be ambivalent, rather than confident, about the benefits of achieving a global free trade regime. That ambivalence will, of course, spill over into our criticism of the WTO as one particular instantiation of a liberal trading regime. Certainly, the WTO has attracted enormous criticism from activists and academics alike since soon after its inception.[16]

One of the most thoughtful criticisms of the WTO comes from Harvard economist Dani Rodrik who asks *what trade is for* such that we should desire more of it. Rodrik points to the mistake of treating trade as an end in itself—as the WTO expressly does—because he argues that free trade is merely a *means* to an end, not something valuable in itself. If we take that end to be, for example, economic development, particularly of the poorest countries in the world, then the rules that we have adopted under the WTO regime may fall short of our objective. Rodrik writes: "Imagine a trading regime in which trade rules are determined so as to maximise development potential, particularly of the poorest nations in the world. Instead of asking, 'how do we maximise trade and market access?' negotiators would ask, 'how do we enable countries to grow out of poverty?' Would such a regime look different than the one that exists currently?"[17] He answers that it certainly would look different, and suggests how the world trading order might be appropriately reformed. He argues in a number of different articles that free trade is not a substitute for a national development policy and, in fact, may even undermine the ability to have a good one in several salient respects.[18] Instead, WTO rules could be made more development-friendly by focusing not on maximizing the volume of trade across borders, but on maximizing the economic development or poverty alleviation that such trade brings. This might be accomplished in part by building in opt-out clauses to protect the long-term interests of developing world countries in certain strategic areas, such as intellectual property or for infant industry protection, bearing in mind the dynamics that Gomory and Baumol introduce in their criticism of classical trade theory.

We should understand these and related suggestions as calling for coordinated collective action in the management of a nation's trade regime —that is, for incursions of sovereignty into the relations of sociability, the better to reshape them for our desired ends. Free trade proponents treat this kind of incursion with great skepticism and hostility, arguing—often on *a priori* grounds—that it is undesirable, a point to which I will return in the following chapter in the discussion of neoliberalism. But for those concerned to make good use of the power of sovereignty, there is a deeper aspect to its erosion beyond the way in which sovereign decision-making is now fractured and conducted at multiple levels, many of which escape the grasp of national politics. For, if a global free market requires a set of background rules, which must not themselves be altered by any one of the participants, then it follows that the rules of a global economy must be placed outside or beyond the reach of politics altogether. On this view, the problem is not that the WTO leads to the *splintering* of national sovereignty (thus degrading the democratic politics operative there), but that it even requires its outright suppression.

The philosopher John Gray has spotted this problem clearly: "Those who seek to design a free market on a worldwide scale have always insisted that the legal framework which defines and entrenches it must be placed beyond the reach of any democratic legislature. Sovereign states may sign up to membership of the World Trade Organisation; but it is that organization, not the legislature of any sovereign state, which determines what is to count as free trade, and what a restraint of it. The rules of the game of the market must be elevated beyond any possibility of revision through democratic choice."[19] After making the case for the unfeasibility of laissez-faire economics (citing the earlier work of Karl Polanyi), Gray concludes: a "reform of the world economy is needed that accepts a diversity of cultures, regimes and market economies as a permanent reality."[20]

This argument will probably be considered vague, unworkable, or downright wrong to most economists today, who are trained in an austere analytics of sociability that makes it hard for many to understand (or even to admit) the inescapability of sovereign power. Notably, this was not always the case; during the interwar years, no less an authority than John Maynard Keynes argued for a greater degree of "national self-sufficiency." Keynes writes that he was "brought up, like most Englishmen, to respect free trade not only as an economic doctrine which a rational and instructed person could not doubt, but almost as a part of the moral law."[21] But in time, he came to believe differently: that for reasons of international peace and national politics, a degree of relative economic isolation among countries was desirable.

> I sympathize, therefore, with those who would minimize, rather than with those who would maximize, economic entanglement among nations. Ideas, knowledge, science, hospitality, travel—these are the things which should of their nature be international. But let goods be homespun whenever it is reasonably and conveniently possible, and, above all, let finance be primarily national. Yet, at the same time, those who seek to disembarrass a country of its entanglements should be very slow and wary. It should not be a matter of tearing up roots but of slowly training a plant to grow in a different direction.[22]

Keynes's argument follows from his view—presented earlier by John Stuart Mill, and more recently by Gomory and Baumol—of the sort of goods that were traded in the economy of his day. Most manufactured goods do not lend themselves necessarily to the kind of international division of labor to which Ricardo famously drew attention in his discussion of the benefits that accrued to both Britain and Portugal when they traded the wool of one for the wine of the other, given that neither could produce domestically what the other had in abundance. Unlike wool and wine, many goods produced today have no "natural" national home, so any and all could, in theory, fall within the ambit of any national economy, given the right sort of industrial policy.[23] But why we should want to move to the sort of "national self-sufficiency" that Keynes recommended is not a question that the abstract analytics of free trade can answer. It must be situated instead in a broader debate about politics and values.

THE END OF THE WTO?

Given the network power of the WTO, no objections to a global free trade regime currently have much traction in modifying what has become a universal standard. However, these objections are arguably at the heart of the failure to produce any new WTO agreements, despite five years of negotiations and intense diplomatic pressure to do so. Indeed, all of the recent WTO ministerial conferences have been derailed by national political differences, leading to a collapse of several years' worth of trade talks.

Following the Uruguay Round that gave birth to the WTO, the next round of trade negotiations was slated to begin as the "Seattle Round" at the Ministerial Conference in 1999. Loud demonstrations and the failure to achieve the required consensus meant that no new agreements emerged there. Instead, a new round began in Doha, Qatar, in 2001, in a secure and isolated location far from any protestors, where diplomatic pressure and the (informal) exclusion of some developing countries enabled fresh talks focused on a "Doha Development Agenda."[24] The Doha Round commenced negotiations for new WTO agreements, pushing forward the liberalization that had begun in the Uruguay Round both by extending it to new sectors of the global economy and by deepening the liberalization required by existing agreements. On the Doha agenda, more specifically, were liberalization in agriculture and manufacturing markets and a new push to standardize investment protection and competition policy—taking up the contentious "Singapore issues" that had been lingering since a Ministerial Conference there in 1996.

If the Doha Round had succeeded, it would have produced new agreements guaranteeing a liberal world economic order, not just in industrial goods but also in agriculture, finance and capital goods, and services. It would have helped to realize what the then-Director-General of the WTO, Mike Moore, called a "world without walls."[25] Of course, the walls were to remain in place when it came to the exchange of people and ideas: labor was to remain trapped within national borders—waiting for mobile capital to arrive from outside—and intellectual property restrictions would have been given new force.

But the ambitions of the Doha Round have yet to be realized. Trade talks faltered in successive WTO ministerial conferences at Cancun in 2003 and Hong Kong in 2005. An attempt to revive the Doha Round took place at a meeting of six key countries in July 2006 in Geneva but came to nothing, following which many commentators declared the Doha Round a "failure." Indeed, it looks as though no new agreements will be forthcoming, despite efforts by the Organization for Economic Cooperation and Development to jumpstart talks in the autumn of 2006. The Doha Round appears to be at an end.

It was a contentious round from the start, with conflicts focused on two sets of issues: agricultural liberalization and the "Singapore issues." As I suggested above, whether we should want to pursue liberalization in any of these areas can be answered only as part of a debate about our politics and our values more generally. However, a dominant theme in both the U.S. and some segments of the British media has been to decry loudly the failure of Doha as a tragedy for the global poor and to lay its collapse at the feet of agricultural protectionism, representing a new "mercantilism" in the rich world.

But should we understand Doha's collapse in these simple terms— crudely put, that the United States and the European Union refused to cut their bloated agricultural subsidies and do the right thing for world trade and the poor? A different interpretation of Doha's failure is simply that a global regime of free trade is not necessarily a desirable aim, perhaps especially in agriculture, finance and other areas of national regulatory concern. Furthermore, although the rich countries of the global north were no doubt playing "mercantilist" games, it is not clear that there are any better games to play, given a concern with both absolute and relative levels of welfare—that is, given a different interpretation of what mercantilist strategies aim to accomplish.

For example, take the most allegedly indefensible position in the latest round of trade talks: the refusal of the industrialized world to relent on protectionist agricultural policies. Now, there are good reasons for the United States and the European Union to rethink many *specific* subsidies, tariffs, and closed markets, both for the benefit of domestic taxpayers and for farmers in the global south. Indeed, although the Europeans are frequently criticized for agricultural protection, the United States is particularly guilty of using agricultural subsidies for short-term political gain (rather than as part of a long-term rural policy) as a payoff to "swing" states empowered by the geographic distortions built into the Electoral College and Senate and to bolster agribusiness lobbies that export to developing world markets.

But at the most general level is it clear that free trade in agriculture is a straightforwardly good thing? Consider the argument recast, not as one about comparative advantage, with agriculture to be viewed as any other commodity, but as concerning *food security*. Put starkly, in a world threatened by transnational terrorism, global plagues, and volatile fossil fuel prices—any one of which could radically disrupt international transport networks—is it prudent (never minding the actuarial details of comparative advantage) to trust one's food supply to global commerce? Why should the citizens of France, say, decide that self-sufficiency in food is not a reasonable *political* goal, whatever the economic calculations that accompany it? These economic calculations might indicate the extra cost of securing a stable food supply at a national level instead of letting global free markets "deliver the goods," but they indicate nothing about the political rationality or irrationality of such a decision.

Citizens who thought, upon surveying the history of global trade and famines, that they would like to keep a significant part of their agricultural production at home need not be considered selfish or irrational—indeed, quite the contrary if, as in France especially, agriculture is managed by generations of small family farmers who have valuable know-how that would be hard to regenerate in a short-term crisis, once lost. These citizens might simply be making a different calculation about the durability of any intercontinental network of trade, unwilling to become even more dependent for their necessities on foreign commerce than they may be already. This may be economically costly according to one kind of calculation, but it is by no means foolish.

But even if it is not irrational for the developed world to prefer domestic agricultural policies to free trade in agriculture, is it nevertheless selfish? A common line of argument now runs that in pursuing protectionist agricultural policies, the countries of the north are undermining the world trading order and thereby hurting the world's poor, who need access to foreign markets to advance economically. A great deal can and should be said about this charge, but a detailed response is beyond my scope here. As to the first claim, the confidence that so many have placed in the rapid emergence of a global world order of free trade may be unreasonable. Global free trade may prove unsustainable, undesirable, or both—depending on a more careful analysis of who is trading what with whom. As to the second claim, we should note that the main beneficiaries of agricultural liberalization would not be poor *campesinos* in the global south, but powerful agribusiness interests in Brazil, India, China, South Africa, and the other main developing world exporters, including also powerful agribusiness lobbies in the *developed* world.[26] It is for this reason that, while the ministers of many large developing-world countries pushed for agricultural liberalization and complained vociferously about the collapse of Doha, many representatives of developing-world NGOs and civil society organizations argued that the failure might be salutary, providing an occasion to rethink the entire Doha Round and to push for a different set of trading rules better tailored to poverty alleviation. These same groups charge that Doha never amounted to the "development round" that the global poor really require—whether or not the rich world ever reduces its agricultural subsidies. Finally, a general point bears repeating: claims about the relationship between poverty and trade are empirical claims and not to be argued *a priori* by simply citing the doctrine of comparative advantage. When such empirical assessments are done, the relationship is much more ambiguous than classical trade theory would suggest.[27]

Does the collapse of Doha represent the end of world free trade as some commentators have claimed? It is true that, following the summer of 2006, many countries began pursuing bilateral and regional trading agreements even more vigorously than they had been already, and that these agreements often pit a small country directly against a richer, more powerful one. (It does not follow, however, that any multilateral agreement is better than every bilateral arrangement.) And it is true that the dispute resolution system of the WTO looks likely to be put under more pressure as countries bring new controversies to it, unwilling to bide patiently in the hope of better agreements to come. The free trade optimism of the late 1990s has clearly dissipated, and yet it should not be forgotten that in many critical respects (such as quantitative restrictions on imports), world trade is now freer than ever before, even without the additional deregulations promised in the Doha agenda.[28]

For those who believe that global networks of commerce provide the best solution to extreme poverty, or military aggression, or national chauvinism —those who, as Keynes puts it, persist in the "mental habits of the pre-war nineteenth-century world"—the collapse of Doha is a tragedy because it halts the progress toward a fully liberalized global economy.[29] But for those who are more skeptical about the consequences of unregulated sociability and more concerned with the need for effective political action to reshape domestic economic space—in the service of international peace and domestic prosperity—the collapse of Doha is neither surprising nor regrettable. It is not surprising because trade liberalization depends ultimately on the suppression of power politics among nations, which is most likely when a single powerful country has nothing to fear from the quicker development of its rivals, and therefore underwrites a liberal trading order. Moore's "world without walls" was much easier to imagine in 1995 when the WTO began than it would be a decade later. But this is not necessarily regrettable, for the relationship between commerce and politics is much more complex than even the most well-intentioned free traders have ever admitted, and without a better understanding of what purpose free trade serves, it remains unclear why we should want more of it—particularly if it requires a suppression of democratic politics at the national level.

CHAPTER NINE

Global Neoliberalism

THE WTO INSTITUTIONALIZES the economic philosophy of "neo-liberalism" in the world's multilateral trading order. Neoliberalism is the philosophy behind what is often referred to as "economic" globalization —which includes the liberalization not just of international trade, but also of international capital flows and, more generally, the deregulation of domestic economies. Indeed, as it is usually understood, neoliberalism is a philosophy of economic governance that privileges markets and distrusts government intervention in the regulation of the economy, whether at the domestic or global level. Neoliberalism works across both domestic and international space in that it prescribes a set of policy arrangements intended to lay the groundwork for national development and integration into the world economy. It thus privileges relations of sociability and mistrusts those of sovereignty, since (on its own account at least) the latter are distorted and corrupted by power in a way the former are not. Instead, neoliberals place their faith in those activities that people undertake as individuals choosing to participate in broader structures of social life.

In this chapter, I first examine the philosophy of neoliberalism and the extent to which specific neoliberal policy proposals have been adopted due to network power. I argue that most neoliberal proposals—with the notable exception of trade liberalization—have not been adopted due to network power, but on account of other forms of pressure or persuasion. The way in which a neoliberal principle (like that of trade liberalization) can come to possess network power is through a process of *juridification*, which I explore in the controversy over international investment standards— proposals for regulating international finance that are at the heart of the neoliberal agenda, but so far remain unrealized.

THE NEOLIBERALISM OF THE WTO

The neoliberal stance is often as much a temperament as it is a worked-through philosophical position, but at the philosophical level we can understand it as making claims on behalf of relations of sociability and against the power at work in sovereignty. It imagines a world purified of power—which it identifies with state action—and governed instead by the free and productive relations of human sociability, especially economic activity in markets. At most, the state may play a supporting role in enforcing the basic protections (especially of property) required to keep these relations free and productive.

Neoliberalism thus carries the political philosophy of libertarianism into an analysis of the global economy, representing an extreme form of the argument for sociability. We may consider all such forms of libertarianism as varieties of *right-wing anarchism*, trusting in private property and markets, not governments, as the basis for the proper organization of human affairs. The contrast here is with *left-wing anarchism*, anarcho-syndicalism of the familiar variety that puts its confidence in labor unions and workers' councils rather than in governments (and the relations of private property they protect)—including the technological utopians I discussed in Chapter 7. In their hostility to organized sovereignty, neoliberals resemble these technological utopians, but unlike these left-wing anarchists, they revere private property and accept its social consequences.

These features of the commitment to neoliberalism are clear in the way that the WTO manages trade relations: WTO agreements have come increasingly into conflict with government regulation of industries at a national level, which has been interpreted as an implicit barrier to trade. Of course, sometimes government action clearly is a bar to trade or a subsidy to domestic industry; besides outright discrimination in tariff rates, or direct financial subsidy to favored industry, governments may set up subtle regulatory schemes that favor domestic companies. Whether any of these barriers to trade are detrimental, however, requires examining the case for free trade, as I did in the last chapter.

The requirements of WTO membership may come into conflict not just with direct or indirect barriers to trade such as subsidies, but with national laws and regulations that may in fact seem to have little to do with trade. In particular, many environmental and social regulations have strong domestic political support and yet have an undeniable effect on international trade, usually disadvantaging some foreign imports, as in the case of countries that fail to adequately protect endangered sea turtles or that use child or sweatshop labor. WTO proponents therefore have good reason to claim that internal economic policies affect the terms of trade—a point that opponents should not (and need not) deny. Both free trade proponents and their critics recognize that putting the ideal of free trade into practice requires something beyond merely eliminating greedy customs officials at the border; it requires rather deep intervention into domestic economies, handcuffing not only tariff officials but also a whole range of government institutions, many of which are central to national policy. How could it be otherwise, given that governments can intervene at any point in the process of production and distribution to discriminate in favor of domestic products?

To put the matter differently, if there is no clear way to separate the constructions of sociability from those of sovereignty, then the neoliberal ideal must demand the elimination of sovereignty, at least insofar as it affects the economy. In fact, the end-point of a non-discriminatory trade regime, such as that the WTO hopes to bring about, is both obvious and likely impossible. Free trade demands more than merely tariff-free boundaries. It requires *the elimination of public action in economic space altogether,* for non-discriminatory tariff regimes do not deliver trade that is fully "free" from all governmental influence. Trade that is fully free could only come from the withdrawal of politics from production altogether, which would require convergence in domestic economic regulation across different countries.

GLOBAL NEOLIBERALISM AND THE WASHINGTON CONSENSUS

The WTO represents just one part of the neoliberal ideal: the commitment to multilateral trade liberalization. But neoliberals would like to

see the ultimate withdrawal of politics from production in all areas of the
economy, not just those affecting international trade. This divorce between
politics and production depends upon the belief that markets are the main
(and only reliable) driver of economic growth and the natural form of
social relations purified of artificial disturbance by governmental or collective action. To make markets (thus conceived) work well requires ceding
control of the economy to private agents, who must nevertheless rely on
the state to enforce the stable macroeconomic environment and legal regime under which they prosper. In the context of economic development,
this neoliberal commitment amounts to what Roberto Mangabeira Unger
has described as "the program of macroeconomic stabilization without
damage to the internal and external creditors of the state."[1]

This program finds concrete expression today in a set of policy recommendations often called the "Washington Consensus," which is used as a
catchall phrase roughly synonymous with neoliberalism. The term "Washington Consensus" was first introduced in 1989 by the economist John
Williamson to describe the set of economic policy initiatives suggested
for the developing world, particularly Latin American countries, by the
"powers-that-be in Washington"—the Bretton Woods institutions, the U.S.
Treasury, and assorted foreign aid agencies.[2] According to Williamson, it
"offers a description of what is agreed about the set of measures typically
called for" in economic development.[3] Williamson now regrets that he
did not call the description the "universal convergence" or "the one-world
convergence" instead of the Washington Consensus, given that "there
is no complete consensus, while the very real convergence extends far
beyond Washington."[4]

The Washington Consensus recommends the following policy initiatives: fiscal discipline, meaning that governments should not have budget
deficits that cannot be financed through ordinary taxation rather than
inflation; the redirection of public expenditure priorities toward "neglected
fields with high economic returns," such as primary and secondary education; tax reform through "broadening the tax base and cutting marginal
tax rates"; financial liberalization through reliance on "market-determined
interest rates"; exchange rates managed for competitiveness in export;
trade liberalization through the reduction of tariffs to a "uniform low
tariff in the range of 10 percent"; foreign direct investment, solicited by
the equal treatment of foreign and domestic firms and the elimination of

barriers to the entry of foreign firms into domestic economies; privatization of all state-owned enterprises; deregulation of domestic economies
by the elimination of all government measures that "impede the entry of
new firms or restrict competition"; and strong property rights protection.[5]
Of course, only some of these elements of the Washington Consensus as
Williamson listed them are standard parts of the agenda pushed by the
"powers-that-be": for example, fiscal discipline, tax reform, financial and
trade liberalization, and privatization are often emphasized by neoliberal
reformers, while efforts to rein in military spending in favor of other
public expenditure priorities such as education receive much less staunch
advocacy (if indeed any at all).[6]

However, the idea of neoliberalism is not reducible to this (or any
specific) set of policy recommendations, but represents a broader commitment to international economic integration and the elevation of individual
voluntarism over politics. Neither is neoliberalism just another word for
"capitalism," for it advocates a specific form of capitalism, a free market
ideology applied to global economic relations and domestic governance.
Consider by contrast a mixed economic system without the same commitments to markets as the only appropriate form of global and domestic
coordination, which is nonetheless a variety of capitalism.[7]

THE NETWORK POWER OF NEOLIBERALISM

Neoliberalism is now the subject of enormous empirical and normative
controversy among economists, politicians, and activists, in marked contrast to the heyday of the Washington Consensus in the 1990s, when only
activists and a few brave academics begged to differ.[8] To examine these
important controversies would require a separate volume. Instead, I want
to ask a different question, which is whether the policies advanced by
the Washington Consensus possess network power. For, if they do, then
the desirability of neoliberalism may be settled by the *extrinsic* need for
coordination, regardless of the outcome of contemporary debates over the
intrinsic merits or demerits of particular policies.

Can the dominance of the neoliberal program be attributed to the
network power of neoliberalism? To evaluate the possibility, we must
examine more closely the institutional components of this supposedly
"universal convergence." At the heart of the neoliberal program—in the
actual proposals of the Washington Consensus, for example—we see a

varied and separable set of policy prescriptions that can be adopted piece-meal, rearranged, and reordered, so as to favor some elements and jettison others. For unlike, say, the WTO, neoliberalism does not represent a single coherent standard. Rather, it can be disassembled and disaggregated.

The development success stories of East Asia—countries that have risen from poverty more quickly than any others in history, notwithstand-ing the "Asian economic crisis" of the late 1990s—illustrate how a par-tial adoption and partial rejection of the central recommendations of the Washington Consensus can prove highly effective. While countries such as Japan, South Korea and Taiwan did, as a general rule, maintain low rates of inflation and protect (some) private property rights during their periods of most rapid development, they also violated neoliberal tenets by promoting government cooperation with private enterprise to quicken technology transfer and industrial development, protecting domestic markets from imports while pursuing an export-led growth strategy, and intervening in support of favored industries.[9] The more recent, equally spectacular growth of China presents a further conundrum, as China does not even protect private property rights, at least as they are conventionally understood.[10]

Since the actual prescriptions of the Washington Consensus can be disaggregated and reassembled in this manner, any view of it as a single, coherent set of policies cannot be maintained. Here, the contrast with the WTO is instructive, for unlike the multilateral trading system—now regulated by the WTO in a relatively inflexible way—other parts of the global economic regime remain surprisingly open, with innovations and policy experiments often far more feasible than either proponents or de-tractors of neoliberalism commonly acknowledge. The network power of neoliberalism as a whole is thus limited, because it does not really operate as a standard that governs access to markets in a clear manner, unlike the central agreements that must all be jointly accepted for entry into the WTO. Instead of attempting to view neoliberalism as a single, undifferentiated standard, therefore, we must break it apart and examine the network power of its constituent policy elements. In some cases we may find that these policies are becoming globally dominant because of their network power, while in other situations we may have to locate a different reason for their widespread adoption.

As with the adoption of any standard, we can discuss the motivation for pursuing a particular neoliberal policy in terms of reason, whether intrinsic or extrinsic, and force, whether direct or indirect. Where the reasons are intrinsic, the neoliberal standard is valued because of the benefits that it brings, independently of the coordination it provides with others. For example, some political parties may press for government deregulation because they believe that the privatization of state-owned enterprises will benefit the economy (or their financial backers), regardless of what happens elsewhere in the world. By contrast, other standards are chosen for mainly extrinsic reasons, because of the desired access that this standard provides to other countries, as I argued is the case with the WTO. Standards are chosen for extrinsic reasons when they govern access to forms of beneficial cooperation with others that cannot be secured more easily by other means. We also see force in the adoption of neoliberal standards. We see direct force in the adoption of neoliberal policies when they are tied to crisis-driven conditionality agreements imposed by the IMF as a requirement for receiving needed loans. In such cases, a country facing an economic crisis turns to the lender of last resort for protection, and receives it conditionally, in return for required domestic policy adjustments. By contrast, the WTO is joined because of the indirect force of network power, the threat of economic isolation from a trading bloc that encompasses the great majority of nations.

Thus any neoliberal standard will be chosen because of particular combinations of reason and force, representing variable degrees of network power. One reason that we should doubt these policies possess much network power is that they are usually adopted because of intrinsic reason or direct force, rather than that merger of extrinsic reason and indirect force that indicates network power. For example, neoliberal policies are often chosen for intrinsic reasons—because they appear likely to better the economic condition of a country (at least in the opinion of the chief decision-makers in the country). In these instances, persuasion has been at work—and the neoliberal agenda has powerfully persuasive advocates in the media, academia, and prominent multilateral institutions, as well as, of course, in Washington. At other times, it is not so much persuasion that lies behind the promotion of a particular policy as arm-twisting of a more familiar variety, as when neoliberal policies are made part of conditionality agreements imposed by the IMF, advancing through country-by-country coercion rather than because of network power.

A neoliberal policy possesses network power when it coordinates access to a desirable social activity, serving as a membership standard. This can come about in one of two broad ways: due to multilateral enforcement in a gate-keeping institution, or because of reputation effects that determine the availability of capital. In both of these cases, some form of economic cooperation is predicated on the explicit adoption of a Washington Consensus policy. The WTO provides the main example of a successful gatekeeper institution, controlling access to a sphere of international cooperation through a multilateral institution. This institutionalization represents the *juridification of neoliberalism*. Through juridification, abstract principles of neoliberalism become membership standards, setting the terms of access to the international economy by being formalized as requirements for membership in multilateral bodies.[11] Juridification abrogates the freedom of developing-world countries to be persuaded—or not persuaded—about the merits of any actual neoliberal proposal by establishing a dynamic of interdependent choice through international standardization. It changes the incentives for adopting a neoliberal standard, increasing the importance of extrinsic over intrinsic reasons to fall in line with it.

The second route by which a standard may come to possess network power is perhaps more common: neoliberal policies can serve as membership criteria when they are used as *signaling devices* to gain the approval of key international decision-makers, such as the officials of the powerful countries or (perhaps more importantly) the heads of international private finance.[12] Enormous pressure is frequently exerted on countries which act in defiance of the conventional economic wisdom—particularly when these countries are poor, debtor nations—both from other countries and from private international actors, such as bond traders and currency speculators. Through diplomatic channels and financial market reaction, countries failing to conform to the neoliberal program may be denied international support and private capital flows. The journalist Thomas Friedman famously called the network of international bond traders "the electronic herd," and argued that it is responsible for keeping countries in the "Golden Straitjacket" of neoliberalism—a constraint he endorses.[13]

However, the extent to which these decentralized forms of sanction and coercion are effective in securing compliance with the Washington Consensus remains unclear.[14] Financiers are above all interested in making money, and so may dispense with some neoliberal commitments as appropriate—as when investing in China, say. However, while bond traders may be willing to invest in economically heterodox states if their model proves effective, they may not, if it is within their power, be willing to allow such states sufficient room for experimentation in the first place. Relative insulation from financial pressure thus proves important for sustained divergence from the Washington Consensus—which has refocused attention on the desirability of policies that limit the easy mobility of capital.[15]

INTERNATIONAL INVESTMENT STANDARDS

The ongoing controversy over investment standards provides a concrete illustration of the juridification of neoliberalism. For over half a century, capital-exporting countries, particularly the United States, have engaged in an effort to achieve international protection for their investors abroad.[16] They have proposed various treaties, all of which have sought to establish a common international standard for managing overseas capital flows. The most dramatic effort to establish such a treaty collapsed in 1998, with the failure of the Multilateral Agreement on Investment (MAI), which I discuss below, but the effort to create international standards for investment protection is an ongoing and multifaceted one. Here we see the first steps and early failures of a process of juridification in which abstract principles concerning investment may become standards possessing network power.

Capitalists desire protection from two main threats that foreign governments pose to their investments: outright expropriation of their property (nationalization), and government oversight (regulation) that could make their investments less profitable. Protection against the possibility of nationalization is the aim of the principle of non-expropriation, under which a country cannot take property from a foreign national without due process of law and just compensation. Protection against state interference with foreign investment is advanced in the principle of "national treatment," under which foreign investments receive the same treatment as those of domestic investors. Despite over fifty years of effort, these two principles have not yet been made part of any multilateral investment agreement, though they are often incorporated into other international accords and on a bilateral basis. Although these abstract principles may be formalized in treaties or international agreements, they possess only the power to *persuade*, not the power to structure choice through network power. Countries adopt them because they believe that "national treatment," for example, will ultimately redound to the benefit of their own investors, or help them attract needed capital. But because these principles do not necessarily regulate desired access to economic cooperation, countries need not adopt them. (Of course, countries may face pressure to adopt them on a bilateral basis, but that direct compulsion is not network power *per se*, but a different form of soft power.)

How would these principles for managing international investment attain network power? First, they would have to become standardized institutionally. The principles would then become standards with a definite articulation, which is the beginning of the process of juridification. The rich, capital-exporting countries of the Organization for Economic Cooperation and Development (OECD) have made the most progress toward the standardization of investment principles: seven different OECD instruments form a framework for investment, and the principles codified in these agreements include national treatment, protection from expropriation, and guidelines for corporate investment.[17] Second, these standards either would then have to become part of country-to-country bargaining, and thus a shared form of coordination among many countries, or else serve as the basis for a broader multilateral framework.[18] The decentralized adoption of principles regarding investment, for example, may create a shared expectation that they must be adopted in order for states to benefit from the international flow of investment. Even in the absence of an explicit multilateral agreement, the widespread dissemination of a set of norms may approximate to global social coordination, if these norms begin to function as a signaling device, say, for attracting needed foreign capital. Or, if given an explicit gatekeeper status as part of a multilateral regime, the standard will come to possess network power even more directly.

THE MULTILATERAL AGREEMENT ON INVESTMENT

The juridification of neoliberal standards for foreign investment has met the first requirement, but has so far failed the second. The Multilateral Agreement on Investment (MAI) offered an explicit standard setting global rules for investment flows among the capital-exporting countries of the OECD, but it was never adopted, for reasons relating to both external opposition and internal conflict among the negotiating parties.[19] The MAI sought to establish a neoliberal investment regime among these countries, inspired by the investor-protection provisions of NAFTA, the "gold standard" as far as protection of foreign investment is concerned.

There is great debate about how the MAI would have functioned and, indeed, whether it would have functioned at all, given the many national exceptions that participating countries were granted in the course of the negotiations. Furthermore, the draft resolution establishing the MAI was never completed (despite running to two hundred pages when negotiations were ended), which allows only general speculations about how it would have worked. Broadly, however, the MAI sought to protect foreign investment in four ways. It would have guaranteed "national treatment" for foreign investors; provided standards under which government expropriation of private property would be allowed and set a framework for mandatory compensation; prohibited government conditions on foreign investment; and provided a binding dispute resolution system probably similar to that of the WTO. How these broad principles would have been interpreted in practice remains unclear, but it should be noted that one of the immediate and obvious effects they would have had is to limit the ability of governments to control capital flows. While advocates of the MAI like to argue the case in terms of foreign direct investment, even government control over foreign portfolio investment—the more volatile flows of "hot" money that can destabilize entire regions—would probably have been severely constrained under its provisions.

At least to some extent, the MAI negotiations failed because of loud public protests against them. These protests were among the first of the large-scale demonstrations against neoliberal economic policies, culminating in the global media spectacle in Seattle during the WTO Ministerial Conference in 1999. (In an interesting foreshadowing, the Seattle City Council had declared the city an "MAI-free zone" in 1998.) Anti-MAI activists worried about the threats that they believed the MAI posed to labor unions, to the environment, to working conditions in the developed world, and to employment in the developing world. Whether the MAI would have actually had any of these effects is unclear, and the protests were arguably less against the MAI in particular than against neoliberal economic globalization more generally—the MAI representing the latest, and allegedly the most potent, installment of the neoliberal program.

Some commentators have argued that the protestors against the MAI were confused in charging that it would hurt the developing world, or trigger job flight from the rich world, since, in fact, the agreement was being negotiated only among OECD countries. It may be true that many protesters were ignorant of the fact that the MAI would have committed only developed nations. But a more nuanced view might be to suggest that the protestors intuited something that their critics failed to understand or acknowledge. Anti-MAI protestors were anxious about the creation of a standard regulating international investment, though without clearly articulating why. In light of the discussion of network power, we can better understand the rationale that a relatively thoughtful person might have offered against it: that when the rich nations of the world agree to something, they often find a way to "force" their agreement on poor countries. What the OECD was crafting was a standard that might rapidly have become a universal standard through the dynamics of network power. The juridification of investment principles might begin with a set of coordinating rules for rich countries alone, but there is no need to assume it would stop there.

Unlike the protestors, who seem to have been spurred by their appreciation of this danger (however vaguely grasped), many of the MAI's supporters were either unaware of or indifferent to it. Consider, for example, the case for the MAI and against the activists laid out by Edward Graham in *Fighting the Wrong Enemy: Antiglobal Activists and Multinational Enterprises*. Responding to the worry that most of the activists had that the MAI would affect the developing world, or the developed world in relation to the developing world (say, by job losses from offshoring), Graham argues: "These criticisms of the MAI . . . can be dismissed with relative ease. The MAI was to have been, as noted at the outset, an agreement within the OECD, whose members are mostly industrial, not developing, countries. It would not have been binding on nonmembers. It therefore would have done little or nothing to foster the transfer of jobs or of polluting activities by foreign investors to most developing countries. Concerns about job loss in the industrial countries as a group, or about exploitation of workers in most developing countries, are therefore essentially a nonissue as far as the MAI was concerned."

Graham then continues: "Ironically in this light, the industrial countries seeking an MAI chose the OECD as the negotiating venue precisely in

order to exclude the developing countries from the negotiating exercise."
Why were the developing countries left out? Graham writes, in what is almost certainly a correct assessment, that "the main reason for keeping these
countries out of the MAI negotiations was the presumption that the OECD
countries were 'like-minded' on the subject of investment policy and already
had in place relatively liberal investment policy regimes." He explains:

> It was thought that these [OECD] countries, because they
> shared similar views on investment policy and similar policies,
> could quickly conclude a "high standards" agreement—that
> is, one in which relatively stringent rules would apply. In a
> negotiating forum such as the WTO, on the other hand, with
> its wider country representation, consensus would have been
> much more difficult to achieve, and any consensus would likely
> have been at a lower standard. In particular, the US and other
> OECD governments believed that a bloc of developing coun-
> tries within the WTO would have prevented any high-standards
> agreement from ever coming into force.[20]

Graham's indifference to concerns about developing-country participation
is striking, given that he notes the explicit ambition to exclude them from
negotiations. Against the imagined fears of environmental or social violations in the developing world, he asserts that "the agreement contained
no provisions that would have significantly enhanced the ability of multinational firms to invest in developing countries." This is true, but only insofar as developing countries were not party to the original agreement, and
crucially, Graham also recognizes that developing countries would have
joined the MAI, had it been established. He writes: "To be sure, had the
MAI come into force, some developing-world countries would have joined
it. Indeed, the draft agreement made provisions for non-OECD countries
to accede to the agreement, and some had expressed an interest in doing
so."[21] In fact, five developing countries had "observer" status at the OECD
negotiations: Argentina, Brazil, Chile, Hong Kong (China), and the Slovak
Republic. As an OECD policy report on the MAI states, "OECD members
hope that non-OECD countries will join the MAI as founding members,
or soon after the agreement is put in place."[22] Thus the negotiations do not
appear to have been so exclusively aimed at the rich world that concerns
about the developing world could be dismissed as irrelevant.

The deeper reason why Graham does not acknowledge these concerns must be that he is convinced that foreign investment is essential for poor countries, and that such investment should be shielded from government interference. With regard to the developing world's stake in the MAI provisions, he writes "In each of these areas, it seems in developing countries' interest to agree to currently accepted international standards, subject to specific exceptions, as would have been agreed to under the MAI."[23] Given this attitude, it follows that he would be unworried about the possibility that developing countries might be coerced into an agreement requiring a hands-off approach to multinational investment. He is principally concerned with achieving greater investment protection, and unconcerned with the process by which it would come about.

A different approach can be seen in an article in *Le Monde Diplomatique*:

Why then is the MAI being discussed by 29 states at the OECD, and not at the WTO which, with 131 member states, is a priori the more legitimate forum? Using the language of diplomacy, Mr. Henri Chavranski [the French negotiator at the OECD] provides us with the answer: "The negotiations began and are continuing within the OECD exclusively, between member states that are providers of capital; those states are firmly convinced that this kind of internal procedure is the only way of producing a binding and therefore useful text that will subsequently be gradually extended to non-OECD countries wishing to attract foreign capital." He goes on to say that, at the WTO, "the presence of countries that have major reservations concerning or are actually hostile to the very principle of a binding agreement on investment mean that the negotiations would be unlikely to succeed."[24]

Chavranski is admitting here that countries that do not want a particular agreement will be shut out of it until it has been drawn up, at which point it will be "gradually extended" to them based on the need to "attract foreign capital." Again, it seems clear that the MAI was not intended to remain merely an agreement among the rich countries, but was to be negotiated among them before presenting the world with a *fait accompli* that would be difficult to refuse.

THE NETWORK POWER OF THE MAI

Considering the network power that the MAI would have possessed helps to clarify how it would have reshaped the global economy. It would have replaced the bilateral investment treaties (BITs), currently negotiated on a country-to-country basis by a single accord, with a multilateral institution. Like the move from bilateral trade agreements to the GATT, and subsequently to the WTO, the move from BITs to the MAI would have established an international standard for coordination capable of exerting network power. Whether the MAI would have been a beneficial part of the international economic order requires an empirical assessment that the theoretical framework of network power cannot provide. But it should be obvious that such a standard, backed by the most powerful countries in the world, would have set up a structural dynamic by which small nations might either be made to join it or face increasing costs of isolation from the network of international capital. In fact, as Chavranski admits (while Graham dissembles) this outcome was the intended effect of using the OECD as the negotiating forum for the agreement.

Had the MAI negotiations succeeded, the wealthy nations of the world would have become parties to an agreement articulating a set of rules they would have had to abide by—but which they had themselves formulated. The MAI would then have operated as a gateway to international investment, allowing relatively unencumbered access to foreign-investment markets. Any benefits of cooperation, however, may have come at the price of inhibiting innovation. And, like all standards that govern access to others, the MAI would have proved attractive to nonmembers, especially the capital-poor. While the MAI negotiations failed and we can only suppose how it would actually have operated, it seems likely that the original MAI would have served as a treaty organization to which new members would gain entry by coming into conformity with its terms, enabling its adoption beyond the OECD alone. Hence, the MAI would have exerted network power on nonmembers, holding out the promise of access to needed foreign-investment markets in return for obedience to its rules and processes of dispute settlement.

Whether nonmembers would have joined the MAI in large numbers depends on too many factors to be anything other than a matter for speculation. But the protestors' intuitions were plausible. By setting up an agreement to which the most powerful nations of the world were parties, the MAI probably would have become something more than a gentlemen's agreement within the OECD. Instead, we might view it as the "thin end of the wedge," with the potential to reshape the international economic order through its standardization of investment rules in an institutional configuration exhibiting network power. Even the mere existence of the MAI would have altered the bargaining position of nonmembers and would have significantly restricted the range of viable choices open to them.

THE FUTURE OF NEOLIBERAL INVESTMENT STANDARDS

The failure of the MAI does not represent the end of efforts to establish transnational standards governing investment. Indeed, an investment treaty remains a controversial but important "Singapore issue" (begun in the Singapore Ministerial Conference of 1996) still currently being negotiated in the WTO. However, as the MAI negotiators foresaw, the success of an investment treaty protecting capital-exporting countries will remain highly uncertain if it must be agreed to in advance by the countries in the developing world, particularly in a forum like the WTO, in which developing countries can build negotiating alliances and pool resources strategically. Indeed, no investment agreement emerged from the Doha, Cancun, or Hong Kong Ministerial Conferences of the WTO—and the collapse of Cancun was directly linked to the developing world's refusal to consider one. Despite the frequent criticism of the WTO, it remains—at least in comparison with an exclusively OECD agreement negotiated in private—a relatively representative forum for hashing out a world investment regime. The fact that no investment (or other) agreement looks likely to come from the WTO indicates that neoliberal globalization has run up against a limit.

If we need a world agreement on foreign investment, how should it be pursued? A strategy that takes advantage of network power would be to approach the matter as attempted in the case of the MAI. The rich countries might bargain among themselves to achieve a solution they find satisfactory, and then—in what would no doubt be presented as an act of generosity or at least inevitability—throw wide the doors of their new club for the rest of the world to join. Of course, in accepting these investment standards, new members would be admitted on previously settled terms they did not help to formulate. Nevertheless, given the share of foreign investment represented in a bloc of the world's wealthy nations, network power would probably catapult the standard to global dominance.

A different strategy, albeit a more difficult one to achieve, would be to approach an agreement on global investment as necessarily a *global* agreement, requiring international negotiation about the costs and benefits of this new form of cooperation well in advance of the establishment of a multilateral regime possessing network power. It is obvious why this latter approach is not usually tried: it would cost currently powerful nations more of the gains they seek. For example, in exchange for guarantees of protection from expropriation, the developing world might insist on receiving significant development assistance and expedited technology transfer far in excess of the relatively small sums currently spent (and often misspent) on foreign aid. It might also be demanded that any agreement accommodate environmental and social regulations that would make industrial production less profitable, but less costly socially, by distinguishing between regulations that legitimately reduce the profitability of foreign investment and those that are targeted against particular foreign companies or countries in an illegitimate manner.

More fundamentally, however, it is not clear that any single, multilateral approach to investment is necessarily right for all the countries in the world, particularly with regard to the difficult issue of capital mobility. Not merely the content but the very existence of a multilateral agreement on investment is presently up for grabs. But where a transnational standard is desirable, and where we cannot make it compatible with existing practices, we have an obligation to develop it in a transparent and participatory fashion. In the case of the MAI, precisely the opposite strategy was pursued: a standard of dubious necessity was crafted in a nontransparent manner by an elite subset of countries with the (unstated) intent that it be catapulted to global dominance through network power.

NEOLIBERAL STANDARDIZATION

Throughout this book, I have argued that in an age of global interconnectedness—an age in which we depend on international standards in order to coordinate many of our activities—network-power dynamics prove a common feature of our shared social life. Further, they present complicated ethical and practical problems. Since network power can be used strategically by the powerful, it would seem that we need a different way of setting standards, enforcing a new regime for transnational standardization that is less dependent on the agency or influence of any particular country or bloc of countries. It is no longer enough for each country to pursue its own interests under the fiction that other countries can independently decide whether or not to participate in projects of transnational coordination. This "free market" in standards under which every country is offered the choice to join up on terms set by the powerful (or face isolation) must be replaced by the functional equivalent of democratic oversight at the global level.

However, what this oversight might look like is difficult to say, since the relations of sovereignty are coextensive with the boundaries of nation-states and—as I argued in Chapter 6—it is hard to imagine the functional equivalent of the relations of sovereignty operative at the global level. To recognize this problem is to acknowledge that the age of international voluntarism has passed and one of pervasive global interdependence has taken its place, but that we do not yet know how to manage the tensions and potential that such interdependence holds. Where we cannot together reshape powerful global networks by acting directly on the agents constituting them, we may wish simply to limit international interdependence, adopting Keynes's position on "national self-sufficiency." If this means giving up some of the benefits of international integration—benefits that, in many cases, may be more convincing in abstract arguments than in on-the-ground realities—it also means preserving valued freedoms that too tight a global integration may put at risk. Making any such trade-off is, of course, a matter that requires *political* determination.

Thus, the problem, once again, is how we should understand the politics of sovereignty in an age of globalization. Democratic decision-making engages politics rather than suppressing it. By contrast, neoliberal economic policies privilege the relations of sociability and favor a hands-tied approach to keep the demands of domestic politics away from standards designed to ensure international economic integration. Whether such a hands-tied approach will prove sustainable is unclear. For as neoliberal principles are fashioned into standards wielding network power through the process of juridification, they will likely be even more resented than they are at present, particularly if they seem to benefit the globally privileged disproportionately—and to deny the capacity for effective choice-making to the rest. How the politics of such an uneven globalization will affect international integration remains to be seen, but it seems unwise to be too sanguine, given the precedents with which history presents us. Ironically, neoliberalism denies experimentation at the local level only to engage in it at the global: it suppresses national interventions for the sake of an unfettered world market but thereby jeopardizes international integration altogether.

CHAPTER TEN

Network Power and Cultural Convergence

BEHIND THE WORRY about the rise of universal standards in technology or policy is a concern not just about the distributive justice of globalization or the autonomy of democratic politics but also about the possible cultural loss that the rise of a dominant standard can entail. Technologies and institutions are rarely, if ever, only neutral solutions to existing problems. Rather, they reflect the selection of one direction among many.

One of the most common complaints against globalization is that it produces or hastens cultural loss and homogenization. On this view, it generates circumstances of increasing global uniformity, the haunting specter of "McWorld." Why this should be so, however, remains unclear—and is made yet murkier by the fact that the literature on globalization often focuses on the wrong variables. In this chapter, I examine the applicability of the idea of network power to the phenomena that make up cultural life and in which we see examples of convergence. Can a network power analysis help us to understand the reasons for cultural homogenization, or even what such homogenization entails? The first problem is to identify the relevant domains of "culture" at stake in globalization. Answering how network power works to produce uniformity in these domains requires examining the practices, norms, and frames of reference that can serve as standards in interconnected cultural networks.

NETWORK POWER AND CULTURAL CONVERGENCE 267

CULTURAL CONVERGENCE AND CULTURAL LOSS

In a great deal of the popular literature on cultural globalization, we find an unproductive debate that sets two compatible views against each other in a contrived conflict. On the one hand, some authors point to an increasing convergence on specific forms of artistic, culinary, or musical culture—usually, but not exclusively, moving from the United States, via newly global media, to the rest of the world.[1] Against this view of "Americanization" or "McDonaldization," other authors point to a number of distinct but related phenomena that they take to be countertrends or rebuttals to the claim that the world is becoming increasingly uniform—for example, the fact that cultural borrowing occurs in multiple directions, as with the appropriation of non-Western and non-American cultural forms by a global audience.[2] On this view, the creation of new hybrid forms in music or cuisine or art reveals that cultural globalization is not a one-way street. A corollary is that even Americanization may not be what it seems, but that American cultural forms can become effectively "localized" through the agency of their consumers abroad. For example, it appears that customers at McDonald's in China enjoy a menu that has been altered to suit local tastes—thus eating beneath the same Golden Arches, but eating something different than they would in Chicago.[3] The most extreme interpretation of this kind of phenomenon denies a place for any cultural "essence" at all, claiming that it is impossible or illegitimate to label something "American" or "Chinese" in a world of rapid and diverse flows of cultural artifacts, people, and ideas.

The problem with these two views is not that either of them is wrong—indeed, they may both be right—but that they are uninteresting because they focus on relatively superficial elements of cultural globalization. No one can deny that American media forms have spread around the world or that these forms have been taken up and altered by the people to whom they have been transmitted. Both views are superficially right, and both miss the most significant uniformity generated by globalization: in *our ways of thinking and living.*

The cultural homogenization that may or may not be occurring globally takes place against the backdrop of this more profound integration. Against an unappealing view of other people as the passive recipients of American cultural hegemony, we need not advance an alternative that denies the existence of any recognizably distinct cultural identities altogether.

Instead, we should understand concerns about cultural homogenization as revealing a broad transformation in the ways of thought and life available to people today—a transformation that marks the real convergence in our time and which is, across significant swathes of the world, already a *fait accompli*.

Indeed, while this convergence in ways of thinking and living may extend to influence cultural forms like music or food, it need not necessarily do so. It is striking that in this moment of global integration producing massive convergence in economic, linguistic, and institutional standards, we should be so worried about restaurant chains and pop music, neglecting much more significant issues. Famously, Sigmund Freud argued that nationalist rivalries between neighboring countries reflected the "narcissism of minor differences," a pathological focus on relatively trivial distinctions driven by the desire to keep at bay an anxiety-provoking recognition of fundamental sameness.[4] Perhaps our focus on relatively superficial aspects of cultural globalization reveals a similar dynamic. For in the midst of profound and wide-reaching global integration at all levels, we have been reduced to worrying about the menu at Kentucky Fried Chicken restaurants in China and analyzing the pop lyrics of global youth culture.

Many of the causes of this deeper convergence can be captured in a network power framework. Indeed, the argument of the book so far should lend force to the claim that the world is becoming increasingly unified as people and countries join up in new global networks. The emergence of transnational standards in diverse areas of social life will obviously affect the diversity of ways that people live together and thus how they form cultural connections. The network power of a dominant standard can produce pressure toward uniformity, one result of which may be the loss of local standards. As I argued in Chapter 5, where these local standards are connected to identity (however we wish to conceive it), we have the feeling that something important is being lost, rather than that some people are just getting the bad end of a bargain. As global networks of sociability drive forward to convergence on many different fronts, they leave in their wake a greater uniformity in our formerly diverse ways of making the world, our ways of thinking and living.

The narcissism of minor differences that directs our attention to convergences (or divergences) in elements of style or fashion distracts us from this more profound convergence on so many other levels. It is perhaps unsurprising that the globalization of pop culture seems to preoccupy observers in Western Europe and the United States while a concern about the diversity of ways of thinking and living is more common in the post-colonial world and among writers from indigenous nations.[5] For convergence at this more profound level is connected to the network power of dominant global standards in trade, technology, language, and institutions, which may appear a step removed from the more immediately "cultural" aspects of globalization—except, of course, to those most immediately subject to the network power of these dominant standards.

Complaints about cultural homogenization should properly include the loss of languages, institutions, and traditions as contributing parts of "culture." For example, languages can be seen as standards that possess network power, and the dominance not only of English on a global scale, but of regional languages on a continental scale brings with it a reduction in the languages spoken on earth. The classic "three-generation shift" in which linguistic loss occurs under conditions of network power has become a global phenomenon. The death of languages is one of the clearest and most worrying forms of cultural loss since it can signal the end of entire cultures and traditions captured in them. Additionally, diverse local institutions and practices are also converging because of network power. For example, in the case of the ISO 9000, local corporate practices may increasingly conform to an international standard of business. And domestic political institutions—for example, laws and regulations affected or even vitiated by the WTO—may be subject to requirements of harmonization with international standards. If a diversity of national regulatory institutions reflects the legitimate expression of different national political cultures, then we should be concerned about network power operating to produce institutional conformity because of both the interests and the identity concerns at stake.

Thus both linguistic and institutional diversity may be lost due to network power, because of the desire to coordinate globally with others, which necessarily involves the elevation of jointly adopted standards and may entail the loss of local ones. How valued forms of identity or culture are bound up with, or in some way dependent upon, a diversity of institutional and linguistic regimes is a complex empirical question. But it certainly makes no sense to pretend that these domains are separate. Indeed, given the eclipse of linguistic and institutional diversity around the world, our focus on the global variation in the menu at McDonald's is revealed for what it is: a will to difference manifest only in our different routes to obesity.

THE FOUR FACES OF GLOBAL CULTURE

Network power can also operate directly to produce what have become more familiar kinds of cultural homogenization, such as the loss of diversity in peoples' traditions: their customs, habits, and behaviors. Understanding whether network power might be at work in the homogenization of such cultural behavior requires first specifying the domains under consideration and the ways in which they are affected by globalization, and then asking if such social patterns can operate like a standard possessing network power.

There are many different ways to present cultural globalization in order to examine the network power dynamics at work in their convergence. I will rely on a helpful account offered by sociologist Peter Berger in his article "Four Faces of Global Culture," which draws on two of the most popular works on cultural globalization, Benjamin Barber's *Jihad vs. McWorld* and Samuel Huntington's *Clash of Civilizations and the Remaking of World Order*.[6] Presumably, many other ways exist in which we could look at the network power operative (or not operative) in some of the broad cultural movements in globalization, but Berger concisely captures many of the relevant aspects of the current debate.

Berger presents a fourfold typology of aspects of cultural globalization and the varieties of resistance to it, identifying "four faces" of global culture. The first, which he follows Samuel Huntington in calling "Davos culture," is the culture of the new, cosmopolitan elite of the business world. Its members are part of a new "yuppie internationale," as Berger puts it; the term comes from the town of Davos, Switzerland, which is the site of the annual meeting of the World Economic Forum. Berger explains, "The 'Davos culture' is a culture of the elite and (by way of what sociologists call 'anticipatory socialization') of those aspiring to join the elite. Its principal social location is in the business world, but since elites intermingle, it also affects at least the political elites."

This elite network coordinates its global activities using common technological and social forms—what we might consider the "standards" of Davos culture. Berger writes, "Participants in this culture know how to deal with computers, cellular phones, airline schedules, currency exchange, and the like. But they also dress alike, exhibit the same amicable informality, relieve tensions by similar attempts at humor, and of course most of them interact in English." Berger notes that these behaviors carry over into the private lives of many of the individuals, describing a process of embodying the standards of international business: "it would be a mistake to think that the 'Davos culture' operates only in the offices, boardrooms, and hotel suites in which international business is transacted. It carries over into the leisure activities and the family life of business people."

The second face of global culture Berger calls (somewhat infelicitously) the "faculty club culture," in which he means to include universities, non-governmental organizations, multilateral institutions, and transnational civil society networks. Berger considers this culture to be "essentially, the internationalization of the Western intelligentsia, its values and ideologies," though he has amended this rather strong stance in his more recent work.[7] He writes, "While this culture has also penetrated the business world (and in turn been penetrated by it), its principal carrier is not business. Rather it is carried by foundations, academic networks, non-governmental organizations, and some governmental and multinational agencies (such as development agencies with social and cultural missions)." It spreads "its beliefs and values through the educational system, the legal system, various therapeutic institutions, think tanks, and at least some of the media of mass communication." In short, this "faculty club culture" appears as the global equivalent of the National Public Radio audience in the United States.

The third global culture, "McWorld," is probably the most visible face of cultural globalization. It is the globalization of pop culture: the spread of McDonald's, blue jeans, American television and music, and Hollywood films around the world—the aspect of cultural globalization that attracts the most attention in the media and in the imagination. Berger argues that this domain of popular culture "is most credibly subsumed under the category of Westernization, since virtually all of it is of Western, and more specifically, American provenance."

The extent to which these pop cultural forms of expression are internalized and shape identity remains contentious. Berger takes a relatively strong but still plausible position: "the diffusion of popular culture is not just a matter of outward behavior. It carries a significant freight of beliefs and values." On this view, McWorld is not simply the result of a passing global fancy, a taste for Hollywood and rock 'n' roll, but marks the dissemination of a particular mode of self-understanding embedded within a newly global pop culture.

The fourth face of global culture that Berger identifies is perhaps the least familiar in the contemporary discussion of globalization, but he claims it "is the most important popular movement serving (mostly inadvertently) as a vehicle for cultural globalization": missionary evangelical Protestantism.[8] Since Berger wrote his article, this face of global culture may have become more familiar, given the prominence of a politicized evangelical movement now active in the United States. But the cultural impact of these evangelicals is felt deeply overseas, where they pursue converts throughout Catholic Latin America, Africa, India, China, and East Asia. Berger argues that evangelical Protestantism emerges from and propagates the particular values of North Atlantic societies: "despite its indigenization (converts in Mexico and Guatemala sing American gospel songs in Mayan translation), Evangelical Protestantism is the carrier of a pluralistic and modernizing culture whose original location is in the North Atlantic societies." Berger notes further "this type of Protestantism is creating a new international culture . . . with vast social, economic, and political ramifications." In contrast with other contemporary missionary movements—for example, Wahhabi fundamentalism in Islam—evangelical Protestantism recruits from all populations of the world.

Three points bear mentioning in relation to Berger's typology of global cultures. First, we should note that none of these four faces of global culture is really *new* to contemporary globalization. Indeed, these four elements have been central to the creation of a global modernity driven by Western Europe and, later, the United States over the last three or four centuries. Merchants, Christian missionaries, and social reformers (the latter two only recently distinct from each other) have long been important "transnational" actors, along with military men, whose role in globalization is important but neglected in Berger's analysis.[9] And even before the rise of modern media forms, popular cultural figures achieved widespread celebrity, with styles and vogues spreading across continents—often from Western countries to their colonies and dependencies—as is the case today. However, what is new to our contemporary globalization is the scale and speed with which these global cultures are emerging, perhaps most dramatically with McWorld, which depends upon modern audio-visual media and new communication technologies even more than the talk- and text-based cultures of Davos, the faculty club, or evangelical Protestantism.

The second point is that in the context of contemporary globalization, these four cultures are linked to other globalizing standards in mutually reinforcing ways; they come already "bundled" to institutional and techno-logical standards possessing network power as coordinating conventions. This fact ties the "deeper convergence" that I discussed above—and which is, in many ways, the broad subject of this whole book—to the specific forms of contemporary "cultural" globalization. For example, technological and social changes have enabled the formation of transnational networks based on shared cultural standards, but these cultural standards reinforce the position of privileged insiders—privileged, that is, with respect to the technologies and conventions that underlie these networks in the first place. Indeed, all four of the global cultures that Berger identifies are Anglo-phone, and developed their current power in the context of the postwar dominance of the United States, drawing on and in turn strengthening American "soft power."

Finally, arguing that these faces of global culture possess network power requires identifying a standard or standards at work in them. In some cases, the standards underlying an aspect of global culture are ob-vious: for example, Davos culture operates according to many different technological and social norms that serve to coordinate business activity. To take part in global commerce requires gaining access to other business-men via these social and institutional conventions. On the other hand, the standards underlying the rise of evangelical Protestantism, or even McWorld, are much less clear. As I discuss below, it *may* be possible to understand a religious system as a standard, but it is not clear what we gain from the analogy, given that the dynamics of network power almost certainly do not operate in the religious sphere in the way that they do in the business world. The applicability of a network power framework to any given instance of cultural globalization will vary greatly.

SOCIAL NORMS

To consider more carefully whether any particular aspect of cultural glob-alization is propelled by network power, we should distinguish between two different kinds of standards that may underlie a global culture, "social norms" and "conceptual frames." To advance a rather rough distinction between the two, the first affects the actions and behaviors that people engage in while the second affects what they believe. We see practices, behaviors, and elements of lifestyle—"social norms"—in all four faces of global culture. Consider the obvious similarities in behavior among participants in, say, McWorld and Davos culture. But we also see forms of thought or ideological and religious commitments—"conceptual frames"—in each of these global cultures, perhaps especially in faculty club culture and evangelical Protestantism. This distinction is meant as an intuitive and "fuzzy" guide rather than a strict formal or structural difference: obviously, our ways of thinking and our social practices reflect one another, since we act based on what we believe, and our actions in turn inform those beliefs.

The idea of the "social norm" has been central to explanations of almost any social phenomenon for a very long time, especially if we include as rough synonyms for the concept of the social norm earlier notions like "custom" and "tradition" that have been part of social thought since the ancients. However, the questions of just what counts as a social norm and how to think about something as a norm remain unsettled. Contemporary social theory employs the idea of a norm in two distinguishable senses: first, as a description of a social or behavioral regularity and second, as a prescriptive ideal to which people ought to conform. As a description of a behavioral regularity alone, a norm might be seen as nothing more than a cultural pattern. Some sociologists will discuss social norms as social regularities, as in the norms of a profession, for example "objectivity" in journalism.[10] But norms are more often discussed as informal rules based on an element of "oughtness," which regulates social conduct through a sense of moral obligation or duty. Norms are "normative" because of this felt compulsion.

While the idea of a "social norm" is often used in such a way that it encompasses both of these elements, social norm theorists frequently fail to bring out the interplay between them. For example, we may say that there is a norm of objectivity among journalists, but that norm is not simply the brute *fact* of journalistic objectivity but the belief among journalists that they *ought* to be objective—which then results in a consistent practice that can be described as a norm. Many social patterns emerge because people feel they ought to behave in a certain way. The feeling that men ought to take off their hats in church leads to the fact that few of them wear hats inside churches, but a different feeling of compulsion motivates the regularity of driving on the left (or right) hand side of the street.

One currently popular way of understanding social norms is to emphasize their function as signaling devices.[11] If social access to others is predicated on adherence to a particular social norm—signaling customs of dress, speech, expressions of taste—then we may think of these norms as cultural standards. More precisely, a social norm may possess the qualities of a standard where it is an implicit criterion for membership because signaling adherence to the norm comports with a sense of "oughtness" and allows for entry into certain social circles.

An obvious problem with this analogy, however, is that it robs the norm of any normative force: non-users of a standard may adopt it not because they feel they ought, but because they feel they must, in order to further their own goals. Therefore I do not want to claim that all social norms are susceptible to a network power analysis, but to focus here on signaling norms considered as membership standards, adopted as a way of signaling membership in a certain group and thereby gaining access to others in it. We see this sort of signaling norm in elite circles, where a particular manner of self-presentation may prove crucial, as with the standards of Davos culture.

Inquiring into the network properties of a given norm or set of norms is one way to get an analytic purchase on social norms that may serve as standards. We should ask whether the norm governs access in some way, whether because people engage only with others who do those things they ought to do, or because the norm structures social exchange, as with a language. (Of course, norms may do both.) If it does govern this access, and is coherent—a sign that consistently means one thing and not another to the relevant audience—then we can ask about its network properties. Extending the analysis of network properties to social norm theory, we should inquire whether the norms in question are configured at the boundary in a similar manner to a coherent standard with network power. Is a particular norm *available:* that is, open to others to adopt? For example, under the sumptuary laws of medieval Europe, fashions were restricted by class status, and thus were not open to universal use. This restriction obviously impeded the diffusion of the norm, precisely as intended. Is the norm *compatible* with other norms? For example, are there many acceptable ways of greeting someone, or signaling affection, any of which would allow the signaler to gain the same measure of social access to others? If so, it is less clear that any one particular norm will become privileged over others for accomplishing the same task. Is the norm *malleable*? Does it have a consistent and coherent expression or can each person be "creative" in its application? The more malleable the norm, the less it will serve as a social gatekeeper and the more it will blend into the general background of personal expression. (Of course, as in "hybridized" cultural forms, both a degree of personal expression and social signaling may be at work, and serve to reinforce social standing or recognition in complex ways.) The standards that I have claimed exhibit network power all share certain common configurations of network properties. In general, they are available, relatively incompatible, and relatively non-malleable. Whenever we identify a norm that exhibits availability but relative incompatibility and non-malleability, we should suspect that it might exhibit network power, provided that the expression of that norm offers a way for people to signal something to others, and that the audience for the signal is relevant for the signaler.

THE GLOBALIZATION OF SOCIAL NORMS

To explore the idea of signaling norms, consider two different examples of what might be considered the diffusion of social norms, both of which offer examples of cultural homogenization. The first is a relatively obscure example: convergence in the design and aesthetic presentation of corporate office parks. Jedediah Purdy cites a revealing conversation with the Indian entrepreneur and computer mogul Naryana Murthy of Infosys, a billion-dollar high technology company located outside Bangalore, and one of India's most widely known companies abroad. (Infosys is one of the most visible faces of India's high tech revolution and its status as an economic power of increasing importance.) Murthy explained to Purdy: "When you enter the Infosys campus [which is modeled on the Microsoft Corporation's headquarters] you will see clean roads, large fields, and clean offices. When you see all of this, you will think that you have left India. You will imagine that you have entered the United States, or—or even Switzerland. This is to show our foreign clients that we are serious, that we are world-class."[12]

The second and more familiar example is the phenomenon of "Mc-

Donaldization," the spread of the McDonald's fast food chain restaurant (and similar American fast food restaurants) around the world.[13] Whatever the demerits of its food—which is now the focus of litigation, public health campaigns, and media investigations—the McDonald's chain proliferates overseas in large part because of its association with the United States. McDonald's markets more than its hamburgers: it trades on its American roots. (Of course, this association is not purely advantageous: protestors in both India and France, for example, have targeted the chain as a proxy for American power more generally.)

What should we make of these two examples, the style of the manicured gardens at the Infosys corporate campus in Bangalore and the "McDonaldization" of the world? The Infosys example is easier to understand in network power terms, because the social norm underlying the cultural convergence operates more clearly like a standard underlying a network. Signaling "world-class" status in the Davos culture of international business means conforming to a specific set of aesthetic and architectural standards that are found from Switzerland to California—and now also in India. Corporate office park designs function as a criterion for admission to the ranks of global multinational status. The Infosys campus conforms to those standards that indicate seriousness and global ambition to its potential partners and clients, simply because other companies do likewise.

In other words, the corporate office parks of Davos culture are increasingly uniform because of the same dynamics that compel "Davos man" to speak English. Berger argues that Davos culture "is globalized as a direct accompaniment of global economic processes" and he notes that it "has obvious behavioral aspects that are directly functional in economic terms, behavior dictated by the accoutrements of contemporary business." These accoutrements are the requirements of coordination on a set of standards—in this case, of corporate self-presentation. Participants in (or aspirants to) "Davos culture" determine their individual behavior as part of a larger strategic choice: Which tie to wear to the business meeting? Which policies to initiate to win the confidence of bond traders? How best to convey our "world-class" status to potential partners?

Berger's use of the term "dictated" to describe the standards of Davos culture is interesting and perhaps deserves further comment. The convergence on such global standards does appear dictated, made necessary by the coordination game of international business. This is a point that

Berger does not elaborate on, at least in his first article on the four faces of global culture.[14] My argument, by contrast, has emphasized that the adoption of a standard is not enough to indicate a truly voluntary choice; rather, we must assess that choice against the backdrop of the available options before imagining that it represented genuine consent. Purdy also takes a more nuanced approach to this issue when he questions Murthy about his remarks on the corporate culture of Infosys: Purdy asks "whether it troubles him that appearing world-class means mimicking Silicon Valley down to the level of casual Fridays, and that seeming 'too Indian' suggests inadequacy." He reports Murthy's answer: "The weak always have to play by the rules the strong have made. If we play well, maybe in two or three generations we can make our own rules."[15] Thus even these "functional" standards of Davos culture appear deeply linked to identity and the experience of coercion, at least to the participants in this global cultural network.

Can we understand McDonaldization as also driven by network power? Berger certainly denies that coercion is at work in the spread of global cultural fashions: while the accoutrements of global business may be dictated by demands of economic functionality, he claims that the charge of cultural imperialism or coercion fails to recognize the free nature of the choices driving globalized culture. This is a popular line of argument with many other authors too (perhaps especially Americans) who see the rise of global popular culture as driven by its intrinsic attractions. As one commentator puts it: "Hollywood strives to present the universal to global audiences."[16] It is tempting—especially against arguments of that naively triumphalist variety—to emphasize instead the significance of extrinsic reasons, of the power of standards driving McWorld. But by contrast with those of the Davos elite, the pop culture standards in McWorld are harder to diagnose in terms of social coordination, even while the identity concerns are obvious.

The nature of the social cooperation and the way in which access is gained to it are both less clear here than in the case of international business culture. For example, the standard—say, the norm of "eating at McDonald's" or listening to pop music—may or may not signal something specific that enables the signaler to cooperate with others. No doubt, some people eat at McDonald's for intrinsic reasons (for example, because of the convenience or the taste of its food). For others, it may offer a chance to feel American or cosmopolitan for the quick duration of a McDonald's meal, the chance to see and be seen as part of a wave of global culture. The distinction that Berger and others draw between "sacramental" and "non-sacramental" consumption is relevant here: eating at McDonald's may signal something relatively specific to some people at some times, but, as Berger writes, to "paraphrase Freud, sometimes a hamburger is just a hamburger."[17]

To make sense of McDonaldization requires examining in greater detail the relation between network power and the dynamics of psychosocial recognition more generally. Where participation in a pop cultural form allows someone to cooperate with others (by signaling some relevant set of characteristics), then we can see network power as part of its success. But more often, signaling occurs not so much to gain cooperation from other people as to secure their recognition. Where the issue of access to cooperation is not explicit, we enter the more ambiguous realm of emulation and recognition.

PERSUASION AND RECOGNITION

Network power may lead someone to learn English, or cause a nation's decision-makers to join the WTO. It may even be responsible for driving a particular cultural mode or aesthetic choice in the international business world. But it is much less obvious that network power is behind "Mc-World," responsible for the rise of global pop culture or "Americanization." Where these cultural behaviors are adopted for extrinsic reasons—rather than their intrinsic attractions—it is not clearly from a desire to gain access to others for the sake of beneficial cooperation. Rather, the rise of McWorld (and perhaps any instance of peer-group socialization) appears to come from a desire to conform to a common pattern and be recognized by others—a complex psychosocial dynamic that early modern theorists discussed under the rubric of "emulation" and saw as central to their accounts of the emergence of sociability.[18] Thus, much of the cultural homogenization occurring in globalization may be governed by a different dynamic than that of network power. Like neoliberal standards that have not yet been juridified, these cultural forms do not buttress any particular type of transnational coordination, so they can be rejected as easily as they are taken up—which may help explain why fads come and go more quickly in McWorld than in Davos culture.

However, there is a way to understand the globalization of McWorld in terms of network power dynamics if we broaden our sense of the kinds of "cooperation" to which standards mediate access. Many forms of cultural convergence can be understood as being driven by a demand for recognition, a sense of belonging, esteem, or affection, which can be achieved by sharing particular norms. Of course, the behavioral signals we use to attract and bestow recognition are not about strategic access via a means of shared coordination but something more psychologically complex—however, they may rely on shared frames that operate as standards. Understanding this deep social psychology of emulation and its impact on global culture is a profound and important area of research to which the idea of network power may be able to make a modest contribution, in conjunction with theories of psychosocial recognition.

Recall Axel Honneth's contrast between the relations of recognition involved in a universalistic domain, like law, and that in a particular "community of values" in which people achieve social solidarity through their group's distinctiveness. Pop cultural forms may operate as cultural signals that express *both* a desire to pull together and to pull apart—a desire for both solidarity and difference—depending on the intended audience. Pulling together may mean adopting a common set of norms that allow identification with an in-group, often identified *against* outsiders, which for international youth culture may mean parents, other authority figures, or even other groups of peers—thus the obvious connection between forms of adolescent rebellion and the spread of McWorld.[19] But the rise of a global youth culture also allows for forms of solidarity in a framework of mutual recognition forged through shared cultural practices.

On such grounds, it is not implausible to argue that a common set of cultural attributes—which may together constitute "Americanization," for example—could rise to dominance as a vehicle through which the demand for intersubjective recognition can be articulated. It may be that there are intrinsic reasons to adopt (some) American cultural practices. As a few scholars have suggested, the United States, as a "nation of immigrants," may already have a hybridized culture uniquely suited to global dissemination.[20] Or perhaps the dominance of American media and other forms of American soft power have smoothed the way for this Americanization because Hollywood adapted itself early on to the commercial demands of a global audience.

However plausible or implausible these suggestions, an analysis based on network power focuses on extrinsic reasons rather than intrinsic ones, viewing "Americanization" as a kind of coordination problem. Indeed, if network power dynamics are operative in a demand for recognition that has propelled the spread of McWorld, then we should wonder whether coercion is at work in cultural globalization as well.

The argument that coercion is at work in cultural choices is not very popular, perhaps especially among American scholars. Berger, for example, asserts that, "though the United States has a great deal of power, its culture is not being imposed on others by coercive means."[21] This blanket exemption for cultural exports does not seem consistent with his assertion that some norms of Davos culture appear "dictated." A general focus of my argument has been, of course, that even formally free actions may be non-voluntary, reflecting forms of dominance in our social relations, and I see no reason why this might not be true in the domain of culture. Indeed, it may be especially true given the purely conventional nature of most cultural forms—their proximity to the arbitrary signs of Saussure's investigation.

The relative contributions of extrinsic and intrinsic reason (and thus of force) in the rise of McWorld will doubtless remain a subject of controversy. What is not controversial is that McWorld is spreading. It is also clear, however, that as it is adopted, it is taken up in different forms, and altered, consciously and unconsciously. This, too, can be understood in a framework of recognition. The third relation of recognition that Honneth describes comes from social solidarity within a particular group. Where such solidarity is undermined—perhaps because of cultural homogenization driven by a demand for universal recognition—then the creation of new forms of identity, or the renewal of older ones, may satisfy an individual's need for recognition of particularity. Of course, these new identities may appear in a variety of forms, from the innocuous (as with the indigenization of McWorld) to the more ominous, visible in the rise of fundamentalist reaction against cosmopolitan culture, both in the United States and abroad.

This need for recognition through social solidarity will not be satisfied by a thin global culture that presents itself as a rational universal and functions primarily as a solvent. Rather, alongside the desire to be alike—to be compatible, to be comprehensible—there remains too a desire to be unique, generating a *will to difference.* On this view, parallel to the consolidation of McWorld, we are likely to see cultural differentiation as well, reflecting, in part, the narcissism of minor differences—particularly in those areas central to youthful identity-formation, in which the demands of psychic individuation give this will to difference a special vigor.

Thus the dynamics of cultural globalization encompass both push and pull. At first we pull together, and then we push apart, in search of both universal recognition and solidarity within a particular group. Focusing on only one aspect of this process will cause us to miss the overall dialectical form of this historical development. Arguably, standards are central to both parts of this process, providing the universal conventions through which we come to know each other, and mediating the relations of recognition through which we come to know ourselves.

Where social norms provide a signaling function, we see a kind of psychosocial coordination game being conducted on a newly worldwide scale. For the participants in Davos culture, the norms are, at least in the first instance, functional and driven by straightforward interests, even while they have an effect on identity. For consumers in the pop cultural domain of McWorld, network power may be efficacious, but only through the complex psychological channels in which people gain access to recognition from others. In both cases, we see the globalization of local traditions—Western, and often specifically American ones—that now serve as standards facilitating the emergence of worldwide cultural networks. The fact that these traditions may also be altered or reinterpreted means that the cultural landscape constituted by these processes of convergence—at least where they are driven by dynamics of recognition rather than functional coordination—may look, at first glance, rather complex in form, with a great deal of apparent heterogeneity produced by the will to difference.

CONCEPTUAL FRAMES

While the globalization of specific social norms is an important part of the cultural process of globalization, it does not capture many other forms of convergence that seem to be taking place in our modes of understanding and self-conception. The Davos standards, for example, function as more than signaling norms for their users: they also change their users' self-understanding in profound and subtle ways through the process of *embodiment*. Likewise, young people across the globe may internalize new social mores and perspectives through their participation in McWorld. In both of these cases, the diffusion of a social norm affects the consciousness of those adopting it.

In the two other arenas of emerging global culture that we have discussed—"faculty club culture" and missionary evangelical Protestantism—the standards in question are not in the first instance practices or social norms that affect consciousness, but rather conceptual positions or epistemic commitments from the very start—what I earlier called "conceptual frames" in contrast to social norms. Here, network power operates not at the level of behavior or customs that subsequently affect thought processes, but directly in thought and perception. Understanding how network power can generate conceptual convergences in this way will allow us to make sense of those elements of globalization driven less by functional considerations than by conceptual or ideational dissemination.

Consider, for example, the growing movement of non-governmental organizations working across borders to solve problems ranging from environmental degradation to nuclear proliferation to human rights abuses.[22] The participants in this transnational culture—who are identified under the heading "faculty club culture" in Berger's analysis—share an understanding of certain issues and arrangements as problems, and a set of attitudes, intellectual approaches, and organizational frameworks that help them to solve these. How do network power dynamics contribute to the emergence of these networks of international activists and decision-makers? Some scholars in the field of international relations argue that international cooperation and problem-solving can emerge as the result of coordination in "epistemic communities," networks of experts committed to a shared way of conceiving and resolving problems.

Using this idea of epistemic communities in a broad sense allows us to see how conceptual categories can emerge as the solution to a particular kind of coordination problem. As one scholar explains, an "epistemic community is a network of professionals with recognized expertise and competence in a particular domain and an authoritative claim to policy-relevant knowledge within that domain or issue-area."[23] These networks can influence national decision-making and international cooperation not only through direct lobbying and argumentation but, more subtly, by articulating the nature of a problem in one way rather than another.

Understanding international issues from global warming to nuclear proliferation requires paying attention to "the role that networks of knowledge-
based experts—epistemic communities—play in articulating cause-and-
effect relationships of complex problems, helping states identify their
interests, framing the issues for collective debate, proposing scientific
policies, and identifying salient points for negotiation."

The ability to set the terms of debate and define relevant issues is a potent form of power—the focus of interest in what Steven Lukes has called
the "two-dimensional" view of power, and what Bachrach and Baratz call
"nondecision-making." In fact, theorists of epistemic communities use
similar language in explaining why attention should be paid to this phenomenon, claiming that these networks possess "control over knowledge
and information [which] is an important dimension of power."[24] Epistemic
communities are the conduits through which common modes of perception and reaction are channeled in the effort to resolve transnational
problems. They share a number of factors: "normative and principled beliefs," which help direct the "social action of community members"; causal
beliefs; notions of "validity," which include "internally defined criteria for
weighing and validating knowledge in the domain of their expertise"; and
a "common policy enterprise."[25]

Broadening the idea of epistemic communities will help us see how
forms of thought may be considered standards with the pull of network
power. The notion of an "epistemic community" might denote, most generally, a group of people with shared patterns of conceptual thinking or a
style of analytic reasoning. So far at least, the idea has been mostly used
to describe the international network of scientists sharing a common
empirical approach to knowledge and a form of reasoning in the scientific
method. But the idea of an epistemic community can be expanded to include groups of professionals or experts united by their "shared belief or
faith in the verity and the applicability of particular forms of knowledge
or specific truths."[26] It can perhaps be expanded yet further to include
whole systems of thought or "conceptual frames."

THE GLOBALIZATION OF CONCEPTUAL FRAMES

The literature on epistemic communities is helpful because it illuminates
the concrete benefits of international conceptual coordination in achieving ends such as nuclear disarmament or environmental amelioration.

These benefits come from shared conceptual understandings and specific knowledge that make parties to an international dispute comprehensible to other parties, putting decision-makers from different backgrounds on a common footing. But the academic literature construes the idea of epistemic communities rather narrowly, restricting the description to various expert professions. If we instead accept that at the heart of the epistemic community is a shared set of ideas on causality, expectations, knowledge and so on—a *conceptual frame*—then there is no need to restrict the use of this idea to scientific or governmental bodies. Indeed, in the way that I broaden the idea of an epistemic community, it approaches the idea of an *interpretive community* introduced by the literary theorist Stanley Fish, who argues that shared interpretive strategies render texts intelligible and meaningful relative to particular communities of readers.[27]

Uniting an epistemic community is an epistemic commitment (or series of commitments) that functions like a standard linking a network. The conceptual frames that link an epistemic network can be understood as a standard, operating almost as a language. Indeed, these frames are often specialized discourses with their own vocabularies and patterns of logic. On this view, international networks based on shared conceptual frames may be particularly important for policy-making on cross-border issues, but these are not the only epistemic communities playing significant roles in contemporary globalization. In fact, a broader view of what constitutes an "epistemic community" may serve to illuminate important areas of cultural convergence, where a shared conceptual frame operates like a standard. Any specific conceptual frame—for example, the patterns of reasoning and bodies of knowledge in ecology—must be examined in its specific context to see whether it functions in this way. But broadly, we can speculate on the standard-like aspects of at least *many* conceptual frames. Understanding them as sites of conceptual coordination allows us to be more specific than simply arguing that ideas spread in cultural globalization—or, as Chateaubriand predicted more elegantly, that "ideas . . . will have wings." Instead, we can proceed by identifying specific ways in which transnational actors want to achieve conceptual coordination and then articulate the different frameworks in which they might plausibly do so. Ideas may "have wings" for any number of general or specific reasons, but at least one reason that a particular conceptual frame may become dominant is because of network power.

Conceptual frames regulate access to others intellectually and imaginatively. A conceptual frame is a kind of mediating standard, a commonality that inherently governs a form of social exchange. It may also operate in the second sense, as a membership standard where entrance to a scientific or governmental body is predicated on its acceptance, either explicitly, as with entrance examinations, or implicitly, as in the need to show familiarity with the terms of a specialized discourse. (In the case that it operates as a membership standard, the conceptual frame may eventually become embodied in its users and then act as a mediating standard.) Sharing a conceptual framework enables coordinated problem-solving in intellectual and social exchanges that would otherwise be difficult or impossible.

Importantly, communication within many epistemic communities may constitute its own kind of action, which breaks down any rigid separation between "actions" and discursive practices. Speaking about a problem in a certain manner goes some way to solving it: it defines the issue, immediately narrowing the range of conceivable responses. In the case of epistemic communities endowed with special authority, communicating about a problem can be a form of settling it. Lawmakers, expert bureaucrats, and government officials in particular act by "doing things with words" (as J. L. Austin put it), setting the authoritative expectations according to which their constituencies cooperate and manage their shared lives.[28]

The configuration of network properties possessed by common conceptual frames supports the view that they would exert network power. We might suppose conceptual frames to be relatively *available;* indeed, many of the most important contemporary conceptual frames are not just open to new adherents, but aggressively missionary. As for *malleability,* these frames allow a good deal of dissent within their terms, but broadly speaking, conceptual frames tend to be constituted in relatively non-malleable ways. Of course, this is to be expected: for conceptual frames to be coherent as ideological units, they cannot be understood merely as collections of ideas and concepts to be altered or changed easily, but must be seen as foundational and basic.

Are these conceptual frames *compatible?* This is a difficult question to answer in the abstract. But if they are compatible, it is not costless or easy compatibility: as with a language, one may be able to adopt multiple, compatible conceptual frames, but each needs time and attention to internalize. Great attention may be necessary if we want to switch between specialized discourses while maintaining credibility in each. Of course, if we imagine a conceptual frame in the most comprehensive sense—as shaping our self-understanding, view of causality, and the like—one frame certainly may not prove very compatible with alternatives. Given these properties, some conceptual frames may very well exert network power, providing a common way not just of talking about issues but even of thinking through them in the first place. And, apart from any actual benefits to be gained by thinking about a complex problem in one fashion rather than another, there may be pressures to adopt one conceptual framework rather than another simply because many of the people with whom one must work to solve a problem are already using or committed to using that conceptual frame. Anyone who has had to take part in a committee meeting knows firsthand the pressures to conform to a particular way of thinking and speaking about problems, and the benefits and frustrations that this narrowing brings. The idea of network power may then suggest a way to consider how shared consciousness or symbolic intersubjectivity may function, without some of the difficulties that have attended earlier arguments (in Durkheim, for example) about "group minds" or collective representations.[29]

EPISTEMIC NETWORKS

Many transnational networks function as epistemic communities sharing a conceptual frame. Consider the following professional groups: scientists, public finance experts, international lawyers and jurists, professors of comparative literature, and civil engineers. Obviously some of these groups use a more coherent conceptual frame than others, and therefore constitute tighter epistemic networks. Any of these conceptual frames might possess network power, however.

For example, the business community in the United States relies on a conceptual frame that we might call "business-speak," based on a view of instrumental economic rationality. Because of the centrality of organized business in American economic life, the business community has the power to make outsiders recast their language—and perhaps therefore understand differently the nature of many problems—according to this conceptual frame. Politicians, academics, government officials, labor union officials, and lawyers all come from backgrounds and epistemic communities with different ways of understanding the world and conceiving and solving problems. But when these groups need to cooperate with businessmen, problems that might be conceived and articulated in a variety of ways come to be discussed and argued over in the language of costs, benefits, and interests according to a pattern of reasoning that amounts, more or less, to the style of argument one finds in the classrooms of American business schools. Indeed, professionals of all stripes now take "mini-MBA" classes that serve as crash courses in business-speak.

For some problems, the conceptual frame of business-speak may be intrinsically helpful; that possibility need not be ruled out *ex ante* on either aesthetic or ideological grounds. But the reason that diverse groups use business-speak is for the sake of coordinating—not only discursively, but conceptually—with a powerful epistemic community. The alternative to this concession would be epistemic and ideological conflict over the terms of the debate—or, perhaps just as likely, straightforward exclusion from it. To connect with the heads of enterprise, it may be necessary not only to speak the language of business, but also to view the world in the way that a businessman does. This coordination has obvious practical effects (both beneficial and detrimental) not only in what is said, but in what is left *unsaid*—as, for example, in the marginalization of concerns about the limits of markets that may be difficult to express *within* the framework of "business-speak," since these ideas require a critical interrogation of that very framework.[30] Thus, the choice of a conceptual frame to address a set of problems in one way may amount to effective "nondecision-making" (as Bachrach and Baratz put it) about particular problems.

The discursive coordination that leads to the elevation of one specialized language over another may well present an example of network power. This power is felt not only by members of elite global networks, but also by newcomers aspiring to join them. Of course, communities of thought do not emerge as the result of network power alone, as I have emphasized throughout the book by drawing a distinction between the intrinsic and extrinsic reasons that may motivate the adoption of standards. Conceptual frames may seem attractive because of their network power—that is, because many others share that mode of thought—but a particular framework of inquiry may also be useful independent of how many others are using it. The prevalence of any conceptual frame may increase initially through being adopted for intrinsic reasons, while extrinsic reasons associated with network power may later have a greater effect. It may often prove difficult to distinguish the attraction of a conceptual frame from the effect of the power wielded by its network—especially when our modes of evaluation are internal to the frame itself—but we need not therefore claim that truth is constituted by power (as some post-modern theorists might have it), at least not in any simple way. Indeed, the distinction I have drawn between the intrinsic and extrinsic reasons for the adoption of a particular conceptual frame is predicated on there being better and worse *intrinsic* ways of approaching a problem or framing a discussion, even if the intrinsic reasons for so doing may sometimes be lost in the face of extrinsic pressure toward intellectual conformity.

GLOBAL SOCIAL IMAGINARIES

How far can the idea of coordination in epistemic networks be pushed in understanding global ideological diffusion in areas other than expert epistemic communities? If we are to take seriously the argument that there are different systems of thought, will a network power analysis help in understanding our most fundamental conceptual frames? We might be able to explain the globalization of "faculty club culture" given the network power of conceptual frames, but could we explain the success of "evangelical Protestantism"? At first glance, some religious doctrines may well seem to exhibit availability, incompatibility, and relative mallea-bility—that configuration of network properties that, as we have seen, makes for a successful standard. For example, consider both Christianity and Buddhism, the two most successful missionary faiths in world history, by contrast with their "parent" religions, Judaism and Hinduism. Since neither Christianity nor Buddhism is tied to any particular people in the way that both Judaism and Hinduism are, they have generally functioned as relatively more open networks than their progenitor religions.

However, in moving beyond networks of experts and beginning to examine broad religious or ideational standards, we have gone some dis-tance from the idea of a conceptual frame and an epistemic community—indeed, some might say too far. Viewing other forms of discourse and ideology through the lens of network power brings the idea of a con-ceptual frame closer to the idea of a "social imaginary." This notion has been used to describe the imaginative associations and identifications that occur in large groups of people. It comes from the work of social theorist Cornelius Castoriadis, but has been given a different inflection in recent scholarship by anthropologists and philosophers such as Arjun Appadurai and Charles Taylor, keen to emphasize the idea of multiple or alternative modernities.[31] Dilip Gaonkar explains that social imaginaries refer to those ways of "understanding the social that become social entities themselves, mediating collective life." Social imaginaries, in this sense, are reflective understandings internal to a particular community or culture, functioning as "first-person subjectivities that build upon implicit understandings that underlie and make possible common practices."[32] Charles Taylor explains that he uses the idea to focus on "the ways in which people imagine their social existence, how they fit together with others, how things go on between them and their fellows, the expectations that are normally met, and the deeper normative notions and images that underlie these expectations."[33]

A social imaginary is thus something deeper than a conceptual frame, and usually more difficult to specify precisely. Social imaginaries are less available to outside or objective verification than, say, a particular way of analyzing scientific data. (This is part of the problem, as I noted above, with attempting to diagnose the different contributions made by intrinsic and extrinsic reasons in the adoption of conceptual frames that may themselves represent particular modes of evaluation.) Gaonkar explains that social imaginaries "are imaginary in a double sense: they exist by virtue of representation or implicit understandings, even when they acquire immense institutional force; and they are the means by which individuals understand their identities and their place in the world."[34] None of this is to suggest, however, that social imaginaries lack practical force. Indeed, if it makes sense to speak of social imaginaries at all, it is in terms of very broad social understandings that have a profound impact on our most important social institutions and practices. Taylor argues that "the social imaginary is that common understanding that makes possible common practices and a widely shared sense of legitimacy."[35] To engage in those practices and share that sense of legitimacy requires participating in the social imaginary by which they are made possible.

Does it make sense to suppose that social imaginaries may function as complex standards, linking together vast groups of people in networks of shared consciousness over long periods of time? If it does, then we can inquire into the network power dynamics inherent in particular ways of seeing and understanding the world, and, accordingly, analyze the globalization of social imaginaries as identified by as the anthropologist Arjun Appadurai and others.[36]

However, considering the network power of the "social imaginaries" through which large numbers of people make themselves normatively and practically intelligible to one another is beyond the scope of this book. I have tried to illustrate the idea of network power through relatively simple examples, taken from the domains of technology, language, culture, and the economy. Yet it is an intriguing thought that the globalization of these standards—and our resulting participation in a networked world—may affect us at a deeper level, even influencing the ways in which we conceive of ourselves and others. Indeed, the "deeper convergence" to which I alluded at the beginning of my discussion of cultural globalization may be expected to have significant ramifications for the social imaginaries prevailing today.

I suspect that convergence at the level of social imaginaries would prove unlike the other instances of convergence I have discussed in this book, such as the diffusion of new technologies, the juridification of neo-liberalism, and the spread of global popular culture. It might, in fact, constitute the emergence of a new global subjectivity, a shared consciousness through which any and all forms of conventional sociability could be rethought (and hence transformed). That rethinking and transformation might make possible a deeper form of globalization: a self-conscious, collective reorganization of global activity, reflected through a new social imaginary that would itself be included as a prominent constituent of the new world order that it described.

However, expanding upon this possibility at the present moment would be, as one psychoanalyst quipped about his profession, "not only impossible but extremely difficult."[37] For the achievement of this deeper form of globalization would be nothing less than revolutionary, and we are always both agents and objects in any revolutionary process.

Conclusion

IN THIS BOOK, I have argued that globalization is best understood as the emergence and consolidation of transnational and international networks that link people—or groups of people, including entire countries—through the use of shared coordinating standards. These standards are social conventions that exhibit economies of scale in their adoption by new users, giving rise to what I have called network power. Although this dynamic emerges as a result of the exercise of formally free choice, it can result in the elimination of the alternatives over which free choice may be exercised effectively. I have exemplified this argument by considering elements of contemporary globalization, including many of the linguistic, technological, cultural, and economic developments that are most obvious to us in our daily lives.

Understanding globalization, I have argued, requires us to recognize the power inherent in relations of sociability. I have located this power in the social structures through which we coordinate our actions. These social structures emerge out of the aggregation of many individual choices and, taken together, produce circumstances in which individual agency can be severely curtailed. The idea of network power starts from this point, and enables us to make better sense of the combination of voluntary (even eager) acceptance and profound resentment that we see in the responses of many people to contemporary globalization. This seeming paradox can be resolved if we specify more carefully what is indicated when an individual accepts any state of affairs. For it is certainly possible to consent to our circumstances without those circumstances being very attractive in the first place. Participation in social relations that are unfair or coercive may often prove preferable to not participating at all—an insight that critics of sociability have emphasized for several centuries now, but the implications of which we have yet to accommodate fully on either a philosophical or a political level.

That accommodation begins with the recognition that there is another way in which we can construct our social life: that is, by using the power of sovereignty to alter our collective circumstances, including those that come about through the accumulation of individual choices. I have not considered the relations of sovereignty in much detail in this book, choosing to focus instead on providing an analysis of sociability that has largely been missing. But I have been keen to argue throughout that the anarchy of pure sociability is neither desirable nor sustainable, even though it is the case that large-scale social structures can emerge from interdependent, individual choices. Protecting ourselves against the entrapping constructions of sociability requires the organized power of democratic politics.

The old argument expressed in these ideas has a new relevance today because the globalization of coordinating standards has led to the emergence of transnational networks which unite geographically distant participants outside the structures of political authority. The emergence of global standards is not complete and it is not unalterable. It is possible—as I suggested in my discussion of how we might go about remedying network power—that new forms of compatibility may allow pluralism and coordinated access to exist together in an increasingly networked world. And if such compatibility proves unfeasible, it is possible that a more equitable division of the costs and benefits of transnational cooperation could help us to avoid violent conflict over global standards. In either case, however, we need to acknowledge an important point concerning contemporary globalization: that difference can no longer be assumed as a fact of history or nature, but must be produced or maintained for the sake of a valued end (or, where our differences are not valuable, simply left to disappear). That production or maintenance cannot be based on relations of sociability, which tend to produce convergence and uniformity, but requires a reassertion of politics undergirded by the power of sovereignty.

Creating the arrangements that will support a diversity of national regimes or enshrine more egalitarian forms of global cooperation becomes a task for politics because politics is the only effective countervailing power that we have with which to refashion the structures that emerge through sociability. Politics presents us with an alternative to reliance on the accumulation of individual decisions conducing to something systemic over time. Instead of wandering blindly into circumstances that emerge, unforeseen, as the result of many different individuals' actions—the aggregated effects of which nonetheless affect us all—we can become part of a unified political body in order to consider the kind of world we would like to live in, and pursue together the collective outcomes we desire. The difference between these two ways that we make our social world—over time through the accumulation of interdependent, individual decisions, or all at once in an act of political construction—reveals the deep way in which we can use politics to overcome the vagaries of history.

This, of course, makes some people uneasy about politics, for many familiar and well-rehearsed reasons. But we should not let that anxiety delude us into thinking that there exists any alternative to politics, or that we should reject politics in order to render ourselves subject to new forms of global sociability. For, as the arguments I have made concerning network power have illustrated, power operates in the sphere of sociability just as it does in the sphere of sovereignty. It should not be forgotten that there are many different ways to be oppressed; it is slavery that has been our constant companion throughout history, not emancipation.

Politics provides a way to get a grip on social conventions that might otherwise become the site of a private but nonetheless powerful structural domination. The relation between modern politics and social emancipation is complicated and debated—the subject for another book altogether —but a moment's reflection should convince us that important forms of individual freedom do depend on collective mobilization. To reshape or reduce the power that the social structures we create have over us, we can only summon the organized power of politics. The large-scale voluntarism of sociability, by contrast, has always delivered the most varied and elaborate forms of individual subjugation. Today's global networks prove no exception.

The previous high point of global sociability—the episode of globalization that preceded the First World War—collapsed in the violent reassertion of national politics. What lessons should we draw from this fact? Surely the problem is not (as many have been tempted to claim) that politics refused to die peacefully, but rather that it was hijacked and inflamed by particular interests and ideologies made all the more potent by the unregulated power of sociability. Consider that even the liberal democracies of that epoch relied upon the strategic reassertion of national sovereignty to manage a global sociability gone wrong. To reform an international society thrust into depression, violence, and imperialism, citizens everywhere turned to collective decision-making—to politics—whether in the form of Keynesian economic planning or in the deliberate revival of national cultures and languages, including movements for decolonization.

To claim that the relations of sovereignty constitute our best hope for overcoming structural domination is not, of course, to deny the obvious fact that relations of sovereignty may themselves be distorted or corrupt. Simply, it is to focus our attention on the fact that political construction is inescapable whether we manage it collectively or cede that privilege to powerful private interests, contenting ourselves with one or another of the many naïve forms of voluntarism available to us in our daily lives. Importantly, however, we cannot ever cede our political agency completely or finally. The turn from politics lasts only so long as we forget that what makes freedom significant is not what we do with it individually but what we make of it together.

As the power of today's global networks becomes increasingly coercive —because increasingly universal—we should anticipate a future reassertion of politics demanding the freedom which is achieved together through the relations of sovereignty. Pretending that globalization is on the verge of eliminating the need for politics will not help us to think clearly about that reassertion of politics when it occurs, and may, in fact, mean that we end up promoting ugly and virulent political forms—fascism, say, as opposed to resurgent democracy—without necessarily intending it.

As to this future reassertion of politics, the idea of network power can provide little guidance. It can suggest how forms of globalized sociability might operate—given the dynamics of network power at work in them—but it cannot tell us what form our political agency should take to counter network power. We can agree with Clausewitz that war is politics carried on by other means and still hope that, in reworking today's globalization, we are able to find less destructive ways of asserting our collective will, including the will to difference. Reworking today's globalization requires using politics to regulate transnational networks, in order to benefit as much as we can from both democracy and globalization. This is the deep, unfinished task of democratic modernity: to use the relations of sovereignty to innovate egalitarian and sustainable forms of sociability at all levels, including the global.

Globalization is here to stay, however, so rework it we must. Even the violence of two world wars did not, in the end, slow down the process for more than a few decades. In fact, in significant respects—in the transmission of ideas, in the migration of people, in the deployment of armies across the face of the earth—the two world wars and the Cold War that followed them only consolidated globalization rather than halting it. We know that we will have a globalized future, therefore, but we do not know what form it will take. Globalization can be reworked, but not rejected: it cannot be rejected because it represents a transformation that we ourselves have brought about, and which has already transformed us. But we cannot know what form it will take for the very same reason: it depends on what we decide to make of it together.

NOTES

INTRODUCTION

1. The problem of coordination (tacit or explicit) is a central theme of Schelling's book. See Thomas Schelling, *The Strategy of Conflict* (Cambridge: Harvard University Press, 1960). The specific examples of tacit coordination that he offers—including that of choosing the clock in the center of Grand Central Station at 12 noon for an unplanned rendezvous—are discussed on pp. 54–58. Schelling writes (p. 57, italics original): "People *can* often concert their intentions or expectations with others if each knows that the other is trying to do the same. Most situations—perhaps every situation for people who are practiced at this kind of game—provide some clue for coordinating behavior, some focal point for each person's expectation of what the other expects him to expect to be expected to do."

2. The term "network power" is an obvious one to name the power that inheres in or is structured through networked social relations. At a moment when the fascination with networks or "flat ontologies" is at a high, and with such networks counterposed to hierarchies of power (e.g., in the state), it seems a salutary term for reminding us that network dynamics constitute relations of power too. I sometimes also refer to this concept as the "power of a standard," which I mean interchangeably with network power, since a standard underlying a network is powerful owing to the significance of the network it unites. I also use the term "network power" because at least two other works on globalization have already done so: see Jean-Marie Guéhenno, *The End of the Nation-State*, trans. Victoria Elliott (Minneapolis: University of Minnesota Press, 1995), and Michael Hardt and Antonio Negri, *Empire* (Cambridge: Harvard University Press, 2000). Although the precise way in which I employ the term differs from these previous usages—which

are helpfully provocative but do not attempt to provide an *analytics* of network power—there are nevertheless some broad resonances with these works that I wish to indicate. Indeed, I hope that a more fully articulated concept of network power will render these accounts of globalization more comprehensible to those who do not share the background vocabularies (mainly of contemporary Continental philosophy) on which they draw.

3. These reciprocally determining, conditional expectations are what the philosopher David Lewis terms "higher-order expectations." See David K. Lewis, *Convention: A Philosophical Study* (Cambridge: Harvard University Press, 1969). I discuss the idea of conventions (particularly Lewis's) more fully in Chapter 2.

4. The literature on empire has become increasingly substantial and varied in the past few years, especially following the terrorist attacks of September 11, 2001, and the subsequent American military operations in the Middle East and elsewhere. We should distinguish the claim (1) that globalization is imperial or hegemonic from the claim (2) that the foreign policy of the United States is now (or has always been) imperial. Tony Judt and Anatol Lieven have reviewed a number of the arguments for these two claims, and offer good introductions to the contemporary debate. See Anatol Lieven, "The Empire Strikes Back," *The Nation*, July 7, 2003, and Tony Judt, "Dreams of Empire (America and Imperialism)," *New York Review of Books* 51, no. 17 (2004). The claim (2) that the United States now has an "empire"—with a secondary question as to whether it should keep or pursue it—brings together neoconservatives and "liberal imperialists" like Max Boot, Niall Ferguson, and Michael Ignatieff who favor American military intervention abroad for geopolitical or humanitarian reasons. See, for example, Max Boot, "The Case for American Empire," *Weekly Standard*, October 15, 2001, and Niall Ferguson, *Colossus: The Price of America's Empire* (New York: Penguin Press, 2004). This view is extremely controversial, of course, and according to its critics at home and abroad, threatens to undermine many of the most important public values of the United States. See Prata Bhanu Mehta, "Empire and Moral Identity," *Ethics and International Affairs* 17, no. 2 (2003). It is also a contested claim, empirically, for the limits of American power are increasingly obvious, as Michael Walzer points out in "Is There an American Empire?," *Dissent* 50, no. 4 (2003). Emmanuel Todd has argued provocatively that the American hegemony is already declining to such an extent that it makes sense to begin discussions about what the "after empire" might look like. See his *After the Empire: The Breakdown of the American Order*, trans. C. Jon Delogu (New York: Columbia University Press, 2003).

Claim (1) is a different, and in many ways more interesting charge: that globalization itself, quite apart from recent American maneuvers, is imperial or hegemonic. It is to this distinct but related debate that the idea of network power contributes most obviously. Hardt and Negri present in *Empire* a provocative account of contemporary globalization as a new kind of empire, which they distinguish from territorial empires. Their account incited controversy well before the neoconservative position on American empire brought this characterization of globalization into mainstream discussion. For a good review of Hardt and Negri's *Empire*, see Sanjay G. Reddy, "Dilemmas of Globalization," *Ethics and International Affairs* 15, no. 1 (2001). I have also reviewed their book: David Singh Grewal, "Empire's Law," *Yale Journal of Law and the Humanities* 14, no. 1 (2002). An argument for understanding globalization as empire is also found in Robert H. Wade, "The Invisible Hand of American Empire," *Ethics and International Affairs* 17, no. 2 (2003), and in Ellen M. Wood, *Empire of Capital* (London: Verso, 2003). Jedediah Purdy also develops an account similar to the one I use here, in his *Being America: Liberty, Commerce, and Violence in an American World* (New York: Knopf, 2003).

5. Two books which offer good historical overviews of the variety of past empires, which prove useful to compare and contrast with today's globalization are: Anthony Pagden, *Peoples and Empires: A Short History of European Migration, Exploration, and Conquest, from Greece to the Present* (New York: Modern Library, 2001), and Michael W. Doyle, *Empires* (Ithaca, N.Y.: Cornell University Press, 1986).

6. The terms "informal" and "formal" empire are developed in several mid-century historical studies of the British Empire. See, e.g., John Gallagher and Ronald Robinson, "The Imperialism of Free Trade," *Economic History Review* 6, no. 1 (1953).

7. John Maynard Keynes, *The Economic Consequences of the Peace* (London: Macmillan, 1919), 9.

CHAPTER 1. DEFINING NETWORK POWER

1. Emma Rothschild, "Globalization and the Return of History," *Foreign Policy*, no. 115 (1999): 106–116.

2. For an excellent examination of seventeenth- and eighteenth-century ideas about international politics and commerce, see Istvan Hont, *Jealousy of Trade: International Competition and the Nation-State in Historical Perspective* (Cambridge: Harvard University Press, 2005).

3. As cited in Rothschild, "Globalization and the Return of History," 107.

4. See Jeremy Bentham, *Introduction to the Principles of Morals and Legislation* (London: T. Payne, 1789), 324–325. Bentham introduced the term to update the older Roman law concept of *ius gentium*. (The *Principles* was first printed in 1780.) Of course, as this example illustrates, many of the concepts used in analyses of globalization or of interstate relations draw on earlier theories of law and empire from the classical world, even if words like "international" are relatively modern inventions. Indeed, classical commentary on empire remains usefully provocative for those thinking through these issues, as the host of recent comparisons between American hegemony and the Roman Empire makes clear. See, for example, Michael Hardt and

Antonio Negri's *Empire*, or Jedediah Purdy's *Being America* for two different discussions, both of which make use of parallels or analogies between our current world situation and that of the ancients. The argument in each is that the kind of "empire" that American-led globalization is forging is less a state-centered empire on the model of the "new imperialism" of the late nineteenth century than an older version of empire as a system of culture and an idea of right without bounds. Certainly, the Romans understood the world they dominated in this fashion. Consider the famous prophecy of Jupiter at the beginning of the first book of the *Aeneid*, lines 278–279: "his ego nec metas rerum nec tempora pono; imperium sine fine dedi." In the Loeb translation: "For these [Romans] I set neither bounds nor periods of empire; dominion without end have I bestowed." *Virgil*, ed. H. Rushton Fairclough and George P. Goold, Loeb Classical Library 63–64 (Cambridge: Harvard University Press, 1999), 260–261.

5. Anthony Giddens, *The Consequences of Modernity* (Stanford: Stanford University Press, 1990), 64. In *The Follies of Globalisation Theory: Polemical Essays* (London: Verso, 2000), Justin Rosenberg offers a powerful criticism of both globalization theory in general and Giddens's *Consequences* in particular, calling that book "the ur-text of globalisation as a social theory" (88). His critique of Giddens (pp. 88–155) takes up almost half the volume. In a different book, Giddens makes a claim that there are two sources of the "disembedding" of social relations—via what he calls "symbolic tokens" and "expert systems." See Anthony Giddens, *Modernity and Self-Identity: Self and Society in the Late Modern Age* (Stanford: Stanford University Press, 1991), 18. The idea of network power is meant to address both, most obviously the case of symbolic tokens (as I examine in Chapter 3 on money, for example) but also the idea of expert systems, which I address in the literature on "epistemic communities" in Chapter 10.

6. Roland Robertson, *Globalization* (London: Sage, 1992), 8, cited in Malcolm Waters, *Globalization* (London: Routledge, 1995), 4.

7. Waters, *Globalization*, 3. David Harvey links this "compression of space" in globalization to the dynamics of capitalism and argues that the current wave of American imperialism arises from tensions within American capitalism now manifest on a global stage. See Harvey, *The New Imperialism* (Oxford: Oxford University Press, 2003).

8. Technology alone was insufficient for the globalization of many networks, which came about instead owing to European overseas expansion—motivated, perhaps in part, by certain universalizing tendencies in modernity. On the European expansion of the nineteenth century and the formation of global networks in culture and commerce, see Christopher A. Bayly, *The Birth of the Modern World, 1780–1914: Global Connections and Comparisons* (Malden, Mass.: Blackwell, 2004). In the literature on globalization, there is some debate as to whether it represents a continuation, however accelerated, of previously existing trends or a decisive break from the past. As I

present it in this book, contemporary globalization is a current episode in a continuing process of social coordination. I agree, therefore, with those theorists who argue that globalization does not represent a radical departure from past trends but the generalization of these trends on a new stage and perhaps at a new tempo. It should be noted, of course, that the technological shifts that have enabled the compression of geographic distance are themselves dependent on standardization, whether we consider the "containerization" in integrated global transport networks of sea, rail, and long-haul trucking or the new communications technologies, which are the subject of my discussion in Chapter 7.

9. The way that different networks can be structured is a central concern of social network theory and social network analysis. As should be obvious, this book is not a contribution to formal network analysis proper, but an attempt to examine the new global networks in a richer social theoretic frame. I will address formal network analysis to the extent that it becomes relevant —as in Chapter 6, for example—in the context of a more general analysis of globalization.

10. The *Oxford English Dictionary* has several pages of definitions for the word "standard," which I use here in one of two different ways, corresponding roughly to the following two definitions: (1) "An authoritative or recognized exemplar of correctness, perfection, or some definite degree of any quality," and (2) "A rule, principle, or means of judgement or estimation; a criterion, measure."

11. The idea of a "network" need not be restricted to groups of people united by some shared technological standard, although that is the most familiar domain in which transnational networks are currently discussed. We can consider the community of English-language speakers as a "network" based on the use of English, even though we will never know the millions—perhaps billions—of other people who speak some English. We can think of the users of a given currency as constituting a network, united by the common use—the offer and acceptance—of a given monetary token, like the Euro or the Yuan. These linguistic and currency networks, of course, may or may not be contiguous with any national community. For example, the U.S. dollar is legal tender not only in the United States, but also in Ecuador and Panama, and is commonly accepted as an informal second currency in many countries overseas, where half to two-thirds of the $700 billion in bills circulate. The widespread use of the U.S. dollar abroad is well known to the Federal Reserve Bank, which must track such usage as part of its ongoing effort to manage the money supply. See: http://www.federalreserve .gov/boarddocs/speeches/2004/20040426/default.htm. See also: http:// www.federalreserve.gov/paymentsystems/coin/default.htm.

12. It is possible to imagine a membership standard becoming a mediating standard when the routine that defines access to an in-group is offered to non-users who come to adopt it as an integral part of their activity. The

distinction I introduce between them is meant to capture a rough distinction I suppose familiar to our thinking about these issues rather than to suppose a precise analytic divide. I should also add that this distinction is just one of many different ways to think about different types of standards. One related but not identical division might be between process-related standards and standards in outcomes or final products. Mapping this division onto the scheme I have outlined, we would say that where a process-related standard or a standard in outcomes is intrinsic to the interaction (such that it mediates the basic activity), it is a *mediating* standard. More commonly, this distinction—as used, say, in industrial design—would be a subdivision within two different types of standard criteria for admission, specifying either the process necessary for admission or the final outcome necessary for admission, with the requirement pegged accordingly.

13. For more on the *acquis* and its function in the European Union, see Simon Hix, *The Political System of the European Union* (New York: St. Martin's Press, 1999). The fact that the *acquis* serves as a mediating standard should, on my analysis, make the EU an alliance or network of sovereign states, an in-group of those countries that choose to participate in it. It should, in other words, represent a form of *sociability*, as I will describe it in Chapter 2. But it is also supposed to be a supranational governing body, and thus there is some controversy about the description of the EU in political theoretic terms. Jan Zielonka has recently laid out the case for understanding (and then celebrating) the EU not as a federated superstate, but as a "neo-medieval empire," a form of post-national empire in which there is no clear demarcation of sovereignty, clear boundaries, or political authority. See his *Europe as Empire: The Nature of the Enlarged European Union* (Oxford: Oxford University Press, 2006). I think that Zielonka's description is basically correct, but that we should be concerned, rather than pleased, about losing national sovereignty in a neo-medieval jumble. For such a loss is a blow to democratic decision-making, which takes place in the context of national polities. Zielonka seems to believe, by contrast, that the alleged "democratic deficit" affecting the EU should make us rethink our commitment, not to the EU so much as to democracy (at least as it is currently practiced).

A different view of what the EU should be—not so much a description of what it currently *is*—comes in Glyn Morgan's recent book, *The Idea of a European Superstate: Public Justification and European Integration* (Princeton: Princeton University Press, 2005). Morgan seeks a stronger, federal superstate at the European level, which will be capable of participating on the world stage and acting, internationally at least, as a single sovereign. But, while this is arguably desirable from a foreign policy perspective (depending on one's judgments about contemporary global threats), it is not clear that it preserves many of the elements of sovereignty that are most valuable, namely, a clear and transparent setting in which democratic decisions can be effectively put into practice. In a vast superstate like Morgan's proposed

EU, the opportunity to participate in democratic politics may become un-available for ordinary people, lost in channels of federated bureaucracy or diluted in a continental superpower that collects together too many people to represent popular will adequately. Indeed, would this new European superstate resemble the United States in possessing an undeniable external sovereignty in world affairs, but also an inadequately democratic internal sovereignty?

14. I do not want to make too much of the distinction between economies of scale and returns to scale, which is a rather technical issue. Part of the confusion may be that Brian Arthur's important work on network effects uses the term "increasing returns" to indicate a positive feedback dynamic, but that it has a somewhat different formal definition in economics. See W. Brian Arthur, *Increasing Returns and Path Dependence in the Economy* (Ann Arbor: University of Michigan Press, 1994). The common use of the phrase "increasing returns to scale" to indicate a positive feedback dynamic is probably better captured, strictly, by "economies of scale." As the *New Palgrave* defines it: "We say that there are *economies* (or *diseconomies*) *of scale* in some interval of output if the average cost is decreasing (or increasing) there." *The New Palgrave: A Dictionary of Economics*, ed. John Eatwell et al., 4 vols. (London: Macmillan, 1987), 80, italics original. By contrast, "A tech-nology exhibits increasing returns to scale if a proportionate increase in all inputs allows for a more than proportionate increase in outputs; in the single-output case, this implies a decreasing average cost curve" (ibid., 761). Under certain circumstances, these two notions of economies of scale and increasing returns are equivalent, but not necessarily in all cases.

15. There are a wide variety of social theories that locate the important action at the level of aggregate phenomena. Sometimes, social aggregates are de-scribed in a way that attributes agency to them (though whether that attribu-tion includes intentionality, as we see with human agents, is up for debate). For example, in the analyses of contemporary "actor-network theory" associ-ated with Science and Technology Studies scholars such as Bruno Latour, the network coheres as a whole (thus, both network and actor) and can be considered the key variable. See Bruno Latour, *Reassembling the Social: An Introduction to Actor-Network Theory* (Oxford: Oxford University Press, 2005), and see also my discussion of Actor-Network Theory in note 21 of Chapter 6.

Some literature on globalization considers standards in this way, explic-itly granting a kind of agency to transnational phenomena. Consider the anthropological literature on transnational cultural phenomena that imag-ines a form of agency in technology, ideas, or forms—e.g., Annelise Riles, *The Network Inside Out* (Ann Arbor: University of Michigan Press, 2000). I am not clear whether this literature is using theoretical shorthand—an abbreviation, as it were—or whether it advances the idea that there is such a thing as non-human or transhuman agency. These and other postmodern approaches to agency are indebted to a variety of earlier philosophers, especially phenomenologists in the Heideggerian tradition. In the "language ontologies" of Heidegger, for example, it is claimed that language "speaks" us rather than we speaking it. I am sympathetic to George Steiner's thought that Heidegger's account here may be, at root, theological in its inspiration (akin, perhaps, to the idea of God "speaking" through man): *Martin Heidegger* (Chicago: University of Chicago Press, 1991), 61–63. This is *not* the kind of argument that I am trying to advance here, even if I sometimes describe networks in a way that seems to attribute agency to them. I do sometimes write, for example, that "a standard possesses network power," which I mean only as a kind of shorthand and not the ascription of agency to a form of social coordination. Likewise, if I write of a standard "driving to conventionality," I do not mean to imply a teleology of standards apart from any teleological dimension already present in the social world and ultimately attributable in some fashion to the actions and choices of human agents.

16. In many different situations, we want to cooperate with greater rather than fewer numbers of people. In economic contexts, the point is easy enough to see. Companies in the "Alliance for Rational Standards" want clients to use their standards and hence to buy their products. As company executives using a different set of standards, we may switch over to the Alliance's standards in order to sell to its market. Or, to use an illustration from a different industry, as computer company executives, we want more people to use our software program or our operating system, and hence to make them more attractive for others to use. And if we are not offering software compatible with the dominant operating system—Microsoft Windows, for example— it may be hard for our products to compete.

But the more general point about network power can be made if we expand this idea from the context of business strategy to include non-commercial networks too. Even in non-economic contexts involving some other form of social exchange, we often want to reach as many people as possible. The value of the language we speak will depend, at least in part, on how many others speak it. An institute in a non-English-speaking country may therefore want someone on staff who can translate its policy papers into English for a global audience. Likewise, public health officials may want to have everyone conform to a set of health procedures, such as routine vaccinations, not only for the individual benefit to patients, but for the collective outcomes that are thereby achieved. (The value of a single vaccination is limited to that individual, but a *public* vaccination campaign exhibits increasing returns to scale.) Or, an environmental organization dedicated to protecting old-growth forests may introduce a set of guidelines for environmentally sustainable forestry and offer to "eco-certify" logging companies that conform to the standard. The environmentalists' hope, of course, is that eco-certification will become widespread enough to emerge as a new industry standard driven by the choices of environmentally conscious consumers. In all these cases, the actors want access to a larger network, and it is through the strategic construction or adoption of standards that they achieve it.

17. Metcalfe's Law (named for Robert Metcalfe, the inventor of the Ethernet), may be understood as holding that the value of a computer network increases at a non-linear rate with increases in the size of the network. This means that the addition of each new computer to a network contributes more than did the one before it. Furthermore, the increases in value may themselves be increasing, even exponentially. In computer networks (at least as modeled by Metcalfe's Law), we assume combinatorial connections, which result in this non-linearly increasing value of a network in relation to its size. A popular statement of Metcalfe's Law is that the value of a network grows by the square of the number of users connected to it. A more general version would hold that the power of a network grows in increasing proportion to the number of users connected to it, because every computer added to the network uses the network as a resource and, in so doing, adds its own resources to it.

   A similar kind of positive feedback is central to my analysis of the standards underlying social networks, including networks mediated technologically, as in the example of the telephone network. Borrowing from Metcalfe's Law, we might conclude that the power of a network grows at an *increasing* rate with its size. But the reason that network value will increase at this increasing rate in computing is that each addition of a new computer to a network results in a greater-than-proportionate increase in possible connections within the network. As a more general proposition for social networks, however, we can only claim that the power of a standard increases with the size of its network. It may increase at an increasing rate, but we cannot make this claim universally, as new additions to a social network may not uniformly increase network activity. In some cases, the power of a standard may grow exponentially in proportion to network size. But the rationale for this exponential relation is that each new node added to a computer network increases exponentially the number of possible connections within it. With computers or technically compatible systems, the claim is more plausible than in social systems, where the addition of another English speaker, say, no doubt adds value to English as a standard that outsiders want to adopt, but does not necessarily do so exponentially, particularly as all network members are not connected to one another except potentially. Furthermore, the social position of the new entrants must be considered in social network analysis, unlike in the analysis of networks in which the nodes are all uniform, as with machines.

18. If we could effortlessly learn every language, we might consider the knowledge of any language, however obscure, an asset. Though it may be unlikely that we will come across someone who speaks Occitan, a language once

spoken across much of southern France (but now largely gone, except for perhaps half a million scattered speakers), we might nevertheless want to speak it if we could do so without any difficulty.

19. Of course, we are assuming that the collective action problems (if there are any) in the formation of a standard have been solved, and we are considering only the factors for which someone might choose to join an already extant standard. Once the use of a standard is relatively widespread, it will represent a coordination equilibrium of the kind I describe in Chapter 2, and it will be rational (not irrational) for people to want to adopt it—as in the case of any conventional good. This makes the problem of coordination on a common standard importantly different from the familiar "collective action problem." For the classic work on collective action problems, see Mancur Olson, *The Logic of Collective Action: Public Goods and the Theory of Groups* (Cambridge: Harvard University Press, 1965). See also Russell Hardin, *One for All: The Logic of Group Conflict* (Princeton: Princeton University Press, 1995). Criticism of too narrow a conceptualization of collective action problems is now widespread; see, for example, Amartya Sen's essays on rationality and social choice theory, recently collected in his *Rationality and Freedom* (Cambridge, Mass.: Belknap Press, 2002). For important contributions to the reformation of the theory of rationality in situations of cooperative, collective action, see Jon Elster, *The Cement of Society: A Study of Social Order* (Cambridge: Cambridge University Press, 1989), and Thomas C. Schelling, *Micromotives and Macrobehavior* (New York: Norton, 1978), 213–243.

As a more general matter, I do not think we should assume that collective action problems routinely prevent the emergence of new standards. On a different understanding, the whole idea of a "collective action" problem needs to be reconsidered. Our presumption should be that even relatively large-scale (and non-conventional) social cooperation is both possible and common; certainly, history presents us many dramatic counterexamples to the conclusions that theories of "free riding" seem to suggest. In fact, as the historian of thought Richard Tuck points out in his book *Free Riding* (Cambridge: Harvard University Press, 2008), the notion of a collective action problem is itself of comparatively recent vintage, and may also be philosophically mistaken.

20. Saussure, *Course in General Linguistics*, ed. Charles Bally, Albert Sechehaye, and Albert Riedlinger and trans. Roy Harris (LaSalle, Ind.: Open Court, 1986), 68.

21. Saussure writes that "any means of expression accepted in a society rests in principle upon a collective habit or a convention, which comes to the same thing. . . . It is this rule which renders them obligatory, not their *intrinsic* value" (ibid., italics mine).

22. In the fuller passage, Saussure writes, "The word *symbol* is sometimes used to designate the linguistic sign, or more exactly that part of the linguistic sign which we are calling the signal. This use of the word *symbol* is awk-

ward, for reasons connected with our first principle. For it is characteristic of symbols that they are never entirely arbitrary. They are not empty configurations. They show at least a vestige of natural connexion between the signal and its signification. For instance, our symbol of justice, the scales, could hardly be replaced by a chariot" (ibid.). In another passage in which he discusses symbols, Saussure writes that one can "discuss the pros and cons of a system of symbols, because a symbol has a rational connexion with what it symbolizes" (ibid., 73). See note 24 of this chapter for the full passage.

23. Ibid., 68.

24. Saussure clearly recognized that his study of linguistic signs would not exhaust the value of the semiotic method: "linguistics serves as a model for the whole of semiology, even though languages represent only one type of semiological system" (ibid.). As I indicated in the text, he focused on linguistic signs because their purely arbitrary relation made them ideal for the general exposition of semiotics. Many of the standards that I focus on in this book, by contrast, operate more like symbols, possessing value for both intrinsic and extrinsic reasons. In another passage in which he discusses the idea of a symbol, Saussure writes:

> The arbitrary nature of the linguistic sign was adduced above as a reason for conceding the theoretical possibility of linguistic change. But more detailed consideration reveals that this very same factor tends to protect a language against any attempt to change it. It means that there is no issue for the community of language users to discuss, even were they sufficiently aware to do so. For in order to discuss an issue, there must be some reasonable basis for discussion. One can, for example, argue about whether monogamy is better than polygamy, and adduce reasons for and against. One could likewise discuss the pros and cons of a system of symbols, because a symbol has a rational connexion with what it symbolizes. But for a language, as a system of arbitrary signs, any such basis is lacking, and consequently there is no firm ground for discussion. No reason can be given for preferring *soeur* to *sister*, *Ochs* to *boeuf*, etc. (ibid., 73).

There are clearly grounds in Saussurian semiotics for the distinction between extrinsic and intrinsic reason, which would be important outside linguistics proper, including for the analytic study of the convention (another field that I draw on, in Chapter 2). However, despite being a widely influential classic, Saussure's *Course in General Linguistics* has been neglected by some later authors, who have therefore had to reinvent some of its insights. For example, the analytic study of the convention took as its starting point particular debates in Anglo-American philosophy of language, often neglecting similar issues in Saussurian linguistics.

25. See ibid., 79–98, for Saussure's commentary on the synchronic versus diachronic study of language. See also Jean Piaget, *Structuralism*, ed. and trans. Chaninah Maschler (New York: Basic Books, 1970), 76–79, for a discussion

of Saussure's approach and, more generally, the issues involved in synchronic and diachronic analyses of linguistic structure.

26. In any non-linear dynamic system, we may see such thresholds—"tipping points"—at which a small change can have a dramatic impact. Malcolm Gladwell has popularized this notion in his book *The Tipping Point: How Little Things Can Make a Big Difference* (Boston: Little, Brown, 2000), borrowing from epidemiology to discuss a variety of social phenomena that seem to have tipping points. But we do not need to analogize non-linear systems to virus ecologies in order to speak about threshold effects. Neither do we need to follow Gladwell in thinking about ideas and norms as viruses that infect us, which is an unfortunate nod in the direction of "mimetic" theory, a very crude framework for understanding intersubjective interactions. Simply because the mathematical modeling of viral infections and, say, network effects in economics show similar non-linearity, we do need not to imagine *actual* similarities between the processes being modeled. To do so is to confuse the mathematical relations that we use to represent different processes and the represented ontologies themselves—a common post-Cartesian mistake, but a mistake nevertheless. Instead, we should simply acknowledge that the formation of social structures—driven by human action and not a virtual viral infection—may be a non-linear process.

    By discussing the trajectory of network power in terms of "thresholds," I want to highlight this non-linearity of a standard in its ascent. But I do not want to imply further that chaos dynamics are at work here or to pretend that viral analogies will offer us much insight. Network power is a theory about social power and choice (and its absence), and how our interdependent choices may lead to threshold and lock-in effects.

27. See Daniel Nettle and Suzanne Romaine, *Vanishing Voices: The Extinction of the World's Languages* (New York: Oxford University Press, 2000), 14, and consider the moving statement by Marie about her social isolation following the loss of her language and culture—a fate worse than physical death in certain respects.

28. We might say that the larger network has absorbed the smaller one, but this vision misattributes the agency, and makes it seem that large networks gobble up smaller ones. What really happens is that smaller networks are gradually abandoned by their members: if gobbling happens, it is just as often bite by bite and member by member, as through the incorporation of entire networks all at once. Of course, entire networks might be incorporated depending on the decision-making process determining when and how members of one network will abandon their standard and switch to another. This possibility depends on there being central control over a network in its entirety—something I analyze in terms of sovereignty in Chapter 2. As an analysis of sociability, the idea of network power takes as its touchstone the more gradual accretion of individual choices. What constitutes a relevant unit for that individual choice depends on the level of decision-making:

when individual persons are choosing—rather than companies or states—
the attrition from a lesser to a dominant network may be person by person.

29. The most famous example of such a collective action problem is probably
that of the "Prisoner's Dilemma." The key distinction between the Prisoner's Dilemma and conventional equilibria is that a Prisoner's Dilemma
imagines independent choice, while conventions emerge from *interdependence* of choice. (Also, the Prisoner's Dilemma is usually played as a "two-
person game" and there are various technical issues that arise in attempting
to generalize its insights.) It may be tempting to think that a standard in
formation (below the threshold of visibility) provides an example of non-
conventional behavior and thus may suffer from problems of collective
action because the convention has not yet been established adequately to
ensure interdependence of choice. To argue in this way may mean accepting a version of the so-called free riding problem, which I criticize in note
19 of this chapter.

30. I discuss the idea of compatibility and other "network properties" at greater
length in Chapter 6. A different, but related point is that even where a minority standard falls below the threshold of visibility (because, say, it is in
competition with an incompatible, universalizing standard), it may be possible that it can be resuscitated or brought back by a concerted effort.

31. As I discuss in Chapter 6 at greater length, dropping the assumption of
strict incompatibility leads to another possibility. To the extent that Standard
A and Standard B prove compatible, at least to some degree, then the universalization of Standard A past the threshold of inevitability may lead to the
co-existence of two networks, a universal Network A, accessible by either
Standard A or Standard B, and a smaller Network B.

32. By claiming that two networks will converge, I do not mean that one will
necessarily overtake the other altogether, rendering it non-existent. Rather, I
mean that the lesser network will be pushed below the "threshold of visibility," under which it will be too small to exert any effective pull on outsiders.
Furthermore, the movement toward universality is only the most striking of
a range of trajectories possible through different network dynamics. Not all
networks necessarily move to such universality. But in the general case, and
for the purposes of this discussion, I develop the idea that network power
pushes toward the ascendance of a single network.

33. The idea of the universal standard is similar to that of the "general equivalent." The term "general equivalent" comes from Marx's argument about
the rise of the money-form as the common currency among commodities,
the "commodity of commodities." See Karl Marx, *Capital*, ed. Ernest Mandel
and trans. David Fernbach and Ben Fowkes (Harmondsworth, U.K.: Penguin Books, in association with New Left Review, 1976).

     The French theorist Jean-Joseph Goux, in a strange and provocative ac-
count, uses the Marxian idea of the general equivalent in a relatively radical
way, introducing the Father, Language, the Phallus, and Gold as general

equivalents in various areas of social life, centering the idea of the general equivalent on exchange both commercial and psychological. See Goux, *Symbolic Economies: After Marx and Freud*, trans. Jennifer Gage (Ithaca, N.Y.: Cornell University Press, 1990).

34. Of course, it may not be reasonable to say that the standard is then powerless because it is still conventional, and like any convention, hard to dislodge. For that reason, it may keep small networks from surpassing the threshold of visibility because everyone will want to maintain connectivity via the existing convention.

35. The idea of a "social fact" has a somewhat specific meaning in positivist sociology following Durkheim's use of the term and his suggestion that sociology orient itself to the study of "social facts." I mean the term very generally and do not want to privilege any precise Durkheimian or positivist notion of social ontology in using it, although the way I discuss networks as social facts is not incompatible with Durkheim's emphasis on the role that collective coordination plays in giving rise to a social phenomenon that structures individual action.

Durkheim comes to his definition of social fact after an interesting methodological discussion, including an argument against what I call "agent-dominated theories" in Chapter 2 or what he refers to as "up-and-up individualism." He writes: "A social fact is every way of acting, whether fixed or not, capable of exerting over the individual an external constraint; or: which is general over the whole of a given society whilst having an existence of its own, independent of its individual manifestations." See Emile Durkheim, *The Rules of Sociological Method*, ed. Steven Lukes and trans. W. D. Halls (New York: Free Press, 1982), 59, but more generally pp. 50–59 on the idea. I have reservations about the effacement of agency in some strains of positivist sociology and in the structuralist sociology that followed Durkheim's efforts (as I discuss in Chapter 2) and do not mean to imply any favor to the rest of his account, at least on that interpretation of it.

CHAPTER 2. THE POWER OF SOCIABILITY

1. Two places where the ideas of sovereignty and sociability are explicitly discussed in historical analyses of political and economic discourse are Istvan Hont's book *Jealousy of Trade*, and Richard Tuck, *The Rights of War and Peace: Political Thought and the International Order from Grotius to Kant* (Oxford: Oxford University Press, 1999). Tuck's unpublished manuscript *Hobbes and Rousseau* also examines these issues very helpfully.

I cannot focus as much as I might wish on this distinction and its history in political thought. Nevertheless, a few brief remarks may be in order to orient the interested reader. To be highly summary about it, the tradition of theorizing sovereignty is associated prominently with Thomas Hobbes and Jean-Jacques Rousseau, among others, and I base my understanding of it on arguments I have drawn from them. (In note 5 of this chapter, I discuss the relationship between Hobbes and Rousseau at greater length.) In its modern form, the idea of sociability is prominently associated with David Hume and his disciple Adam Smith, among others, although arguments about the naturalness of sociability go back to Aristotle and medieval Christian Aristotelianism.

The contrast between sociability and sovereignty can be seen in the difference between Hume and Hobbes on the origin and function of social conventions. I discuss Hume's views on sociability in the second half of Chapter 2, so will not examine them here, but the contrast between his views and Hobbes's should be kept in mind as the central distinction around which my argument about contemporary globalization is structured. The philosophies of Hume and Hobbes, in their different ways (and in the hands of successors) still echo in many contemporary debates, particularly (I think) over the role of the market—a topic on which Hume had a great deal more to say (and to observe, perhaps) than the earlier Hobbes.

Hobbes's views, which I do not examine in any detail in this book, suggest a different route for the establishment of conventions from Hume's, understanding them not as constructs of sociability but of sovereign politics —a politics that overcomes the fearful anarchy of the "state of nature." A passage from Hobbes's *Elements of Law* that Richard Tuck is fond of citing makes this point well (and captures Hobbes's overall argument on ethics, epistemology, and politics). Hobbes writes:

In the state of nature, where every man is his own judge, and differeth from other concerning the names and appellations of things, and from those differences arise quarrels, and breach of peace; it was necessary there should be a common measure of all things that might fall in controversy; as for example: of what is to be called right, what good, what virtue, what much, what little, what *meum* and *tuum,* what a pound, what a quart, &c. For in these things private judgments may differ, and beget controversy. This common measure, some say, is right reason: with whom I should consent, if there were any such thing to be found or known in *rerum natura*. But commonly they that call for right reason to decide any controversy, do mean their own. But this is certain, seeing right reason is not existent, the reason of some man, or men, must supply the place thereof; and that man, or men, is he or they, that have the sovereign power, as hath been already proved; and consequently the civil laws are to all subjects the measures of their actions, whereby to determine, whether they be right or wrong, profitable or unprofitable, virtuous or vicious; and by them the use and definition of all names not agreed upon, and tending to controversy, shall be established. As for example, upon the occasion of some strange and deformed birth, it shall not be decided by Aristotle, or the philosophers, whether the same be a man or no, but by the laws.

312   NOTE TO PAGE 45

Cited in Richard Tuck, *Hobbes, Past Masters* (Oxford: Oxford University Press, 1989), 57–58.

These laws issue from sovereign political relations—which depend on what Hobbes calls a "union" and which he contrasts with "consent." He writes, "It remaineth therefore still that *consent* (by which I mean mere concurrence of many men's wills to one action) is not sufficient security for their common peace. . . . And that this [the achievement of peace] may be done, there is no way imaginable but only *union;* which is defined . . . to be the involving or including the wills of many in the will of one man, or in the will of the greatest part of any one number of men." See Thomas Hobbes, *The Elements of Law, Natural and Politic: Part I, Human Nature, Part II, De Corpore Politico,* ed. John C. A. Gaskin (Oxford: Oxford University Press, 1994), 106, italics mine.

In another passage that clarifies what he means by consent, Hobbes writes: "When the wills of many concur to some one and the same action, or effect, this concourse of their wills is called CONSENT; by which we must not understand one will of many men, for every man hath his several will; but many wills to the producing of one effect" (ibid., 72). This is the process of social construction that I have described as working through relations of sociability and not (as in the production of a political body or union) through relations of sovereignty.

A century later, Rousseau advanced a theory of politics that was very Hobbesian, however much Rousseau may have wanted to distance himself from the accusation of radical "Hobbisme." Rousseau, like Hobbes, denied the assumption of a rich natural sociability—an assumption that goes back to Aristotle and was associated prominently with Samuel Pufendorf, among others, who was a target of Rousseau's criticism. (On the "Hobbesianism" of Rousseau, see Tuck, *The Rights of War and Peace,* 197–207.) Following Hobbes, some philosophers (like Pufendorf) offered theories of sociability and sovereignty together. For example, John Locke—whose concise definition of sovereignty I cite in the text—has a very "Hobbesian" account of the formation of politics, but also presents a relatively expansive conception of natural sociability before political society is formed, as I discuss in examining his views on money in Chapter 3. Immanuel Kant also understands the two together—influenced, of course, by Rousseau but also by David Hume. Kant's political theories combine a concern for republican sovereignty that resembles the Hobbesian or Rousseauvian with an interest in the progressive aspects of trade and international commerce in line with the Scottish enlightenment writers. See *Kant: Political Writings,* ed. Hans Siegbert Reiss and trans. Hugh B. Nisbet (Cambridge: Cambridge University Press, 1991), and Tuck, *The Rights of War and Peace,* 207–225 on Kant. But both Locke and Kant recognize that sovereignty is primary analytically, if not historically, and that durable, elaborated forms of human sociability depend ultimately upon politics. What is distinctive about Hume, by contrast, is his attempt to advance an account of pure sociability outside sovereignty—and to argue that we can more or less get along just fine without politics, given markets and customs. This account is developed in its most general terms in his discussion of "artificial virtue" in the final book of his *Treatise of Human Nature*, ed. David F. Norton and Mary J. Norton (Oxford: Clarendon Press, 2000).

In the nineteenth century, both G. F. W. Hegel and Karl Marx were famous for their treatment of the two concepts together. Hegel theorizes a separate sphere of "civil society" in which private rationality leads to the creation of social structures (as I have described happening through "sociability") and imagines civil society alongside, but still within the purview of, the state. The concept of the "state" in Hegel is complicated, for although it is the bearer of sovereignty, it is not uniquely or even primarily a procedural invention but embodies a collective moral, historical, and spiritual aspect. Note also that by Hegel's time, the term "civil society" has come to mean not a politically organized society—a translation of the Latin *civitas*, as in its seventeenth-century usage—but the way we define it now, a sphere of sociability distinct from organized politics. See Georg Wilhelm Friedrich Hegel, *Elements of the Philosophy of Right*, ed. Allen W. Wood and trans. Hugh B. Nisbet (Cambridge: Cambridge University Press, 1991). See also Charles Taylor, *Hegel and Modern Society* (Cambridge: Cambridge University Press, 1979), 102–110, on the idea of "civil society" in Hegel.

Following Hegel's lead in important respects, Marx argued that sociability had to be understood not just as a domain of human interaction that exists alongside or within the "state," but as a relation of power that can overwhelm the relations of sovereignty and come to control them. Throughout his writings, Marx evinces skepticism about any formal division of public and private roles, and worries that the private relations of sociability tend to hijack our public determinations, rendering real politics impotent or distorted. This aspect of Marx's thought is perhaps especially clear in his early political essays, but it should be obvious on a careful reading of *Capital* all the same. See Karl Marx, *Early Political Writings*, ed. Joseph J. O'Malley and Richard A. Davis (Cambridge: Cambridge University Press, 1994).

In the twentieth century, a central figure who clearly grasped this tension between sovereignty and sociability (and did something about it on the world stage) was John Maynard Keynes, who illustrates vividly that a concern for national sovereignty over important domains (for example, the economy) is not in tension with broader liberal and cosmopolitan commitments—and, indeed, may spring from a careful thinking through of what those commitments really demand of us politically. Keynes was, of course, a sophisticated cosmopolitan with a flamboyant personal life and eccentric and elevated tastes—in no way narrow-mindedly nationalistic, statist, or otherwise parochial.

2. The use of "ideal types" in social explanation is prominently associated with

Max Weber. The distinction I intend here between sociability and sovereignty is not exhausted by, though resembles in some respects, Weber's distinction between a "voluntary association" or *Verein* and a "compulsory association" or *Anstalt*. Although Weber discusses the state as the exemplar of the compulsory association, he does not emphasize the democratic aspect of sovereignty in his general sociological description of the distinction. (This is perhaps a salient difference between the political theory motivating my distinction and Weber's sociological method.) Relevant to my purposes here, Weber notes: "The distinction between voluntary and compulsory associations is relative in its empirical application. The rules of a voluntary association may affect the interests of non-members, and recognition of these rules may be imposed upon them by usurpation and the exercise of naked power, but also by legal regulation." See Weber, *Economy and Society: An Outline of Interpretive Sociology,* ed. Guenther Roth and Claus Wittich and trans. Ephraim Fischoff et al. (Berkeley: University of California Press, 1978), 52–53. I will examine Weber's analysis of domination through social structures in Chapter 4.

3. The distinction between the "general will" and the "will of all" comes most famously from *The Social Contract,* but was also present in Rousseau's earlier *Discourse on Political Economy.* See Jean-Jacques Rousseau, *The Social Contract and Other Later Political Writings,* ed. and trans. Victor Gourevitch (Cambridge: Cambridge University Press, 1997), 6 for the mention of the "general will" in the *Discourse on Political Economy,* and 49–53 for the famous discussion of it in *The Social Contract.*

4. John Locke, *Two Treatises of Government,* ed. Peter Laslett (Cambridge: Cambridge University Press, 1988), 331, italics original. Locke elaborates this definition of sovereignty in the remainder of his famous chapter "Of the Beginning of Political Societies," discussing the nature of the consent that people give to form a sovereign, the corporate character of the resulting sovereign, the unification of wills that is thereby achieved, and the reason that majoritarian decision is the only and proper way in which that sovereign body can direct itself. Arguably, these themes are all Hobbesian, but they come out very clearly in Locke—at least in this chapter, however he may otherwise obscure them—so I cite Locke rather than the earlier Hobbes. More generally, see ibid., 330–333.

5. I realize that this may be a controversial interpretation of Rousseau and Hobbes, for which I am indebted to Richard Tuck's unpublished manuscript *Hobbes and Rousseau.* A brief but published analysis of the relation between Hobbes and Rousseau appears in Tuck, *The Rights of War and Peace,* 197–207.

To be clear, nothing in the argument I am putting forward about globalization—that is, my use of sociability and sovereignty as I have defined them here—depends upon my getting this particular piece of intellectual history "right." Nevertheless, I do find a plausible and helpful reading of the relation between Hobbes and Rousseau to be, in highly abbreviated fashion, that Hobbes first laid down the general outlines of what sovereignty is and how it is constituted, and then Rousseau offered particular amendments to a theory that he otherwise accepted—even while, for reasons of reputation, offering certain vulgar criticisms of Hobbes, from whom he wished to distance himself. These two figures are often presented today as holding opposing views, but significantly, early commentary on Rousseau claimed just the reverse, which may have been a worrying association for him.

What Hobbes asserts is that sovereignty is formed initially by the agreement of a relevant group to a procedure for determining the resolution of contentious (and thus potentially quarrelsome) issues. That multitude—formed now into a unified body—can then, if it will, hand the government off to a single man (as in a monarchy) or group of men (as in an aristocracy). It is this alienation of sovereignty that Rousseau finds unacceptable, arguing instead that ultimate power must always rest with the general will that determines the government. In a sense, Rousseau rejects Hobbes's attempt to read even monarchical government as a kind of democracy, in which the people have handed off power of their own accord. (Rousseau also presents a different account of man's passions in the state of nature from Hobbes's, though on Tuck's plausible reading it is not an incompatible one.) Compare on this issue Hobbes's *De Cive* and Rousseau's *The Social Contract*. See Thomas Hobbes, *On the Citizen*, ed. and trans. Richard Tuck and Michael Silverthorne (Cambridge: Cambridge University Press, 1998), and Rousseau, *The Social Contract and Other Later Political Writings*.

6. David Held, in his *Models of Democracy* (Stanford: Stanford University Press, 1996), 352–353, poses the problem of democracy in an age of globalization squarely: "The modern theory of the sovereign democratic state, liberal and radical, presupposes the idea of a community which rightly governs itself and determines its own future. This idea is challenged fundamentally by the nature of the pattern of global interconnectedness." Held argues that, under such conditions of global interconnectedness, "the proper 'home' of politics, and of the model of democratic autonomy especially, becomes a puzzling matter." His solution is the reconstitution of democratic politics in new forms of international and transnational association, an ideal of cosmopolitan democracy: "The possibility of democracy today must, in short, be linked to an expanding framework of democratic institutions and agencies" including regional parliaments, a restructuring of the United Nations, international courts and human rights instruments, and even a "new democratic international assembly" (354).

Held has articulated this position in numerous books on democracy, on globalization, and on the two together. See, most significantly, David Held, *Democracy and the Global Order: From the Modern State to Cosmopolitan Governance* (Stanford: Stanford University Press, 1995). But see also Held, *Models of Democracy*, and Daniele Archibugi and David Held, eds., *Cosmopolitan*

Democracy: An Agenda for a New World Order (Oxford: Blackwell, 1995). Held resembles here another famous political theorist, Jürgen Habermas, who has advanced an argument for cosmopolitan democracy. Habermas argues that we need to reconstitute the functional equivalent of national democratic norms at the global level (to respond to what he calls a "postnational" age) in his *The Postnational Constellation: Political Essays,* trans. and ed. Max Pensky (Cambridge: MIT Press, 2001).

The idea of cosmopolitan democracy remains controversial, with many scholars unconvinced that globalization can be effectively "democratized" above or outside the space of national governments. This skeptical position is probably more widespread in the literature than the belief in "postnational" democracy of some kind; scholars in many different disciplines have examined how transnational activities now outstrip the national regulatory bases that previously managed them. See, for example, Saskia Sassen, *Losing Control?: Sovereignty in an Age of Globalization* (New York: Columbia University Press, 1996); Susan Strange, *The Retreat of the State: The Diffusion of Power in the World Economy* (New York: Cambridge University Press, 1996); and also the collection of essays by John Dickey Montgomery, Nathan Glazer, and Donald L. Horowitz, eds., *Sovereignty under Challenge: How Governments Respond* (New Brunswick, N.J.: Transaction, 2002), in which there is the suggestion (14–15) that the rise of transnational "standards" poses a threat to national sovereignty. A thoughtful contribution that examines how we might achieve the equivalent of democratic representation in global institutions (and hence achieve legitimate countervailing power to many other global processes) is Andrew Kuper, *Democracy beyond Borders: Justice and Representation in Global Institutions* (Oxford: Oxford University Press, 2004). Anne-Marie Slaughter, in *A New World Order* (Princeton: Princeton University Press, 2004), presents an important related contribution, showing how new forms of global governance operate through transnational networks linking elements of the decomposed national regulatory apparatus (say, national courts) to their foreign counterparts. See also the overview of this discussion of politics under globalization in Waters, *Globalization,* 123–159.

Finally, it should be noted that not all scholars are anxious about the possible undermining of national sovereignty under globalization—perhaps because they consider it in its "external" aspect rather than looking to the "internal" dynamics of political representation. The international law scholars Abram and Antonia Chayes argue that in an age of globalization, "sovereignty no longer consists in the freedom of states to act independently, in their perceived self-interest. . . . To be a player, a state must submit to the pressures that international regulations impose." Abram Chayes and Antonia Chayes, *The New Sovereignty: Compliance with International Regulatory Agreements* (Cambridge: Harvard University Press, 1995), 27. This argument —which is made commonly in one form or another in the international law and international relations literature—may be appealing when we think about, suppose, human rights issues. However, it may be a self-defeating or limiting move more generally, if we consider sovereignty in its "internal" and political theoretic aspect, as political theorists on either side of the "cosmopolitan democracy" debate do. Consider, by contrast, the denial of effective decision-making powers by national bodies in the more contentious arenas of international economic regulation and policy, which I examine in Chapters 8 and 9.

I cannot here address the issue of cosmopolitan democracy as much as I might like. It is perhaps unnecessary to add that I am skeptical of grand claims made on behalf of a cosmopolitan-democratic order, at least if the analogy between national and global sovereignty is made straightforwardly. And, to the extent that there is no straightforward analogue, the issue of how best to control global sociability will be a question left, for the most part, to national politics. But this is a theme that I will explore throughout this book.

7. See, for example, Thomas Friedman on the "Golden Straitjacket," which we can interpret as the neoliberal version of the old argument about "forcing people to be free"—an argument usually associated with the theorists of sovereignty but here put forward as a defense of the coercive power at work in the relations of sociability: See Friedman, *The Lexus and the Olive Tree* (New York: Anchor Books, 2000), 104–105, and my discussion in note 13 of Chapter 9. The original phrase "forced to be free" comes from *The Social Contract*, in which Rousseau argues that the social contract—that is, sovereign government—obliges those who participate in it to be free, securing them from personal dependence for the sake of their political independence (*The Social Contract and Other Later Political Writings*, 53). On my view, this is one of the clearest statements of the argument that political sovereignty provides the bulwark against the forms of subjugation that sociability may bring, whether outright slavery or more subtle forms of oppression (including those to which individuals may consent, not knowing any better). It is sometimes interpreted—anachronistically and inaccurately, I fear—as an argument justifying "democratic tyranny." However, the actual text, as well as the background of Rousseau's own concerns, suggests a different reading: a concern with slavery or personal subjugation, and the escape route that modern politics provides. Friedman's version shares none of this concern, representing instead an apology for the way in which international capital markets limit the freedom of national polities.

8. Anthony Giddens, who first suggested the term "structuration" calls the two poles "subjectivist" and "objectivist," taking society as the "object" and the individual as the "subject." Giddens's use of these terms is found in his *Constitution of Society: Outline of the Theory of Structuration* (Berkeley: University of California Press, 1984), xx, among other places. An earlier articulation of the structuration argument is Giddens, *Central Problems in Social*

Theory: Action, Structure, and Contradiction in Social Analysis (Berkeley: University of California Press, 1979), 49–85.

I prefer not to follow Giddens's use of "subjectivist" and "objectivist" here, hoping instead to capture the same content but with less possible confusion. Since the dualism that Giddens rightly opposes is often called the "agency/structure" dichotomy, the use of the terms "agency-dominated" and "structure-dominated" seems clearer, if somewhat workaday, and less prone to confusion outside of sociological theory proper. The agency/structure dichotomy is also sometimes expressed by the terms "individualist" and "collectivist," but these are too easily confused with *political* accounts of individualism and collectivism that are remote from these methodological concerns. So, too, the use of atomism and structuralism, which can have any number of relatively distinct uses in arguments about methodology in the natural and human sciences. For example, in his book *Structuralism*, Jean Piaget opposes "atomism" and particular narrow forms of "structuralism," but this methodological controversy is broader than the agency/structure dichotomy in social theory and takes place in several different disciplinary settings.

9. See note 43 of this chapter for a brief discussion of the controversies about methodological individualism, atomism, and holism in social and natural science. The idea of network power adopts a (broadly) individualist methodology that may fail to account for some of the ways in which social structures cannot be considered reductively. This issue of "emergentism" is not one I can take up in this book, however important it may ultimately be for social theorists to consider. On methodological individualism in the social sciences, see chapter 17 of Steven Lukes, *Individualism* (New York: Harper & Row, 1973), 118–119. Lukes argues at pp. 121–122 that a broad methodological individualism can amount to question-begging—a charge I cannot consider here adequately.

10. The question of the relation of the social background to theories of individual agency or autonomy is a long-standing concern of philosopher Charles Taylor. See Taylor, *Philosophical Arguments* (Cambridge: Harvard University Press, 1995); Taylor, *Human Agency and Language* (Cambridge: Cambridge University Press, 1985); and Taylor, *Philosophy and the Human Sciences* (Cambridge: Cambridge University Press, 1985).

11. For criticism of this strong "agential liberalism" in Rawlsian philosophy, see Michael Sandel, *Liberalism and the Limits of Justice* (Cambridge: Cambridge University Press, 1982). The effort to bring Rawlsian insights to bear on real-world problems is perhaps clearest in the current controversies over international distributive justice, especially concerning international poverty and inequality. See Christian Barry, Thomas Winfried Menko Pogge, and Jedediah Purdy, eds., *Global Institutions and Responsibilities: Achieving Global Justice* (Malden, Mass.: Blackwell, 2005), and Pogge, ed., *Global Justice* (Oxford: Blackwell, 2001). See also Robert Hockett, "Three (Potential) Pillars

of Transnational Economic Justice: The Bretton Woods Institutions as Guarantors of Global Equal Treatment and Market Completion," *Metaphilosophy* 36, no. 1–2 (2005).

12. The reason that neoclassical economics has developed in this fashion seems related to the focus of the early marginalists on the bilateral transaction as the basis for the mathematical treatment of economic exchange. Once the analytics in this context were clear, they were more or less expanded as a model for the entire economy, however inapposite that might seem on reflection, particularly for understanding production or the setting of the background framework of laws and mores within which exchanges take place. The clearest account of the bilateral bargain in early marginalist thought is in the work of Francis Edgeworth. See his *Mathematical Psychics: An Essay on the Application of Mathematics to the Moral Sciences* (London: C. K. Paul, 1881). The extension of this kind of reasoning to the entire economy is notable in the famous works establishing general equilibrium theory in the 1950s. See, for example Gerard Debreu, *Theory of Value: An Axiomatic Analysis of Economic Equilibrium* (New York: Wiley, 1959).

13. By structure-dominated, I do not mean to indicate only the formally "structuralist" disciplines, as I discuss in the following note, but to emphasize any theories in which human action or agency is set aside so that explanatory emphasis can be put on some set of broader conditions that are alleged to determine or decide it. (Many forms of "structuralism" take this approach— though perhaps not all—and at the same time, a structure-dominated approach is not restricted to "structuralist" theories.) This move is not necessarily wrong, but it is always partial—requiring a synthetic position capable of incorporating human action where it is plausibly efficacious to complete a more comprehensive form of social explanation. Structure-dominated theories include, in linguistics or semiotics, the work of Ferdinand de Saussure, whom I have relied upon extensively in the text so far; in sociology, the work of Emile Durkheim and those who followed his positive method (or the earlier positivism of Auguste Comte), including in some respects Talcott Parsons; and in anthropology, the structuralist anthropologies of Claude Lévi-Strauss (who drew on Saussure) and Alfred Radcliffe-Brown. Even work that is not technically "structuralist" may adopt a structure-dominated position, as I argue below in the case of "poststructuralists" like Michel Foucault (and many who follow his lead). See Durkheim, *The Rules of Sociological Method;* Emile Durkheim, *The Elementary Forms of Religious Life,* ed. Karen E. Fields (New York: Free Press, 1995); Auguste Comte, *System of Positive Polity,* trans. John Bridges, Frederick Harrison, and Edward Beesly (London: Longmans, Green, 1875); Claude Lévi-Strauss, *Structural Anthropology,* trans. Claire Jacobson and Brooke G. Schoepf (New York: Basic Books, 1963); and Talcott Parsons, *The Structure of Social Action* (New York: McGraw-Hill, 1937).

14. For example, Michel Foucault protests against being called a "structuralist,"

complaining: "In France, certain half-witted 'commentators' persist in label-
ing me a 'structuralist.' I have been unable to get it into their tiny minds
that I have used none of the methods, concepts, or key terms that characterize structural analysis": *The Order of Things: An Archaeology of the Human
Sciences* (New York: Pantheon Books, 1971), xiv. And yet, Foucault's method
shares with other "structure-dominated accounts" skepticism about the efficacy—and perhaps even the reality—of ordinary human agency. He adopts
what might be called a discourse-dominated view of intellectual history, focusing on discursive formations (and their contingent changes in history)
rather than individual subjects. Explaining his efforts, he writes: "I should
like to know whether the subjects responsible for scientific discourse are
not determined in their practical possibilities by conditions that dominate
and even overwhelm them. In short, I tried to explore scientific discourse
not from the point of view of the individuals who are speaking, nor from
the point of view of the formal structures of what they are saying, but from
the point of view of the rules that come into play in the very existence of
such discourse" (ibid., xiv). Of course, Foucault here discounts the perspective of formal structure, seeking to distinguish himself from structural anthropologists like Lévi-Strauss. But on a broader view of what "structure"
might mean, he is expressing here what I call a "structure-dominated"
(or discourse-dominated) method of analysis that discounts human agency.
Jean Piaget aptly characterizes Foucault's approach as a "structuralism
without structures" and complains: "Foucault's ouster of the subject is
more radical than any hitherto" (*Structuralism*, 134–135).

Another reason I use "structure-dominated" rather than "structuralist"
in my discussion of such accounts of social life is that there are many possible structuralisms, as Piaget's excellent account makes clear. And whatever
commonalities the structuralist accounts of language, child development,
social life, or natural science may share, the term "structuralism" neither
captures all the issues involved in the structure/agency dichotomy nor is
exhausted by them. Thus, the term "structuralism" would be misleading,
invoking debates I do not take up here while also failing to indicate precisely the issues that I do want to examine.

15. Giddens develops his theory of structuration in a number of works, but the
most extended presentation is in *The Constitution of Society*, especially in
chapters 1, 4, and 6. Habermas presents a social theory that I consider an
account of structuration in his famous work *The Theory of Communicative
Action*, trans. Thomas McCarthy (Boston: Beacon Press, 1984). (I should
note that Giddens disagrees with this assessment, claiming instead that
Habermas reproduces the errors of Parsonian functionalism: Giddens, *The
Constitution of Society*, xxxvi–ii.) Pierre Bourdieu develops a framework of
habitus and *field* to offer a social theory that moves beyond the structure/
agency dichotomy in his *Distinction: A Social Critique of the Judgement of
Taste*, trans. Richard Nice (Cambridge: Harvard University Press, 1984).

Roberto Mangabeira Unger develops his social theory in the three-volume work *Politics*, which consists of *Social Theory, False Necessity*, and *Plasticity into Power*. *Social Theory* diagnoses the problems of social thought in relation to our understandings of context and context change, while *False Necessity* develops this diagnosis into a theory of context change for empowered democracy. See Unger, *Social Theory: Its Situation and Its Task* (Cambridge: Cambridge University Press, 1987); Unger, *False Necessity: Anti-Necessitarian Social Theory in the Service of Radical Democracy* (Cambridge: Cambridge University Press, 1987); and Unger, *Plasticity into Power: Comparative-Historical Studies on the Institutional Conditions of Economic and Military Success* (Cambridge: Cambridge University Press, 1987). Note that Verso is now producing new editions of these works, and that an abridged edition of all three provides an introduction to Unger's thought: Roberto Mangabeira Unger, *Politics: The Central Texts; Theory against Fate* (London: Verso, 1997).

Notably, all three thinkers bring psychology into their social theory, as one would expect from an account of structuration. Giddens relies on the insights of post-Freudian ego psychology, for example in his *Modernity and Self-Identity;* Habermas draws on the work of Mead and Piaget, among others in *A Theory of Communicative Action,* and Unger advances his own account of human motivation and ambition in his *Passion: An Essay on Personality* (New York: Free Press, 1984).

16. Giddens, *The Constitution of Society*, 374.
17. See, for example, Leszek Kolakowski, *Toward a Marxist Humanism: Essays on the Left Today,* trans. Jane Z. Peel (New York: Grove Press, 1968), and the collection of essays Leszek Kolakowski and Stuart Hampshire, eds., *The Socialist Idea: A Reappraisal* (London: Weidenfeld and Nicolson, 1974). The concern about the role of agency in Marxist theory is by no means restricted to those living under Soviet control, but has been a question for democratic socialists for several generations, going back to Marx himself, who put democratic agency at the heart of all his analyses.
18. For example, three of the social theorists I cited earlier have developed, or are developing their thought as it applies to contemporary globalization. Anthony Giddens does so in *The Consequences of Modernity,* Jürgen Habermas in his book *The Postnational Constellation,* and Roberto Mangabeira Unger in *Free Trade Reimagined: The World Division of Labor and the Method of Economics* (Cambridge: Harvard University Press, 2007).
19. See Bayly, *The Birth of the Modern World, 1780–1914.* Bayly's effort is to produce a global history, which is necessarily concerned with "the concatenation of changes produced by the interactions of political, economic, and ideological change at many different levels" (475).
20. Ibid., 477–478.
21. Ibid., 476.
22. Ibid., 475.
23. Ibid., 476.

24. The contrast, of course, is with Hobbes, who may be considered the greatest philosopher of sovereignty, and who is an implicit (usually unstated) target of Hume's criticism. The difference between these two British philosophers highlights the important question of the extent to which we are dependent upon politics in the construction of our shared social life, and how much can be done outside of politics, in what Hume's disciple Adam Smith would later call the state of "natural liberty." For more on these themes, see note 1 of this chapter.

25. David Hume, *An Enquiry Concerning the Principles of Morals: A Critical Edition*, ed. Tom L. Beauchamp (Oxford: Clarendon Press, 1998), 98, italics and capitalization in original.

26. Hume's discussion of justice as conventional comes in his broader argument about "artificial"—that is, constructed and not intrinsic or given—virtues. Hume argues in this same text that justice is such a human convention. The famous passage on justice is drawn from ibid., 97–98, Appendix 3. In considering justice to be a convention, he was following Aristotle. See Aristotle, *Nicomachean Ethics*, trans. and ed. Roger Crisp (Cambridge: Cambridge University Press, 2000), Book V.

27. It should be added that Nash was an indispensable contributor to the development of both kinds of games. For an introduction to coordination games, see Russell W. Cooper, *Coordination Games: Complementarities and Macroeconomics* (Cambridge: Cambridge University Press, 1999).

28. Schelling, *The Strategy of Conflict*, 57. The original idea of focal points comes from pp. 54–58, but see also 53–118 more generally. Among his other works in this area, see Schelling, *Micromotives and Macrobehavior*, and Thomas C. Schelling, *Choice and Consequence* (Cambridge: Harvard University Press, 1984). In many ways, it might be argued that Schelling's original account consisted in an edifying form of description rather than a theory—which I think better emerged in Lewis's later work on conventions. Robert Sugden makes this point in a recently published discussion of focal points (in a journal issue devoted to Schelling's work): "one has the sense that Schelling is struggling to articulate a vividly-perceived idea—one might even say a vision—which resists literal formulation." Sugden, "Finding the Key: The Riddle of Focal Points," *Journal of Economic Psychology* 27, no. 5 (2006), 612.

29. Lewis develops his final definition of a convention very precisely:
    "Our final definition [of convention] is therefore: A regularity R in the behavior of members of the population P when they are agents in a recurrent situation S is a convention if and only if it is true that, and it is common knowledge in P that, in almost any instance of S among members of P,
    (1) almost everyone conforms to R;
    (2) almost everyone expects almost everyone else to conform to R;
    (3) almost everyone has approximately the same preferences regarding all possible combinations of actions;

(4) almost everyone prefers that any one more conform to R, on condition that almost everyone conform to R;

(5) almost everyone would prefer that any one more conform to R′ on condition that almost everyone conform to R′;

where R′ is some possible regularity in the behavior of members of P in S, such that almost no one in almost any instance of S among members of P could conform both to R′ and R." Lewis, *Convention*, 78.

30. Ibid., 14, italics original.

31. Ibid., 8.

32. "Coordination by precedent, at its simplest, is this: achievement of co-ordination by means of a shared acquaintance with the achievement of coordination in a single past case exactly like our present coordination problem" (ibid., 41).

33. Schelling, *The Strategy of Conflict*, 55.

34. Elster, *The Cement of Society*, 12. He continues, explaining more formally: "Conventional equilibria are also characterized by a *strict* preference for one's own and others' conformity to the convention, whereas the ordinary equilibrium concept requires only weak preference" (ibid., italics original). The reason for this strict preference is clear: every additional follower of a convention makes that convention more valuable for others, by adding additional people with whom one's actions are coordinated. Elster describes co-ordination equilibria as one of five main types of cooperation (pp. 11–13).

35. Of course, for analytic clarity, it is useful to separate out the various kinds of network externalities. We may want to distinguish the effect created by: the number of other users (as in the telephone example I gave above, or in the case of Microsoft Word, the word processing software); the effect created by actual communication with other users (as with fax machines and the dominant fax data protocol); the "learning effect" created by adherence to a standard (as in the case of the QWERTY keyboard); and the secondary effect created by third-party producers of standard goods (as in the VHS example). I am indebted to Robin Goldstein for a discussion of these differences.

36. The idea of the externality is actually a relatively nuanced and complex one—far more so than most who use the term routinely admit. Understanding the idea of network effects as inherent in any form of social interdependence requires a conceptual framework in which externalities are understood in relation to actual and possible institutions, market and non-market. For a theoretically sophisticated account of externality, which seems to me underappreciated, see Andreas A. Papandreou, *Externality and Institutions* (Oxford: Clarendon Press, 1994).

37. The thought that history can bequeath suboptimal outcomes may not strike some people as surprising. But one side of the debate on path-dependence in neoclassical economics treats the idea with skepticism and hostility. Part of the explanation for this reception may be the "Panglossian" commitments

of neoclassical economic theory. See Geoffrey M. Hodgson, *Economics and Evolution: Bringing Life Back into Economics* (Cambridge, U.K.: Polity Press, 1993). I examined some of these themes in David Singh Grewal, "Optimality and Evolution in Economics: Darwinism in the Study of Firms and Institutions" (Harvard University, 1998).

38. The VCR wars are part of a broader debate about the extent of path-dependence and positive feedback dynamics in the economy. The two main critics of the idea of path-dependence, Liebowitz and Margolis, have contested the main empirical examples put forward by economists Brian Arthur and Paul David, and claim that path-dependence is quite rare. For some of the original contributions (now compiled in a single volume), see Arthur, *Increasing Returns and Path Dependence in the Economy*. See also the criticism of these ideas in Stan J. Liebowitz and Stephen E. Margolis, "Path Dependence, Lock-in, and History," *Journal of Law, Economics, & Organization* 11, no. 1 (1995), 218–222, for the attack on the Beta-VHS example. The other main example used in this literature is the argument about the keyboard configuration and the extent to which it is suboptimal and path-dependent. The original contribution here was by Paul David, "Clio and the Economics of Qwerty," *American Economic Review* 75, no. 2 (1985). David argued that the QWERTY keyboard is inefficient for current technology, but has remained dominant over other keyboard configurations, such as the Dvorak keyboard, because of path-dependence based on the high cost of switching to another routine from the established QWERTY system. This view was criticized in Stan J. Liebowitz and Stephen E. Margolis, "The Fable of the Keys," *Journal of Law & Economics* 33, no. 1 (1990). We should recognize, however, that the path-dependence that has kept QWERTY dominant is not analogous to the VCR wars, but arises from the cost of retraining oneself as a typist. The costs that keep us constrained to the historically given keyboard are those of individual re-learning, not the lost connectivity with a technological network, as in the more common cases of path-dependence based on network effects, such as in the VCR wars. David argues that technical interrelatedness as well as "quasi-irreversible investments" (sunk costs) in touch-typing with QWERTY cause path-dependence. But since we can switch costlessly onto the new technology, given that software allows computer keyboards to be instantly reconfigured to the main alternative, the Dvorak layout, the only network effects are from the continued teaching of QWERTY. Otherwise, it is simply the cost of unlearning QWERTY that keeps us locked in. There is no incompatibility between users of two different keyboard standards, which is why I do not think the path-dependence here arises from network effects as commonly understood.

These empirical examples aside, the critics' argument against path-dependence rests on several confused presuppositions that a more sophisticated reader of the literature would not assume. For example, the distinction between "second degree" and "third degree" path-dependence (Liebowitz and Margolis, "Path Dependence, Lock-in, and History") rests on an impoverished view of human agency and the assimilation of all failure to constraint, generating the tautology that all action is optimization, however constrained.

39. See Paul Krugman, "Increasing Returns and Economic-Geography," *Journal of Political Economy* 99, no. 3 (1991). See also Arthur, *Increasing Returns and Path Dependence in the Economy*, 49–67, for work on industrial cores and path-dependence. On the question of institutional path-dependence, see Douglass C. North, "Institutions," *Journal of Economic Perspectives* 5, no. 1 (1991), 98, for his statement of this position, which would excite controversy only in a discipline as unhistorical as neoclassical economic history. See also Paul A. David, "Why Are Institutions the 'Carriers of History'?: Path Dependence and the Evolution of Conventions, Organizations, and Institutions," *Structural Change and Economic Dynamics* 5, no. 2 (1994), 208, for a more intelligent discussion of the dynamics of path-dependence with regard to North's argument. David discusses path-dependence in relation to conventions at ibid., 209–210. For more on the way that North uses the idea of path-dependence in his later works (and the productive confusion resulting from it), see Grewal, "Optimality and Evolution in Economics," chapter 5.

40. The neologism "anti-rival" was suggested to describe the nature of software code by Steven Weber in his book *The Success of Open Source* (Cambridge: Harvard University Press, 2004), 153–154. Weber writes: "Software in many circumstances is more than simply nonrival. Operating systems like Linux in particular, and most software in general, actually are subject to positive externalities. Call it a network good, or an anti-rival good (an awkward, but nicely descriptive term)" (ibid.). I have no problem with the concept—which I have tried to argue is a more general one than perhaps many scholars realize—but I do think the term "anti-rival" not just a bit awkward (as Weber himself recognizes) but potentially misleading. For, since "rivalry" already connotes opposition, the term "anti-rival" suggests the negation of the negation. But "anti-rival" goods are not goods for which a preexisting rivalry has been overcome, but goods that exhibit a conventional aspect dictating complementarities in use from the very beginning. It might be simpler just to call these goods "network goods," as Weber suggests, or perhaps "conventional goods," even if this term does not signal an opposition to the usual neoclassical assumption of "rivalry" in consumption.

41. For this aspect of Wittgenstein's thought, see, among other sources, his later work, especially *Philosophical Investigations*, trans. G. E. M. Anscombe (Oxford: Blackwell, 1953). Two insightful contemporary commentators on the later Wittgenstein are Stanley Cavell and Charles Taylor, who have developed their positions in a number of books. See, for example, Taylor, *Philosophical Arguments*, and Stanley Cavell, *The Claim of Reason: Wittgenstein, Skepticism, Morality, and Tragedy* (New York: Oxford University Press, 1999). For a helpful intellectual historical examination of Wittgenstein's later work,

see S. Stephen Hilmy, *The Later Wittgenstein: The Emergence of a New Philosophical Method* (Oxford: Blackwell, 1987), and for a lucid philosophical interpretation of the "early" and the "late" Wittgenstein that emphasizes the continuity between the two, see Anthony Kenny, *Wittgenstein* (Oxford: Blackwell, 2006).

42. See the essay "Irreducibly Social Goods," in which Taylor takes issue with the Lewisian idea of conventions as "higher-order" expectations (without naming Lewis as his target): "it is futile and wrong-headed to try to define common or mutual understanding as a compound of individual states. Our having a common understanding about something is distinct from my understanding it, plus your understanding it, plus perhaps my knowing that you understand, and your knowing that I understand; nor does it help to add further levels, say that I know that you know that I understand" (Taylor, *Philosophical Arguments*, 138). I believe that Taylor is distinguishing here between what he later calls the "convergent" and the "common," where we might articulate his argument as being that the convergent is not the common because it involves an "us" that emerges, and that is distinct from "you plus me." On these grounds, I suspect that the idea of network power may fail to address adequately the issue of how a "we" (say, a network) emerges as an ontologically distinct level from the compounded actions of individuals.

43. The idea that we cannot adequately understand a whole reductively, but must consider properties that emerge in the whole *as a whole*, irreducible to the properties of its constituent parts, is sometimes called "emergentism." It is related to methodological holism (more properly: wholism), which is opposed to the perspective of methodological atomism, and even methodological individualism. On a holistic account, we cannot understand wholes reductively, even on a full account of the properties of their constituent elements. Something new emerges with the whole—perhaps the relevant "laws" changing at a more complex level of interaction, or a feedback between the whole and the parts—such that more sophisticated social (or natural) entities must be considered autonomously. There is a distinction sometimes made between descriptive emergentism, which describes, for example, how a whole interacts with its parts, rendering reductionism inapplicable, and explanatory or methodological emergentism, which takes as its starting point the methodological premise that more complex structures cannot be reduced to the properties of their constituent elements (even given a good account of the "laws of composition" governing the formation of the structures). One of the most familiar (and arguably, most plausible) holistic accounts is that of semantic holism, the idea that a symbol (such as a word in a natural language) cannot be understood except in the context of the entire system of representations in which it is contained. In linguistics, this argument is associated with Saussurian arguments about "langue" and "parole." How far we can go in pushing this perspective into other areas of

social life outside language (and the extent to which there are any areas of social life not shot through with the meanings and representations inherent in language) is an area of active debate in the philosophy of social science, which I cannot take up adequately in this book. I should note that these issues come up in other settings too; Piaget's excellent volume, *Structuralism*, takes up the issue of how to understand wholes (structures) in relation to their constituent parts, without using the language of emergentism, which comes from a more analytic tradition. John Stuart Mill deals with issues of emergence in the third book of his famous *System of Logic, Ratiocinative and Inductive* (New York: Longmans, 1965). For a later discussion of emergence in the context of evolutionary theory, see the Gifford Lecture of 1922 at St. Andrews, published as C. Lloyd Morgan, *Emergent Evolution* (London: Williams and Norgate, 1922). For a criticism of holistic thought in the social sciences, see Denis C. Phillips, *Holistic Thought in Social Science* (Stanford: Stanford University Press, 1976).

CHAPTER 3. ENGLISH AND GOLD

1. Saussure, *Course in General Linguistics*, 77, italics original.
2. Ibid., 204.
3. The passage on particularism and unification is worth citing in full. Saussure writes: "What that means in practice is that in studying linguistic evolution over an area we can leave particularism out of account: or, equivalently, treat it as the negative aspect of the force of unification. If the force of unification is powerful enough, it will establish uniformity over the whole area. If not, the feature will spread only so far and be restricted to one part of the area in question. That part, none the less, will itself form a coherent whole internally. Therefore one can explain everything by reference simply to the force of unification, without appeal to parochialism. Parochialism is nothing other than the force of intercourse characteristic of each region" (ibid., 206).
4. On the theory of linguistic waves, see ibid., 209. On the issue of time, Saussure writes: "it is time on which linguistic differentiation depends. Geographical diversity has to be translated into temporal diversity" (197). This is not to say that geographic diversity is irrelevant, but only that it has a temporal dimension in its origin. Saussure notes the central role that this diversity has in bringing about an awareness of language as a conventional and variable system: "territorial divergences [in language] leap immediately to the eye. . . . It is even by means of such comparisons that a people becomes aware of its own language" (189).
5. See David Crystal, *The Cambridge Encyclopedia of the English Language* (Cambridge: Cambridge University Press, 1995), 106–112.
6. The debate over the precise number of English-language speakers continues unresolved. Much of the question turns on how proficiency is measured—who is included in the Anglophone population. Crystal estimates 320

million native English speakers, and approximately 2 billion people with some exposure to English, however minimal. There are perhaps 100 million to 300 million non-native speakers of English who have some real capacity in the language. Of course, part of the question turns on what language we take English to be. Ibid., 108. For definitions of "Standard English," see 110–111. Another excellent book of David Crystal's explicitly concerns the role of English as a "global language." He discusses the different ways of calculating who knows how much English: Crystal, *English as a Global Language* (Cambridge: Cambridge University Press, 2003), 60–71.

7. Robert McCrum, "Has la langue française lost out to la langue du Coca-Cola? You betcha," *Observer Review,* January 6, 2002, 17.

8. In 1996, President Jacques Chirac termed the dominance of English on the Internet a "major risk for humanity." Of course, the Internet has already grown exponentially since that dire forecast. "Move over Latin and French, English Is Here to Stay," *Pittsburgh Post-Gazette,* December 27, 1996.

9. The English that is spoken around the world is highly variable, and may be as much a local dialect as the global standard. It is not surprising that pared-down versions of the dominant standard should be emerging around the world, as these versions provide access and coordination, however un-polished they may sound to other English speakers. The supposed "frag-mentation" of English is not surprising in a network power framework. Again, depending on who is trying to access whom, pared-down or dialectic versions of English may prove entirely sufficient. On the rise of "New Englishes," see Crystal, *English as a Global Language,* 141–172.

10. Strevens is cited in Sally Weeks, "Embracing English," *Miami Herald,* August 18, 1996.

11. Crystal, *The Cambridge Encyclopedia of the English Language,* 112.

12. See ibid., 274–275, for a discussion of this point. On English's grammar, syntax, and phonetics, see also George L. Brooks, *A History of the English Language* (London: Cox and Wyman, 1958).

13. Crystal, *English as a Global Language,* 9. Rather, Crystal writes, "A language has traditionally become an international language for one chief reason: the power of its people—especially their political and military power."

14. Alfred the Great (849–899) was a justly famous early English king, but it is probably not really accurate that he saved English at Ethandun. The Danes later broke the Treaty of Wedmore, signed in 886 to limit the extent of Dan-ish advance to northeast England, and overran the Anglo-Saxon kingdoms to the south. English survived. See Crystal, *The Cambridge Encyclopedia of the English Language,* 8–29 for a better account of the historic record of Old English. Alfred arranged for important Latin texts such as *The Ecclesias-tical History of the English Nation* by the monk Bede, the "Venerable Bede" (c. 673–735), to be translated into Old English. Most of the Old English texts we have are in this West Saxon dialect although it was Mercian, the dialect of the commercial center of London, which is the forerunner of our contem-

porary English. It "is one of the ironies of English linguistic history that modern Standard English is descended not from West Saxon, but from Mercian, which was the dialect spoken in the area around London when that city became powerful in the Middle Ages," writes Crystal (*The Cambridge Encyclopedia of the English Language*, 29). In a network power analysis, this fact is less surprising; it may reflect a scholarly bias to consider the availability of translations a more important factor than commercial advantage when choosing which language to learn. For accounts of the forerunner of modern Standard English and its relation to internal British trade, see ibid., 54–55. On the history of Old and Middle English, see also Brooks, *A History of the English Language*, 40–54.

15. The decline of the Celtic languages of the British Isles, such as Gaelic, Cornish, and Welsh, resulted from both direct force and the growing network power of English within Britain. See Nettle and Romaine, *Vanishing Voices*, 133–143.

16. Crystal, *English as a Global Language*, 9.

17. Henry L. Mencken, "The Future of English," *Harper's Magazine* 17 (1935): 543. The colonial language policy was initiated after the opinion of men like Thomas Macaulay on the importance of English won out over those of the "Orientalists," who favored native education in Sanskrit and Urdu. Macaulay laid out his views in an influential speech, *A Minute on Indian Education,* which proved decisive in the debates. See Thomas B. Macaulay, *Speeches: With His Minute on Indian Education* (New York: AMS Press, 1979). The use of English in India maps across regional divides, picking up class ones instead. As Pavan Varma writes of the social milieu after Independence: "The truth is that English had become an instrument for social exclusion: the upper crust of the Indian middle class presided over the linguistic apartheid; the rest of India consisted of victims and aspirants": *The Great Indian Middle Class* (New York: Viking, 1998), 58, but see more generally 58–63.

18. This is a point that Jean-Paul Sartre makes, in his case about the role of French—the colonizer's language in French West Africa—providing a common forum in which the oppressed can unite. See his essay "Black Orpheus," reprinted in Sartre, *"What Is Literature?" and Other Essays,* trans. Jeffrey Mehlman (Cambridge: Harvard University Press, 1988).

19. Crystal, *English as a Global Language*, 120.

20. This erosion occurs in any diglossic relationship in which one language is used in official and high cultural functions and the other at home. English becomes, increasingly, the language of global literature, research, and government—and hence languages that once functioned in these domains lose out and are progressively impoverished. They become less viable because less happens in them—fewer books, articles, papers, movies, conversations— as more activity is carried on in English. More generally, the network power of a dominant standard erodes the viability of lesser standards in this way, which is the element of "indirect force." On diglossic languages, see Nettle

and Romaine, *Vanishing Voices*, 30–31. Crystal argues in *Language Death* (Cambridge: Cambridge University Press, 2000) that having a language of intimate affairs and a second language for professional communication may be the best solution one can reach in a world of threatened languages, though the dangers of diglossic relationships are also clear enough, since they invite the degeneration of bilingualism into monolingualism.

21. The policy of English as the medium of instruction that began with Macaulay's *Minute on Indian Education* continued throughout the Raj. My father recalls his frustration at having to memorize passages of Coleridge's poem "The Rime of the Ancient Mariner" as a young boy in a Punjabi village school in British India, prior to Independence and Partition (and very far from the sea). The use of direct force to advance the English language also occurred in the United States. It is not only the Native American languages that suffered, though because of their small populations of speakers, the effect of that prohibition was often language death. Spanish, too, was prohibited from being spoken on school grounds in many states. In Texas, for example, the prohibition of Spanish on school grounds lasted until 1971.

22. These different elements are touched on by most books about contemporary language, in one guise or another. See Nettle and Romaine, *Vanishing Voices*; Crystal, *Language Death*; John H. McWhorter, *The Power of Babel: A Natural History of Language* (New York: Times Books, 2001).

23. Crystal, *Language Death*, 70.

24. Richard Garner, "Tongue-Tied: Must the U.K. Always Be a Nation of Language Dunces?," *The Independent*, December 19, 2002.

25. For an accessible account of linguistic change, creolization, dialects, and hybridization, see McWhorter, *The Power of Babel*.

26. Two of the best works that deal exclusively with the subject are Nettle and Romaine, *Vanishing Voices*, and Crystal, *Language Death*. McWhorter addresses it also in a final chapter: *The Power of Babel*, 253–286.

  I argue that network power is responsible for all the five linguistic changes in globalization, but I do not mean to suggest that, say, the rise of English as a global language is *directly* tied to language death; the place of regional languages is probably more important, and furthermore, the social status of the speakers of minority languages seems particularly important. Crystal argues that "the emergence of any one language as global has only a limited causal relationship" to linguistic death: *English as a Global Language*, 21; and more generally, on the relationship between a global language and minority language death 21–24.

27. See the first chapter of Crystal's *Language Death*, 2–23; the *Ethnologue* study is cited at 5. See also Nettle and Romaine, *Vanishing Voices*, 27–49, on the question of the number of languages and the extent of endangerment.

28. Crystal, *Language Death*, 14. Crystal makes this argument with the caveat that "The analysis of individual cultural situations has shown that population figures without context are useless" (p. 11). An exception to the generali-

zation that a language with a small population of speakers is threatened is Karitiana, a Brazilian language, spoken by 185 speakers out of a total group size of 191—a 96% rate—preserved by the fact that all Karitiana learn Portuguese as a second language after Karitiana. Karitiana, though, may be the exception that proves the rule (ibid., 12).

29. Nettle and Romaine, *Vanishing Voices*, 40.
30. Crystal, *Language Death*, 14.
31. Nettle and Romaine, *Vanishing Voices*, 51.
32. On the diglossic relationship, see ibid., 30, and on the periphery/metropole distinction, ibid., 126–149.
33. Ibid., 91.
34. Ibid., 136, and Crystal, *Language Death*, 78–79.
35. Crystal, *Language Death*, 79.
36. Nettle and Romaine, *Vanishing Voices*, 31.
37. Ibid., 21.
38. On projects of linguistic revival, see McWhorter, *The Power of Babel*, 266–271.
39. Money is an interesting standard, whose network effects have been discussed a great deal. See, e.g., Martin Shubik, *The Theory of Money and Financial Institutions* (Cambridge: MIT Press, 1999), 142–143. There are also important considerations of justice in the establishment of a monetary system, precisely because of the reciprocal dependence that such a system involves. For an interesting contribution to this question, see Sanjay G. Reddy, "Developing Just Monetary Arrangements," *Ethics and International Affairs* 17, no. 1 (2003). In a network power analysis, we should recognize money as both a mediating standard and a standard criterion for admission. On the one hand, where it is accepted, it regulates economic exchange inherently, as a mediating standard. On the other hand, it also serves as a kind of standard criterion of admission, for, famously, lacking it you are unable to join in economic cooperation with others except through barter. Perhaps we should think of any successful monetary token as a standard criterion for admission, which has become embodied in its users as a substitute for real value, and now acts as a mediating standard.
40. By contrast, he explains, "More awkward or exotic items such as cattle, shells, whiskey and stones, though greatly relished by teachers on money, have never been durably important for people much removed from primitive rural existence." See John Kenneth Galbraith, *Money, Whence It Came, Where It Went* (Boston: Houghton Mifflin, 1975), 5.
41. Glyn Davies, *A History of Money: From Ancient Times to the Present Day* (Cardiff: University of Wales Press, 1994), 35.
42. These citations from ibid., 35; the Nigerian banker was Dr. G. O. Nwankwo.
43. Dentalium shells were harvested off the west coast of Vancouver Island and used along the entire Pacific coast of North America, even into the upper Midwest. Because dentalia are rare and difficult to harvest—at depths

reaching 60 feet—they kept their value in exchange, and were used by some inland tribes into the twentieth century, well after smallpox destroyed the coastal peoples who harvested them and woolen blankets had become the currency of the Northwest. The shells were also used ceremonially.

44. On Yap stones, see Davies, *A History of Money*, 37–38. The Yap islands are all closely situated to one another and enclosed within a single barrier reef. Thus, they are sometimes called simply Yap Island.

45. See Thomas More, *Utopia*, ed. George M. Logan and trans. Robert M. Adams (Cambridge: Cambridge University Press, 2002), 60–61, for the passages in which More discusses how the Utopians treat valuable metals and valuable gems.

46. Cited in Galbraith, *Money, Whence It Came, Where It Went*, 6.

47. Ultimately, Marx develops this theory of money as part of a broader analysis of capitalist economic relations. The money form is a precursor to the development of capital, and, in one phase of the circulation of commodities, becomes it. Marx expresses the use of money as a general equivalent in the circulation of commodities as C-M-C, where commodities (C) are transformed into money (M) for other commodities. Money becomes capital in the reverse form of this expression, M-C-M, where money itself becomes productive—that is, it becomes capital—when it is used to buy labor-power as a commodity.

48. Marx, *Capital*, 93.

49. Ibid., 109.

50. Ibid., 118.

51. Smith also mentions the rise of paper money, but he means paper certificates representing metal in a bank, not the paper money of, say, the dollars of the contemporary United States, which are backed by the "full faith and credit" of the government rather than a store of bullion.

52. Marx draws on the Aristotelian account of money in developing his analysis in *A Contribution to the Critique of Political Economy*, ed. Maurice Dobb and trans. S. W. Ryazanskaya (London: Lawrence & Wishart, 1970). Aristotle's early treatment of money is brief but instructive and sets the basis for later arguments concerning the rise of the money-form. (It is particularly significant as few philosophers in the classical world were much interested in these questions of daily life.) In Book V of *Nicomachean Ethics*, Aristotle explains that exchange—what he calls the reciprocation of "good for good"—requires commensurability: some standard or mean by which equality can be assessed. As he puts it, "everything that is exchanged must be in some way commensurable." This commensurability is achieved through the use of a *mean* by which things are rendered measurable and comparable: "This is where money comes in; it functions as a kind of mean, since it is a measure of everything, including, therefore, excess and deficiency." Without such a mean, "there can be no exchange and no association." He explains that "Everything . . . must be measured by some one standard" and goes on

to say: "This standard is in fact demand, which holds everything together; for if people needed nothing, or needed things to different degrees, either there would be no exchange or it would not be the same as it now is. But by social convention money has come to serve as a representative of demand. And this is why money is called *nomisma,* because it exists not by nature but by convention (*nomos*), and it is in our power to change its value and to render it worthless." He points out that exchange is entered into only out of need, without which there would be no necessity of a convention like money. But money is not just any convention; it renders things commensurable for exchange and thus, in a sense, equal (or equalizable). Aristotle captures the logic of the universal standard, explaining: "So money makes things commensurable as a measure does, and equates them; for without exchange, there would be no association between people, without equality no exchange, and without commensurability, no equality. It is impossible that things differing to such a degree should become truly commensurable, but in relation to demand they can become commensurable enough. So there must be some one standard, and it must be on an agreed basis— which is why money is called *nomisma.* Money makes all things commensurable, since everything is measured by money." All of these passages are from Book V, Chapter V of the *Nicomachean Ethics* (90–91).

Marx starts from this Aristotelian account but denies that it is money itself that makes commodities commensurable; rather, it is because they are already commensurable that money can commensurate them. Marx writes: "Labour-time is the measure of both gold and commodities, and gold becomes the measure of value only because all commodities are measured in terms of gold; it is consequently merely an illusion created by the circulation process to suppose that money makes commodities commensurable. On the contrary, it is only the commensurability of commodities as materialised labour-time which converts money into gold" (*A Contribution to the Critique of Political Economy,* 67–68).

53. Locke, *Two Treatises of Government,* 294, italics original. Locke's discussion of money comes out of his argument on the right of property more generally, which he believes arises from man's natural right to appropriate to himself the fruits of his labor, provided such an act of appropriation leaves "enough and as good" property for others, and does not result in spoilage or waste, which would indicate that someone has taken more than he himself can use. Money, as a conventional measure of value that does not spoil, is the means by which someone can appropriate more perishable goods than he could individually consume by entering them into the system of exchange, receiving money in return for, say, acorns. Money comes from a social agreement (informally achieved) to make gold worth so much in terms of these other goods.
54. Ibid., 300.
55. Ibid., 300–301.

56. These two citations are from ibid., 301 and 300 respectively.

57. Ibid., 301–302.

58. Ibid., 302. Note that Locke's argument made the commercial activity and appropriation of resources by settlers in British North America appear a pre-political right guaranteed by the laws of nature. Since there is "enough and as good" in North America, and because the use of money and commerce are pre-political rights, the British settlers had no need to negotiate with or include Native American sovereigns in establishing a system of private property and commerce. Locke also claims that the use of money is a major (perhaps *the* major) difference that allows European domination of North America, which was insufficiently developed by its native inhabitants owing to the lack of the use of money. See Locke's argument in both Section 49 and later in Section 108 of his *Two Treatises of Government*, 301, 339 respectively. This claim ignores, of course, the use of money in a different form throughout the North American continent. But perhaps Locke had something like network power dynamics in mind: lacking gold, the Native Americans could not participate in the monetary networks of the Old World once they came into contact with its inhabitants. More generally on Locke and the Native Americans, see James Tully's essay "The *Two Treatises* and Aboriginal Rights," in Graham A. J. Rogers, *Locke's Philosophy: Content and Context* (Oxford: Clarendon Press, 1994).

59. Adam Smith, *Lectures on Jurisprudence*, ed. Ronald L. Meek, David D. Raphael, and Peter Stein (Oxford: Clarendon Press, 1978), 368.

60. Ibid., 367.

61. Ibid., 368.

62. "In the same manner as they changed the naturall measures of length into artificiall ones, so did they those of value" (ibid., 367).

63. See ibid., 369–370 for these arguments. Smith writes explicitly against Locke on gold and silver: "Their value is not as Mr. Locke imagines founded by an agreement of men to put it upon them; they have what we may call a naturall value, and would bear a high [one] considered merely as a commodity, tho not used as the instrument of exchange."

64. Nevertheless, it also seems clear in Smith's account that while he wants to argue that gold and silver have a "natural" or market price independent of their use as the instrument of exchange, he also recognizes that the metals take value from convention. For example, he writes in a later lecture that the effort devoted to digging gold and silver out of the ground to serve as money is less beneficial than simply growing more corn. If gold has a merely natural price, it would not follow that these efforts are wasted, for one can always have more gold spoons.

65. A large section of *The Order of Things* is devoted to a provocative genealogy of classical theories of exchange focused on the way in which money was understood to represent value. See Foucault, *The Order of Things*, 166–214.

66. John Maynard Keynes, *A Treatise on Money* (New York: Harcourt, 1930), 2:289.

67. Ibid., 290.

68. It is true that the gold standard came back, albeit indirectly, under the Bretton Woods system, in which the currency to which all others were tied—the United States dollar—was in turn tied to gold. But this "gold-exchange standard" collapsed in the early 1970s, leading to our current world of floating currencies. It was suspended in 1971 before being formally abandoned in 1978.

69. See Barry J. Eichengreen, *Globalizing Capital: A History of the International Monetary System* (Princeton: Princeton University Press, 1996). See also the collection of essays he edited with Marc Flandreau, *The Gold Standard in Theory and History* (London: Routledge, 1997).

70. See Eichengreen, *Globalizing Capital*, 10–11, for a helpful hypothetical example to illustrate this phenomenon, which we might consider an example of "Gresham's Law," the idea that "bad money drives out the good." Eichengreen supposes that a country exchanges gold for silver at a ratio of 1 ounce of gold to 15 ounces of silver:

> Say, however, that the price of gold on the world market rose more than the price of silver, as it did in the last third of the nineteenth century. Imagine that its price rose to the point where 16 ounces of silver traded for an ounce of gold. This creates incentives for arbitrage. The arbitrager could import 15 ounces of silver and have it coined at the mint. He could exchange that silver coin for one containing an ounce of gold. He could export that gold and trade it for 16 ounces of silver on foreign markets (since 16 to 1 was the price prevailing there).
>
> Through this act of arbitrage he recouped his investment and obtained in addition an extra half ounce of silver. As long as the market ratio stayed significantly above the mint ratio, the incentive for arbitrage remained. Arbitragers would import silver and export gold until all the gold coin in the country had been exported. . . . Alternatively, if the market ratio fell significantly below the mint ratio, arbitragers would import gold and export silver until the latter had disappeared from circulation. Only if the mint and market ratios remained sufficiently close would both gold and silver circulate.

This latter condition, by which silver is driven out of domestic circulation, is what evidently occurred following Newton's failure to lower the mint ratio sufficiently in 1717, creating a de facto gold standard in Britain which was later given the force of law. With the mint ratio of gold in terms of silver higher than the market ratio, gold was essentially "deposited" in Britain while British silver fled to other regions, where it was valued more highly against gold. Adam Smith complained about this "small mistake in the relative proportion of gold and silver." He then claims, "A proposal was made in Parliament to have remedied this, but as it was found to be extremely troublesome it was laid aside" (Smith, *Lectures on Jurisprudence*,

377). Parliament would later be forced to demonetize silver for large purchases altogether.

71. Keynes, *A Treatise on Money*, 2:290.
72. Eichengreen, *Globalizing Capital*, 5–6, italics original.
73. Ibid., 6.
74. Weber, *Economy and Society*, 179.
75. Eichengreen, *Globalizing Capital*, 195.
76. Keynes, *A Treatise on Money*, 2:299.
77. Ibid., 291.
78. Ibid., 292.
79. Ibid., 299.
80. Keynes writes, "even if an international gold standard does serve to keep slovenly countries up to the mark, it may also keep progressive countries below the standard of monetary management which they might otherwise attain. Thus the gold standard is, as I have said above, part of the apparatus of Conservatism. For Conservatism is always more concerned to prevent backsliding from that degree of progress which human institutions have already attained, than to promote progress in those quarters which are ready for progress, at the risk of 'upsetting the ideas' of the weaker brethren and bringing into question precarious and hard-won conventions which have the merit that they do at least preserve a certain modicum of decent behaviour" (ibid., 300).
81. Keynes writes: "This, then, is the dilemma of an international monetary system—to preserve the advantages of the stability of the local currencies of various members of the system in terms of the international standard, and to preserve at the same time an adequate local autonomy for each member over its domestic rate of interest and its volume of foreign lending" (ibid., 304).
82. Ibid.
83. Ibid., 301.
84. Ibid., 307.
85. Ibid., 309.
86. Ibid., 336.
87. Keynes writes, "The device which we have now to consider is expressly directed towards damping down this sensitiveness without departing from effective conformity with an international standard" (ibid., 319–320).
88. Ibid., 330. Keynes's argument has been echoed recently by the economist Jagdish Bhagwati, who has sounded an extremely skeptical note on capital mobility, arguing that overhasty financial liberalization was pushed by a "Wall Street–Treasury complex" for the benefit of U.S. banks and to the detriment of fragile developing world economies. See Bhagwati, *In Defense of Globalization* (New York: Oxford University Press, 2004), 204–206.
89. Keynes, *A Treatise on Money*, 2:332.
90. Ibid., 336.

91. John Maynard Keynes, *The General Theory of Employment, Interest and Money* (London: Macmillan, 1936), 372.

92. Keynes writes, "In short, the aggregate return from durable goods in the course of their life would, as in the case of short-lived goods, just cover their labour-costs of production *plus* an allowance for risk and the costs of skill and supervision" (ibid., 375, italics original).

93. Ibid., 376. The reason that such a policy can be pursued is that, unlike in the case of land, Keynes sees "no intrinsic reasons for the scarcity of capital." Indeed, even if "net saving in conditions of full employment comes to an end before capital has become sufficiently abundant"—that is, if capitalists stop saving when the returns to capital fall too low—Keynes suggests that, "it will still be possible for communal saving through the agency of the State to be maintained at a level which will allow the growth of capital up to the point where it ceases to be scarce" (ibid.).

94. Mises insists on the practicality and desirability of a return to the gold standard in a host of different works. For example, in his *Economic Policy: Thoughts for Today and Tomorrow* (Chicago: Regnery/Gateway, 1979), p. 65, he argues, "The gold standard has one tremendous virtue: the quantity of the money supply, under the gold standard, is independent of the policies of governments and political parties. This is its advantage. It is a form of protection against spendthrift governments." Likewise, in his *Planning for Freedom* (South Holland, Ill.: Libertarian Press, 1980), p. 185, he writes, "The gold standard alone makes the determination of money's purchasing power independent of the ambitions and machinations of governments, of dictators, of political parties, and of pressure groups." Hayek also desired a return to the gold standard because of its anti-political consequences, but he doubted that it could be practically achieved. He therefore suggested the "denationalization" of money by eliminating "legal tender" laws and inviting the creation of private forms of money (issued by corporations and other private actors) to compete with national currencies. See his book *The Denationalisation of Money* (London: Institute of Economic Affairs, 1990), which was first published in 1976. Even though he would prefer a system of privately printed currencies in competition because of his recognition that "there is just not enough gold about" (p. 110), Hayek would still support a return to the gold standard instead of sovereign control of the money supply. He writes (p. 130): "I still believe that so long as the management of money is in the hands of government, the gold standard with all its imperfections is the only tolerably safe system. But we can certainly do better than that, though not through government."

CHAPTER 4. POWER AND CHOICE IN NETWORKS

1. Nozick argues, for example, that a worker should not be considered as "forced" to work, even where his only alternative is starvation, except where "unjust" actions created the absence of alternatives. He holds that ordinary

market outcomes that are the result of a series of legitimate prior activities can lead to unhappy alternatives but not coercion, which can only be the result of an earlier violation. I think it is more obvious to follow Gerald Cohen's criticism of this position than Nozick's denial of coercion where one has the "choice" of only an unacceptable option. See Nozick, *Anarchy, State, and Utopia* (New York: Basic Books, 1974), 262–264, and Cohen's critique, "The Structure of Proletarian Unfreedom," *Philosophy & Public Affairs* 12, no. 1 (1983), 4. Serena Olsaretti offers a particularly lucid argument against this libertarian justification of market outcomes, in her *Liberty, Desert and the Market: A Philosophical Study* (Cambridge: Cambridge University Press, 2004), 109–136.

2. Cohen became interested in this question while examining the structure of formally free choices under conditions of modern employment (in response to Nozick's libertarian philosophy justifying formally free but substantively unfree choices as non-coercive). For example, do workers "choose" hazardous jobs, and what moral judgments depend upon our characterization that these jobs were chosen freely? See Cohen, "The Structure of Proletarian Unfreedom," 27 (italics original), and Gerald A. Cohen, "Are Disadvantaged Workers Who Take Hazardous Jobs Forced to Take Hazardous Jobs?" in his *History, Labour, and Freedom: Themes from Marx* (Oxford: Clarendon Press, 1988). A related issue is the freedom of the wage bargain as a whole, which Cohen takes up in "Are Workers Forced to Sell Their Labor Power?," *Philosophy & Public Affairs* 14, no. 1 (1985).

3. Olsaretti, *Liberty, Desert and the Market*, 138, italics original.

4. Ibid., 140. Although I do not consistently employ Olsaretti's distinction throughout, hers is a helpful one, distinguishing what we might call merely formal or empty freedom from real freedom (which she calls voluntariness). Where I discuss freedom in the way she uses it, I often say formal or empty freedom, to indicate that it is not freedom to choose over a range of acceptable alternatives.

5. Ibid., 138, italics original.

6. Ibid., 149, 150.

7. Ibid., 151.

8. Ibid., 154, italics original.

9. Ibid., 139, italics original.

10. Ibid., 156, italics original.

11. Saussure, *Course in General Linguistics*, 71. Note that here Saussure does not mean you cannot legislate new words in some instances, but that linguistic change does not usually occur in this manner.

12. Ibid.

13. Ibid., 78. He explains in an earlier passage: "Continuity with the past constantly restricts freedom of choice. If the Frenchman of today uses words like *homme* ('man') and *chien* ('dog'), it is because these words were used by his forefathers. . . . It is because the linguistic sign is arbitrary that it knows

no other law than that of tradition, and because it is founded upon tradition that it can be arbitrary" (74).

14. See Weber, *Economy and Society*, 53, for definitions of "power" (*Macht*) and "domination" (*Herrschaft*). Weber defines power as "the probability that one actor within a social relationship will be in a position to carry out his own will despite resistance, regardless of the basis on which this probability rests." This definition is "amorphous," he claims, and thus he prefers to use the concept of domination, which he defines as "the probability that a command with a given specific content will be obeyed by a given group of persons." He uses the concept of domination rather than power in his discussion of domination "by virtue of a constellation of interests" and "authoritarian power of command." In this section (941–948), he also explains that "domination constitutes a special case of power."

15. Ibid., 941. In the broader passage, Weber writes, "Domination in the most general sense is one of the most important elements of social action. Of course, not every form of social action reveals a structure of dominancy. But in most of the varieties of social action domination plays a considerable role, even where it is not obvious at first sight. . . . Without exception every sphere of social action is profoundly influenced by structures of dominancy." It may be that Weber here means dominancy in the more restricted sense (i.e., authoritarian power of command), but the broader passage is somewhat ambiguous, and comes before he has made his narrower definition explicit, so I take it as referring to domination in its multiple forms.

16. Ibid., 943.

17. Ibid., 945.

18. Ibid., 943.

19. Ibid.

20. Ibid., 944–945. Of course, Weber's analysis of capitalism in *Economy and Society* is far from "Marxist" but whatever the (much debated) differences between them (usually focusing on the "idealist" elements in Weber), it seems clear that Marx's analyses had a significant impact on Weber's thought, in this work especially.

21. Ibid., 945. He goes on to explain, "In the German Customs Union the Prussian officials were dominant because their state's territory constituted the largest and thus the decisive market; in the German Reich they are paramount because they dispose of the largest net of railroads, the greatest number of university positions, etc., and can thus cripple the corresponding administrative departments of the other, formally equal, states." Interestingly, he also cites the example of New York's position within the United States as a form of domination "by virtue of a constellation of interests," writing that "New York can exercise political power, because it is the seat of the great financial powers" (946).

22. Ibid., 946, italics original.

23. Weber writes, "because of the very absence of rules, domination which

originates in the market or other interest constellations may be felt to be much more oppressive than an authority in which the duties of obedience are set out clearly and expressly" (ibid). Add to this point that the relations of sovereignty are democratically constituted—a point on which Weber is not convinced—and you have a strong argument for using sovereign power to manage the relations of sociability.

24. This view of power is commonly associated with Hobbes, Weber, and Dahl, though I suspect it is a substantial misreading of both Hobbes and Weber to identify their arguments too strictly with such a view; it may better represent Dahl's position. See Giddens, *Central Problems in Social Theory*, 88.

25. See Brian Barry's essay on power from a perspective of costs and benefits and for a discussion of power as the ability to realize one's will, and the ways in which one can go about it: "Power: An Economic Analysis," in Brian M. Barry, ed., *Power and Political Theory: Some European Perspectives* (New York: Wiley, 1976), 68–101.

26. Steven Lukes, *Power: A Radical View* (London: Macmillan, 1974).

27. Ibid., 26.

28. Ibid., 27.

29. Lukes writes that the theorists of one-dimensional and two-dimensional views of power both "follow in the steps of Max Weber, for whom power was the probability of *individuals realising their wills* despite the resistance of others." Unfortunately, Lukes does not discuss Weber's more complex analysis of domination (which would have fitted well into his general discussion) but references only the standard "Weberian" concept—an oversight in an otherwise insightful analysis (ibid., 22).

30. Peter Bachrach and Morton S. Baratz, "The Two Faces of Power," *American Political Science Review* 56, no. 4 (1962). Bachrach and Baratz introduce an interesting typology of kinds of power, covering allied terms such as "authority," "influence," and "force."

31. For Giddens's interesting review of Lukes and his criticism of the link between interests and power in Lukes's "three-dimensional view," see Giddens, *Central Problems in Social Theory*, 89–91.

32. All citations in this paragraph are from Lukes, *Power: A Radical View*, 22.

33. Lukes argues that the two-dimensional view still requires actual conflict, if only in the sense that the nondecision-making is observable.

34. Ibid., 22.

35. Ibid., 21–22.

36. Ibid., 23.

37. Ibid., 39.

38. More precisely, a counterfactual or "contrary-to-fact conditional" is a subjective conditional for which the antecedent is presupposed false. This is a complicated way of saying that counterfactuals are statements of the form, "If that, then this," where we know the "that" is not true or did not actually occur. Counterfactuals thus enable us to think about how things might be

now given a different set of prior conditions: a different institutional framework, different actions on the part of someone, a different set of contingen-
cies, and so on. Lukes explains: "in general, any attribution of the exercise
of power . . . always implies a relevant counterfactual, to the effect that (but
for A, or but for A together with any other sufficient conditions) B would
otherwise have done [something different from what he did under A's exercise of power]." Lukes argues, and I think persuasively, that the reason that
the one- and two-dimensional views of power insist upon actual conflict is
that conflict provides evidence of the clear counterfactual necessary to identify an exercise of power. When the observer can see conflict, she can tell
easily that there is something that B wants to do, and would have done, but
for A's power. See ibid., 41, for this statement and the argument.

39. Lukes notes: "Some appear to feel discomfort in speaking either of groups,
institutions, or collectivities 'exercising' power, or of individuals or collectivities doing so unconsciously. This is an interesting case of individualistic and
intentional assumptions being built into our language—but that in itself
provides no reason for adopting such assumptions" (ibid., 39).

40. The mechanism of power is less clear on an account that ties the mechanism into evidence of power being "exercised" directly, because the argument of network power does not require direct or personal interference,
even if hidden, for the systemic conditions to constitute a kind of power. In
this it follows most three-dimensional views of power. If direct actions are
sought, they will most likely be found in the creation (or deliberate maintenance) of standards that are incompatible with other standards, and govern
access to a large network of members. I turn to these institutional conditions of power in the second half of Chapter 6, and discuss the creation of
the WTO as a strategic exercise of network power in Chapter 8.

41. In this text, I have sometimes spoken of standards and networks as if they
"spread" or "grow," but this loose language must be seen as shorthand for
the real agency of people in networks deciding which standards they will
use. Networks and standards must not be imagined to possess volition independent of the choices of individuals deciding how best to accomplish their
own ends, facing consequences determined by others similarly positioned.
I discuss this issue at greater length above in note 15, Chapter 1.

42. Lukes, *Power: A Radical View,* 52. Lukes discusses the work of Althusserians
such as Nico Poulantzas, in ibid., 52–55. Consider Poulantzas's statement
that class relations *"are at every level relations of power: power, however, is*
only a concept indicating the effect of the ensemble of the structures on *the
relations of the practices of the various classes in conflict"* (cited ibid., 55, italics
original).

43. Ibid., 55, italics original.
44. Ibid., 54.
45. Ibid., 54–55.
46. For a brief discussion of the opposition of these two concepts, see Joseph V.

Femia's introduction to his *Gramsci's Political Thought: Hegemony, Consciousness, and the Revolutionary Process* (Oxford: Clarendon Press, 1981).

47. See Antonio Gramsci, *Selections from the Prison Notebooks of Antonio Gramsci*, ed. and trans. Quintin Hoare and Geoffrey Nowell Smith (New York: International Publishers, 1971), footnote at 55, for a discussion of the translation of these terms from Italian. Gramsci usually uses *direzione* and *egemonia* interchangeably. Sometimes *egemonia* is defined as *direzione* plus *dominazione:* hegemony is leadership plus domination. At other times, *egemonia* seems to mean only the consensual aspect of leadership, though it is always accompanied by domination, or can be reinforced by it.

48. Ibid., 57.

49. Ibid., 59.

50. Femia proposes four different forms of consent in *Gramsci's Political Thought*, 38–40. Perhaps unsurprisingly, given his Marxist commitments, Gramsci does not offer a single conception of consent, but alters his usage depending on the particulars of his historical analysis or the context in which he deploys the term. Likewise, Gramsci's idea of hegemony is also subject to ongoing interpretation. Femia identifies three different types of hegemony in Gramsci's work—integral, decadent, and minimal (46–48). Adamson argues that there are at least two main senses in which hegemony is used by Gramsci; first, "the consensual basis of an existing political system within civil society. . . . understood to be in contrast to the concept of 'domination'"; and second, as "an overcoming of the 'economic-corporative'" and the "advance to a 'class consciousness' where class is understood not only economically but also in terms of a common intellectual and moral awareness, a common culture." See Walter L. Adamson, *Hegemony and Revolution: A Study of Antonio Gramsci's Political and Cultural Theory* (Berkeley: University of California Press, 1980), 170–171.

51. Femia, *Gramsci's Political Thought*, 31.

52. From Antonio Gramsci, *Il materialismo storico e la filosofia di Benedetto Croce*, 11, cited at Femia, *Gramsci's Political Thought*, 43.

53. Ibid., 44–45.

54. Ibid., 31. Note that on this interpretation of Gramsci, the false consciousness in question need not be conceived an out-and-out "brainwashing" or mystification, but results from the division of labor itself in a relatively straightforward way. The practical world in which the working classes move and act is itself the product of an earlier alienation that then comes to be reflected in the forms of thought and reflection available to the proletariat. We may find it unsurprising that the experience of slavery results in a slavish disposition in which the conditions of liberation are difficult to grasp, either practically or theoretically.

55. The literature on Foucault's conception of power is immense. See, for example, Michel Foucault, *Power/Knowledge: Selected Interviews and Other*

Writings, 1972–1977, trans. and ed. Colin Gordon (New York: Pantheon Books, 1980); Michel Foucault, *Power*, ed. James D. Faubion (New York: New Press, 2000). Among the many followers of Foucault, one of the most interesting on power is Judith Butler, who explores the way in which power is involved in the formation of subjects. See Judith Butler, *The Psychic Life of Power: Theories in Subjection* (Stanford: Stanford University Press, 1997).

56. Michel Foucault, *The History of Sexuality*, trans. Robert Hurley (New York: Vintage Books, 1980). Michel Foucault, *"Il Faut Défendre la Société": Cours au Collège de France (1975–1976)* (Paris: Editions du Seuil, 1997). I believe that these lectures at the Collège de France have not yet been translated, despite their salience for any analysis of Foucault's political thought.

57. Foucault, *The History of Sexuality*, 90.

58. Ibid., 89.

59. Ibid., 92.

60. Ibid., 93.

61. Ibid.

62. Ibid., 94.

63. Ibid., 95.

64. Gilles Deleuze, *Foucault*, trans. and ed. Seán Hand (Minneapolis: University of Minnesota Press, 1988), 25.

65. Cited at ibid., 28. The English translation of this passage contains a small error.

66. Charles Taylor, "Foucault on Freedom and Truth," *Political Theory* 12, no. 2 (1984), 158.

67. Taylor, "Foucault on Freedom and Truth," 158. Taylor's essay occasioned a response by William Connolly to which he in turn responded: William E. Connolly, "Taylor, Foucault, and Otherness," *Political Theory* 13, no. 3 (1985). Charles Taylor, "Connolly, Foucault, and Truth," *Political Theory* 13, no. 3 (1985). Taylor returns to these themes in "Taylor and Foucault on Power and Freedom—a Reply," *Political Studies* 37, no. 2 (1989).

68. See Anthony Giddens, *Politics, Sociology and Social Theory: Encounters with Classical and Contemporary Social Thought* (Cambridge, U.K.: Polity Press, 1995), 265, and Piaget, *Structuralism*, 134–135.

69. Taylor, "Foucault on Freedom and Truth," 166.

70. Ibid., 167.

71. Ibid., 168.

72. This makes them different from the more helpful account offered by some versions of "critical theory," which situates theory together with the agents' own understanding in an emancipatory analysis. See Raymond Geuss, *The Idea of a Critical Theory: Habermas and the Frankfurt School* (Cambridge: Cambridge University Press, 1981).

73. Taylor, "Foucault on Freedom and Truth," 169.

74. Ibid., 170.

75. Lukes, *Power: A Radical View*, 26.

76. Karl Marx and Friedrich Engels, *The Eighteenth Brumaire of Louis Bonapart*, in *Selected Works [of] Karl Marx and Frederick Engels* (Moscow: Foreign Languages Pub. House, 1962), 247.

CHAPTER 5. EVALUATING NETWORK POWER

1. Although it is a possibility I discuss below, I do not think it is helpful to collapse these two categories of concern by claiming that the loss of identity constitutes a "cost" to someone. Such a reduction has the effect of distorting what we commonly mean by both identity and interest rather than helping us to elucidate either—and a helpfully reductivist account should elucidate rather than obscure our commonsense insights.

2. There is a vast literature on these themes. Ashis Nandy's work has particularly shaped my thinking. See, e.g., Nandy, *The Intimate Enemy: Loss and Recovery of Self under Colonialism* (New York: Oxford University Press, 1983), and Nandy, *The Savage Freud and Other Essays on Possible and Retrievable Selves* (Princeton: Princeton University Press, 1995). So, too, have a number of standard classics, such as Albert Memmi, *The Colonizer and the Colonized*, trans. Howard Greenfeld (New York: Orion Press, 1965), and Frantz Fanon, *Black Skin, White Masks*, trans. Charles L. Markmann (New York: Grove Press, 1967). More recent contributions that I have found helpful include Ranajit Guha, *Dominance without Hegemony: History and Power in Colonial India* (Cambridge: Harvard University Press, 1997); Ranajit Guha and Gayatri Chakravorty Spivak, *Selected Subaltern Studies* (New York: Oxford University Press, 1988); and Leela Gandhi, *Postcolonial Theory: A Critical Introduction* (New York: Columbia University Press, 1998).

3. Keynes, *A Treatise on Money*, 2:332.

4. For a more precise definition of counterfactuals, see the discussion in note 38, chapter 4. When I discuss "counterfactuals," I am drawing on the common recognition that the world as we know it might have been different if one of many other possible historical pathways had been taken. What I do not want to take up here is the argument about "possible worlds," as it originated in Leibnitz. Leibnitz's claim was that God had chosen our actual world out of an infinite array of many possible worlds. This claim, and the various arguments that follow from it, were largely ignored in Anglo-American philosophy due to the influence of Humean skepticism. Recently, however, several prominent analytic philosophers, including David Lewis, have taken up the concept of possible worlds. For a collection of their work, see Michael J. Loux, ed., *The Possible and the Actual: Readings in the Metaphysics of Modality* (Ithaca, N.Y.: Cornell University Press, 1979). One of Lewis's contributions to that volume, an essay entitled "Possible Worlds," begins straightforwardly, invoking our commonsense notion that "things might have been different" given an alternate historical trajectory. But he moves from this appeal to rather abstract speculation on the reality of "possible worlds," by which he means not the unrealized but possible worlds

that might have existed in place of the actual world we now inhabit, but parallel or alternate realities that he argues exist as fully as we suppose our own world to exist. (Whether Lewis's arguments are persuasive here requires an assessment I must leave to others.) In my discussion of counterfactuals, I mean merely to suggest the possibility of other ways in which our world might have been, not other "possible worlds" as Leibnitz introduced them. Of course, no one needs to worry that the inquiry into counterfactuals in the more limited sense I intend depends upon the philosophical resolution of questions of "possible worlds." As Robert Stalnaker writes in response to Lewis, "One could accept . . . that there really are many ways that things could have been—while denying that there exists anything else that is like the actual world" (ibid., 228). Of course, there may be a philosophical relation between counterfactuals and possible worlds, as Lewis suggests in his book *Counterfactuals* (Cambridge: Harvard University Press, 1973), which explores counterfactual reasoning and discusses the idea of possible worlds as foundational for a philosophical development of the idea of the counterfactual. Nevertheless, for the more modest purposes of this inquiry, I believe the two notions are adequately separable.

5. I am indebted to Roberto Mangabeira Unger for many helpful discussions about imagination and social explanation, some of which have made their way into this section in particular. The insight that we can understand those things we have made ourselves comes out clearly in Hobbes—and has been a central theme of modern social and political thought since.

6. Of course, with many standards, the disadvantage that a new user faces will be much more extreme than in the adoption of a new measurement system. A meter may always be a meter, but we know the difference between an immigrant's English and the Queen's.

7. Nash explains: "A two-person bargaining situation involves two individuals who have the opportunity to collaborate for mutual benefit in more than one way." In this bargaining game, cooperation is achieved through a division of the benefits to which the parties can agree. See John F. Nash, "The Bargaining Problem," *Econometrica* 18, no. 2 (1950), 155, and more generally, Elster, *The Cement of Society*, 50–96.

8. Amartya K. Sen, "How to Judge Globalism," *The American Prospect*, January 14, 2002, A5, italics original.

9. Alberto Alesina and Robert J. Barro, *Currency Unions* (Stanford, Calif.: Hoover Institution Press, 2001), 13–14.

10. This may not be an adequately nuanced understanding of the problem of inflation, however widespread it is among macroeconomists now. For a different view, which emphasizes the political determinants of a particular rate of inflation, see the collection of essays edited by Fred Hirsch and John H. Goldthorpe, *The Political Economy of Inflation* (Cambridge: Harvard University Press, 1978).

11. Alesina and Barro, *Currency Unions*, 17.

346 NOTES TO PAGES 152–161

12. Philippe van Parijs, "Linguistic Justice," *Politics, Philosophy & Economics* 1, no. 1 (2002).

13. Crystal, *Language Death*, 29.

14. On why we should care about linguistic diversity, see ibid., 27–67; and Nettle and Romaine, *Vanishing Voices*, 150–175.

15. Charles Taylor, *Multiculturalism and the Politics of Recognition: An Essay*, ed. Amy Gutmann (Princeton: Princeton University Press, 1992), 25.

16. See Habermas, *The Theory of Communicative Action*, vol. 2: "Lifeworld and System: A Critique of Functionalist Reason," 392.

17. Axel Honneth, *The Struggle for Recognition: The Moral Grammar of Social Conflicts*, ed. and trans. Joel Anderson (Cambridge: MIT Press, 1996). One reason that Honneth's account is better developed than Taylor's may be that, while both look to Hegel, Taylor looks to Hegel's mature thought, as in the *The Phenomenology of Spirit*, while Honneth mines early and relatively obscure writings from Hegel's time at Jena as a young man. Honneth claims that these early writings are more helpful because they are based on a view of history in which the struggles of people—rather than the world-historical realization of *geist*—are given the central explanatory role. See Honneth, *The Struggle for Recognition*, chapters 2 and 3 for more on the way that Honneth makes use of Hegel's early writings.

18. I say inappositely because I think that the most interesting interpretations of Hobbes emphasize the role played by *epistemic* conflict in which individual interests are to a significant extent unknown or uncertain, rather than the interest-based conflict with which Hobbes is commonly associated. This is a line of thought that comes out most clearly in one of his lesser-known works, *The Elements of Law*, which reveals Hobbes's rich and provocative political psychology in a way that some of his more familiar works may not. For this interpretation of Hobbes, see Tuck, *Hobbes*.

19. Unfortunately, I think that Honneth misrepresents Marx somewhat, emphasizing those elements of Marxian thought that accord least place to a richly intersubjective notion of recognition, such as class conflict over narrowly conceived economic interests. (Honneth's handling of Marx here parallels what I take to be his misreading of Hobbes.) But surely the point of a *critique* of political economy like Marx's presupposes many of the elements of recognition and relation-to-self that Honneth is keen to emphasize. I do not mean to detract overly from Honneth's work. It should be obvious (given the effort I make introducing it) that I find Honneth's account a helpful one. Accordingly, I have confined my objections to his intellectual historical work to these notes.

20. Honneth, *The Struggle for Recognition*, 95.

21. Honneth argues convincingly that these psychological relations are the most basic, and are therefore the most historically invariant, in contrast with the other two forms of recognition whose content changes with and influences the historical trajectory of entire societies. It is not clear that network power,

which influences network membership, is very important in these most basic settings, despite some obvious connections between the domains. We use standards to gain access to others, and—in the context of globalization, at least—the concern is how to connect to relatively distant, rather than intimate, others. It is obviously the case that a lack of legal recognition or social esteem will influence the likelihood of receiving adequate emotional recognition at home, but our focus must therefore be on the failure of legal recognition or social solidarity in the first place. For example, the loss of a way of life under circumstances of greatly unequal network power will certainly impact the intimate practices of child-rearing and parental bonding, but the network power dynamics operate indirectly on these practices by first affecting the social contexts in which they occur. What direct effects the social conditions of modernity and globalization have on these emotional bonds is a complicated and important question, but one well beyond the scope of the present study.

22. On gay marriage, see the interesting article by Adam Haslett that illustrates these dynamics of recognition: "Love Supreme: Gay Nuptials and the Making of Modern Marriage," *The New Yorker*, May 31, 2004.

23. Taylor, *Multiculturalism and the Politics of Recognition*, 38.

24. Purdy, *Being America*, 43.

25. Ibid., 46.

26. See John Rawls, *Justice as Fairness: A Restatement*, ed. Erin Kelly (Cambridge: Harvard University Press, 2001), 59. See also, of course, John Rawls, *A Theory of Justice* (Cambridge, Mass.: Belknap Press, 1971).

27. Robert Hockett, "The Deep Grammar of Distribution: A Meta-Theory of Justice," *Cardozo Law Review* 26 (2005).

28. See the discussion of the capabilities framework and the criticism of competing conceptions in Amartya K. Sen, *Inequality Reexamined* (Cambridge: Harvard University Press, 1992). See also Martha Nussbaum, *Women and Development: The Capabilities Approach* (New York: Cambridge University Press, 2000).

29. Nancy Fraser has done important work in this area. See her *Justice Interruptus: Critical Reflections on the "Postsocialist" Condition* (New York: Routledge, 1997). She has also recently advanced a critical theory of recognition that she claims comes closer than Axel Honneth's or Charles Taylor's to reconciling interests and identities by focusing on the political economy of society and not just the intersubjective conditions of recognition. See Nancy Fraser and Axel Honneth, *Redistribution or Recognition?: A Political-Philosophical Exchange* (London: Verso, 2003). With regard to Honneth, at least, I am not sure that Fraser's theory has any serious advantages (leaving aside Honneth's misreading of Marx). It may have a number of disadvantages. By refusing Honneth's focus on the intersubjective conditions of identity formation, Fraser offers a theory of interests at the group level with a focus on status, rather than identity-formation. But it is not clear that we can separate

these out: why should we care about status in the abstract? For a supportive view of Fraser's recent work, see Christopher F. Zurn, "Identity or Status? Struggles over 'Recognition' in Fraser, Honneth, and Taylor," *Constellations* 10, no. 4 (2003). Amartya Sen's approach is contrasted with other distributive justice theories in relation to Nancy Fraser's criticism of them in Ingrid Robeyns, "Is Nancy Fraser's Critique of Theories of Distributive Justice Justified?," *Constellations* 10, no. 4 (2003).

30. The term "positional goods" comes originally from Fred Hirsch, and his interesting argument about the limits to what growth can deliver (in terms of human happiness) given that we cannot "grow" our way out of a scarcity of such goods. Of course, as Hirsch no doubt recognized, the concept of positional goods is long-standing and central to a variety of earlier theories in social thought and political economy. See his *Social Limits to Growth* (Cambridge: Harvard University Press, 1976).

31. Freedom is obviously a term that groups together many different notions, an "essentially contested concept." A good essay on the different notions of freedom that emphasizes a "self-realization" conception is Charles Taylor's "What's Wrong with Negative Liberty," in his *Philosophy and the Human Sciences*, 211–229. As should be obvious from my usage, I do not mean freedom here in the more limited sense of "freedom of choice" that Olsaretti contrasts with voluntariness.

CHAPTER 6. COUNTERING NETWORK POWER

1. This distinction between positive and negative rights is sometimes conflated with the distinction that Isaiah Berlin advanced between positive and negative liberty in *Two Concepts of Liberty* (Oxford: Clarendon Press, 1961). The liberal understanding of rights is deeply linked to the idea that there is a separate domain of the "private" (opposed to the "public"), which merits protection from interference. For a discussion of the history of these concepts, see Raymond Geuss, *Public Goods, Private Goods* (Princeton: Princeton University Press, 2001). Within the category of negative rights, a further distinction is sometimes made between "active" and "passive" rights. Active rights, also called "liberty" rights, guarantee the freedom to do as one chooses, as in the right to freedom of movement. Passive rights are the guarantees against basic interference regardless of what one does, as in the right to be let alone or to be safe from persecution.

2. This is one way of interpreting the view that Justice Breyer has recently advanced in relation to the rights tradition in the United States. See Stephen G. Breyer, *Active Liberty: Interpreting Our Democratic Constitution* (New York: Knopf, 2005).

3. I. Shapiro, "Gross Concepts in Political Argument," *Political Theory* 17, no. 1 (1989), 52, italics original. Shapiro is here referencing MacCallum's criticism of Berlin's two concepts.

4. There is now a rather substantial literature in the political philosophy of

liberalism that seeks to reconcile cultural pluralism with liberal theories of procedural neutrality, independence from any particular conception of the good, and so on. Many of these contributions deal with the problem of cultural pluralism via one or another rights theory. See, for example, Will Kymlicka, *Multicultural Citizenship: A Liberal Theory of Minority Rights* (Oxford: Clarendon Press, 1995); Will Kymlicka, *Liberalism, Community, and Culture* (Oxford: Clarendon Press, 1989); Taylor, *Multiculturalism and the Politics of Recognition*; James Tully, *Strange Multiplicity: Constitutionalism in an Age of Diversity* (Cambridge: Cambridge University Press, 1995); Yael Tamir, *Liberal Nationalism* (Princeton: Princeton University Press, 1993); Neil J. Smelser and Jeffrey C. Alexander, eds., *Diversity and Its Discontents: Cultural Conflict and Common Ground in Contemporary American Society* (Princeton: Princeton University Press, 1999). There are several good volumes on the question of group rights and liberal political theory, including: Judith Baker, ed., *Group Rights* (Toronto: University of Toronto Press, 1994); Mahmood Mamdani, *Beyond Rights Talk and Culture Talk: Comparative Essays on the Politics of Rights and Culture* (New York: St. Martin's Press, 2000); and Oliver Mendelsohn and Upendra Baxi, eds., *The Rights of Subordinated Peoples* (New York: Oxford University Press, 1994).

5. McWhorter, *The Power of Babel*, 272.
6. See Jean-Marie Guéhenno, *The End of the Nation-State*, on the age of "open systems." Guéhenno argues that power is decentralized and diffused in globalization, operating from the bottom up in global networks, rather than from the "top down," as in the hierarchies of the nation-state, whose epoch, he argues, is closing in an age of globalization.
7. These "costs" of compatibility are the costs of translation for a user of one standard seeking to cooperate with the users of a different standard. They are not the costs of maintaining two different networks. For example, it may be "costly" to maintain bilingualism in a population because it requires extra schooling and additional resources that a monolingual population would not need. I leave these costs aside in the discussion of compatibility, and focus on the cost of a monolingual person employing a translator to communicate with a foreigner, for example. Note also that I do not use compatibility here in the sense that it is sometimes used in the industrial organization literature—that is, that two fax machines are "compatible" if they share a common standard for facsimile transmission. This is compatibility between machines made possible by the use of a shared standard. What I want to indicate, rather, is whether a network is accessible by multiple standards.
8. Of course, if the anthropologist wanted to work with these people for any extended period of time, she would learn their language herself rather than relying on a translator, since language is central to cultural self-understanding.
9. Crystal, *English as a Global Language*, 26–27.

10. While the original metric length has been constant since the French Revolution, it has been elaborated in ever more precise examples. The original definition of 1793 was based on a ten millionth fraction of the distance from the pole to the equator. Following several successive definitions, including a platinum cast mold of a prototype meter, the current definition is based on the distance that light travels in a vacuum in a fixed fraction of a second. In a sense there have been "French" meters, "German" meters, and perhaps there is now an "American" meter, but each attempts to describe the same distance with greater accuracy, rather than putting forward a different measure.

11. In standards with a layered structure in which core logic underlies variable expression—as in a language with flexible vocabulary but fixed grammatical rules—we may have to distinguish malleability at various levels. English, for example, easily incorporates new vocabulary, perhaps as a result of its historical borrowing from Anglo-Saxon, Latin, and French. It is malleable at the lexical level but much less so, if at all, at the grammatical.

12. Crystal, *The Cambridge Encyclopedia of the English Language,* 110, identifies these two trends as "internationalism" and "identity," in which the former moves toward greater international intelligibility while the latter moves toward greater individuality among English dialects. He discusses the New Englishes in *English as a Global Language,* 141–172. This difference between "internationalism" and "identity" is captured by Saussure's earlier distinction between the opposing forces of "particularism" and "intercourse." Of course, the presence of written English may serve as a check against too much variation, or at least as an invitation to return to a shared version of the language. Indeed, the Romance languages have two distinct layers of lexical commonality, the first from their common origin in Vulgar or spoken Latin, and the second from the deliberate reintroduction of Latinisms throughout the Middle Ages, under the influence of written Latin.

13. The best introduction to social network analysis is Stanley Wasserman and Katherine Faust, *Social Network Analysis: Methods and Applications* (Cambridge: Cambridge University Press, 1994). See also Stanley Wasserman and Joseph Galaskiewicz, eds., *Advances in Social Network Analysis: Research in the Social and Behavioral Sciences* (Thousand Oaks, Calif.: Sage, 1994); Ronald S. Burt and Michael J. Minor, eds., *Applied Network Analysis: A Methodological Introduction* (Beverly Hills: Sage, 1983); and Barry Wellman and Stephen D. Berkowitz, eds., *Social Structures: A Network Approach* (Greenwich, Conn.: JAI Press, 1997).

14. See Mark Granovetter, "Economic Action and Social Structure: The Problem of Embeddedness," *American Journal of Sociology* 91, no. 3 (1985).

15. See Ronald S. Burt, *Structural Holes: The Social Structure of Competition* (Cambridge: Harvard University Press, 1992).

16. For the analysis of the Zapatistas as a SPIN, see David Ronfeldt and Armando Martinez, "A Comment on the Zapatista 'Netwar,'" in John

Arquilla and David Ronfeldt, eds., *In Athena's Camp: Preparing for Conflict in the Information Age* (Santa Monica, Calif.: Rand, 1997), 369–391.

17. Among others, Lévi-Strauss used a form of social network analysis. As Jean Piaget explains of "the particular structural models of Lévi-Strauss: while he took his departure originally from linguistics, and while phonological or, more generally, Saussurian, structures inspired his search for anthropological structures, the really decisive discovery for him was, as is well known, that kinship systems are instances of algebraic structures—networks, groups, and so on" (*Structuralism*, 110). See Lévi-Strauss, *Structural Anthropology*.

18. For example, there is a new journal entitled *Global Networks* that adopts various forms of network methodology and applies them to transnational and global phenomena of all kinds. See the review essay by Matthew Sparke, "Networking Globalization: A Tapestry of Introductions," *Global Networks: A Journal of Transnational Affairs* 1, no. 2 (2001). See also Peter Dicken, Philip F. Kelly, Kris Olds, and Henry Wai-Cheung Yeung, "Chains and Networks, Territories and Scales: Towards a Relational Framework for Analysing the Global Economy," *Global Networks: A Journal of Transnational Affairs* 1, no. 2 (2001).

19. Peter Spiegler gives an insightful account of the way that formalism works in social science, as a translation between two different worlds, the "real world" and the world of "mathematical objects" that obey abstract laws of mathematics. The power of formalism in social science (and its limitations) is related to the appropriateness of an analogy between these two worlds, such that formal analysis can deliver real-world insight. See Peter M. Spiegler, "A Constructive Critique of Economics" (Harvard University, 2005). Spiegler addresses formalism in the context of neoclassical economics, but his critique would apply too to formal models in social network analysis. Actual social relations must first be analogized to a field of nodes and ties in topology, which can then be analyzed mathematically. The results of that analysis must then be reinterpreted in light of the original analogy before mathematical results can be thought to show something about the way the world actually is. Thomas Wilson makes a similar point about the necessity of heuristics in the use of formal methods in sociology in his "Sociology and the Mathematical Method," in Anthony Giddens and Jonathan Turner, eds., *Social Theory Today* (Stanford: Stanford University Press, 1987), 383–404.

20. See Ronald E. Rice, "Network Analysis and Computer-Mediated Communication Systems," in Wasserman and Galaskiewicz, eds., *Advances in Social Network Analysis*, 167–203, and, on epidemiology, R. M. Christley et al., "Infection in Social Networks: Using Network Analysis to Identify High-Risk Individuals," *American Journal of Epidemiology* 162, no. 10 (2005).

21. Latour, *Reassembling the Social*. Latour's approach to Actor-Network Theory (ANT) seems in large part a quarrel with contemporary social science, and

is less a formal methodology for mapping networks than an admonition not to think about human action (in relation to its technological and social contexts) in particular, limiting ways. Latour is especially eager to avoid the use of the "social" as a category of thought without recognizing this very concept as a form of totalizing (and anti-political) discourse. See ibid., 241–250. The part of ANT that I find puzzling is its seeming ascription of agency to non-human actors, which I understand to be a strategy of resistance to "the narrow limits fixed by the premature *closure* of the social sphere," as Latour puts it (p. 260), by the demobilizing discourse of social science. Whether this strategy will succeed in opening up our common life to unembarrassed scrutiny beyond the confines of the "sociology of the social," as Latour intends, or will rigidify it through a new series of reifications remains unclear, however. The latter seems to me a serious risk of the proposed ANT ontology. On the ascription of agency to non-human actors, see ibid., 46–50, 70–80, 216–218; on standards and networks in ANT, see ibid., 221–232.

22. See, e.g., David Knoke, "Networks of Elite Structure and Decision-Making," *Sociological Methods & Research* 22, no. 1 (1993); and Joseph Galaskiewicz, "The Formation of Inter-Organizational Networks," *Contemporary Sociology* 28, no. 1 (1999). This sort of careful scrutiny, using techniques of social network analysis but keen to recognize the particular role that some agents have in a network has been undertaken by some global network theorists. One team of authors has argued: "in a global economy that is constituted by networks of flows . . . it is important for us to focus on the *exercise* of power by actors in networks, rather than just on the embeddedness of power in these networks. We suggest that the task of a network methodology for understanding the global economy must be to identify the actors in these networks, their power and capacities, and the ways through which they exercise their power through association with networks of relationships" (Dicken et al., "Chains and Networks, Territories and Scales," 93). I agree entirely with this ambition, and suggest that the deficiency, then, is not so much with the formal network analysis as with the philosophical understanding of power underlying that analysis—a deficit to which I hope the idea of network power might contribute in some fashion toward overcoming.

23. An example of this kind of work is Barry Wellman, *Networks in the Global Village: Life in Contemporary Communities* (Boulder, Colo.: Westview Press, 1999). I do not share the sanguinity with which Wellman approaches the loss of traditional social networks under conditions of global modernity, but the work provides an example of social network analysis concerned with empirical rather than methodological issues. Along these lines, see also Robert Perrucci and Harry R. Potter, *Networks of Power: Organizational Actors at the National, Corporate, and Community Levels, Social Institutions and Social Change* (New York: A. de Gruyter, 1989).

24. This general aspect of Unger's thought is clear throughout all his works,

but two in particular bear mention in this context: his three-volume work *Politics* and the recent philosophical summation of his views, *The Self Awakened: Pragmatism Unbound* (Cambridge: Harvard University Press, 2007).

25. Unger, *False Necessity*, 530.

26. See, for example, Charles F. Sabel and William H. Simon, "Destabilization Right: How Public Law Litigation Succeeds," *Harvard Law Review* 117, no. 4 (2004). This view comports well with Unger's own position. As Unger argues, destabilization rights have "counterparts in variants of the complex injunctive relief found in contemporary law," based on which courts have intervened in "important institutions, such as schools and mental asylums, or in major areas of social practice, such as electoral organization" (*False Necessity*, 532). Intervention to correct an abuse often requires reworking the relationships that led to the abuse in the first place: "Destabilization is not enough; intervention provoked by the exercise of a destabilization right must change the disrupted practice or institution" (531).

27. Unger, *False Necessity*, 531.

28. This point about the need for politics is a point that Unger's work on globalization has made abundantly clear—and which is in line with the whole thrust of his thought. His proposal about destabilization rights was targeted domestically. To restructure international relations, he proposes a program of national renewal via the promulgation of national development strategies linked to democratic-experimentalist politics, with the aim of making countries capable of resisting the convergence that neoliberalism otherwise imposes on the developing world in particular.

29. Again, I recognize (as in note 6 of Chapter 2) that some theorists advancing a position of "cosmopolitan democracy" argue that democratic norms and possibly even procedures may be attainable in the relations between national sovereigns, and even over and above them (as in the possible creation of global democratic assemblies of one kind or another). But, insofar as what would look like real sovereignty has yet to be constituted (and looks unlikely to be so) beyond the national level, I maintain that the primary tension in contemporary globalization is that everything has been globalized, except politics. Held, Habermas, and others think that this tension calls straightforwardly for the reinvention of politics at a global level. A different solution, should that prove less promising than they hope, would be a modern version of Keynes's program: to withdraw strategically from some aspects of global sociability in favor of a reasserted national sovereignty.

CHAPTER 7. NETWORK POWER IN TECHNOLOGY

1. James R. Beniger, *The Control Revolution: Technological and Economic Origins of the Information Society* (Cambridge: Harvard University Press, 1986).

2. There are actually a wide variety of standards organizations for cement. See: http://www.wbcsdcement.org/industry_portal_sites.asp.

3. See its description at: http://www.iec.ch/about/organ-e.htm.

4. See its homepage at: http://www.ansi.org.
5. See its homepage at: http://www.eia.org.
6. See its homepage at: http://www.tiaonline.org.
7. See the website for the ITU at: http://www.itu.org.
8. A similar phenomenon is found in many large-scale technological enterprises, in which the conditions of industrial advance require sophisticated
   coordination among public and private actors both within and above the
   market. The ideas of cooperative competition and public-private partnerships are discussed in Roberto Mangabeira Unger and Zhiyuan Cui, "China
   in the Russian Mirror," *New Left Review* 1, no. 208 (1994), among other
   places.
9. The effort is conducted under the sponsorship of the Auto/Steel Partnership. See: http://www.a-sp.org.
10. Robert Reich, "Electrosoft: A Fable for Today," *Los Angeles Times*, July 2,
    2001.
11. During the 2000 presidential election cycle, Microsoft and its employees
    were the fifth largest political donor. Microsoft employees donated $50,000
    to the Bush campaign while the company gave $500,000 in unlimited
    "soft" money to the Republican National Committee to wage the political
    campaign. Microsoft gave no money to the Gore campaign. Additionally,
    in the recount effort following the electoral mishaps in Florida, Microsoft
    employees gave $22,500 to Bush's effort. With that recount complete—or
    at least, with the issue settled such as it was—a Microsoft executive donated
    $100,000 to the Bush-Cheney Inauguration Committee for the celebration.
    See John Wildermuth, "Will Political Donations Keep Microsoft Intact?,"
    San Francisco Chronicle, July 1, 2001.
12. As cited in David Teather, "It's Not over yet, EC Tells Gates," *The Guardian*,
    November 5, 2002.
13. http://news.bbc.co.uk/1/hi/business/3563697.stm.
14. See, for example, Michael J. Piore and Charles F. Sabel, *The Second Indus-
    trial Divide: Possibilities for Prosperity* (New York: Basic Books, 1984).
15. I am indebted to Talli Somekh for sharing with me his insights on open
    source and free software, and especially for helping me to see the distinc-
    tion between the two (and why it matters critically for politics). A good re-
    cent analysis of the open-source movement, including some of its history, is
    Weber, *The Success of Open Source*. I also like Eben Moglen's free-wheeling
    essays, including "Anarchism Triumphant: Free Software and the Death of
    Copyright," *First Monday*, no. 8 (1999), http://www.firstmonday.org/issues/
    issue4_8/moglen/index.html.
16. All the citations from Eben Moglen are from his online essay "Anarchism
    Triumphant."
17. See his *GNU Manifesto* for the discussion of the motivation to share among
    friends. Richard M. Stallman, "Gnu Manifesto," http://www.gnu.org/gnu/

manifesto.html. The first version came out in 1985 and has been updated in a minor way since then.

18. http://www.opensource.org/docs/history.php.

19. These positions (and many others) are all available on Eric Raymond's blog: http://catb.org/esr/.

20. The discussion of the GPL v. 3 is available online (along with drafts of the new version) at: http://gplv3.fsf.org/.

21. The source for these statistics is the ISO's homepage. For updates, see: http://www.iso.org/iso/en/iso9000–14000/understand/inbrief.html. For a general introduction to the ISO 9000, see John T. Rabbit and Peter A. Bergh, *The ISO 9000 Book: A Global Competitor's Guide to Compliance and Certification* (White Plains, N.Y.: Quality Resources, 1994). There are literally hundreds of academic articles, mostly in industry journals, and thousands of newspaper articles discussing the ISO 9000 in different industry sectors and in different countries. I cite a few specific academic articles and books below, but also draw in this section on what I take to be central themes in the discussion of the ISO 9000.

22. See, for example, the recent case of Brazilian law courts seeking ISO 9000 certification. Wallace Nunez, "Courts and law offices adhere to ISO 9000," *Gazeta Mercantil* Online (Brazil), Monday, February 20, 2006, Sao Paolo, Front page.

23. Ann Terlaak and Andrew A. King, "The Effect of Certification with the ISO 9000 Quality Management Standard: A Signaling Approach," *Journal of Economic Behavior & Organization* 60, no. 4 (2006).

24. A recent article examines the patterns of geographic diffusion of the ISO 9000 using a model of diffusion via transnational networks. See Eric Neumayer and Richard Perkins, "Uneven Geographies of Organizational Practice: Explaining the Cross-National Transfer and Diffusion of ISO 9000," *Economic Geography* 81, no. 3 (2005). Unsurprisingly, firms which are connected to networks in which it is widely used are much more likely to go through the effort to be certified, which lends credence to the understanding of the ISO 9000 as a signaling norm.

25. See, for example, John Seddon, *In Pursuit of Quality: The Case against the ISO 9000* (Dublin: Oak Tree Press, 1997).

26. On the different responses to ISO 9000 certification and how it is approached differently in different workplaces, see the interesting article by Olivier Boiral, "ISO 9000: Outside the Iron Cage," *Organization Science* 14, no. 6 (2003).

27. Robert Reich makes the point that New Economy anti-trust policy is really an argument over the nature of intellectual property in ideas, rather than the older concerns of the first trustbusters. He writes, "I think the Microsoft case can be better understood as a harbinger of a new kind of role for government in the emerging 'new economy'—even if the company wins on appeal and escapes a breakup. Rather than regulating particular markets,

government will be setting the contours of property rights as they apply to new ideas, and thus defining the new economy." See Reich, "The Transformation of Government from Regulator of the Old Economy to Definer of the New," *Washington Post*, June 11, 2000. For an excellent argument on these themes, see Nathan Newman, "Storming the Gates," *The American Prospect*, March 27–April 10, 2000.

28. I interpret anarchism as a position that gives ethical and practical priority to the relations of voluntarism over the relations of sovereignty, which are seen as coercive. The libertarian position is a version of what we might call "right anarchism" or right-wing anarchism, holding that the market is a non-coercive institution (because based on formally free exchange) that facilitates decentralized interactions outside the realm of organized politics. The "left anarchist" position, by contrast, views both the market and the state as coercive—the market because it is based on unjust relations of property backed by the state.

This left anarchist position is associated with the work of Pierre-Joseph Proudhon and his followers who drove a split in the "First International" between anarchists (following Mikhail Bakunin) and Marxists. I interpret the salient difference between these two groups as concerning the weight that should be given to sociability as against sovereignty in the struggle for a just society. I take it that the anarchists thought state power was corrupting and dangerous, while the Marxists thought that mastering the relations of sovereignty was indispensable for the achievement of egalitarian political ends. In this chapter, I interpret "technological utopianism" or techno-utopianism as a technologically oriented variant of left anarchism. For anarchist classics by Proudhon, see: Pierre-Joseph Proudhon, *General Idea of the Revolution in the Nineteenth Century* (New York: Haskell House, 1969), and Pierre-Joseph Proudhon, *What Is Property?* (Cambridge: Cambridge University Press, 1994). For a collection of seminal writings by anarchists, including William Godwin, Pierre-Joseph Proudhon, Mikhail Bakunin, Pyotr Kropotkin, Max Stirner, and others, see Marshall S. Shatz, ed., *The Essential Works of Anarchism* (New York: Bantam Books, 1971).

29. Yochai Benkler, *The Wealth of Networks: How Social Production Transforms Markets and Freedom* (New Haven: Yale University Press, 2006), 16.

30. Ibid., 21.

31. Ibid., 22.

32. Ibid.

33. Ibid., 27.

34. Ibid., 105. He explains, "the physical machinery necessary to participate in information and cultural production is almost universally distributed in the population of the advanced economies."

35. Ibid.

36. Ibid., 121. He repeats the basic point elsewhere, writing, for example: "As long as capitalization and ownership of the physical capital base of this

economy remain widely distributed and as long as regulatory policy does not make information inputs artificially expensive, individuals will be able to deploy their own creativity, wisdom, conversational capacities, and connected computers, both independently and in loose interdependent cooperation with others, to create a substantial portion of the information environment we occupy" (ibid., 106).

37. The "Cambridge Capital Controversies" concerned that extent to which we can imagine capital as an abstract quantity, as it appears in the production function of neoclassical microeconomics, pitting post-Keynesian economists (from Cambridge, U.K.) like Joan Robinson and Piero Sraffa against American neoclassical economists (from Cambridge, U.S.) like Paul Samuelson. A good introduction to the controversies is: Avi J. Cohen and Geoffrey C. Harcourt, "Retrospectives: What Happened to the Cambridge Capital Theory Controversies?" *Journal of Economic Perspectives* 17, no. 1 (2003). A classic of the "English" side of the debate is Piero Sraffa, *Production of Commodities by Means of Commodities: Prelude to a Critique of Economic Theory* (Cambridge: Cambridge University Press, 1960).

38. Benkler, *The Wealth of Networks*, 463. Indeed, Benkler is keen to downplay the significance of the schism between "free software" and "open source," and even argues that the "depoliticization" of the free software movement (in its transformation into the more anodyne "open-source movement") is a good thing. He writes: "It took almost a decade for the mainstream technology industry to recognize the value of free or open-source software development and its collaborative production methodology. As the process expanded . . . more of those who participated sought to 'normalize' it, or, more specifically, to render it apolitical. Free software is about freedom." Benkler argues, by contrast with this commitment to freedom: "'Open-source' software was chosen as a term that would not carry the political connotations. It was simply a mode of organizing software production that may be more effective than market-based production." Benkler does not decry the resultant rift that developed between the initial pioneers of the Free Software Movement and communities of open-source programmers, but argues that "the abandonment of political motivation and the importation of free software into the mainstream have not made it less politically interesting but more so" (ibid., 66). Steven Weber takes a somewhat similar line in his discussion of the origins of the open-source movement: *The Success of Open Source*, 52–53.

39. Benkler, *The Wealth of Networks*, 463–464.

40. Indeed, Benkler and other analysts of the networked information economy point to the phenomenon of *zero* (or near zero) marginal costs of production—the fact that an extra unit of software costs next to nothing to produce—as grounding the rationality of more egalitarian methods of networked production and distribution. While the marginal cost of production in the industrial economy is not zero, it was—on many accounts—a *declining* cost

schedule, such that each additional unit of production costs less to produce than did the previous one, given various economies of scale and scope in production. This fact seemed of great relevance to earlier socialists for it militated in favor (so the argument went) of centralization and democratic control of the economy, which would provide the only efficient response to what would otherwise result in a system of monopoly.

41. The history of various left and anarchist labor movements is well covered in many books, including Richard Geary, *Labour and Socialist Movements in Europe before 1914* (New York: St. Martin's Press, 1989); Eric J. Hobsbawm, *Labouring Men: Studies in the History of Labour* (London: Weidenfeld and Nicolson, 1965); Eric J. Hobsbawm, *Workers: Worlds of Labor* (New York: Pantheon Books, 1984); and Donald Sassoon, *One Hundred Years of Socialism: The West European Left in the Twentieth Century* (New York: New Press, 1996).

42. The statement is attributed to RMS by fellow hacker Brian Reid, who developed a way to charge users for software in 1979—something that RMS found objectionable. See Sam Williams, *Free as in Freedom: Richard Stallman's Crusade for Free Software* (Sebastopol, Calif.: O'Reilly, 2002), especially chapter 6.

43. Stallman, "GNU Manifesto."

44. Benkler, *The Wealth of Networks*, 470.

45. Ibid., 471.

46. Indeed, RMS links his advocacy of free software directly to a very democratic vision of a "post-scarcity world" in which we would legislate together as one of our common activities:

> In the long run, making programs free is a step toward the post-scarcity world, where nobody will have to work very hard just to make a living. People will be free to devote themselves to activities that are fun, such as programming, after spending the necessary ten hours a week on required tasks such as legislation, family counseling, robot repair and asteroid prospecting. There will be no need to be able to make a living from programming.
>
> We have already greatly reduced the amount of work that the whole society must do for its actual productivity, but only a little of this has translated itself into leisure for workers because much nonproductive activity is required to accompany productive activity. The main causes of this are bureaucracy and isometric struggles against competition. Free software will greatly reduce these drains in the area of software production. We must do this, in order for technical gains in productivity to translate into less work for us.
>
> From Richard Stallman, "GNU Manifesto." Eben Moglen's "dotCommunist Manifesto" is available at: http://emoglen.law.columbia.edu/publications/dcm.html.

47. Lawrence Lessig, *Free Culture: How Big Media Uses Technology and the Law*

to *Lock Down Culture and Control Creativity* (New York: Penguin Press, 2004), 287.

48. James Boyle, *Shamans, Software, and Spleens: Law and the Construction of the Information Society* (Cambridge: Harvard University Press, 1996), 183.

CHAPTER 8. GLOBAL TRADE AND NETWORK POWER

1. WTO website: http://www.wto.org/english/thewto_e/whatis_e/inbrief_e/inbro2_e.htm.

2. It is appropriate to consider all the WTO agreements as constituting a single, albeit complex standard, since any state must accept all these agreements together for admission to the organization. In an earlier essay, I interpreted the WTO as a standard possessing network power. See David Singh Grewal, "Network Power and Globalization," *Ethics & International Affairs* 17, no. 2 (2003).

3. In large part, members of the United States Congress were unhappy with the failure of international investment to be included within the scope of the ITO's activities. With the failure of the Multilateral Agreement on Investment in 1998—which I examine in Chapter 9—the issue of international investment standardization remains unsettled.

4. The full text of the Dispute Settlement Understanding and a brief explanation of it are available at: http://www.wto.org/english/tratop_e/dispu_e/dsu_e.htm.

5. At the time of writing in January 2007, the WTO had 150 members. That number is in flux, of course; the WTO website lists all members and also all parties contracting to become members at: http://www.wto.org/english/thewto_e/whatis_e/tif_e/org6_e.htm.

6. Of course, the transfer of control over trade involves (at least where the country is democratic) a decision taken by a national representative body to join the WTO in the first place. Once that is accomplished, however, ongoing democratic oversight of the trade regime in which a country participates is ceded to the decisions of WTO bureaucrats and—if any new agreements are ever reached—to the trade delegations of all the assembled nations in the formation of additional agreements.

7. The idea of comparative advantage in international trade is systematized in David Ricardo's classic *Principles of Political Economy and Taxation* (New York: Dutton, 1973). The case for trade between nations specializing in the production of different commodities is analytically identical to the case for trade between individuals in the division of labor but for the difference that nations are represented with a fixed labor force that cannot move freely. I am indebted to conversations with Roberto Unger and Sanjay Reddy on the idea of free trade, which centered on Roberto Unger's book, *Free Trade Reimagined*, which was then in draft. Unger's arguments as to the *incompleteness* of the theory of comparative advantage are particularly compelling, but I have not here been able to take full account in this chapter of his ideas on

this subject. Unger concentrates on problems stemming from the theoretical incompleteness of the idea of comparative advantage itself; here, I have accepted the analytics of free trade in order to argue their inadequacy in relation to political questions raised by reflection on relative (and not absolute) differences in welfare.

8. See David Hume's essay "Of the Jealousy of Trade" (1742), published in Hume, *Essays, Moral, Political, and Literary,* ed. Eugene F. Miller (Indianapolis: Liberty Classics, 1987), 331.

9. For a standard account of the English mercantilist literature, see Douglas A. Irwin, *Against the Tide: An Intellectual History of Free Trade* (Princeton: Princeton University Press, 1996), 26–42. For a richer view of this literature in relation to the history of thought more generally, see Hont, *Jealousy of Trade,* 1–77 on the neo-Colbertist politics of the time.

10. See Norman Angell, *The Great Illusion: A Study of the Relation of Military Power in Nations to Their Economic and Social Advantage* (New York: G. P. Putnam, 1911), especially the chapters "The Great Illusion" and "The Impossibility of Confiscation," at 29–62.

11. Keynes explained the change in his views in his Finlay Lecture at University College, Dublin, in April 1933. (The lecture was later published in the *Yale Review* and in condensed form in the *New Statesman.*) I discuss Keynes's views at greater length in the text accompanying notes 21–23 of this chapter. On the issue of international peace and trade, Keynes writes:

We are pacifist today with so much strength of conviction that, if the economic internationalist could win this point, he would soon recapture our support. But it does not now seem obvious that a great concentration of national effort on the capture of foreign trade, that the penetration of a country's economic structure by the resources and the influence of foreign capitalists, and that a close dependence of our own economic life on the fluctuating economic policies of foreign countries are safeguards and assurances of international peace. It is easier, in the light of experience and foresight, to argue quite the contrary. The protection of a country's existing foreign interests, the capture of new markets, the progress of economic imperialism—these are a scarcely avoidable part of a scheme of things which aims at the maximum of international specialization and at the maximum geographical diffusion of capital wherever its seat of ownership. Advisable domestic policies might often be easier to compass, if the phenomenon known as "the flight of capital" could be ruled out. The divorce between ownership and the real responsibility of management is serious within a country, when, as a result of joint stock enterprise, ownership is broken up among innumerable individuals who buy their interest to-day and sell it to-morrow and lack altogether both knowledge and responsibility towards what they momentarily own. But when the same principle is applied internationally, it is, in times of stress, intolerable—I am irresponsible towards what I own and those who operate what I own are irresponsible towards me. There may be some financial calculation which shows it to be advantageous that my savings should be invested in whatever quarter of the habitable globe shows the greatest marginal efficiency of capital or the highest rate of interest. But experience is accumulating that remoteness between ownership and operation is an evil in the relations among men, likely or certain in the long run to set up strains and enmities which will bring to nought the financial calculation.

I sympathize, therefore, with those who would minimize, rather than with those who would maximize, economic entanglement among nations. Ideas, knowledge, science, hospitality, travel—these are the things which should of their nature be international. But let goods be homespun whenever it is reasonably and conveniently possible, and, above all, let finance be primarily national. Yet, at the same time, those who seek to disembarrass a country of its entanglements should be very slow and wary. It should not be a matter of tearing up roots but of slowly training a plant to grow in a different direction.

For these strong reasons, therefore, I am inclined to the belief that, after the transition is accomplished, a greater measure of national self-sufficiency and economic isolation among countries than existed in 1914 may tend to serve the cause of peace, rather than otherwise. At any rate, the age of economic internationalism was not particularly successful in avoiding war; and if its friends retort, that the imperfection of its success never gave it a fair chance, it is reasonable to point out that a greater success is scarcely probable in the coming years.

John Maynard Keynes, "National Self-Sufficiency," reprinted in Donald Moggridge, ed., *The Collected Writings of John Maynard Keynes* (London: Macmillan, for the Royal Economic Society, 1982), 21: 235–237.

Many of today's pro-globalization commentators would do well to reflect upon these thoughts lest they resuscitate that doctrine once called "Norman Angellism." Norman Angell's argument was that "military and political power give a nation no commercial advantage; that it is an economic impossibility for one nation to seize or destroy the wealth of another, or for one nation to enrich itself by subjugating another." See Angell, *The Great Illusion*, vii. The *Financial Times* columnist Martin Wolf echoes these themes, and adds to them the unification of purpose that he hopes the "global war on terror" will bring to otherwise competing nations: in his book, *Why Globalization Works* (New Haven: Yale University Press, 2004), 309–10. I criticize Jagdish Bhagwati's and Martin Wolf's recent works in this vein, in a review essay, "Is Globalization Working?" *Ethics and International Affairs* 20, no. 2 (2006).

12. See, for example, a controversial recent essay along these lines by the famous economist Paul Samuelson: "Where Ricardo and Mill Rebut and Confirm Arguments of Mainstream Economists Supporting Globalization," *Journal of Economic Perspectives* 18, no. 3 (2004), and a response to his critics, "The Limits of Free Trade—Response from Paul A. Samuelson," *Journal of Economic Perspectives* 19, no. 3 (2005).

13. Ralph E. Gomory and William J. Baumol, *Global Trade and Conflicting National Interests* (Cambridge: MIT Press, 2000). Gomory and Baumol recognize that John Stuart Mill and others concerned with the political economy of industrial development made similar points in the nineteenth and early twentieth centuries, and they draw explicitly on these arguments in an admirable (and all-too-rare) adaptation by contemporary economists of the insights of earlier political economy. Their book also includes a closing chapter by Edward Wolff presenting empirical evidence that confirms the persistent specialization among industrialized countries that their analysis would predict.

14. Ibid., 73.

15. The empirical evidence concerning the relationship between openness and economic growth (and between growth and poverty reduction) is the subject of ongoing scholarly controversy. See Francisco Rodriguez and Dani Rodrik, "Trade Policy and Economic Growth: A Skeptic's Guide to the Cross-National Evidence," in *NBER Macroeconomics Annual 2000* (2001); Robert H. Wade and Martin Wolf, "Prospect Debate: Are Global Poverty and Inequality Getting Worse?," *Prospect* 72 (2002); and Richard B. Freeman, "Trade Wars: The Exaggerated Impact of Trade in Economic Debate," *World Economy* 27, no. 1 (2004).

16. The philosopher Peter Singer groups criticisms of the WTO into four broad categories. Activists charge that the WTO "places economic considerations ahead of concerns for the environment, animal welfare, and even human rights"; that it "erodes national sovereignty"; that it "is undemocratic"; and that it "increases inequality," or even, in what Singer recognizes is a stronger claim, that it "makes the rich richer and leaves the world's poorest people even worse off than they would otherwise have been." Singer takes up each point in turn and finds a good deal of truth to the first three criticisms. About the last, he charges that the evidence is insufficient to assess what is an empirical controversy about the role of trade in economic inequality and development. See Peter Singer, *One World: The Ethics of Globalization* (New Haven: Yale University Press, 2002), 53. On the last point that Singer notes, it is important to recognize that deeply contentious issues of definition and measurement are at stake: the question of how many poor people there are in the world, and whether that number has been increasing or decreasing as a result of neoliberal globalization is a topic of current empirical and normative controversy. I discuss this issue briefly in "Is Globalization Working?," 251–253, drawing on the work of Sanjay Reddy and

Thomas Pogge, particularly their paper "How Not to Count the Poor,"
available (along with responses and press coverage) at: http://www
.socialanalysis.org.

17. Dani Rodrik, "How to Make the Trade Regime Work for Development,"
(2004), available online at: http://ksghome.harvard.edu/~drodrik/
How%20to%20Make%20Trade%20Work.pdf.

18. See, for example, Dani Rodrik, "Trading in Illusions," *Foreign Policy* 123,
(March/April 2001), 54–62. This is a point that Robert Wade has also made
forcefully. See Robert H. Wade, "What Strategies Are Viable for Developing
Countries Today? The World Trade Organization and the Shrinking of 'Development Space,'" *Review of International Political Economy* 10, no. 4 (2003).

19. John Gray, *False Dawn: The Delusions of Global Capitalism* (London: Granta
Books, 1998), 18.

20. Ibid., 20. Gray argues: "Global democratic capitalism is as unrealizable
a condition as worldwide communism" (21). Gray's analysis borrows from
Karl Polanyi's famous work, *The Great Transformation* (New York: Rinehart,
1944), which offers an analysis of what we now call "neoliberalism" that
remains as cogent and astute as it was when first published.

21. Keynes, "National Self-Sufficiency," 233.

22. Ibid., 236.

23. Keynes admits: "A considerable degree of international specialization is
necessary in a rational world in all cases where it is dictated by wide differences of climate, natural resources, native aptitudes, level of culture and
density of population. But over an increasingly wide range of industrial
products, and perhaps of agricultural products also, I have become doubtful whether the economic loss of national self-sufficiency is great enough
to outweigh the other advantages of gradually bringing the product and the
consumer within the ambit of the same national, economic, and financial
organization" (ibid., 238).

24. For a critical account of the backroom negotiations and manipulations that
enabled the Doha Round to begin, see Robert H. Wade, "The Ringmaster
of Doha," *New Left Review* 25 (2004).

25. For the former WTO Director-General's book, see Mike Moore, *A World
without Walls: Freedom, Development, Free Trade and Global Governance* (Cambridge: Cambridge University Press, 2003). For a critical review of Moore's
role in forging the Doha Round, see Wade, "The Ringmaster of Doha."

26. Dani Rodrik offers a forceful criticism of the argument that agricultural
liberalization is somehow central to a properly conceived "development
round" of trade talks. See his "How to Make the Trade Regime Work for
Development."

27. On the empirical evidence for greater "openness" and its relation to
economic growth and poverty reduction (which are, of course, distinct
concepts), see notes 15 and 16 of this chapter.

28. See Dani Rodrik, "Failure at Doha Would Be No Big Deal" (November

2005), available online at: http://ksghome.harvard.edu/~drodrik/
shortpieces.html.

29. Keynes, "National Self-Sufficiency," 234.

CHAPTER 9. GLOBAL NEOLIBERALISM

1. Roberto Mangabeira Unger, *What Should Legal Analysis Become?* (New York: Verso, 1996), 9. The full passage is worth reproducing: "Neoliberalism is the program of macroeconomic stabilization without damage to the internal and external creditors of the state; of liberalization, understood both more narrowly as acceptance of foreign competition and integration into the world trading system and more generally as the reproduction of traditional Western contract and property law; of privatization, meaning the withdrawal of the state from production and its devotion, instead, to social responsibilities; and of the development of social safety-nets designed to compensate, retrospectively, for the unequalizing effects of market activity." See also Roberto Mangabeira Unger, *Democracy Realized: The Progressive Alternative* (New York: Verso, 2000), 52–58. For a proposal for the reorientation of the Bretton Woods institutions away from neoliberal dogma, see Roberto Mangabeira Unger, "The Really New Bretton Woods," in: Marc Uzan, ed., *The Financial System under Stress: An Architecture for the New World Economy* (New York: Routledge, 1996), 11–25.

2. See Williamson, "In Search of a Manual for Technopols," in his *Political Economy of Policy Reform* (Washington, D.C.: Institute for International Economics, 1994), and also "Appendix: The Washington Consensus," in Pedro-Pablo Godard and John Williamson, *After the Washington Consensus: Restarting Growth and Reform in Latin America* (Washington, D.C.: Institute for International Economics, 2003), 26–28 for a concise summary of the program.

3. Williamson, *The Political Economy of Policy Reform*, 17.

4. See John Williamson, "What Should the World Bank Think about the Washington Consensus?," *World Bank Research Observer* 15, no. 2 (2000), 251 for the argument that the Washington Consensus should be called the "universal convergence" or "one-world consensus."

5. See Godard and Williamson, *After the Washington Consensus*, 26–28.

6. Unhappy with these elisions, Williamson wishes to distinguish neoliberalism or "market fundamentalism" from what he claims to be the more balanced program of the Washington Consensus as he originally described it. In "What Should the World Bank Think about the Washington Consensus?," he decries the fact that in the "popular, or populist, interpretation of the Washington Consensus, market fundamentalism or neoliberalism . . . refers to laissez-faire Reaganomics—let's bash the state, the markets will resolve everything" (257). However, in practice, the Washington Consensus never amounted to anything more than such market liberalization. Indeed, Williamson himself admits that those aspects of his Washington Consensus

NOTES TO PAGE 251 365

that go beyond market liberalization—for example, the reorientation of public expenditure toward education—were never adequately emphasized. Suffice it to say that Williamson's set of policy initiatives does not correspond to the Washington Consensus as it was ever implemented, so perhaps the crude version of it that he decries is in fact a *better* reflection of the actual consensus among the "powers-that-be" in Washington (which is, after all, what he set out to describe in the first place).

7. For a recent analysis of what was once called the "mixed economy," see Michel Albert, *Capitalism vs. Capitalism: How America's Obsession with Individual Achievement and Short-Term Profit Has Led It to the Brink of Collapse* (New York: Four Walls Eight Windows, 1993), particularly his discussion of what he calls the "Rhineland" model of capitalism contrasted with the "Anglo-Saxon" model. A classic analysis of the mixed economy that remains helpful and provocative is Anthony Crosland, *The Future of Socialism* (London: J. Cape, 1956). For a good introduction to the idea of multiple forms of capitalism, see Peter A. Hall and David W. Soskice, *Varieties of Capitalism: The Institutional Foundations of Comparative Advantage* (Oxford: Oxford University Press, 2001). Note that not all capitalists advocate neoliberalism; indeed, it seems unlikely that even those who do would fare well under a purely neoliberal regime, for businesses rely on the state to create, support, deepen, and extend markets through a variety of legal protections and "sweeteners." What is specific to a neoliberal program is not so much "capitalism"—if by that term we mean an economic system in which labor is a freely alienable commodity while capital is privately owned and scarce—but the attempt to use market relations as the model for all legitimate social action, such that even non-economic social relations are pushed to approximate the form of a decentralized market. For example, the suggested reforms of the Washington Consensus usually push government policies to mimic the logic of markets wherever they cannot be replaced by actual markets altogether. By binding a government's ability to impose controls on the export of capital or raise tax revenue for state-led development programs, for example, the Washington Consensus seeks to eliminate collective alternatives to decentralized market action, leaving markets as the sole determinant of the economic (and hence, socio-political) order.

8. Following the spate of recent criticisms of neoliberalism, economists have had to reconsider questions that they once regarded as settled facts of economic science. Not only have economists such as Dani Rodrik and Robert Wade questioned shibboleths of economic orthodoxy, but figures as established as Joseph Stiglitz, Jeffrey Sachs, and Jagdish Bhagwati have recently advanced intellectual and political positions criticizing elements of neoliberalism. See, for example, Dani Rodrik, *Has Globalization Gone Too Far?* (Washington, D.C.: Institute for International Economics, 1997); Robert H. Wade, "Is Globalization Reducing Poverty and Inequality?," *World Development* 32, no. 4 (2004); Joseph E. Stiglitz, *Globalization and Its Discontents*

(New York: W. W. Norton, 2002), and Bhagwati, *In Defense of Globalization*, in which he reiterates his skepticism about unregulated mobility of capital despite providing an overall neoliberal defense.

Before this debate became mainstream there were nevertheless many critics of neoliberal development strategies. A good collection of the early contributions to the debate over economic development is found in Rajani K. Kanth, ed., *Paradigms in Economic Development: Classic Perspectives, Critiques, and Reflections* (Armonk, N.Y.: M. E. Sharpe, 1994), which includes the analyses of famous early dependency theorists Andre Gunder Frank and Paul Baran. See also Andre Gunder Frank, *Lumpenbourgeoisie: Lumpendevelopment; Dependence, Class, and Politics in Latin America* (New York: Monthly Review Press, 1972). For a more recent work from this standpoint, see Peter B. Evans, *Dependent Development: The Alliance of Multinational, State, and Local Capital in Brazil* (Princeton: Princeton University Press, 1979). The literature on dependency theory and "unequal development" is indebted to earlier ideas emerging from the Marxian critique of imperialism. For an overview of the history of these ideas, see Anthony Brewer, *Marxist Theories of Imperialism: A Critical Survey* (London: Routledge & Kegan Paul, 1980). Brewer's approach is to retain a critical but sympathetic stance with regard to these theories, subjecting them to careful examination and scrutiny rather than rejecting or adopting them wholesale.

9. East Asia's rise to affluence has generated a vast literature exploring empirical and methodological controversies in development theory. See Robert Wade's excellent analysis, *Governing the Market: Economic Theory and the Role of Government in East Asian Industrialization* (Princeton: Princeton University Press, 1990), and also Dwight H. Perkins, "There Are at Least 3 Models of East-Asian Development," *World Development* 22, no. 4 (1994). These and other works tend to emphasize the deviations from orthodox economic policy that led to successful development in the region. The counter-argument to this declaration of an East Asian "miracle" is that the miraculous would simply have occurred much more quickly if these countries had followed the Washington Consensus more closely and eliminated the heretical aspects of their eclectic economic policies. Of course, such an argument is untestable—we cannot ask South Korea to return to an agricultural economy and develop again, this time more closely following the dictates of the Washington Consensus. However, we can gain some insight by comparing countries that have abided more strictly by neoliberal orthodoxy. Consider Argentina's crisis beginning in late 2001 in this regard. See Dani Rodrik, "Reform in Argentina, Take Two," *New Republic* 226, no. 1 (2002). Ha-Joon Chang provides an interesting consideration of development strategies in historical retrospect: *Kicking Away the Ladder: Development Strategy in Historical Perspective* (London: Anthem, 2002).

10. There is a vigorous debate about the way that property rights have functioned in China's recent rise. For a seminal paper on the role of property in

the "Town-Village Enterprises," see Martin L. Weitzman and Chengang Xu, "Chinese Township-Village Enterprises as Vaguely Defined Cooperatives," *Journal of Comparative Economics* 18, no. 2 (1994). Given recent changes to Chinese property law, the debate over how alternative forms of property influence Chinese economic development will remain a live one.

11. Juridification may occur either through the creation of new multilateral institutions (or treaty organizations) based on neoliberal standards, or by linking neoliberal principles to existing international standards bodies, as is proposed in new agreements of the WTO. Such linkage is the jurisprudential equivalent of "bundling" in the Microsoft case discussed in Chapter 7; linking a standard without network power to one that already possesses it may prove an effective way to promote adherence to both. Neither its critics nor its advocates emphasize sufficiently that neoliberalism is slowly developing into a global system of law. This legal regime is established by international "soft law," national legal changes, the harmonization of existing commercial law, and the accumulation of private international commercial decisions (including of international arbitration panels), all of which together constitute an increasingly unified international common law of commerce. A good article that deals with this issue directly is Graham Mayeda, "Developing Disharmony? The SPS and TBT Agreements and the Impact of Harmonization on Developing Countries," *Journal of International Economic Law* 7, no. 4 (2004). See also Slaughter, *A New World Order*.

12. The argument that a neoliberal standard is not a membership standard but a mediating standard is harder to make, and requires a more involved examination of the way in which thought is mediated through institutional conformity, a subject I necessarily leave aside for now to pursue the more obvious cases in which neoliberal standards govern entry to desired relations, not because they mediate them inherently, but because they set criteria for membership.

13. Friedman writes, "To fit into the Golden Straitjacket a country must either adopt, or be seen as moving toward, the following golden rules," which consist in the usual set of neoliberal policy recommendations. He notes that "As your country puts on the Golden Straitjacket, two things tend to happen: your economy grows and your politics shrinks." This is not a bad thing on Friedman's view, because accommodation to reality can never really be a bad thing, however unappealing it may sometimes be. This argument is quite simple, to say the least. See Friedman, *The Lexus and the Olive Tree*, 105, but also more generally 104–111 for a discussion of the "electronic herd"— Friedman's characterization of bond traders, who also appear in his imagery as "watch dogs" barking to disclose unwanted heresy—and the fiscal discipline that this herd imposes on developing countries.

For a more critical response of this sort of imposition, see Singer, *One World*, 10–11 on the effects of the golden straitjacket. See also the discussion of the "confidence game" that international investors play with developing world countries in recession or at risk of recession in Paul Krugman, "How Washington Worsened Asia's Crash: The Confidence Game," *New Republic* 219, no. 14 (1998).

14. For an analysis of multinational corporations and the extent to which they drive policy convergence, see Dean Baker, Gerald A. Epstein, and Robert Pollin, eds., *Globalization and Progressive Economic Policy* (Cambridge: Cambridge University Press, 1998), especially after 107.

15. The extent to which countries can achieve relative insulation from foreign capital to pursue a development-oriented policy agenda remains unclear, but it is linked to the effectiveness of capital controls in one form or another. For a discussion of capital controls in the aftermath of the East Asian crisis of the late 1990s, see Robert H. Wade and Frank Veneroso, "The Gathering World Slum and the Battle over Capital Controls," *New Left Review* 231 (1998). Even the free trade advocate Jagdish Bhagwati has come out in favor of some capital controls, making the undeniable point that trade in currency is not like trade in goods (see note 89 of Chapter 3). The more standard line, however, still calls for greater capital mobility while sounding small notes of concern about the increased risk of financial crisis; see Lawrence H. Summers, "International Financial Crises: Causes, Prevention, and Cures," *American Economic Review* 90, no. 2 (2000).

16. Immediately following the Second World War, in the negotiations for the establishment of the ITO, the United States failed to achieve rules for investment. It has had no greater success in its subsequent efforts, given its failure to produce an investment agreement through the GATT or WTO. In 1986 in the Uruguay Round of the GATT, the United States tried to get investment on the bargaining table, but was opposed by anxious developing countries. The U.S. objectives in the Uruguay Round included the reduction or elimination of artificial trade-distorting barriers to investment, an expansion of the principle of national treatment, the reduction of "unreasonable" barriers to the establishment of investment, and the development of rules for a dispute resolution system and the free flow of investment.

Neither have these objectives made any progress in the WTO, though there is support for such a move among many countries, particularly those controlling most of the foreign investment. One area of the WTO that addresses investment is the Agreement on Trade-Related Investment Measures (TRIMs), a limited measure that resulted from an attempt to negotiate a broader WTO agreement on investment. Instead, due to a conflict between industrialized and developing countries, what might have been a general investment agreement was restricted to regulation of investment as it relates to trade only. Within this framework, issues such as national treatment and the access to foreign exchange were dealt with as they affected trade, and other investment principles such as those relating to expropriation or regulation were not addressed at all.

The other major area of the WTO that deals with investment issues is the GATS, where trade in services is interpreted to include "commercial presence" in a foreign country. The GATS includes national treatment principles and prohibitions on restrictions on capital transfers and payments but does not address all investor concerns. It does not, for example, include national treatment uniformly, but only in those sectors of the member state's economy voluntarily specified. The future of investment protection in the WTO remains unclear, given the serious division between capital-exporting and capital-importing countries on the proper rules for the global economy.

The one treaty in which the United States has managed to get a multilateral investment agreement is in the North American Free Trade Area (NAFTA) it established with Mexico and Canada in 1994. NAFTA guarantees national treatment and protection from expropriation and even from some domestic regulations that "unreasonably" impact foreign investment. At the heart of NAFTA's protection for investment is most favored nation treatment (MFN) whereby foreign nations receive national treatment. The same principles—national treatment, international minimum standards of property protection, and an investor-state dispute settlement mechanism—are incorporated in NAFTA's chapter on investment agreements. These principles are often incorporated into bilateral agreements, but NAFTA represents the first successful effort to multilateralize them. NAFTA also feeds its standards back into Bilateral Investment Treaty (BIT) clauses: its Chapter 11 Provision on Expropriation is being adapted for other BITs negotiated with the United States.

From their position within NAFTA, these standards can continue to spread in BITs, although efforts to multilateralize them further have so far failed, as we see in the case of the Multilateral Agreement on Investment. But it is important to note that as NAFTA membership expands, incorporating more countries in the Americas into its free trade area, these investment principles will become part of a broad multilateral agreement protecting the foreign investments of the United States in its Latin American neighbors.

17. The actual instruments are: The Code of Liberalization of Capital Movements, The Code of Liberalization of Current Invisible Operations, The National Treatment Instrument, The International Incentives and Disincentives Instrument, The OECD Guidelines for Multinational Enterprises, The Decision of the OECD Council Regarding Conflicting Requirements Imposed on Multinational Enterprises, and The Convention on the Combating of Bribery.

18. In the absence of a multilateral agreement on investment, many countries seek reciprocal protection for their investors in BITs negotiated on a country-to-country basis. There are over 1,300 BITs today, so many of the investment standards are already instantiated concretely in international relations, perhaps easing the demand for a multilateral system. Such case-

by-case protection does not generally have the same power as a centralized multilateral agreement. It may also be more costly to negotiate separate BITs than a single centralized system, though this is a difficult assessment to make. Of course, the negotiations for a BIT are by no means without pressure, coercion, and the exercise of diplomatic power of all kinds. Countries may face pressure to adopt a particular arrangement on a bilateral basis; however, that direct compulsion is not network power per se but a different form of what is sometimes called "soft power."

19. Trade ministers launched negotiations for the MAI at an OECD conference in 1995. The OECD eventually failed to come to an agreement after two years, and the period of negotiations was extended for another year. That year passed without resolution, and in fall 1998 the French government withdrew from negotiations, under pressure from domestic anti-MAI opinion. The French pullout followed delays and extensions in what had become a difficult series of negotiations. In December 1998, the OECD deputy secretary-general announced an end to what had been an inconclusive process.

20. Edward M. Graham, *Fighting the Wrong Enemy: Antiglobal Activists and Multinational Enterprises* (Washington, D.C.: Institute for International Economics, 2000), 9. In an earlier article, I analyzed the MAI in a network power framework and criticized Graham: see David Singh Grewal, "Network Power and Global Standardization: The Controversy over the Multilateral Agreement on Investment," *Metaphilosophy* 36, no. 1–2 (2005).

21. Graham, *Fighting the Wrong Enemy*, 10.

22. The policy report can be found online at: http://www.oecd.org/publications/pol_brief/1997/9702_POL.HTM.

23. Graham, *Fighting the Wrong Enemy*, 175.

24. Bernard Cassen, "Wielding Power Behind the Scenes," trans. Julie Stoker, review of Reviewed Item, *Le Monde Diplomatique*, no. (1998), http://mondediplo.com/1998/03/07ami.

CHAPTER 10. NETWORK POWER AND CULTURAL CONVERGENCE

1. A good general discussion of globalization and culture can be found in Frank J. Lechner and John Boli, *World Culture: Origins and Consequences* (Malden, Mass.: Blackwell, 2005). Lechner and Boli advance the beginnings of a theory of power at work in cultural globalization, a project to which the idea of network power might have something to contribute. A number of essays that focus on cultural loss and homogenization under globalization can be found in Jerry Mander and Edward Goldsmith, eds., *The Case against the Global Economy: And for a Turn toward the Local* (San Francisco: Sierra Club Books, 1996). Of course, not everyone is so unhappy with such cultural convergence: see David Rothkopf, "In Praise of Cultural Imperialism?," *Foreign Policy*, no. 107 (1997). Debates about cultural globalization are featured in Alan Scott, ed., *The Limits of Globalization: Cases and Arguments*

(London: Routledge, 1997), the second part of which, "Homogenized Culture or Enduring Diversity?," examines the issue in several different national contexts.

2. For example, see John Street, "'Across the Universe': The Limits of Global Pop Culture," in Scott, *The Limits of Globalization,* 75–89, in which the author argues that there is no single global culture in either the unitary or the "multicultural" sense; Rajika Jalan, "An Asian Orientalism: *Libas* and the Textures of Postcoloniality," ibid., 90–115, in which the author argues that you cannot simply export culture without transforming it in local appropriation; and Ahmed Gurnah, "Elvis in Zanzibar," ibid., 116–142, which argues for a nuanced reading of cross-cultural borrowing, which does not amount to diffusionist or culturally imperialist formulations. As Gurnah writes, "A foreign culture in this context is neither taken at face value nor mindlessly imposed. The processes that make up this culture-complex squeeze it for benefits, sieve it for relevance, and partly reconstitute it before absorbing it" (124).

3. See James L. Watson, *Golden Arches East: McDonald's in East Asia* (Stanford: Stanford University Press, 1997).

4. Freud makes this point about the "narcissism of minor differences" in *Civilization and Its Discontents* (London: Hogarth Press, 1930). He explains: "I once discussed the phenomenon that it is precisely communities with adjoining territories, and related to each other in other ways as well, who are engaged in constant feuds and in ridiculing each other. . . . I gave this phenomenon the name of 'narcissism of minor differences'" (61). The idea is more extensively developed in an earlier form—though without the later appellation—in Sigmund Freud, *Group Psychology and the Analysis of the Ego,* ed. and trans. James Strachey (New York: Bantam Books, 1960), 42.

5. I discuss postcolonial literature in note 2 of Chapter 5 above.

6. Peter L. Berger, "The Four Faces of Global Culture," *The National Interest* 49 (1997). The article draws explicitly on two popular books of the mid-nineties: Benjamin R. Barber, *Jihad vs. McWorld: How the Planet Is Both Falling Apart and Coming Together and What This Means for Democracy* (New York: Times Books, 1995), and Samuel P. Huntington, *The Clash of Civilizations and the Remaking of World Order* (New York: Simon & Schuster, 1996).

7. See the introduction to his later book, Peter L. Berger and Samuel P. Huntington, eds., *Many Globalizations: Cultural Diversity in the Contemporary World* (Oxford: Oxford University Press, 2002), 1–16.

8. Ibid., 8.

9. The globalization of military force is one of the four processes central to Anthony Giddens's analysis of modernity and globality in *The Consequences of Modernity.*

10. Michael Schudson, chapter 6 in Michael Hechter and Karl-Dieter Opp, *Social Norms* (New York: Russell Sage Foundation, 2001).

11. Eric Posner offers a somewhat limited account of social norms in his book

372   NOTES TO PAGES 276–278

Law and Social Norms (Cambridge: Harvard University Press, 2000). He argues that behavioral norms represent a form of signaling by which people supposedly assess the "discount rates" of potential partners in cooperation. This form of signaling is, on Posner's account, both widespread and socially important. However, the idea of social norms functioning as signals should be understood as a much more general notion, and one that I employ (with nothing whatsoever alleged about discount rates) in a network power framework. For a more helpful account of social norms, see Elster, *The Cement of Society*, 97–151.

12. See Purdy, *Being America*, 217–218 for an account of Purdy's conversation with Murthy.

13. The remarkable pervasiveness of the McDonald's chain will be obvious to anyone who has traveled overseas and found the Golden Arches well established in foreign terrain. Interestingly, McDonald's seems to be undergoing retrenchment and consolidation: it may have finally reached its saturation point, beyond which there are fewer prospects for growth. The phenomenon of McDonaldization has not escaped scholarly attention. Two recent books stake out rather different sides of the debate. James Watson in *Golden Arches East* is mixed about the effects of the chain on East Asian culture and its traditions of food. George Ritzer, in his *The McDonaldization of Society* (Thousand Oaks, Calif.: Pine Forge Press, 2004), is less sanguine, concerned with the effects of fast food undermining the world's culinary traditions. The book *Fast Food Nation* offers a well researched and shocking exposé of the social and health disaster in fast food culture, in which McDonald's reigns preeminent: Eric Schlosser, *Fast Food Nation: The Dark Side of the All-American Meal* (Boston: Houghton Mifflin, 2001).

14. Berger adopts a more nuanced position in a longer study based on the original article. See his introductory essay to Berger and Huntington, *Many Globalizations*, 1–16.

15. Purdy, *Being America*, 217–218.

16. Tyler Cowen, *Creative Destruction: How Globalization Is Changing the World's Cultures* (Princeton: Princeton University Press, 2002), 94. Cowen, like many American commentators on American-led cultural globalization, argues for the intrinsic merit of the cultural products exported from the United States. For example, he explains the international success of Hollywood writing (in all seriousness): "The American values of heroism, individualism, and romantic self-fulfillment are well suited for the large screen and for global audiences" (94). In fairness to Cowen, he does acknowledge that the entertainment industry is affected by "clustering effects" and other self-reinforcing dynamics that can skew outcomes in favor of the already powerful. In large part, though, his is a celebratory, even triumphalist view. Cowen is by no means alone in advancing this kind of argument; it is common, particularly in American discussions of cultural globalization. See also, for example, the optimistic assessment of cultural globalization in

John Micklethwait and Adrian Wooldridge, *A Future Perfect: The Challenge and Hidden Promise of Globalization* (New York: Times Books, 2000), 183–198. For a more nuanced, international perspective, see UNDP, "Cultural Liberty in Today's Diverse World," in *Human Development Report*, ed. United Nations Development Programme (New York: 2004), especially chapter 5, "Globalization and Cultural Choice."

17. Berger and Huntington, *Many Globalizations*, 7.
18. The theme of emulation is a long-running one in the history of political and social thought, generating (on some accounts) civilized social life itself. Consider the famous (and ambivalent) assessment in Rousseau's Second Discourse: *A Discourse on Inequality* (New York: Penguin Books, 1984), 113–120 especially. Emulation is obviously a powerful form of sociability, and I suggest in this chapter one way in which we may be able to account for the dynamics of emulation in the framework of network power. Developing this account more fully, however, would require a deeper engagement with theories of psychosocial development than I have here undertaken. It may also be worth reflecting on theories of power as subject-forming, as in Butler, *The Psychic Life of Power*.
19. Berger discusses this phenomena in his analysis of modernization as individuation: Berger and Huntington, *Many Globalizations*, 9.
20. For example, in his essay, "In Praise of Cultural Imperialism," David Rothkopf writes (p. 48): "American culture is fundamentally different from indigenous cultures in so many other locales. American culture is an amalgam of influences and approaches from around the world. It is melded—consciously in many cases—into a social medium that allows individual freedoms and cultures to thrive." Similar sorts of arguments about the intrinsic merits of American culture for globalization can also be found in Cowen, *Creative Destruction*, and in Micklethwait and Wooldridge, *A Future Perfect*, to cite just two examples. For an interesting account of how American-led globalization is understood and rationalized by elite members of U.S. corporations, NGOs, and church movements working internationally, see James D. Hunter and Joshua Yates, "In the Vanguard of Globalization: The World of American Globalizers," in Berger and Huntington, *Many Globalizations*, 323–356.
21. Berger and Huntington, *Many Globalizations*, 3.
22. For a history of international NGOs, see Akira Iriye, *Global Community: The Role of International Organizations in the Making of the Contemporary World* (Berkeley: University of California Press, 2002). Anne-Marie Slaughter argues in *A New World Order* that globalization has facilitated the formation of transnational regulatory networks linking different parts of the regulatory apparatus of nation-states, for example, courts of law. We may think of these regulatory networks as constituting powerful epistemic communities.
23. Peter M. Haas, "Epistemic Communities and International-Policy Coordination—Introduction," *International Organization* 46, no. 1 (1992), 3.

24. Ibid., 2.
25. These factors are explicated more thoroughly in ibid., 3. Haas also suggests other possible criteria as relevant for the exposition of the idea of the epistemic community: "shared intersubjective understandings," "a shared way of knowing," "shared patterns of reasoning," "shared causal beliefs and discursive practices," and "a shared commitment to the application and production of knowledge."
26. Ibid.
27. Stanley Fish, *Is There a Text in this Class? The Authority of Interpretive Communities* (Cambridge: Harvard University Press, 1980). See the reprint in this volume of Fish's famous essay "Interpreting the *Variorum*," in which he argues: "Interpretive communities are made up of those who share interpretive strategies not for reading (in the conventional sense) but for writing texts, for constituting their properties and assigning their intentions" (171). A great deal of the rest of the volume revolves around the issue of interpretation and its relation to shared interpretive strategies. The question of whether the reader or the text is analytically prior drops away given a focus on the intersubjective construction of the styles and strategies of interpretation that set the context for what gets read and how.
28. It was the philosopher J. L. Austin's famous little book *How to Do Things with Words* (Cambridge: Harvard University Press, 1962), which offered the seminal analysis of "speech acts" (or what Austin originally called "illocutionary acts")—the use of words to perform an action, as, for example, when the City Clerk proclaims, "I now pronounce you husband and wife." This idea has since been taken up into philosophy and discourse ethics more generally. See, e.g., Habermas, *The Theory of Communicative Action*.
29. On group mind and collective forms of consciousness or symbolic representation, see Durkheim, *The Elementary Forms of Religious Life*, especially 231–233, 421–448. Durkheim's analysis of religious life (through which he motivated a more general study of thought) presents what we might call a theory of structuralist idealism, in which forms of consciousness act to structure the ideas and mental life of individuals. It presents a *gestalten* type view in which wholes presuppose parts, and vice-versa—an argument which, as I noted in Chapter 2, can sometimes prove persuasive, but which may be difficult to parse in terms of individual agency (without, that is, some theory of structuration, as I attempt to provide here). Durkheim writes that "it is in the school of collective life that the individual has learned to form ideals. . . . To be sure, collective ideals tend to become individualized as they become incarnate in individuals" (ibid., 425). He also suggests that "impersonal reason is but collective thought by another name. Collective thought is only possible through the coming together of individuals; hence it presupposes the individuals, and they in turn presuppose it, because they cannot sustain themselves except by coming together" (447). This mutual constitution of whole and part raises the methodological issues that I con-

sidered in Chapter 2, namely, how to understand social ontology, and whether we can understand social wholes as, ultimately, the construction of individuals without presupposing that these structures have an active agency of their own.

30. For arguments concerning the moral limits of market transactions, see Elizabeth Anderson, *Value in Ethics and Economics* (Cambridge: Harvard University Press, 1993), and Michael J. Sandel, "What Money Can't Buy: The Moral Limits of Markets," in Grethe B. Peterson, ed., *The Tanner Lectures on Human Values,* vol. 21 (Salt Lake City: University of Utah Press, 2000), 87–122.

31. Cornelius Castoriadis, *The Imaginary Institution of Society* (Cambridge: Polity Press, 1987).

32. Dilip Gaonkar, "Toward New Social Imaginaries," *Public Culture* 14, no. 1 (2002), 4.

33. Charles Taylor, "Modern Social Imaginaries," *Public Culture* 14, no. 1 (2002), 106.

34. Gaonkar, "Toward New Social Imaginaries," 4.

35. Taylor, "Modern Social Imaginaries," 106.

36. Arjun Appadurai, *Modernity at Large: Cultural Dimensions of Globalization* (Minneapolis: University of Minnesota Press, 1996).

37. In answer to an earlier remark of Freud's that psychoanalysis might be among the "impossible professions," the English psychoanalyst Adam Limentani offered the following quip: "As psychoanalysts we are only too aware that our profession is not only impossible but extremely difficult." (Freud's remark is also amusing: "It almost looks as if analysis were the third of those 'impossible' professions in which one can be sure beforehand of achieving unsatisfying results. The other two, which have been known much longer, are education and government.") Janet Malcolm's study of psychoanalysis features these quips as epigraphs. See the front matter of Malcolm, *Psychoanalysis, the Impossible Profession* (New York: Vintage Books, 1982).

Adamson, Walter L. *Hegemony and Revolution: A Study of Antonio Gramsci's Political and Cultural Theory.* Berkeley: University of California Press, 1980.

Albert, Michel. *Capitalism vs. Capitalism: How America's Obsession with Individual Achievement and Short-Term Profit Has Led It to the Brink of Collapse.* Trans. Paul Haviland. New York: Four Walls Eight Windows, 1993.

Alesina, Alberto, and Robert J. Barro. *Currency Unions.* Stanford: Hoover Institution Press, 2001.

Anderson, Elizabeth. *Value in Ethics and Economics.* Cambridge: Harvard University Press, 1993.

Angell, Norman. *The Great Illusion: A Study of the Relation of Military Power in Nations to Their Economic and Social Advantage.* New York: G. P. Putnam, 1911.

Appadurai, Arjun. *Modernity at Large: Cultural Dimensions of Globalization.* Minneapolis: University of Minnesota Press, 1996.

Archibugi, Daniele, and David Held, eds. *Cosmopolitan Democracy: An Agenda for a New World Order.* Oxford: Blackwell, 1995.

Aristotle. *Nicomachean Ethics.* Ed. and trans. Roger Crisp. Cambridge: Cambridge University Press, 2000.

Arquilla, John, and David F. Ronfeldt, eds. *In Athena's Camp: Preparing for Conflict in the Information Age.* Santa Monica, Calif.: Rand, 1997.

Arthur, W. Brian. *Increasing Returns and Path Dependence in the Economy.* Ann Arbor: University of Michigan Press, 1994.

Austin, John L. *How to Do Things with Words.* Cambridge: Harvard University Press, 1962.

Bachrach, Peter, and Morton S. Baratz. "The Two Faces of Power." *American Political Science Review* 56, no. 4 (1962): 947–952.

Baker, Dean, Gerald A. Epstein, and Robert Pollin, eds. *Globalization and Progressive Economic Policy.* Cambridge: Cambridge University Press, 1998.

Baker, Judith, ed. *Group Rights.* Toronto: University of Toronto Press, 1994.

Barber, Benjamin R. *Jihad vs. McWorld: How the Planet Is Both Falling Apart and Coming Together—and What This Means for Democracy.* New York: Times Books, 1995.

Barry, Brian M., ed. *Power and Political Theory: Some European Perspectives.* London: Wiley, 1976.

Barry, Christian, Thomas Pogge, and Jedediah Purdy, eds. *Global Institutions and Responsibilities: Achieving Global Justice.* Malden, Mass.: Blackwell, 2005.

Bayly, Christopher A. *The Birth of the Modern World, 1780–1914: Global Connections and Comparisons.* Malden, Mass.: Blackwell, 2004.

Beniger, James R. *The Control Revolution: Technological and Economic Origins of the Information Society.* Cambridge: Harvard University Press, 1986.

Benkler, Yochai. *The Wealth of Networks: How Social Production Transforms Markets and Freedom.* New Haven: Yale University Press, 2006.

Bentham, Jeremy. *Introduction to the Principles of Morals and Legislation.* London: T. Payne, 1789.

Berger, Peter L. "The Four Faces of Global Culture." *The National Interest* 49 (1997): 23–29.

Berger, Peter L., and Samuel P. Huntington, eds. *Many Globalizations: Cultural Diversity in the Contemporary World.* Oxford: Oxford University Press, 2002.

Berlin, Isaiah. *Two Concepts of Liberty.* Oxford: Clarendon Press, 1961.

Bhagwati, Jagdish N. *In Defense of Globalization.* New York: Oxford University Press, 2004.

Boiral, Olivier. "ISO 9000: Outside the Iron Cage." *Organization Science* 14, no. 6 (2003): 720–737.

Boot, Max. "The Case for American Empire." *Weekly Standard,* October 15, 2001.

Bourdieu, Pierre. *Distinction: A Social Critique of the Judgement of Taste.* Trans. Richard Nice. Cambridge: Harvard University Press, 1984.

Boyle, James. *Shamans, Software, and Spleens: Law and the Construction of the Information Society.* Cambridge: Harvard University Press, 1996.

Brewer, Anthony. *Marxist Theories of Imperialism: A Critical Survey.* London: Routledge & Kegan Paul, 1980.

Breyer, Stephen G. *Active Liberty: Interpreting Our Democratic Constitution.* New York: Knopf, 2005.

Brooks, George L. *A History of the English Language.* London: Cox and Wyman, 1958.

Burt, Ronald S. *Structural Holes: The Social Structure of Competition.* Cambridge: Harvard University Press, 1992.

Burt, Ronald S., and Michael J. Minor, eds. *Applied Network Analysis: A Methodological Introduction.* Beverly Hills: Sage, 1983.

Butler, Judith. *The Psychic Life of Power: Theories in Subjection.* Stanford: Stanford University Press, 1997.

Cassen, Bernard. "Wielding Power Behind the Scenes." Trans. Julie Stoker. *Le Monde Diplomatique.* (1998), http://mondediplo.com/1998/03/07ami.

Castoriadis, Cornelius. *The Imaginary Institution of Society.* Trans. Kathleen Blamey. Cambridge: Polity Press, 1987.

Cavell, Stanley. *The Claim of Reason: Wittgenstein, Skepticism, Morality, and Tragedy.* New York: Oxford University Press, 1999.

Chang, Ha-Joon. *Kicking Away the Ladder: Development Strategy in Historical Perspective.* London: Anthem, 2002.

Chayes, Abram, and Antonia Chayes. *The New Sovereignty: Compliance with International Regulatory Agreements.* Cambridge: Harvard University Press, 1995.

Christley, R. M., G. L. Pinchbeck, R. G. Bowers, D. Clancy, N. P. French, R. Bennett, and J. Turner. "Infection in Social Networks: Using Network Analysis to Identify High-Risk Individuals." *American Journal of Epidemiology* 162, no. 10 (2005): 1024–1031.

Cohen, Avi J., and Geoffrey C. Harcourt. "Retrospectives: What Happened to the Cambridge Capital Theory Controversies?" *Journal of Economic Perspectives* 17, no. 1 (2003): 199–214.

Cohen, Gerald A. "Are Workers Forced to Sell Their Labor Power?" *Philosophy & Public Affairs* 14, no. 1 (1985): 99–105.

———. *History, Labour, and Freedom: Themes from Marx.* Oxford: Clarendon Press, 1988.

———. "The Structure of Proletarian Unfreedom." *Philosophy & Public Affairs* 12, no. 1 (1983): 3–33.

Comte, Auguste. *System of Positive Polity.* Trans. John Bridges, Frederick Harrison, and Edward Beesly. London: Longmans, Green, 1875.

Connolly, William E. "Taylor, Foucault, and Otherness." *Political Theory* 13, no. 3 (1985): 365–376.

Cooper, Russell W. *Coordination Games: Complementarities and Macroeconomics.* Cambridge: Cambridge University Press, 1999.

Cowen, Tyler. *Creative Destruction: How Globalization Is Changing the World's Cultures.* Princeton: Princeton University Press, 2002.

Crosland, Anthony. *The Future of Socialism.* London: J. Cape, 1956.

Crystal, David. *English as a Global Language.* Cambridge: Cambridge University Press, 2003.

———. *Language Death.* Cambridge: Cambridge University Press, 2000.

———. *The Cambridge Encyclopedia of the English Language.* Cambridge: Cambridge University Press, 1995.

David, Paul A. "Clio and the Economics of Qwerty." *American Economic Review* 75, no. 2 (1985): 332–337.

———. "Why Are Institutions the 'Carriers of History'?: Path Dependence and the Evolution of Conventions, Organizations, and Institutions." *Structural Change and Economic Dynamics* 5, no. 2 (1994): 205–220.

Davies, Glyn. *A History of Money: From Ancient Times to the Present Day.* Cardiff: University of Wales Press, 1994.

Debreu, Gerard. *Theory of Value: An Axiomatic Analysis of Economic Equilibrium.* New York: Wiley, 1959.

Deleuze, Gilles. *Foucault.* Ed. and trans. Seán Hand. Minneapolis: University of Minnesota Press, 1988.

Dicken, Peter, Philip F. Kelly, Kris Olds, and Henry Wai-Cheung Yeung. "Chains and Networks, Territories and Scales: Towards a Relational Framework for Analysing the Global Economy." *Global Networks—a Journal of Transnational Affairs* 1, no. 2 (2001): 89–112.

Doyle, Michael W. *Empires.* Ithaca, N.Y.: Cornell University Press, 1986.

Durkheim, Emile. *The Elementary Forms of Religious Life.* Ed. and trans. Karen E. Fields. New York: Free Press, 1995.

———. *The Rules of Sociological Method.* Ed. Steven Lukes and trans. W. D. Halls. New York: Free Press, 1982.

Eatwell, John, Murray Milgate, and Peter K. Newman, eds. *The New Palgrave: A Dictionary of Economics.* 4 vols. London: Macmillan, 1987.

Edgeworth, Francis Ysidro. *Mathematical Psychics: An Essay on the Application of Mathematics to the Moral Sciences.* London: C. K. Paul, 1881.

Eichengreen, Barry J. *Globalizing Capital: A History of the International Monetary System.* Princeton: Princeton University Press, 1996.

Eichengreen, Barry J., and Marc Flandreau, eds. *The Gold Standard in Theory and History.* London: Routledge, 1997.

Elster, Jon. *The Cement of Society: A Study of Social Order.* Cambridge: Cambridge University Press, 1989.

Evans, Peter B. *Dependent Development: The Alliance of Multinational, State, and Local Capital in Brazil.* Princeton: Princeton University Press, 1979.

Fanon, Frantz. *Black Skin, White Masks.* Trans. Charles L. Markmann. New York: Grove Press, 1967.

Femia, Joseph V. *Gramsci's Political Thought: Hegemony, Consciousness, and the Revolutionary Process.* Oxford: Clarendon Press, 1981.

Ferguson, Niall. *Colossus: The Price of America's Empire.* New York: The Penguin Press, 2004.

Foucault, Michel. *The History of Sexuality.* Trans. Robert Hurley. New York: Vintage Books, 1980.

———. *"Il Faut Défendre la Société": Cours au Collège de France (1975–1976).* Paris: Editions du Seuil, 1997.

———. *The Order of Things: An Archeology of the Human Sciences.* New York: Pantheon Books, 1971.

———. *Power.* Ed. James D. Faubion. New York: New Press, 2000.

———. *Power/Knowledge: Selected Interviews and Other Writings, 1972–1977.* Ed. and trans. Colin Gordon. New York: Pantheon Books, 1980.

Frank, Andre Gunder. *Lumpenbourgeoisie: Lumpendevelopment; Dependence, Class, and Politics in Latin America.* Trans. Marion D. Berdecio. New York: Monthly Review Press, 1972.

Fraser, Nancy. *Justice Interruptus: Critical Reflections on the "Postsocialist" Condition.* New York: Routledge, 1997.

Fraser, Nancy, and Axel Honneth. *Redistribution or Recognition?: A Political-Philosophical Exchange.* London: Verso, 2003.

Freeman, Richard B. "Trade Wars: The Exaggerated Impact of Trade in Economic Debate." *World Economy* 27, no. 1 (2004): 1–23.

Freud, Sigmund. *Civilization and Its Discontents.* London: Hogarth Press, 1930.

———. *Group Psychology and the Analysis of the Ego.* Ed. and trans. James Strachey. New York: Bantam Books, 1960.

Friedman, Thomas L. *The Lexus and the Olive Tree.* New York: Anchor Books, 2000.

Galaskiewicz, Joseph. "The Formation of Inter-Organizational Networks." *Contemporary Sociology* 28, no. 1 (1999): 55–56.

Galbraith, John Kenneth. *Money, Whence It Came, Where It Went.* Boston: Houghton Mifflin, 1975.

Gallagher, John, and Ronald Robinson. "The Imperialism of Free Trade." *Economic History Review* 6, no. 1 (1953): 1–15.

Gandhi, Leela. *Postcolonial Theory: A Critical Introduction.* New York: Columbia University Press, 1998.

Gaonkar, Dilip. "Toward New Social Imaginaries." *Public Culture* 14, no. 1 (2002): 1–19.

Garner, Richard. "Tongue-Tied: Must the UK Always Be a Nation of Language Dunces?" *The Independent,* December 19, 2002, 17.

Geary, Richard. *Labour and Socialist Movements in Europe before 1914.* New York: St. Martin's Press, 1989.

Geuss, Raymond. *The Idea of a Critical Theory: Habermas and the Frankfurt School.* Cambridge: Cambridge University Press, 1981.

———. *Public Goods, Private Goods.* Princeton: Princeton University Press, 2001.

Giddens, Anthony. *Central Problems in Social Theory: Action, Structure, and Contradiction in Social Analysis.* Berkeley: University of California Press, 1979.

———. *The Consequences of Modernity.* Stanford: Stanford University Press, 1990.

———. *The Constitution of Society: Introduction to the Theory of Structuration.* Berkeley: University of California Press, 1984.

———. *Modernity and Self-Identity: Self and Society in the Late Modern Age.* Stanford: Stanford University Press, 1991.

———. *Politics, Sociology and Social Theory: Encounters with Classical and Contemporary Social Thought.* Cambridge: Polity Press, 1995.

Gladwell, Malcolm. *The Tipping Point: How Little Things Can Make a Big Difference.* Boston: Little, Brown, 2000.

Gomory, Ralph E., and William J. Baumol. *Global Trade and Conflicting National Interests.* Cambridge: MIT Press, 2000.

Goux, Jean-Joseph. *Symbolic Economies: After Marx and Freud.* Trans. Jennifer Gage. Ithaca, N.Y.: Cornell University Press, 1990.

Graham, Edward M. *Fighting the Wrong Enemy: Antiglobal Activists and Multinational Enterprises.* Washington, D.C.: Institute for International Economics, 2000.

Gramsci, Antonio. *Selections from the Prison Notebooks of Antonio Gramsci.* Ed. and trans. Quintin Hoare and Geoffrey Nowell Smith. New York: International Publishers, 1971.

Granovetter, Mark. "Economic Action and Social Structure: The Problem of Embeddedness." *American Journal of Sociology* 91, no. 3 (1985): 481–510.

Gray, John. *False Dawn: The Delusions of Global Capitalism.* London: Granta, 1998.

Grewal, David Singh. "Empire's Law." *Yale Journal of Law and the Humanities* 14, no. 1 (2002): 211–219.

———. "Is Globalization Working?" *Ethics and International Affairs* 20, no. 2 (2006): 247–59.

———. "Network Power and Globalization." *Ethics & International Affairs* 17, no. 2 (2003): 89–98.

———. "Network Power and Global Standardization: The Controversy over the Multilateral Agreement on Investment." *Metaphilosophy* 36, no. 1–2 (2005): 128–144.

———. "Optimality and Evolution in Economics: Darwinism in the Study of Firms and Institutions." Thesis, Harvard University, 1998.

Guéhenno, Jean-Marie. *The End of the Nation-State.* Trans. Victoria Elliott. Minneapolis: University of Minnesota Press, 1995.

Guha, Ranajit. *Dominance without Hegemony: History and Power in Colonial India.* Cambridge: Harvard University Press, 1997.

Guha, Ranajit, and Gayatri Chakravorty Spivak. *Selected Subaltern Studies.* New York: Oxford University Press, 1988.

Haas, Peter M. "Epistemic Communities and International-Policy Coordination— Introduction." *International Organization* 46, no. 1 (1992): 1–35.

Habermas, Jürgen. *The Theory of Communicative Action.* Trans. Thomas McCarthy. Boston: Beacon Press, 1984.

———. *The Postnational Constellation: Political Essays.* Ed. and trans. Max Pensky. Cambridge: MIT Press, 2001.

Hall, Peter A., and David W. Soskice. *Varieties of Capitalism: The Institutional Foundations of Comparative Advantage.* New York: Oxford University Press, 2001.

Hardin, Russell. *One for All: The Logic of Group Conflict.* Princeton: Princeton University Press, 1995.

Hardt, Michael, and Antonio Negri. *Empire.* Cambridge: Harvard University Press, 2000.

Harvey, David. *The New Imperialism.* Oxford: Oxford University Press, 2003.

Haslett, Adam. "Love Supreme: Gay Nuptials and the Making of Modern Marriage." *The New Yorker,* May 31, 2004, 76–80.

Hayek, Friedrich von. *The Denationalisation of Money.* London: Institute of Economic Affairs, 1990.

Hechter, Michael, and Karl-Dieter Opp, eds. *Social Norms*. New York: Russell Sage Foundation, 2001.

Hegel, Georg Wilhelm Friedrich. *Elements of the Philosophy of Right*. Ed. Allen W. Wood and trans. Hugh B. Nisbet. Cambridge: Cambridge University Press, 1991.

Held, David. *Democracy and the Global Order: From the Modern State to Cosmopolitan Governance*. Stanford: Stanford University Press, 1995.

———. *Models of Democracy*. Stanford: Stanford University Press, 1996.

Hilmy, S. Stephen. *The Later Wittgenstein: The Emergence of a New Philosophical Method*. Oxford: Blackwell, 1987.

Hirsch, Fred. *Social Limits to Growth*. Cambridge: Harvard University Press, 1976.

Hirsch, Fred, and John H. Goldthorpe, eds. *The Political Economy of Inflation*. Cambridge: Harvard University Press, 1978.

Hix, Simon. *The Political System of the European Union*. New York: St. Martin's Press, 1999.

Hobbes, Thomas. *The Elements of Law, Natural and Politic: Part I, Human Nature, Part II, De Corpore Politico; with Three Lives*. Ed. John C. A. Gaskin. Oxford: Oxford University Press, 1994.

———. *On the Citizen*. Ed. and trans. Richard Tuck and Michael Silverthorne. Cambridge: Cambridge University Press, 1998.

Hobsbawm, Eric J. *Labouring Men: Studies in the History of Labour*. London: Weidenfeld and Nicolson, 1965.

———. *Workers: Worlds of Labor*. New York: Pantheon Books, 1984.

Hockett, Robert. "Three (Potential) Pillars of Transnational Economic Justice: The Bretton Woods Institutions as Guarantors of Global Equal Treatment and Market Completion." *Metaphilosophy* 36, no. 1–2 (2005): 93–127.

———. "The Deep Grammar of Distribution: A Meta-Theory of Justice." *Cardozo Law Review* 26 (2005): 1179–1322.

Hodgson, Geoffrey M. *Economics and Evolution: Bringing Life Back into Economics*. Cambridge: Polity Press, 1993.

Honneth, Axel. *The Struggle for Recognition: The Moral Grammar of Social Conflicts*. Ed. and trans. Joel Anderson. Cambridge: MIT Press, 1996.

Hont, Istvan. *Jealousy of Trade: International Competition and the Nation-State in Historical Perspective*. Cambridge, Mass.: Belknap Press, 2005.

Hume, David. *An Enquiry Concerning the Principles of Morals*. Ed. Tom L. Beauchamp. Oxford: Clarendon Press, 1998.

———. *Essays, Moral, Political, and Literary*. Ed. Eugene F. Miller. Indianapolis: Liberty Classics, 1987.

———. *Treatise of Human Nature*. Ed. David F. Norton and Mary J. Norton. Oxford: Clarendon Press, 2000.

Hunter, James D., and Joshua Yates. "In the Vanguard of Globalization: The World of American Globalizers." In *Many Globalizations: Cultural Diversity in the Contemporary World*. Ed. Peter L. Berger and Samuel P. Huntington. Oxford: Oxford University Press, 2002: 323–356.

Huntington, Samuel P. *The Clash of Civilizations and the Remaking of World Order.* New York: Simon & Schuster, 1996.

Iriye, Akira. *Global Community: The Role of International Organizations in the Making of the Contemporary World.* Berkeley: University of California Press, 2002.

Irwin, Douglas A. *Against the Tide: An Intellectual History of Free Trade.* Princeton: Princeton University Press, 1996.

Judt, Tony. "Dreams of Empire (America and Imperialism)." *New York Review of Books* 51, no. 17 (2004): 38–41.

Kant, Immanuel. *Kant Political Writings.* Ed. Hans Reiss and trans. Hugh B. Nisbet. Cambridge: Cambridge University Press, 1991.

Kanth, Rajani K. *Paradigms in Economic Development: Classic Perspectives, Critiques, and Reflections.* Armonk, N.Y.: M. E. Sharpe, 1994.

Kenny, Anthony. *Wittgenstein.* Oxford: Blackwell, 2006.

Keynes, John Maynard. *The Economic Consequences of the Peace.* London: Macmillan, 1919.

———. *The General Theory of Employment, Interest and Money.* London: Macmillan, 1936.

———. "National Self-Sufficiency." *Yale Review* 22, no. 4 (1933): 755–69.

———. *A Treatise on Money.* New York: Harcourt, 1930.

Knoke, David. "Networks of Elite Structure and Decision-Making." *Sociological Methods & Research* 22, no. 1 (1993): 23–45.

Kolakowski, Leszek. *Toward a Marxist Humanism: Essays on the Left Today.* Trans. Jane Z. Peel. New York: Grove Press, 1968.

Kolakowski, Leszek, and Stuart Hampshire, eds. *The Socialist Idea: A Reappraisal.* London: Weidenfeld and Nicolson, 1974.

Krugman, Paul. "How Washington Worsened Asia's Crash. The Confidence Game." *New Republic* 219, no. 14 (1998): 23–25.

———. "Increasing Returns and Economic Geography." *Journal of Political Economy* 99, no. 3 (1991): 483–499.

Kuczynski, Pedro-Pablo, and John Williamson, eds. *After the Washington Consensus: Restarting Growth and Reform in Latin America.* Washington, D.C.: Institute for International Economics, 2003.

Kuper, Andrew. *Democracy beyond Borders: Justice and Representation in Global Institutions.* Oxford: Oxford University Press, 2004.

Kymlicka, Will. *Liberalism, Community, and Culture.* Oxford: Clarendon Press, 1989.

———. *Multicultural Citizenship: A Liberal Theory of Minority Rights.* Oxford: Clarendon Press, 1995.

Latour, Bruno. *Reassembling the Social: An Introduction to Actor-Network-Theory.* Oxford: Oxford University Press, 2005.

Lechner, Frank J., and John Boli. *World Culture: Origins and Consequences.* Malden, Mass.: Blackwell, 2005.

Lessig, Lawrence. *Free Culture: How Big Media Uses Technology and the Law to Lock Down Culture and Control Creativity.* New York: Penguin Press, 2004.

Lévi-Strauss, Claude. *Structural Anthropology.* Trans. Claire Jacobson and Brooke G. Schoepf. New York: Basic Books, 1963.

Lewis, David K. *Convention: A Philosophical Study.* Cambridge: Harvard University Press, 1969.

————. *Counterfactuals.* Cambridge: Harvard University Press, 1973.

Liebowitz, Stan J., and Stephen E. Margolis. "The Fable of the Keys." *Journal of Law & Economics* 33, no. 1 (1990): 1–25.

————. "Path Dependence, Lock-in, and History." *Journal of Law, Economics, & Organization* 11, no. 1 (1995): 205–226.

Lieven, Anatol. "The Empire Strikes Back." *The Nation,* July 7, 2003, 25–30.

Locke, John. *Two Treatises of Government.* Ed. Peter Laslett. Cambridge: Cambridge University Press, 1988.

Loux, Michael J. *The Possible and the Actual: Readings in the Metaphysics of Modality.* Ithaca, N.Y.: Cornell University Press, 1979.

Lukes, Steven. *Individualism.* New York: Harper & Row, 1973.

————. *Power: A Radical View.* London: Macmillan, 1974.

Macaulay, Thomas B. *Speeches: With His Minute on Indian Education.* New York: AMS Press, 1979.

Malcolm, Janet. *Psychoanalysis: The Impossible Profession.* New York: Vintage Books, 1982.

Mamdani, Mahmood. *Beyond Rights Talk and Culture Talk: Comparative Essays on the Politics of Rights and Culture.* Cape Town: David Philip, 2000.

Mander, Jerry, and Edward Goldsmith, eds. *The Case against the Global Economy: And for a Turn toward the Local.* San Francisco: Sierra Club Books, 1996.

Marx, Karl. *Capital: A Critique of Political Economy.* Ed. Ernest Mandel and trans. David Fernbach and Ben Fowkes. 3 vols. Harmondsworth, U.K.: Penguin Books, in association with New Left Review, 1976.

————. *A Contribution to the Critique of Political Economy.* Ed. Maurice Dobb and trans. S. W. Ryazanskaya. London: Lawrence & Wishart, 1970.

————. *Marx: Early Political Writings.* Ed. Joseph J. O'Malley and Richard A. Davis. Cambridge: Cambridge University Press, 1994.

Marx, Karl, and Friedrich Engels. *The Communist Manifesto.* Ed. and trans. Samuel Moore and David McLellan. Oxford: Oxford University Press, 1992.

————. *Selected Works [of] Karl Marx and Frederick Engels.* Moscow: Foreign Languages Pub. House, 1962.

Mayeda, Graham. "Developing Disharmony? The SPS and TBT Agreements and the Impact of Harmonization on Developing Countries." *Journal of International Economic Law* 7, no. 4 (2004): 737–764.

McWhorter, John H. *The Power of Babel: A Natural History of Language.* New York: Times Books, 2001.

Mehta, Pratap Bhanu. "Empire and Moral Identity." *Ethics and International Affairs* 17, no. 2 (2003): 49–62.

Memmi, Albert. *The Colonizer and the Colonized.* Trans. Howard Greenfeld. New York: Orion Press, 1965.

Mencken, Henry L. "The Future of English." *Harper's Magazine* 170 (1935): 541–548.

Mendelsohn, Oliver, and Upendra Baxi, eds. *The Rights of Subordinated Peoples.* New York: Oxford University Press, 1994.

Micklethwait, John, and Adrian Wooldridge. *A Future Perfect: The Challenge and Hidden Promise of Globalization.* New York: Times Books, 2000.

Mill, John Stuart. *A System of Logic, Ratiocinative and Inductive.* New York: Longmans, 1965.

Mises, Ludwig von. *Economic Policy: Thoughts for Today and Tomorrow.* Chicago: Regnery/Gateway, 1979.

———. *Planning for Freedom.* South Holland, Ill.: Libertarian Press, 1980.

Moglen, Eben. "Anarchism Triumphant: Free Software and the Death of Copyright." *First Monday,* no. 8 (1999), http://www.firstmonday.org/issues/issue4_8/moglen/index.html.

Montgomery, John D., Nathan Glazer, and Donald L. Horowitz, eds. *Sovereignty under Challenge: How Governments Respond.* New Brunswick, N.J.: Transaction, 2002.

Moore, Mike. *A World without Walls: Freedom, Development, Free Trade and Global Governance.* Cambridge: Cambridge University Press, 2003.

More, Thomas. *Utopia.* Ed. George M. Logan and trans. Robert M. Adams. Cambridge: Cambridge University Press, 2002.

Morgan, C. Lloyd. *Emergent Evolution.* London: Williams and Norgate, 1923.

Morgan, Glyn. *The Idea of a European Superstate: Public Justification and European Integration.* Princeton: Princeton University Press, 2005.

"Move over Latin and French, English Is Here to Stay." *Pittsburgh Post-Gazette,* December 27, 1996, A-25.

Nandy, Ashis. *The Intimate Enemy: Loss and Recovery of Self under Colonialism.* New York: Oxford University Press, 1983.

———. *The Savage Freud and Other Essays on Possible and Retrievable Selves.* Princeton: Princeton University Press, 1995.

Nash, John F. "The Bargaining Problem." *Econometrica* 18, no. 2 (1950): 155–162.

Nettle, Daniel, and Suzanne Romaine. *Vanishing Voices: The Extinction of the World's Languages.* New York: Oxford University Press, 2000.

Neumayer, Eric, and Richard Perkins. "Uneven Geographies of Organizational Practice: Explaining the Cross-National Transfer and Diffusion of ISO 9000." *Economic Geography* 81, no. 3 (2005): 237–259.

Newman, Nathan. "Storming the Gates." *The American Prospect,* March 27–April 10, 2000.

North, Douglass C. "Institutions." *Journal of Economic Perspectives* 5, no. 1 (1991): 97–112.

Nozick, Robert. *Anarchy, State, and Utopia.* New York: Basic Books, 1974.

Nunez, Wallace. "Courts and law offices adhere to ISO 9000." *Gazeta Mercantil Online* (Brazil), Monday, February 20, 2006, Sao Paolo, Front page.

Nussbaum, Martha. *Women and Human Development: The Capabilities Approach.* Cambridge: Cambridge University Press, 2000.

Olsaretti, Serena. *Liberty, Desert, and the Market: A Philosophical Study.* Cambridge: Cambridge University Press, 2004.

Olson, Mancur. *The Logic of Collective Action; Public Goods and the Theory of Groups.* Cambridge: Harvard University Press, 1965.

Pagden, Anthony. *Peoples and Empires: A Short History of European Migration, Exploration, and Conquest, from Greece to the Present.* New York: Modern Library, 2001.

Papandreou, Andreas A. *Externality and Institutions.* Oxford: Clarendon Press, 1994.

Parijs, Philippe van. "Linguistic Justice." *Politics, Philosophy & Economics* 1, no. 1 (2002): 59–74.

Parsons, Talcott. *The Structure of Social Action: A Study in Social Theory with Special Reference to a Group of Recent European Writers.* New York: McGraw-Hill, 1937.

Perkins, Dwight H. "There Are at Least 3 Models of East-Asian Development." *World Development* 22, no. 4 (1994): 655–661.

Perrucci, Robert, and Harry R. Potter. *Networks of Power: Organizational Actors at the National, Corporate, and Community Levels.* New York: A. de Gruyter, 1989.

Phillips, Denis C. *Holistic Thought in Social Science.* Stanford: Stanford University Press, 1976.

Piaget, Jean. *Structuralism.* Ed. and trans. Chaninah Maschler. New York: Basic Books, 1970.

Piore, Michael J., and Charles F. Sabel. *The Second Industrial Divide: Possibilities for Prosperity.* New York: Basic Books, 1984.

Pogge, Thomas, ed. *Global Justice.* Oxford: Blackwell, 2001.

Polanyi, Karl. *The Great Transformation.* New York: Rinehart, 1944.

Posner, Eric A. *Law and Social Norms.* Cambridge: Harvard University Press, 2000.

Proudhon, Pierre-Joseph. *General Idea of the Revolution in the Nineteenth Century.* Ed. and trans. John Beverley Robinson. New York: Haskell House, 1969.

———. *What Is Property?* Ed. and trans. Donald R. Kelley and Bonnie G. Smith. Cambridge: Cambridge University Press, 1994.

Purdy, Jedediah. *Being America: Liberty, Commerce, and Violence in an American World.* New York: Knopf, 2003.

Quiller-Couch, Arthur T. *The Oxford Book of English Verse; 1250–1918.* New York: Oxford University Press, 1940.

Rabbit, John T., and Peter A. Bergh, *The ISO 9000 Book: A Global Competitor's Guide to Compliance and Certification.* White Plains, N.Y.: Quality Resources, 1994.

Rawls, John. *A Theory of Justice.* Cambridge, Mass.: Belknap Press, 1971.

———. *Justice as Fairness: A Restatement.* Ed. Erin Kelly. Cambridge: Harvard University Press, 2001.

Reddy, Sanjay G. "Developing Just Monetary Arrangements." *Ethics and International Affairs* 17, no. 1 (2003): 81–93.

———. "Dilemmas of Globalization." *Ethics and International Affairs* 15, no. 1 (2001): 159–172.

Reddy, Sanjay, and Thomas Pogge. "How Not to Count the Poor," 2002. http://www.socialanalysis.org.

Reich, Robert. "Electrosoft: A Fable for Today." *Los Angeles Times*, July 2, 2001.

———. "The Transformation of Government from Regulator of the Old Economy to Definer of the New." *Washington Post*, June 11, 2000.

Ricardo, David. *Principles of Political Economy and Taxation*. New York: Dutton, 1973.

Riles, Annelise. *The Network Inside Out*. Ann Arbor: University of Michigan Press, 2000.

Ritzer, George. *The McDonaldization of Society*. Thousand Oaks, Calif.: Pine Forge Press, 2004.

Robertson, Roland. *Globalization: Social Theory and Global Culture*. London: Sage, 1992.

Robeyns, Ingrid. "Is Nancy Fraser's Critique of Theories of Distributive Justice Justified?" *Constellations* 10, no. 4 (2003): 538–553.

Rodriguez, Francisco, and Dani Rodrik. "Trade Policy and Economic Growth: A Skeptic's Guide to the Cross-National Evidence." In *NBER Macroeconomics Annual 2000* (2001): 261–325.

Rodrik, Dani. "Can Integration into the World Economy Substitute for a Development Strategy?" Paper presented at the ABCDE-Europe, Paris, June 26–28, 2000.

———. "Failure at Doha Would Be No Big Deal," November 2005. http://ksghome.harvard.edu/~drodrik/shortpieces.html.

———. *Has Globalization Gone Too Far?* Washington, D.C.: Institute for International Economics, 1997.

———. "How to Make the Trade Regime Work for Development," 2004. http://ksghome.harvard.edu/~drodrik/How%20to%20Make%20Trade%20Work.pdf.

———. "Reform in Argentina, Take Two." *New Republic* 226, no. 1 (2002): 13–15.

Rogers, Graham A. J. *Locke's Philosophy: Content and Context*. Oxford: Clarendon Press, 1994.

Rosenberg, Justin. *The Follies of Globalisation Theory: Polemical Essays*. London: Verso, 2000.

Rothkopf, David. "In Praise of Cultural Imperialism?" *Foreign Policy*, no. 107 (1997): 38–53.

Rothschild, Emma. "Globalization and the Return of History." *Foreign Policy*, no. 115 (1999): 106–116.

Rousseau, Jean-Jacques. *A Discourse on Inequality*. Ed. and trans. Maurice W. Cranston. Harmondsworth, U.K.: Penguin Books, 1984.

———. *The Social Contract and Other Later Political Writings*. Ed. and trans. Victor Gourevitch. Cambridge: Cambridge University Press, 1997.

Sabel, Charles F., and William H. Simon. "Destabilization Rights: How Public Law Litigation Succeeds." *Harvard Law Review* 117, no. 4 (2004): 1015–1101.

Samuelson, Paul A. "The Limits of Free Trade—Response from Paul A. Samuelson." *Journal of Economic Perspectives* 19, no. 3 (2005): 242–244.

———. "Where Ricardo and Mill Rebut and Confirm Arguments of Mainstream Economists Supporting Globalization." *Journal of Economic Perspectives* 18, no. 3 (2004): 135–146.

Sandel, Michael J. *Liberalism and the Limits of Justice.* Cambridge: Cambridge University Press, 1982.

———. "What Money Can't Buy: The Moral Limits of Markets." *The Tanner Lectures on Human Values,* vol. 21. Ed. Grethe B. Peterson. Salt Lake City: University of Utah Press, 2000), 87–122.

Sartre, Jean-Paul. *"What Is Literature?" and Other Essays.* Trans. Jeffrey Mehlman. Cambridge: Harvard University Press, 1988.

Sassen, Saskia. *Losing Control?: Sovereignty in an Age of Globalization.* New York: Columbia University Press, 1996.

Sassoon, Donald. *One Hundred Years of Socialism: The West European Left in the Twentieth Century.* New York: New Press, 1996.

Saussure, Ferdinand de. *Course in General Linguistics.* Ed. Charles Bally, Albert Sechehaye, and Albert Riedlinger and trans. Roy Harris. LaSalle, Ill.: Open Court, 1986.

Schelling, Thomas C. *Choice and Consequence.* Cambridge: Harvard University Press, 1984.

———. *Micromotives and Macrobehavior.* New York: Norton, 1978.

———. *The Strategy of Conflict.* Cambridge: Harvard University Press, 1960.

Schlosser, Eric. *Fast Food Nation: The Dark Side of the All-American Meal.* Boston: Houghton Mifflin, 2001.

Scott, Alan. *The Limits of Globalization: Cases and Arguments.* London: Routledge, 1997.

Seddon, John. *In Pursuit of Quality: The Case against the ISO 9000.* Dublin: Oak Tree Press, 1997.

Sen, Amartya K. "How to Judge Globalism." *The American Prospect,* January 14, 2002, A5.

———. *Inequality Reexamined.* New York and Cambridge: Russell Sage Foundation and Harvard University Press, 1992.

———. *Rationality and Freedom.* Cambridge, Mass.: Belknap Press, 2002.

Shapiro, Ian. "Gross Concepts in Political Argument." *Political Theory* 17, no. 1 (1989): 51–76.

Shatz, Marshall S., ed. *The Essential Works of Anarchism.* New York: Bantam Books, 1971.

Shubik, Martin. *The Theory of Money and Financial Institutions.* Cambridge: MIT Press, 1999.

Singer, Peter. *One World: The Ethics of Globalization.* New Haven: Yale University Press, 2002.

Slaughter, Anne-Marie. *A New World Order*. Princeton: Princeton University Press, 2004.

Smelser, Neil J., and Jeffrey C. Alexander, eds. *Diversity and Its Discontents: Cultural Conflict and Common Ground in Contemporary American Society*. Princeton: Princeton University Press, 1999.

Smith, Adam. *Lectures on Jurisprudence*. Ed. Ronald L. Meek, David D. Raphael, and Peter Stein. Oxford: Clarendon Press, 1978.

Sparke, Matthew. "Networking Globalization: A Tapestry of Introductions." *Global Networks—A Journal of Transnational Affairs* 1, no. 2 (2001): 171–179.

Spiegler, Peter M. "A Constructive Critique of Economics." Dissertation, Harvard University, 2005.

Sraffa, Piero. *Production of Commodities by Means of Commodities: Prelude to a Critique of Economic Theory*. Cambridge: Cambridge University Press, 1960.

Stallman, Richard M. "GNU Manifesto," 1985. http://www.gnu.org/gnu/manifesto.html.

Steiner, George. *Martin Heidegger*. Chicago: University of Chicago Press, 1991.

Stiglitz, Joseph E. *Globalization and Its Discontents*. New York: W. W. Norton, 2002.

Strange, Susan. *The Retreat of the State: The Diffusion of Power in the World Economy*. New York: Cambridge University Press, 1996.

Sugden, Robert. "Finding the Key: The Riddle of Focal Points." *Journal of Economic Psychology* 27, no. 5 (2006): 609–621.

Summers, Lawrence H. "International Financial Crises: Causes, Prevention, and Cures." *American Economic Review* 90, no. 2 (2000): 1–16.

Tamir, Yael. *Liberal Nationalism*. Princeton: Princeton University Press, 1993.

Taylor, Charles. "Connolly, Foucault, and Truth." *Political Theory* 13, no. 3 (1985): 377–385.

———. "Foucault on Freedom and Truth." *Political Theory* 12, no. 2 (1984): 152–183.

———. *Hegel and Modern Society*. Cambridge: Cambridge University Press, 1979.

———. *Human Agency and Language*. Cambridge: Cambridge University Press, 1985.

———. "Modern Social Imaginaries." *Public Culture* 14, no. 1 (2002): 91–124.

———. *Multiculturalism and the Politics of Recognition: An Essay*. Ed. Amy Gutmann. Princeton: Princeton University Press, 1992.

———. *Philosophical Arguments*. Cambridge: Harvard University Press, 1995.

———. *Philosophy and the Human Sciences*. Cambridge: Cambridge University Press, 1985.

———. "Taylor and Foucault on Power and Freedom—a Reply." *Political Studies* 37, no. 2 (1989): 277–281.

Teather, David. "It's Not Over Yet, EC Tells Gates." *The Guardian*, November 5, 2002.

Terlaak, Ann, and Andrew A. King. "The Effect of Certification with the ISO 9000 Quality Management Standard: A Signaling Approach." *Journal of Economic Behavior & Organization* 60, no. 4 (2006): 579–602.

Todd, Emmanuel. *After the Empire: The Breakdown of the American Order.* Trans. C. Jon Delogu. New York: Columbia University Press, 2003.

Tuck, Richard. *Free Riding.* Cambridge: Harvard University Press, 2008.

———. *Hobbes.* Oxford: Oxford University Press, 1989.

———. *The Rights of War and Peace: Political Thought and the International Order from Grotius to Kant.* Oxford: Oxford University Press, 1999.

Tully, James. *Strange Multiplicity: Constitutionalism in an Age of Diversity.* Cambridge: Cambridge University Press, 1995.

UNDP. "Cultural Liberty in Today's Diverse World." *Human Development Report.* New York: United Nations Press, 2004.

Unger, Roberto Mangabeira. *Democracy Realized: The Progressive Alternative.* New York: Verso, 2000.

———. *False Necessity: Anti-Necessitarian Social Theory in the Service of Radical Democracy.* Cambridge: Cambridge University Press, 1987.

———. *Free Trade Reimagined: The World Division of Labor and the Method of Economics.* Princeton: Princeton University Press, 2007.

———. *Passion: An Essay on Personality.* New York: Free Press, 1984.

———. *Plasticity into Power: Comparative-Historical Studies on the Institutional Conditions of Economic and Military Success.* Cambridge: Cambridge University Press, 1987.

———. *Politics: The Central Texts.* Ed. Zhiyuan Cui. London: Verso, 1997.

———. "The Really New Bretton Woods." In *The Financial System under Stress: An Architecture for the New World Economy.* Ed. Marc Uzan. New York: Routledge, 1996: 11–25.

———. *Social Theory: Its Situation and Its Task.* Cambridge: Cambridge University Press, 1987.

———. *What Should Legal Analysis Become?* New York: Verso, 1996.

Unger, Roberto Mangabeira, and Zhiyuan Cui. "China in the Russian Mirror." *New Left Review* 1, no. 208 (1994): 78–87.

Uzan, Marc, ed. *The Financial System under Stress: An Architecture for the New World Economy.* New York: Routledge, 1996.

Varma, Pavan K. *The Great Indian Middle Class.* New York: Viking, 1998.

Virgil. Ed. and trans. H. Rushton Fairclough and George P. Goold. Loeb Classical Library; 63–64. Cambridge: Harvard University Press, 1999.

Wade, Robert H. *Governing the Market: Economic Theory and the Role of Government in East Asian Industrialization.* Princeton: Princeton University Press, 1990.

———. "The Invisible Hand of American Empire." *Ethics and International Affairs* 17, no. 2 (2003): 77–88.

———. "Is Globalization Reducing Poverty and Inequality?" *World Development* 32, no. 4 (2004): 567–589.

———. "The Ringmaster of Doha." *New Left Review* 25 (2004): 146–152.

———. "What Strategies Are Viable for Developing Countries Today? The World Trade Organization and the Shrinking of 'Development Space.'" *Review of International Political Economy* 10, no. 4 (2003): 621–644.

Wade, Robert H., and Frank Veneroso. "The Gathering World Slump and the Battle over Capital Controls." *New Left Review* 231 (1998): 13–42.

Wade, Robert H., and Martin Wolf. "Prospect Debate: Are Global Poverty and Inequality Getting Worse?" *Prospect* 72 (2002): 16–21.

Walzer, Michael. "Is There an American Empire?" *Dissent* 50, no. 4 (2003): 27–31.

Wasserman, Stanley, and Katherine Faust. *Social Network Analysis: Methods and Applications*. Cambridge: Cambridge University Press, 1994.

Wasserman, Stanley, and Joseph Galaskiewicz, eds. *Advances in Social Network Analysis: Research in the Social and Behavioral Sciences*. Thousand Oaks, Calif.: Sage, 1994.

Waters, Malcolm. *Globalization*. London; New York: Routledge, 1995.

Watson, James L. *Golden Arches East: McDonald's in East Asia*. Stanford: Stanford University Press, 1997.

Weber, Max. *Economy and Society: An Outline of Interpretive Sociology*. Ed. Guenther Roth and Claus Wittich and trans. Ephraim Fischoff et al. Berkeley: University of California Press, 1978.

Weber, Steve. *The Success of Open Source*. Cambridge: Harvard University Press, 2004.

Weeks, Sally. "Embracing English." *Miami Herald*, August 18, 1996.

Weitzman, Martin L., and Chengang Xu. "Chinese Township-Village Enterprises as Vaguely Defined Cooperatives." *Journal of Comparative Economics* 18, no. 2 (1994): 121–145.

Wellman, Barry. *Networks in the Global Village: Life in Contemporary Communities*. Boulder, Colo.: Westview Press, 1999.

Wellman, Barry, and Stephen D. Berkowitz, eds. *Social Structures: A Network Approach*. Greenwich, Conn.: JAI Press, 1997.

Wildermuth, John. "Will Political Donations Keep Microsoft Intact?" *San Francisco Chronicle*, July 1, 2001.

Williams, Sam. *Free as in Freedom: Richard Stallman's Crusade for Free Software*. Sebastopol, Calif.: O'Reilly, 2002.

Williamson, John. *The Political Economy of Policy Reform*. Washington, D.C.: Institute for International Economics, 1994.

———. "What Should the World Bank Think about the Washington Consensus?" *World Bank Research Observer* 15, no. 2 (2000): 251–264.

Wilson, Thomas P. "Sociology and the Mathematical Method." In *Social Theory Today*. Ed. Anthony Giddens and Jonathan Turner. Stanford: Stanford University Press, 1987: 383–404.

Wittgenstein, Ludwig. *Philosophical Investigations*. Ed. and trans. Gertrude E. M. Anscombe. Oxford: Blackwell, 1953.

Wolf, Martin. *Why Globalization Works*. New Haven: Yale University Press, 2004.

Wood, Ellen M. *Empire of Capital*. London: Verso, 2003.

Zielonka, Jan. *Europe as Empire: The Nature of the Enlarged European Union*. Oxford: Oxford University Press, 2006.

Zurn, Christopher F. "Identity or Status? Struggles over 'Recognition' in Fraser, Honneth, and Taylor." *Constellations* 10, no. 4 (2003): 519–537.

223–224. *See also* open-source
movement
Free Trade Area of the Americas (FTAA),
236
Freud, Sigmund, 65, 268, 279, 371n4,
375n37
Friedman, Thomas, 236, 254, 317n7,
367n13

Galbraith, John Kenneth, 88
Gaonkar, Dilip, 290
General Agreement on Trade and Tariffs
(GATT): and emergence of WTO, 230–
232; history of, 230–231; network properties of, contrasted with WTO's, 232–
233. *See also* World Trade Organization
General Public License. *See* GNU General
Public License
Geuss, Raymond, 343n72
Giddens, Anthony, 19, 55–56, 137, 300n5,
317n8
Gladwell, Malcolm, 308n26
globalization: alternative forms of, 189–
192; of conceptual frames, 284–289;
criticism of, 143–144; economic hegemony under, 236–237; effects on language, 79–82, 85–87; of forms of
sociability, 50–52; historical episodes
of, 17–18, 57–58, 70–71, 96; as imperial,
6–8, 136; of investment standards, 255–
265; of neoliberalism, 247–255; network
power as driving, 4–5; as result of social
coordination, 2–3; of social imaginaries,
289–291; of technical standards, 193–
197; of social norms, 276–282; theories
of, 18–20, 50–52; theorizing power of,
8–9, 136, 140; and theory of structuration, 57–58. *See also* anti-globalization
activism; cultural globalization, empire
GNU General Public License (GPL),
204–207. *See also* free software
gold standard: accidental switch on to,
96–97; anchor currencies functioning
as, 150; bimetallism and, 96–98; collapse of 19th-century version, 98–101;
discussion by Keynes of, 95, 99–105;
discussion by Locke of, 92–94; discussion by Marx of, 91–92, 94–95; discus-

sion by Smith of, 92–94; discussion by
Weber of, 98; echoes of in contemporary globalization, 102, 234; as exemplifying tensions in a universal standard,
100–103, 178; historical use of gold as
money and, 90–91; intrinsic reason
for adoption of, 32; network effects of,
97–98; psychological reasons for, 95;
relation to bullion of, 95; right-wing
arguments for return to, 104–105,
337n94; rise of 19th-century version,
95–98. *See also* money
Gomory, Ralph, 238–239, 240, 241
Goux, Jean-Joseph, 309n33
Graham, Edward, 258–261
Gramsci, Antonio, 106, 124, 129, 131–134
Grand Central Station, 1–2, 4, 83, 178
Gray, John, 240–241
Guéhenno, Jean-Marie, 297n2, 349n6

Haas, Peter, 373n23–374n25
Habermas, Jürgen, 55, 157–158, 320n15
Hardt, Michael, 136, 297n2, 298n4
Haslett, Adam, 347n22
Hayek, Friedrich von, 104–105, 337n94
Hegel, Georg, 159, 313n1, 346n17
hegemony: and European empires, 58;
in Gramsci's thought, 131–134, 342n50;
network power as model of, 140;
in Weber's thought, 118–119; as under-
writing globalization, 236–237. *See
also* empire; imperialism
Heidegger, Martin, 304n15
Held, David, 315n6
Hirsch, Fred, 348n30
Hobbes, Thomas, 47, 159, 310n1, 314n5,
322n24, 348n18
Hobson's choice, 109, 112, 114, 115, 169
Hockett, Robert, 318n11
holism, 318n9, 326n43. *See also* emergence; methodological individualism
Honneth, Axel, 158–160, 161, 162, 163, 165,
280–281
Hont, Istvan, 310n1, 360n9
human rights, 161–162, 177, 283
Hume, David, 59–61, 65, 88, 237, 310n1,
322n24
Huntington, Samuel, 270

network properties (*continued*)
definition of, 172; and destabilization, 187; divisions of, 173; of Free Software and Microsoft contrasted, 206–207, 214; of GATT contrasted with WTO, 232–233; general discussion of, 172–179 passim; of language, 80–81; mapping of, 181–182; of social imaginaries, 289; of social norms, 275–276; of WTO, 229–230. *See also* availability; compatibility; malleability

norms. *See* social norms

North American Free Trade Act (NAFTA), 236, 257, 369n16

Nozick, Robert, 108–109, 337n1

Nussbaum, Martha, 165

Occitan, 154, 170

Olsaretti, Serena, 109–115, 146, 160

Olson, Mancur, 306n19

Openness: and global architecture, 172–173; subdivided into network properties, 173. *See also* network properties

open-source movement: as depoliticized "free software," 205, 357n38; distinguished from Free Software, 205–206; skepticism about politics, 215–216. *See also* free software

Parijs, Philippe van, 151–152, 154

Parsons, Talcott, 122, 13n319

path dependence, 64–65, 323–325nn37–39

Piaget, Jean, 137, 318n8, 320n14, 327n43

Polanyi, Karl, 241

positional goods, 165, 348n30

positive feedback, 25–26, 30, 63, 66, 305n17. *See also* economies of scale

Posner, Eric, 371n11

postcoloniality: cultural convergence and, 269; English and, 77; theory of, 144, 344n2

Poulantzas, Nico, 341n42

poverty: and development debates, 239–240, 245–246, 252; measurement of, 362n16

power: considered in relation to agency, 129–131, 137–139; domination as model of, 116–119; Foucault's analysis of, 134–139; in globalization, 7–9, 136, 140; Gramsci's analysis of, 131–134; and hegemony, 131–134; Lukes's analysis of, 122–127, 128–129, 131, 139; network power as form of, 119–122, 127–131, 139–140; of sociability contrasted with sovereignty, 44–48; sovereignty as model of, 106, 119–120, 131; three views of, 122–127; Weber's analysis of, 116–119; use of counterfactuals in identifying, 127–128, 130, 138. *See also* coercion; domination; force

property: anarchist position on, 220–221, 248; in East Asian development, 252, 366n10; on Locke's account, 93; protection of in international investment standards, 255, 257. *See also* intellectual property

Proudhon, Jean-Joseph, 218, 220, 222, 356n28

Pufendorf, Samuel, 312n1

Purdy, Jedediah, 163, 276, 278, 299n4

Quebec, 71, 152–153, 162

Rawls, John, 164

Rawlsian theory, 54, 318n11

Raymond, Eric, 205

reason: and adoption of ISO 9000, 210–211; in adoption of neoliberal standards, 252–254; in analysis of choice under network power, 107–108; as cause in the adoption of a standard, 32–35; in cultural globalization, 281; extrinsic and reassertion of social context, 66–68; intrinsic and extrinsic defined and contrasted, 29–30, 31–35; metric system as example of, 35; relation of extrinsic reason to indirect force, 37–38; in rise of English, 76–79; in trajectory of network power, 38–42; in VCR wars, 63–64

recognition: in the American context, 163–164; cultural globalization and psycho-social, 278–282; and identity concerns, 143–144, 156–158; "moral grammar" of, 159–160; and network